SEX AND RACE

SEX AND RACE

Volume III

WHY WHITE AND BLACK MIX IN
SPITE OF OPPOSITION

By

J . A . ROGERS

Wesleyan University Press
Middletown, Connecticut

Wesleyan University Press
Middletown CT 06459
www.wesleyan.edu/wespress

First Wesleyan University Press edition 2020
ISBN 978-0-8195-7509-8

Manufactured in the United States of America
5 4 3 2 1

CONTENTS

REMARKS ON THE FIRST TWO VOLUMES
OF SEX AND RACE

"Our race is essentially slavish; it is the nature of all of us to believe blindly in what we love, rather than that which is most wise. We are inclined to look upon an honest, unshrinking pursuit of truth as something irreverent. We are indignant when others pry into our idols and criticize them with impunity, just as a savage flies to arms when a missionary picks his fetish to pieces." ... Galton.

Certain orthodox scholars, white and colored, have not liked the history as given in the two preceding volumes of "Sex and Race," as well as in my earlier books. One English editor after reading the "100 Amazing Facts About the Negro," wrote me that it made him feel as if the white race had never accomplished anything. Others said that I claim everybody who has ever done anything as Negro, nevertheless, I had never said, or dreamed of saying, that Homer, or Pericles, or Aeschylus, or Julius Caesar, or Alfred the Great, Shakespeare, Milton, Michael Angelo, Bach, Handel, Wagner, Washington, Lincoln, Edison, Franklin D. Roosevelt, Einstein or thousands of other noted white men were of Negro ancestry; nor did I attribute to Negroes any role of any importance in Europe, itself, from say the sixteenth century onwards. Yet because I mention a few individuals, whom they had all along believed to be of unmixed white strain, I have been called "fantastic" and "credulous!"

And I have been ridiculed not on the result of research, not on examination of the sources which I have given abundantly, but on sheer belief. These scholars did not happen to run across such facts in their reading, in a word, the research I had done was off the beaten track of the college curriculum, therefore, it did not exist.

Perhaps I exaggerate, perhaps I am really being fantastic when I say this of the orthodox scholars, well, I shall give a not uncommon illustration and let the reader judge for himself.

In 1943, Gunnar Myrdal, noted economist of the University of Stockholm, Sweden, aided by 75 experts, working for five years, completed for the Carnegie Corporation at a cost of $209,000, a work on the race problem entitled "An American Dilemma" and published by Harper and Brothers. On page 1393 of this book (1st ed.) I am listed as an example of those who write "pseudo-history, fantastically glorifying the achievements of Negroes."

On what grounds was this judgment arrived at? On anything I had written? No, I was judged on a non-existent book—a book that no mortal could ever have seen.

Here are the facts: In 1927, I finished a manuscript entitled "This Mongrel World, A Study of Negro-Caucasian Mixing In All Ages and All Countries." At about that time I was asked to fill out a blank for "Who's Who in Colored America," and intending to publish the manuscript soon I listed it as being published. However, circumstances prevented my doing so. Thirteen years later, due to the much greater research I had done on the subject, I changed the title to "Sex and Race." Parts of the manuscript I used in Volumes One and Two of that work and discarded most of the rest. In short, when "An American Dilemma" was published not even the manuscript of "This Mongrel World" existed. Nevertheless this *non-existent manuscript* is listed as a *published book* in Myrdal's bibliography. What had happened? In reading through my biographical sketch in "Who's Who in Colored America," Myrdal, or some of his assistants, saw the title and on that alone condemned me. Not a word was said of any of my published books. They probably didn't take the trouble to look into any of them.

Now what is the difference between an attitude of this sort and that of any uneducated man, or any bigot, who would similarly condemn Myrdal's work, or that of any other scientist in such off-hand manner? So far as I am concerned, none whatever.

Furthermore, though I have no philanthropist or foundation, or staff of experts behind me, I go to as great pains as any of the most conscientious of these experts to get my facts straight, checking and re-checking, and travelling hither and yon to see with my own eyes whenever possible what I am writing about; and quoting only from the original sources and from those I have reason to believe are the most reliable. One can do no more. Of course, there will always be errors, but when seventy-six experts, working with unlimited funds as in "An American Dilemma," make errors surely a lone worker, like myself, might be forgiven a few.

Another reason why some object to the facts as given in my books is that they feel that their own learning is being impeached. If such facts were true, why, they certainly would have known them. One able Negro musician, who had a fine education in England, admitted to me later that when he heard me say for the first time that Beethoven was colored, he was "offended." Had he not long been acquainted with Beethoven?

In 1930 while I was carrying in the Negro press a series of articles on great Negroes, an Aframerican, studying in Germany, and now a college professor, wrote the Pittsburgh Courier, leading Negro weekly, that my stories were dubious even though I had included Bilal, Dumas, Pushkin, General Dodds, Chevalier de St. George, Henri Diaz, and others who are very plainly mentioned in biographies as being of Negro ancestry. The simple truth is that he didn't know the first thing of the true ancestry of these individuals but never having heard it, why, that alone made what I said false. As for my statement that the Virgin Mary and Christ were once worshipped as black and that at the present time pilgrimages are made to the shrines of the Black Virgins in France, Spain, and even in Germany, that seemed a veritable Munchausen tale, One Negro columnist, a Catholic, actually resented the idea that the Madonna could have been black. Had he not all his life seen her depicted as white?

Still another reason for their rejecting my researches is that they didn't want the present knowledge in their brains disturbed. They had been taught that the Negro's position in history had been that of a slave and it was much more pleasant to go on believing that than to investigate.

Race prejudice is responsible too, in part. There are those who at the merest mention that this or that noted person was, or might have been, of Negro ancestry, at once set their backs up like an angry cat. So racial are such people that when one attributes Negro ancestry even to an ancient Greek or Egyptian it is "social equality"—a lowering of their own personal dignity. One white woman angrily resented the idea that Alexander Dumas, the great novelist, could possibly have been of Negro ancestry.

The classic example of this sort, however, is Mary Preston, a Southern white woman, whose readings on Shakespeare were popular in her day. Miss Preston twisted "Othello" to suit herself. While admitting that Shakespeare did make Othello "black," that was positively not what Shakespeare meant so far as she was concerned. She said (italics hers) : "In studying the play "Othello" I have always *imagined* its hero a *white man*. It is true the dramatist paints him black, but this shade does not suit the man. It is a stage decoration which *my taste discards;* a fault of color from an artistic point of view. I have, therefore, as I before stated in my *readings* of this play, dispensed with it. Shakespeare was too correct a delineator of human nature to have colored Othello *black* if he had personally acquainted himself with the idiosyncracies of the African race. We may regard, then, the daub of black upon Othello's portrait as an *ebullition* of fancy, a *freak* of imagination —the visionary concept of an ideal figure . . . Othello *was a white* man."[1]

Wherein we ask does such an attitude differ from that of any blind believer in revealed religion?

---

[1] Studies in Shakespeare, p. 71. 1869. Apropos of this a noted psychoanalyst once objected to my saying during a discussion period that when Shakespeare said, "Black men are pearls in beauteous ladies eyes," he actually meant black men. No, he said, there were no Negroes in England in Shakespeare's time, and he was positive about. it. I informed him that there was not only Negro slavery in England at the time but that G. B. Harrison, an Elizabethan authority, thinks that Shakespeare, himself, had a Negro sweetheart. (For sources see Sex and Race, Vol. 1, p. 201, 1941, and Vol. II, p. 400.)

Of course this attitude is hugely amusing. It is one of a piece, too, with the feeling of certain Gentiles when they take up a book on Jewish biography and see for the first time that this or that great pioneer, scientist, or soldier whom they had all along fancied to be non-Jewish was a Jew.

The result of this attitude toward "Negro" history is that the better-known historians, sociologists, and anthropologists, with few exceptions, have been great claimers of Negroid peoples as white. The idea has been to maintain white supremacy. Pick up any national or world history and you'll find even the Ethiopians, who such early writers as Xenophanes, Aristotle, Herodotus and Strabo, tell us were black and wooly-haired, that is, the type now called Negro, are white. They still say the Ethiopians are white though they are uniformly blacker and more wooly-haired than the American Negroes.

Whenever, too, Negroes are mentioned as having appeared anywhere, whether in prehistoric America, the Caucasus, or Albania, they are invariably spoken of as "slaves." For instance, Ignatius Donnelly in trying to prove that the so-called New World was known to the people of the Old reproduces from the ancient Mexican monuments certain portraits of Negroes which he calls "idols."[2] But in the same breath he says they were "slaves" who "were brought to America at a very remote epoch." (Please note the contradiction: "slaves" who were "idols!") His reason for saying they were slaves is that "Negroes have never been a sea-going race," for which statement he hasn't a shred of evidence. Of course, the "slave" had to be brought in to square with white imperialism and the exploitation of the darker peoples even though what he mentions occurred in prehistoric times. The Negro must always be marked down so that his labor can be had in the cheapest market.

The motive for this twisting of history is that white imperialism must be shown a sbeing of old, aristocratic ancestry. This imperialism was built upon the backs of the darker races. A noted example was the British empire, of whose 500,000,000 people, eighty percent are colored. Now some of these colored people as the Ethiopians, Egyptians, East Indians, and Moors were the originators of Western civilization; they were highly civilized when the Europeans were savages[3]—a fact that cannot be denied as long as the works

---

[2] Donnelly, I. Atlantis, pp. 174-5. 1882.

[3] Julian Huxley and A. C. Haddon say, "It is asserted vociferously in certain quarters that the Nordic 'race' is gifted above all others with initiative and originality and that the great advances in civilization have been due to Nordic genius.

"What are the facts? The fundamental discoveries on which civilization is built are the art of writing, agriculture, the wheel and building in stone. All these appear to have originated in the Near East, among peoples who by no stretch of the imagination could be called Nordic or presumed to have but the faintest admixture of Nordic or proto-Nordic genes." (We, Europeans, p. 94, 1935).

of Julius Caesar and Tacitus exist. But it would never do to show that the
lord and master once had very humble beginnings so it must be shown that
the originators of civilization were white—that the white has always been on
top. Therefore, for the purposes of adding lustre to white imperialism, the
Ethiopians, Egyptians and the others are called "white" but for the purposes
of profit they are treated as colored. Thus the white imperialist eats his cake
and has it too.

It is a blow to the pride of certain white Americans, Englishmen, and
Germans to hear it said that peoples and individuals they had all along fondly
believed to be "pure" white were not so. Because I said on the testimony of
white people who knew Beethoven, as well as on reports of his ancestry by
German scholars, that he showed evidence of Negro strain, I have received
letters as cross as if I had attacked the writers themselves.

Any talk of Negro progress angers many. If the blacks advance who
will they have to be better than? There will go their splendid isolation of
fancied superiority. Even worse, they already see themselves losing out, a
state of mind expressed by Bacon when he said, "Men of noble birth are
noted to be envious towards new men when they arise for the distance between them is altered and it is like a deceit of the eye that when others come
on they think themselves go back."

So thorough has been the penetration of white imperialist propaganda
that only a small percentage of the white or the colored in any part of Western civilization today have any idea that any other than white people had a
hand in the origin of civilization. Although I had been an omnivorous
reader from my earliest years I was well past twenty before it began to dawn
upon me that the darker peoples could have had a part in it. Even now I
can recall my astonishment when this occurred to me.

Even as the white manufacturers have bleached out our salt, sugar, flour,
so the white historian has bleached out world history. The dark or mineral
portion has been rejected. Of course this process has produced a product
beautifully pleasing to the eyes of those who have been psychologized to admire it, but which, nevertheless, is constipative and harmful to the mental
digestion.

But as there are those who, realizing the value of the minerals that have
been rejected from our foods, have placed them in again, thereby increasing
the health value, as say how bran has been restored to the bleached, starved-
out white bread, so in like manner I have attempted to gather up the Negro,
or dark, rejected portion of history in the hope that some day they will be re-

stored to world history, thereby permitting a less clogging effect on the mind.

Such being my purpose I do not ever claim that I am writing world or national history. Call it the bran of history if you will. As for those who will regard this "bran" as proving that the white race has never accomplished anything and that the Negro did everything. I can do nothing about it.

I can say, in addition, that I dislike too much the whitening of history; I have too great a loathing for racial propaganda, even knowingly to indulge in it. Moreover, the facts I have given have been culled nearly always from white writers, some of them very ancient, who related facts as they saw them, and who did not worship at the shrine of white imperialism, or did not think of the effect of what they said would have in later years.

To get those little known facts I have travelled tens of thousands of miles in many lands; consulted books and printed matter so vast in number that were I to try to say how many I would sound like a Munchausen; visited the leading museums of many of the civilized lands, and engaged in research in their libraries and ever going to great pains to get my facts as humanly correct as possible. In short, I felt I have looked into books and dug up buried knowledge that many college professors or doctors of philosophy do not know exist, because just as there is a life in the deeper depths of the ocean of which the average fisherman knows nothing so there are depths in the ocean of research of which some of the most learned have never dreamed. For instance, it is estimated that in the National Library of France alone there are 8,000,000 books and pieces of printed matter. How much does the most educated man now alive know of the totality of knowledge in these books? Very, very little. One is ever learning. Truly, as Sir Isaac Newton once said as he looked out on the ocean that there he was picking up pebbles on the beach as it were while the vast ocean of unexplored knowledge lay before him.

Those who will forget their orthodoxy for a while and read my books might not find them so fantastic after all. And even should they reject them they might still profit to the extent of knowing the arguments on the other side and thus be able to refute them, not by denunciation, but in a manner more compatible with common sense.

I hasten to add that I am not accusing all the leading historians of catering to white imperialism. Some as H. G. Wells, Hendrik Van Loon, and Arnold J. Toynbee, have made striking utterances against race prejudice. I believe that these latter accepted the popular white view of history without thinking that there was another side. As the New World was not on the charts of the scholars prior to Columbus so the achievements of the Negro and Negroid peoples were not on theirs.

Furthermore, there are white writers as Volney, Godfrey Higgins, Gerald Massey, Henry M .Stanley, David Livingstone, and Frobenius, greatest of all the Africanologists, who gave a perspective of Negro history that is increasingly found to be the truth. Why, we ask, were the works of these men by-passed by Wells and Toynbee? Were what they said of the Negro in history too fantastic to be considered?

For instance, Toynbee, who is one of the most unprejudiced of historians, attributes a civilization even to the Polynesian but denies any to the Negro. He says, "When we classify Mankind by color, the only one of the primary races . . . which has not made a creative contribution to any of our twenty-one civilizations is the Black Race . . .

"The Black Race has not helped to create any civilization while the Polynesian White Race has helped to create one civilization, the Brown Race two, the Yellow Race three, the Red Race and the Nordic Whit Race four apiece, the Alpine White Race nine, and the Mediterranean White Race ten."[4]

What is the Polynesian White Race? There is no such people. The Polynesians, prior to the migration of white people to their islands, were chiefly of mixed Negro and Mongolian strain, with probably a slight admixture of white strain from Asiatic Russia. The Paris Museum of Ethnology in the Jardin des Plantes has what is, without a doubt, the most comprehensive collection of casts of Polynesian types from nearly all the islands and they are shown to be what would be loosely called Negroes in the United States. Of course, much white "blood" has been mixed in with the South Sea islander since these casts were made over a century ago. Gobineau calls the Polynesians black and he was right at the time he wrote.

Let me express here once again my theory of so-called race. It is this: There is a single human race, which by imperceptible degrees shades from the blond of the Scandinavian to the blackness of the Senegambian or the Solomon Islander with the Sicilian or the Maltese somewhere in the centre. Some peoples as the Portuguese are nearer to the blond, while others as those of Mauretania or Southern India are nearer to the black, therefore, when I see anywhere, no matter where, an individual whose appearance is Negroid, that it, if his facial contour, his lips, nose, hair, present what a lifetime of observation has taught me are signs of Negro inheritance, I say that that person had a Negro ancestor near or distant according to the Negroid signs he presents. One's ancestry, I know, does not come out of the air, but is a reality of realities.

[4] Toynbee, A. J. A Study of History, Vol. I, p. 234. 1934.

Similarly, if I see anywhere an individual whose appearance is Caucasian, that is, his lips, nose, hair, etc., present what a lifetime of observation has taught me are signs of "unmixed" Caucasian inheritance, I set that person down as white. If it is logical to speak of Caucasian strain among Negroes it is just as logical to speak of Negro strain among Caucasians. In this latter respect the Nazi anthropologists are at least right.

For instance, I once attended a reception given to an American Negro publisher and his wife in London. The latter was very fair and in her evening gown looked whiter in skin and more regular in profile than some of the Englishwomen present. If I attributed Negro ancestry to the publisher's wife, whose mother was undoubtedly colored, what should I have said of these Englishwomen who were more colored than she is in appearance?

One may sometimes find Negro ancestry where one least expects it. Take Colette, France's leading woman writer. She is blonde and to all appearances a European. Only a very experienced eye would discover signs of a strain not "pure" Nordic in her. Yet she had a Negro ancestor. When I said that in 1930, I was again charged with claiming all noted white persons as Negroes. But who said it first? Colette, herself.[5] The European, unlike the American, is not inclined to hide his Negro strain, if any. Also J. Larnac in his biography of her says that she inherited some Negro strain from her grandfather ("tenant de son grandpère un peu de sang coloré"). Her mother, "Madame Colette," he says, "is the daughter of Sophie Celeste Chatenay and a colored man with violet fingernails, who manufactured chocolates in Belgium, Henri Marie Landay."[5a] If Colette, who is so blonde, has a Negro strain, I fail to see where the same would be impossible in the case of Beethoven, who did show Negro ancestry.

Again, there are those dear souls who will say that I exaggerate when I call these apparently white persons "Negroes." Would such kindly address themselves to the United State Census Bureau which decrees that if one has a known Negro ancestor, he is a Negro. The wife of the Negro editor mentioned above, was listed as a Negro. And the unwritten law is that if one is known to be of such ancestry, however distant, he is at once marked down. As long as this "one drop" theory remains refutation of alleged Negro inferiority must follow the arbitrary lines set by the Bureau of the Census.

However, no one can possibly know what so-called racial elements enter into his make-up. O. A. Wall estimated that the total number of one's ancestors since the time of Christ was around 144 quadrillions, and said that if one did not count the intermarriage of relatives the figure would be 288,230,-

5 La Maison de Claudine, p. 99. 1922.
5a Colette, pp. 11, 17, 18. 1927. See also Sex and Race, Vol. I, p. 240. 1941

376,151,711,742.[6] Thus since life goes back at least a million years the ancestors of any individual would be as many as the sands of the sea or the stars of the firmament.

Talk of a pure race after that!

I, furthermore, visualize changes in human types as I visualize changes in cosmography, that is, as land that was once at the bottom of the sea now rears lofty peaks among the Alps and the Himalayas and vice versa; and as lands that were once tropical are now frigid, all due to the eternal change in Nature, so peoples who were once black are now white, and the opposite. Or to use a symbol: As parts of the earth are white or black or intermediate tints depending on whether such parts are facing, or are behind, or are sideways to the sun, so, in cosmic time it is with the coloring of the human race.

That humanity is one, that the earliest human beings were of a single color, is evident to even the Australian Bushman, supposedly the lowest in intelligence on earth. Dr. Berkeley Hill says they believe "that a white man is only one of themselves re-born. 'Tumble-down black fellow, jump up white fellow', is the common phrase among them "to express this belief," he says.

There are two principal sides to every question both of which when mixed together go to form the truth as oxygen and hydrogen to form water. My aim is to glean from both sides, using experience and an open mind as my guide. Because one is definitely opposed to our theory, he is not necessarily wrong, and because one favors us, neither does that make him right.

Everything that is, is truth by sheer force of its existence. Therefore by truth I mean that principle, which, at every moment, upholds the right of each individual, regardless of whoever or whatever he may be, to equality of dignity and opportunity, in short, equal justice.

As regards the term, Nature, I use it in no anthropomorphic sense. I do not think of it as a deity but as meaning the totality of all things—that un-

---

[6] Sex and Sex Worship, pp. 304-06. 1922. I do not see, however, where the intermarriage of relatives would affect the computation of one's ancestors except in the cases of those who are the product of incest, and that only in the case of where brother weds sister. Even if a man cohabited with his mother and had children by her as the ancient Britons used to do (at least that is what I infer from Caesar when he said that fathers and sons had the same wives), it seems to me something else would enter into the ancestry of the child. And there is no doubt of it when first cousin marries first cousin. The uncle or the aunt of the latter would have wed someone not related to the family, thus creating new combinations of genes. One has, it is true, only eight great-grandparents but we must not forget that behind each one of these stood enough millions of ancestors probably to go around the world several times. Truly, as Einstein has said, the number of one's ancestors is "astronomical."

Caesar's statement on incest among the ancient Britons reads. "Groups of ten or twelve men have wives together in common and particularly brothers along with brothers and fathers with sons." (Gallic Wars, Bk. V, 14.)

known Force which is forever being unfolded, and within which lies the destiny of all things. The term, Nature, is inadequate of course, but since it is impossible to find a correct name that seems to me as good as any other.

I have also tried to get away from the crass materialism of Western civilization, which because of its eagerness to get hold of material things is forever rending itself and bringing untold misery on itself and all mankind. Three appallingly catastrophic wars in a quarter of a century!

Happily, there is a certain trend in the West today towards the animism of the East and of Africa, to explore into and to make one's self a part of the great inner forces of Nature. For the really cultured Western thinker of today, a bit of board is no longer just board but a segment of the universe seething with the life of the atom; trees are no longer just trees but breathing organisms, marvellous with their own psychology, their own loves and aversions; bees, insects, spiders, animalculae are discovered to have histories almost as intricate and hardly less interesting than those of man; cats, dogs, apes, elephants are discovered to have intelligence which has been cut out of the same cloth, so to speak, as man's. Though its reach is far lower, it operates essentially the same, all intelligence, human and animal, being but a part of the Great Whole.

Finally, as regards human beings, we are getting farther and farther away from the old "science" of physiognomy, and are appraising individuals, not on their looks, but on their acts. We are learning that to gauge intelligence by skull measurement, size of brain, skin color and hair are the sheerest infantilism, no matter how high the reputation of the scientist who advances such theories.

Let not those who think they are up be jealous of those who have been down and are rising. Let them rather rejoice that the human race, of which we are all part, is advancing. Let the thrill of feeling superior come not as the result of looking down on others but in seeing them rise, and in knowing that we are in a position to help them to do so.

To love one's fellow-man is the beginning of all true wisdom and the end of war, the greatest of all insanities.

In the better days that are coming it will be immaterial what color or what race of human beings did this or that great thing. This insanity of color fastened on us by the Virginia slaveholder and the New England slave-dealer will pass as other fantastic theories have passed. In the meantime the reciting of Negro accomplishment, past and present, will be necessary to counteract anti-Negro propaganda even as the reciting of Jewish accomplishment is a foil to anti-Semitism.

THE WHY AND WHEREFORE OF VOLUME THREE
OF SEX AND RACE

The question of why white and black do mate in spite of all opposition, or to be more precise, why certain white people should mate with black people, has intrigued me as far back as I can remember.

I grew up in a part of the world where there was not one color line, but several, none of which, however, was anything as near as rigid, perhaps, I had better say as violent, as in the United States.

At the very top of the social ladder were the European-born whites, principally British. There were no others like them in that island-world. Oh, felt the native white and near-whites, if we were only like them, born in *England!* The fact that such or such was born in England invested him with an aura little short of royalty. Even the black man who had been to England, if only as a sailor, was regarded as is a Mohammedan who has been to Mecca.

Next to the European were the native-born whites, some of whom were as fair as Europeans, but who, I later discovered, to my astonishment, had sometimes a colored grandmother still living. The European whites, because of the manner in which they were catered to by the native whites naturally looked down upon the latter, even when the native white was as fair. There was, for instance, the difference of accent. English accent, like English birth, also came first. Among my friends was a tall and very handsome native white man—I believe unmixed—golden-haired and blonde as any North European; one day when I said to an Englishman that this friend of mine was just as white as he, he replied with a touch of scorn, "Yes, until you hear him talk."

As regards the mixed population, island society was, on the whole, graded, according to the degree of pigment in the skin, which meant that the unmixed black was, except in rare instances, at the foot of the ladder.

Even a slightly lesser degree of pigment constituted some touch of "nobility." Once when a woman, rather dark, called another woman slightly fairer than herself by her first name, instead of "Mrs." the latter placed her hand beside that of the darker woman and said indignantly, "How dare you? Look? *Me and you not the same color."*

Such being the pride of race and color, I was extraordinarily struck by one thing, and that is, how some of the European whites, "the lords of creation," sought out the unmixed black woman, a type that most of the mulattoes would not touch. Sometimes one would run across the Europeans, mostly English and German, cohabiting with the black women in the fields, or in their huts, soiled and dirty as they were. In fact, some of the older mulatto families, who, for no valid reason considered themselves superior to both the

European whites and the blacks, regarded this cohabitation as just another proof of the supposed inferiority of both groups. Why, I kept asking myself, this glaring social contradiction.

In one district settled principally by Germans, I would see some of these well-fed, rosy-cheeked white men consorting with the coal-black women and having children by them. The mulatto women seemed to have had very little attraction for them. There was even an occasional marriage of a European to a black woman. I recall the case of a Scotch doctor, the leading social figure in one town, who had a Barbadian wife of ebony blackness.

The same was in a measure true of some of the European white women. Some of them had black husbands to whom they had been married while the husbands were studying in Europe. Marriages between the native white women and the light mulatto and quadroon men were not rare; but those between the native white women, as well as the light mulatto women, with black men were very much so.

Later, I lived in a garrison town where certain of the wives of the white non-commissioned officers went to hotels with the black soldiers of the garrison, all of which, as I said, puzzled me immensely. Why, I wanted to know, had these people who had been placed on a pedestal, should get off it, of their own free will, to associate with a people considered so "low" as the blacks.

Had I seen the blacks trying to reach the white men and women I could have understood it; but the blacks, on the whole, did not seem anxious to mate even with the mulatto women. Some black men told me that the mere thought of going with a white woman gave them a creepy feeling.

When I came to the United States my astonishment was, if anything, greater. There where the color-line was much stronger and where it was not so much the white man, as the white woman, who was put on a pedestal, I found some of the "deified" creatures mixing with coal-black men, whom, they sometimes preferred to mulattoes. Even in the South, where the very air seemed to exude the "sanctity" of the white woman, I saw white women and black men, meeting "under cover." What's more, when I read American history, I found that this sort of thing had gone on even when the black man was a slave.

Later, when I went to Europe, my astonishment continued, though it took a different turn. While there was no color prejudice anywhere on the Continent—there was some in England, but nothing like that of the United States—I wondered why should certain white men and women, some of whom had had little or no contact with black people, showed almost no visible aversion to them. I recall once going to a very fine French restaurant with an unmixed African, who was studying law in London, and the proprietor, who happened to be a good friend of mine, seated the African on a side-seat next to a white girl of dazzling appearance, and evidently of the upper-class. He had not been there a minute before she engaged him in conversation and seemed fascinated with him.

A case with which I was well acquainted was that of a European girl of multi-millionaire parentage, a blue-blood of the blue-bloods moving in the highest social circle, who had to my positive knowledge four American Negro intimates, and from reports there were others.

Whenever I saw a black man on the Continent—and the Africans were usually much darker than the Aframericans—he was almost invariably with a white woman, who was sometimes an ash-blonde. Much the same was true of the black women; they were nearly always with white men. Except during the Paris Intercolonial Exposition in 1931, when some Africans brought their wives, it was a rare thing to see a couple that was not mixed.

And not only in life but in literature I found many astonishing things of the way in which white people sought out the blacks. One passage that struck me more than the ordinary was one I quoted in Volume One where Dr. Shufeldt said that he knew a German of very fine education and good family who said he preferred a black woman to the finest white woman he had ever known and that he had not been backward in having what he wanted.

Another passage that impressed me even more—a recent one, however, —I found in Stuart Cloete's Congo Song where a "strong, indefatigable, Aryan German, almost a god," who heils Hitler and accepts his doctrine that Negroes are "half-apes," has a great passion for black women. "He wanted Maria's insatiable black flesh. He needed a woman—a black woman. The richness of that black ivory beneath him."[1]

Most remarkable of all the revelations of this passion that I found in literature—remarkable because it gave me a deeper understanding of what I had seen so much in real life—were three letters published in John Cameron Grant's The Ethiopian in which a white woman reveals her innermost desires for mating with a Negro of simon-pure blackness. (She had advertised for such a lover in the daily press).

In the first letter, she says in part, "This longing has conquered me for a very long period. I have never known a man of your race and I feel an irresistible yearning to be possessed by a colored man. Knowing no one could introduce me, or cause me to know any Negroes, I made up my mind to advertise.

"When I did so I was not thinking of the strength of the black, although I have heard that many such men were so largely developed that they could

[1] p. 300. 1943.

have no intimacy with French women. I should not like you to think that this is what I am seeking. No, it is rather the reverse. Pardon me my slightly brutal expressions, but what I desire, what I wish to find is the following voluptuous pleasure, as yet unknown to me. I should like to place myself in the arms of a black man—intensely black—but not for a day or a night but for an infinity of nights devoted to love. . . ."

Another letter reads in part, "I have desired for a long time to know a very black man. I often get laughed at about it for I am very communicative. I used to say when I was with close friends: 'Oh, how I should like to sleep with a nigger.' One day the husband of one of my friends said to me in front of the assembled company, 'Well, I will black myself all over and come and see you.' I answered him, 'No, for I desire the complete illusion. I want to see a real handsome black man stark naked.' "

The third letter reads in part, "I must appear very strange to you. Here is a woman of Paris, where there are so many good-looking fellows, longing for a blackamoor. You must think that I cannot find any of my own tint to have the idea of loving deep black men. . . .

"It would be very difficult for me to explain to you whence comes my passion for your race, especially when it is a rooted idea and not the caprice of a night." In this same letter she adds later, "As much as I long for a man of your colour now, so much did I detest them about five or six years ago. At that moment I believe that if a Negro had tried to kiss me, I should have been ill through fright, and today I long to be able to satisfy this passion, too long restrained, at my ease."

The letter continues in part, "I only desire that you open your black arms ready to receive me, and press me to you. Tell me the day and the hour you will expect me and I will come at once thrilling all over with emotion and throw myself in your embrace. . . . I will abandon myself to you, you in me. Come then, and take possession of my body. Press me in your dusky embrace . . ."[2]

Several writers in dealing with this passion have called it mere "lust." But I asked myself why interracial "lust?" If mere sex satisfaction were the motive then these white persons could have found any number of their own "race" and with probably less trouble.

The significance of this kind of "lust" appeared even stronger to me when I discovered that it extended even to the homosexual relations, that there were white sex perverts of both sexes who preferred blacks to whites. I also learnt that in institutions as prisons and reformatories where the sexes

---

2 p. viii-xii. 1935. The irony of this affair is that it was not a Negro, but a white man who answered her advertisement, and passed himself off as black, thus, her longings were not satisfied.

are segregated, but the "races" aren't, that this attraction of the white by the black also existed. For instance, J. L. Moreno, writing of the State Training Schools for Girls at Hudson, New York, says, "One form of attraction came to our attention, which, as far as we know, has never been analyzed. This is the sexual attraction of white girls to colored girls. . . . It is the white girl who almost invariably takes the initiative and courts the colored girl." I shall have more to say on what Dr. Moreno says of this subject as well on what I, myself, have observed.

In dealing with this sexual attraction few scientists have been bold enough and frank enough to discuss it openly, or even to admit its existence, and these are chiefly Europeans as Havelock Ellis, Iwan Bloch, Owen Berkeley-Hill, Ian D. MacCrone, or Latin-Americans as Gilberto-Freyre. In this respect I wish to make special mention of MacCrone's Race Attitudes in South Africa. This scientist, who is professor of psychology in the University of Witwatersrand, South Africa, had the depth, the courage and the understanding to treat the matter as it is. In fact I found in his writings so many of the conclusions that I had come to myself over the years that I was both astonished and delighted.

He says, for instance, "Evidence of a more serious nature can be brought forward to show that the black does exercise a potent sexual attraction upon the white." He tells how Negroes of both sexes were brought in numbers into the ancient Roman empire for the sexual satisfaction of white people; of how they were brought from Egypt to France during Napoleon's conquest of that land for the same purpose; and of the American whites in Harlem, and adds, "The sexual attraction of the black for the white does exist and is a factor which deserves consideration. . . .

"What is the source of this attraction both for white men and for white women and what effect does it have upon the attitude of the white men and women?" I shall give more in its proper place.

Interested also in knowing the universal cause—the deep inner why of happenings—I sought further and found two writers, one of the last century, and one of today, who gave satisfying answers. The first is Arthur Schopenhauer (1788-1860), who although he did not have the advantage of the researches of Darwin, Huxley, Wallace, and later scientists, saw so deeply into life that he was able to blaze out new paths for those who were to follow. What Schopenhauer has to say in a generalized way on the tendency of fair people to mate with dark opened up wide vistas of understanding for me. I shall give what he had to say on this in its proper place, also.

The second writer is J. R. Marett, professor of anthropology, Oxford

University, England, in whose work "Race, Sex, and Environment," I found a reason so logical that I do not know where to find a better.

Finally, let me say that I do not mean to say that the majority of white people wish to mate with Negroes, or that the majority of Negroes are seeking white people. I am merely trying to give the reason why those who wish to do so. Please remember also that my curiosity on this subject over more than forty years had led me into many likely and unlikely places, thereby permitting me to see somewhat more than the average individual. There is much more under the surface than those who live conventional lives and think conventional thoughts imagine. "There are more things in heaven and earth, Horatio, than are dreamt of in your philosophy."

NOTE: For more extended research on racial intermixture as well as more recent happenings in that field see my "NATURE KNOWS NO COLOR-LINE" In which are reproductions of hundreds of coats-of-arms of noble European families including royalty in which are unmixed Negroes, evidently the ancestors of these families.

SEX AND RACE

Chapter One

MIXED MARRIAGES AS SEEN BY THE LAW -- ANCIENT AND EARLY HISTORIC

> *"Neither shalt thou make marriages with them; thy daughter thou shalt not give unto his son, nor his daughter shalt thou take unto thy son."* Deuteronomy, 7:3.

RULING classes and stronger peoples from time immemorial have prohibited marriage of their members with groups they considered socially inferior. Their object was three-fold: To have a permanently "inferior" group whose labor could be exploited at a minimum of cost; to be able to cohabit freely with the women of the weaker groups, and thus breed more of the latter to be exploited; and to sustain their ego and their morale by having an under-privileged class to look down upon.

This procedure was not at all racial. Black and brown peoples have used it against other blacks and browns; whites against whites; yellows against yellows; blacks and browns against whites; and whites against blacks and browns. It was simply and solely a case of the strong against the weak.

• The Code of Manu, one of the oldest law-books of the world forbade the marriage of a Brahman, or "twice-born' 'individual, with a Sudra, or artisan. Should a Brahman woman so far forget herself as to have a child by a Sudra, the child sank to the Chandala caste, "the lowest of mortals," who was so despised that if he sat on a seat used by a Brahman he was to have his buttocks slit. Manu also considered a woman who had red, or golden hair, inferior, and marriage with her by any of the three upper castes was forbidden (Chap. III, 8). A Brahman was sometimes black and a Sudra sometimes fair, and both might have had a Negro strain. Social position, not color, was the criterion. Caste distinctions in marriage still prevail in India.

The ancient Egyptians must undoubtedly have forbidden marriage with the Jews because when the latter first arrived in Egypt as visitors, and not yet slaves, the Egyptians thought it "an abomination" to break bread with them (Genesis, 42:32). In spite of the high favor shown to Joseph, the Egyptians regarded the Jews as "an abomination" when they came to settle in Egypt because they were shepherds, and relegated them to Goshen (Genesis, 45:34). The Egyptians, like the Jews, were then of mixed white and Negro strain.

Four centuries later when the Jews arrived in Palestine and had conquered that land they followed the example set by Abraham of non-marriage with the peoples there. The latter, however, were according to the Bible of the same original stock as the Jews, namely, the family of Noah. But true to the policy of the conqueror the Jews reserved the right to cohabit with and make concubines of the virgins of the beaten Canaanites, after killing the mothers and the fathers (Numbers, 31:17,18; Deuteronomy 7:2,3).

But these prohibitions against marriage did not work. Some very prominent Hebrews married "strange women." Samson married Delilah, a Philistine; Boaz married Ruth, a Moabitess, ancestress of David; David married Maachah, a Geshurite and Bathsheba, a Hittite; Solomon married Pharaoh's daughter and had so many other non-Jewish wives that there was a revolt against him led by Jeroboam (1 Kings, Chaps. 11-14). He even appears to have lost his throne because of them (Eccles. 1:12). Ahab married Jezebel of Sidon. In fact there was once so general an intermarriage of the Jews with the Canaanites, Hittites, and other peoples, that, according to the Bible, Jehovah sold them into bondage to the king of Mesopotamia for eight years (Judges 3:5-8).

Moses, it is true, married an Ethiopian woman and Joseph, an Egyptian one, but both had been adopted by those people and had been cut off from contact with their own. Later, when Moses found himself again among his people he was roundly scolded by Aaron and Miriam, his brother and sister, because his wife was non-Jewish (Numbers 12:1-16).

The mixing of Jews with non-Jews went on in spite of all laws. After the return from the Babylonian captivity, we find the prophet, Nehemiah, telling how he cursed those who had "transgressed against our God" by taking non-Jewish wives, and how he smote such, pulled their hair, and broke up their families (Neh. 31;17,18). The prophet Ezra, too, in a fit of fanaticism, tore his garment and his beard at seeing how the "holy seed" of Israel had married with the Canaanites, a people of similar "race," and gives a list of the Jews he compelled to leave their wives and children because the latter had not been born into the faith (Ezra, Chaps. 9 & 10).

Purity of religion, not of "race," was the motive behind these restrictions because the Jews who had been very much mixed before they left Egypt were much more so in the time of Ezra and Nehemiah. The idea behind the objection was that the child of parents who were of mixed faiths might have ideas of his own about religion. Such children were barred from entering "the congregation of the Lord," even when they were mixed with favored nations as the Egyptian and the Edomite (Deut. 23:8). For instance, there was the case of Shelomith, a Jewish woman, who had a son by an Egyptian. This son, while still in the wilderness, had an argument and a fight with a Jew over religion and was ordered stoned to death by Moses (Leviticus 24;10.14).

As regards marriage with Gentiles there are still orthodox Jews who feel as strongly against it as did the prophets of Israel.

Mixed Marriages in Rome

In Rome, there were severe laws against the marriage of patricians, or aristocrats, with plebians,[1] a people of the same color, but of the working class. There was also the bar of nationality. However, in 444 B.C., the plebians won the right to marry with the patricians through the Canuleian Law but the restrictions against the non-Roman continued into the Christian era. If say, a white Roman had a child by a white Englishwoman, the child was regarded precisely as was one of a white Virginian and a Negro woman in slavery days. Such offspring even though white were called *Hybridae,* or mixed-blood, the same term used for mules. If the English mother were free, her child ranked just one degree above a slave; if she were a slave, her child also was a slave. The same held true if a black Roman married an Ethiopian.

No matter how high-born the foreigner, he or she could not contract a legal marriage with a Roman. Gibbon says, "The blood of a king could

---

1 Bailey, T. P. (Race Orthodoxy in the South, pp. 350-55. 1914) gives a parallel between the plebians of Rome and the Negroes in the South as based on Coulanges' The Ancient City.

Martial, Roman writer of the first century A.D. in his eulogy of Caeser (III), tells of the great diversity of races living in Rome, among them being peoples from the Nile and "woolly-haired Ethiopians."

It is highly probable that the earliest patricians were of a lighter color than the plebians. The former, it seems, were chiefly of European stock, or natives, while the latter were mostly of Eastern "blood." Prof. Tenney Frank estimates that 90 percent of the plebians were Orientals (Race Mixture in the Roman Empire, Amer. Hist. Rev. Vol. 21, p. 690. 1916). These Orientals were largely from lands conquered by Rome, or lands from which the Roman slave-dealers bought their slaves, that is, they were chiefly Moors, Numidians, Egyptians, Ethiopians, and Sudanese. The island of Delos, off the coast of Greece was the great slave mart of the Roman Empire, and peoples of all colors were bought and sold there.

Great numbers of these Eastern people were brought in to re-populate Rome after the devastations of Hannibal in the third century B.C. After the invasion of Britain, France, Belgium and other northern lands by Julius Caesar, whiter-skinned peoples were also brought in hordes to Rome. These Northern whites seemed to have ranked lowest in the social scale for we find Cicero advising his friend, Atticus not to buy British slaves, because he said they could not be taught.

The patricians undoubtedly had some Oriental strain too, but it might have been more thinned out. Though they claimed descent from the gods some of the most illustrious of them had servile names as Porcia (swine) and Asinia (ass). As regards race" some revealed it in their surnames as Maurus (Moor); Fuscus (dusky) and Niger (Negro). No less than three Roman emperors were named Niger, one of whom married a daughter of a king of England (See Sex and Race, vol. 1, p. 86. 1941).

never mingle in legitimate nuptials with the blood of a Roman, and the name of Stranger degraded Cleopatra and Berenice to live the concubines of Mark Anthony and Titus."[2] Cleopatra was queen of Egypt; and Berenice, the wife of King Herod, who had been captured by Titus in the conquest of Jerusalem in 70 A.D.

With the coming of Christianity in Rome, the ban against marriage took a religious turn. Northern whites, as the Scandinavians, Germans, and English, could not marry a Christian Roman, white or black, because they were regarded as heathens. For instance, an Irishman could contract such a marriage because the Irish were Christians. "There was," says Oswald Spengler, "not the slightest difficulty about an Irishman in Constantinople marrying a Negress if both were Christians."[3]

There was such an absence of color prejudice that when Pope Vitalian (657-672 A.D.) wanted someone to head the Church in England and become the first archbishop of Canterbury, he selected a Negro, Hadrian.[4] When

[2] Decline and Fall of the Roman Empire, Vol. 3, Ch. 44, p. 174. 1831. 4 vols. Tacitus Book XII, 53.

[3] Decline of the West, Vol. 2, p. 69. 1932. Also R. F. A. Hoernle very rightly says, "In ancient Greece and Rome there is no trace of any colour prejudice, whether in sexual or in any other human relations. In the Middle Ages and right into modern times what mattered in dividing men against each other was their religion, but not their race or the color of their skin." (Race Mixture and Native Policy in South Africa in Schapera, I, Western Civilization and the Natives of South Africa, pp. 263-280. 1934). Had there been color prejudice then it certainly would have been recorded along with the national, tribal, and religious ones.

[4] Lappenberg says that the Pope "wishing to set over the Anglo-Saxon bishops a primate devoted to his views, venerable by age and experience and distinguished by his rare knowledge and learning" offered "the dignity to an African, named Hadrian, a monk of Niridano, near Monte Cassino in the kingdom of Naples, who declining the honor for himself, recommended as worthier of it the monk, Theodore, born at Tarsus in Cilicia, a man eminently qualified by his attainments. The recommendation was adopted by the pontiff on condition that Hadrian should accompany the primate to England." (History of England under the Anglo-Saxons, Vol. 1, p. 172. 1845). To these two men England owed the real beginnings of her culture.

Bede, the Venerable, first English historian, who lived in the time of Theodore and Hadrian, and probably knew them both, says of Hadrian, "uir natione Afir," that is, he was one of the "African nation." (Historiae Ecclesiastica Gentis Anglorum, Book 4, ch. 1). At the time "race" was not used as we use it now but "nation" was. A black man was said to be of the African nation. Margaret Murray, a much later English writer, refers to Hadrian twice as "Hadrian the Negro." She says, "Theodore of Tarsus with the aid of Hadrian the Negro organized the Church of England in the seventh century.' (God of the Witches, p. 6. 1933). Africans in our days are at once thought of as Negroes and there is no proof that it was otherwise then. Hadrian died in England and was buried in St. Augustines Chapel, Canterbury.

Either Theodore or Hadrian had very short hair because Bede says that the hair took four months to grow in order "that it might be shorn in the shape of a crown for he had the tonsure of St. Paul." As worded by Bede, it might mean either man. Some writers have translated it to mean Theodore and others, Hadrian.

Hadrian declined and suggested another, the Pope sent Hadrian along as practical supervisor of Theodore who had been given the post.

The Emperor Justinian married his Negro cook to a noble Roman lady, an honor that would have been denied a German or Russian prince.[5] The white princes of the North, says Gibbon, were very eager to contract marriage with the aristocrats of the South, which latter undoubtedly included some mulattoes and blacks. Liuprand, bishop of Cremona, who saw the Roman Emperor, Nicephorus Phocas, said that he was in color a Negro.[5b] The Emperor Constantine, says Gibbon, was so opposed to unions of Christians with even the white kings of the North that he had the prohibition written in "irrevocable law" on "the altar of St. Sophia," Christendom's then most exalted shrine.

In his decree Constantine used language on national and religious dissimilarities which resembles that of certain scientists and legislators of our day when speaking of "race." He said, to quote Gibbon, "Every animal, says the discreet emperor, is prompted by nature to seek a mate among the animals of his own species and as the human species is divided into various tribes by the distinction of language, religion, and manners, a just regard to the purity of descent preserves the harmony of public and private life; but the mixture of foreign blood is the fruitful source of disorder and discord."[6] Purity of descent, we find here, is based not on "race" but on similarity of culture.

Later, the Jews, who in their days of power had called themselves "God's Chosen People," as the Chinese called themselves "Sons of Heaven," were to get a dose of their own medicine. The Romans of the time of Juvenal, first century A.D., made slaves of them and treated them very badly. As for marriage, Christian Rome severely banned marriage of one of them with a Christian, white or black. The earliest English code, that of the seventh century A.D., forbade any union of Christian and Jew, and inflicted a penance of as high as twelve years on any woman who had illicit sex relations with a Jew.[7] A Spanish law of 1348 condemned to death any Jew going with a Christian woman, even though she were a prostitute. In Avignon, France, the penalty for the same was a fine of twenty-five French pounds and the loss of a limb "for each offense." The outlawing of any sexual relations between Jews and Christians was revived by Hitler in 1935.

5 (a & b). See sources in Sex and Race, Vol. 1, p. 118. 1941.
6 Gibbon, Vol. 4, Chap. 53, pp. 13-14.
7 Ancient Laws and Institutes of England. Theodori Arch. Cant. XVI, 35. It read: "Si qua Christiana faemina a perfidis Judaeis munera suscipit, ac cum eis voluntarie fornicationem fecerit, annum integrum separatur ab aeclesia et cum magna tribuationate vivat; deinde ix. annos poeniteat. Si autem liberos genuerit xii. annos poeniteat." etc., etc.

1. Leopold I, Emperor of Germany, by Thomas of Ypres (New York Public Library Coll.)
Compare his features with those of Kamehameha II, on opposite page.

11. Kamehameha II of Hawaii (Compare his features with those of Leopold I, Emperor of Germany, on opposite page).

Whites of the Same Race and Religion Who Could Not Marry

In northern Europe white peoples also had laws banning marriage between themselves and other whites of the same religion and nationality but of the lower class. Professor E. A. Ross says: "Thus among the Saxons of the eighth century social divisions were cast-iron and the law punished with death the man who should presume to marry a woman of rank higher than his own. The Lombards killed the serf who ventured to marry a free woman, while the Visigoths and Burgundians scourged and burned them both . . ."[8]

The English upper class of the eleventh century treated white women of the lower class in a manner that reminds one of how their descendants, the Virginia colonists, treated black women. William of Malmesbury, English historian of the twelfth century, tells how the nobles used "to sell their female servants when pregnant and after they had satisfied their lust either to public prostitution or foreign slavery." He tells of another noblewoman who used to buy up the most beautiful slave girls and sell them at a profit in Denmark.[9]

When the Normans ruled England they regarded the Anglo-Saxons, a whiter complexioned people than they, in the same manner as the Americans slaveholders regarded the Negroes. Macaulay says: "In the time of Richard I the ordinary imprecation of a Norman gentleman was: 'May I become an Englishman.' His ordinary form of indignant denial was: 'Do you take me for an Englishman?' In no country has the enmity of race been carried farther than in England. In no country has that enmity been more completely effaced."

---

[8] Caste and Class. American Jour. of Sociology, Vol. 22, pp. 749-50. 1917. Professor Ross adds: "Even to female beauty and charm the caste line may show itself adamant. The daughter of a rich American who marries a titled European is rarely admitted to the husband's rank. She is made to feel the farmer's or workingman's blood in her veins, the taint of usefulness in her ancestors. The American wife of a high-caste Austrian is not invited to homes of her husband's friends, nor recognized socially."

I saw an example of this snobbery as practiced against Americans in 1930 at Addis-Ababa. Among the visitors to Haile Selassie's coronation were the titled daughter of a former viceroy of India and one of New York's social set, who is related to one of America's great millionaires. Both ladies travelled together, stopped at the same hotel and were being invited together everywhere, as at the receptions at the French and Italian legations. However, at the reception given to the Duke of Gloucester, son of George. V, by the British Legation the American woman was not invited though her name had been given in by the American Minister. She was much hurt by the snub. "To think," she said to me, "that Lady —— and I are both travelling together and she was invited and I left out."

[9] History of the Kings of England, pp. 255, 230 (trans. by John Sharpe. 1915). For the manner in which the Southern masters did the identical thing to colored and near-white women in the nineteenth century see chapter, "Slaveholders and Their Trade with Houses of Prostitution" in Sex and Race, Vol. 2.

Of the marriage of the Norman king, Henry I, to Edith, an Anglo-Saxon princess, Macaulay says it "was regarded as a marriage between a white planter and a quadroon girl would now be regarded in Virginia."[10]

During the Middle Ages, and well into the eighteenth century, the Catholics, who were then in power forbade whites who were of the faith to marry whites who were not of the faith. This was particularly so in Spain, Austria, Italy and France. Marriage between Catholic and non-Catholic is still either forbidden or frowned on by the Catholic Church.

The English and the Irish

None of the above-mentioned prohibitions, however, reached the severity of the ban against the marriage of English to Irish, who were then both Catholic. The Statutes of Kilkenny issued in 1367 by Edward III of England show how far one white group can go in prohibiting marriage with another white group. The worst that Virginia has to offer between that of white and black is almost beneficent in comparison. The English soldier in Ireland, cut off from all women, except Irish ones, who dared to have an amour with an Irishwoman, was guilty of high treason, the punishment for which was death in the most horrible manner. He was "half-hanged, cut down, disembowelled alive and forfeited his estate.[11] Under Cromwell, too, there were heavy penalties against an Englishman for taking an Irish wife. Soldiers who had an amour with an Irish girl were severely flogged.

According to Ringrose's Marriage and Divorse Laws of the World (1924), the following marriages are still illegal: In Servia between Christian and non-Christian; in Sweden, heathens and atheists with Christians; in Morocco and Persia between Moslem and Jew. In all of the lands above-mentioned, with the exception of France during the time when the white colonists of Haiti had considerable influence there, no prohibition existed against the marriage of white and black on racial grounds. Portugal, the European land which had the largest percentage of Negroes, never had a color line.

Primitive dark-skinned peoples also had, and still have, anti-miscegenation laws. Among the Balinese, for instance, the penalty for marrying out of one's own caste was death, a punishment which the Dutch later had changed to imprisonment.[12]

---

10 History of England, pp. 13-14. 1849.
11 Prendergast, J. P., The Cromwellian Settlement of Ireland, pp. 40, 143, 1868.
12 Hirschfeld, M., Mand and Woman, p. 114. 1935. F. A. Sweetenham says that Malay men had the strongest objection to a Malay woman loving, or marrying with, a Chinese. Sometimes the Chinese was killed; sometimes the woman. It was never so bad, he says, "if a Malay had a Chinese woman." (British Malaya, p. 147. 1929).

In West Africa, the Mandingoes, once a ruling people, objected for centuries to marriage with the Kru, another black people. It is said they still do. Much the same is true of certain other African peoples.

Irish, Quakers, and Jews in Colonial America

The United States has probably never had a law against the marriage of one white group to another white group, but it had what amounted virtually to one in the case of three groups: the Irish, the Quakers and the Jews.

The Puritans of New England, it seems, brought with them their hostility to the Irish. In 1652, when David Sellacke, a ship captain merely permitted some Irish members of his crew to come ashore in Boston he was heavily fined. It appears they had only done so to bring ashore one of their sick. Sellacke's fine was later remitted but he was ordered to see that the Irishman was taken aboard as soon as he got well. Martha Benton, a housewife, was given permission to import two servants from Ireland provided she could prove they were of English ancestry. In 1654, Virginia forced all Irish into bondage for five years, and later classed them with aliens. Maryland, between 1704 and 1720 passed twelve laws against the Irish, one of which increased the tax on any importation of them to five pounds sterling. South Carolina offered a bonus of thirteen pounds for every colonist brought in but he was not to be Irish; and on May 10, 1729, Pennsylvania barred all Irish.

In August 1834, mobs in Boston beat every Irish person found on the street, burnt their homes and the Ursuline Convent at Charlestown. On September 12, 1837 when the Montgomery Guards (named after General Montgomery, Revolutionary War hero) appeared to march in a parade, they were ordered home, and when they did not go, they were stoned by the mob.

In Philadelphia during the whole month of May 1844, the Irish were mobbed. On July 4th the same year there was another riot in that city, which lasted for three days in which cannon were used in the streets, more than a hundred persons killed or wounded; and two Irish churches and two rectories burned.

In New York City attempts were made to burn down St. Patrick's Cathedral. It was saved only by stationing sharpshooters at the windows. So great was the hatred of the Irish that the Negroes were forgotten. Scharf and Westcott say, "The spirit of riot and disorder which for some years had vented itself upon Negroes and mulattoes found an entirely new object."

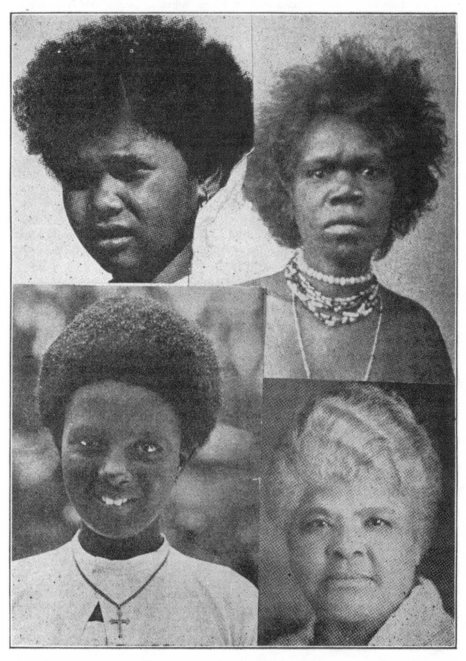

III. Upper left to right: Filipino girl, and Australian Bushwoman. Lower: Ethiopian girl and the late Mrs. Ida B. Wells Barnett, Chicago suffrage leader. The first three are not considered Negroes; the last one is. She is American.

In the cities of the North in apartments and stores the sign "No Irish need apply" was frequently seen.[13]

The Quakers

The white Quakers in Massachusetts were treated with great barbarity. It is safe to say that they ranked even lower than the Negroes, because while the Negroes were permitted to enter the colony and, according to an order of May 27, 1652, were trained in the militia—there were no jim-crow companies, then — the Quakers were forbidden to enter the colony at all and came in only by stealth. Any ship captain, who brought in a Quaker from Europe was liable to a fine of twenty pounds sterling, a large sum in those days. On December 3, 1658, one man was fined nine pounds for attending a Quaker meeting, and on September 4, 1656, another was fined five pounds for entertaining one in his house. There was also a heavy fine for selling, or hiring, a horse to a Quaker. In other words, though they were the most civilized and humane of the white colonists—they had met the Indians unarmed and had bought, not stolen, their lands and food— they were virtually outlaws. Those who refused to leave the colony were stripped to the waist, regardless of sex, tied to the tail of a cart and whipped through the town. They were branded on the face and hand with the letters "H" or "R"; their tongues were pierced with red-hot irons; they were banished to slavery in the West Indies; and if they returned after being once expelled from the colony, were hanged. Three men and one woman once suffered this fate together. Needless to say that when there was a fine of forty shillings an hour (about $40 in the value of our time) for having a Quaker in your house that marriage between a white Puritan and a white Quaker, both of whom were usually English, was unthinkable.[14]

The Jews

The Jews, too, were not welcome in America. In Spanish America, especially Mexico and Peru, they were met with all the horrors of the Inquisition. As late as 1639, they were burnt at the stake.

[13] Records of Massachusetts Bay Colony, Oct. 19 and 26, 1652; Hart, A. B., Commonwealth History of Massachusetts. Vol. 4, pp. 488-92; Vol. 5, 517-21. 1927; Haynes, G. H., The Cause of Know Nothing Success in American Hist. Rev. 1897-8. Vol. 2, pp. 67-82; Cullen, J. B., The Irish in Boston. 1899; Roberts, E. F., Ireland in America, pp. 82-3. 1931; McGuire, J. F., The Irish in America. 1863; Scharf and Westcott, History of Philadelphia. Vol. 1, pp. 663-73. 1884.
[14] Records New Plymouth Colony, Dec. 3, 1658; Sept. 4, 1656; Laws New Plymouth Colony, June 10, 1660. Records Massachusetts Bay Colony Oct. 26, 1652; Oct. 19. 1652; Oct. 14, 1656; Oct. 8, 1662; Oct. 2, 1678. Palfrey, History of New England, Vol. 2, pp. 460-484. 1860.

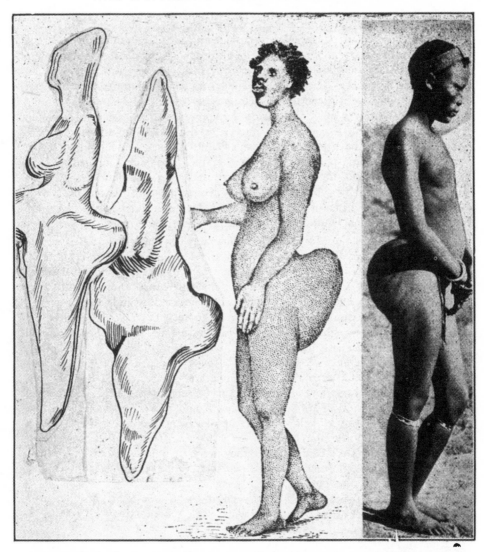

IV. Left to right: Two Grimaldi carvings of about 15,000 B. C., showing the steatopygy, or development of fat on the buttocks. Venus Kallipygos, or the celebrated Hottentot Venus of the last century, from a model of her in the Museum d'Ethnologie, Paris. (Winchell). A living Hottentot woman of the Kalahari, South Africa. (See also No. 5, Sex and Race, Vol. I.)

None of the North American colonies wanted them. Peter Stuyvesant tried to drive them out of New York. He wanted, he said, none of "the deceitful race—such hateful enemies and blasphemers of Christ . . . to infect and trouble the new colony." In 1685, Jewish worship was forbidden in New York, nor could Jews buy land even for a burial-ground. It was not until 1730 they were permitted to own a synagogue.

In 1737, it was only cool heads that prevented a massacre of them in New York. During a contest for a seat in the Assembly between Phillips and Van Horne, the latter made an anti-Semitic speech, in which he depicted in such violent language the sufferings that the Jews were supposed to have inflicted on Christ, that the mob was roused to anti-Semitic frenzy. The Jews saved their lives by staying away from the polls. Later they were disfranchised. A writer of the times said, "The unfortunate Israelites were content to lose their votes could they escape with their lives."[15]

In Massachusetts, Maryland, Virginia, and elsewhere there were restrictions against them, too. Virginia classed them with Negroes and Moslems, and forbade them to buy white people. Had there been no Negroes in America, or had the Negroes been in sufficiently small numbers to have been absorbed by the whites as they had been in England, Portugal, and France, the Jews would undoubtedly have occupied the place of persecution now held by the Negroes, and the laws now extant against blacks, would be fixed on them. The American people, if we are to judge by its psychology, needs some group on which to fix its hate—a scapegoat—someone to look down on. The members of the various emigrant groups coming from Europe where they had been looked down upon for centuries found that one of the joys of the New World was that they could now despise someone else. The Irish, for instance, held in contempt for centuries, assumed an air of great superiority over the Negroes. In 1863, they led in the massacre of Negroes in New York City. Indeed they were, to within twenty years ago, the worst enemies of the Negroes in the North, with the Poles, another long oppressed people, the next.

In 1920, the Ku Klux Klan revived for a few years anti-Semitism and anti-Catholicism on a nation-wide scale. Both are still strong in certain areas, North and South.

[15] Familiar Hist. of the Evangelical Churches of N. Y., pp. 156-9. 1839. Henning's Statutes of Virginia, Vol. 5, Chap. 14, art. 9, p. 550. Lebeson, A. L., Jewish Pioneers in America, p. 46. 1931.

Chapter Two

MIXED MARRIAGES AS SEEN BY THE LAW -- OUR TIMES

"When the state is most corrupt then the laws are most multi-plied" Tacitus.
"What has been decreed among prehistoric protozoa cannot be annulled by Act of Parliament." Thomas Huxley.

A S was said although Negroes were fairly abundant in Europe, there was no law on record against their marriage with white people except in France during the period when the white colonists of Haiti exercised much influence there. The white Americans, though they were able to revive Negro slavery in England after its abolition by Lord Chief Justice Holt[1] about 1702, either did not try, or did not succeed in getting an anti-miscegenation law passed. Thus the reasons for opposing mixed marriages which, as we have seen so far were social and economic, did not also become "racial" until the colonization of the New World began. As Hoernle says, "The evidence strongly suggests that colour prejudice entered into the colonial expansion of Europe in proportion as economic, industrial and nationalistic motives replaced the older religious motives as the chief determinant in the relations of white and non-white."

It may fairly be said that any prohibition of marriage between white and black at all began in the New World. Venezuela, Mexico, Haiti and one or two other Latin American lands, had such laws, but they were abolished either under the Spanish regime or upon the winning of independence. The United States is the only country in the New World which has carried its law against the marriage of white and black from its colonial period into its national one.

1 Campbell, J. L., Lives of the Chief Justices of England, Vol. 2, p. 406. 1874. The American slaveholders, however, succeeded in setting the decision aside by Yorke, the attorney-general and Talbot, the solicitor-general in 1729. Twenty years later Yorke, as Chief Justice, again declared slavery in England legal. In 1772, Chief Justice Lord Mansfield again declared it illegal in the Somerset case, but contrary to general belief that did not end it as Negro slaves continued to be advertised for sale. (Stuart, C., Memoirs of Granvills Sharp, p. 20. 1836.) Negroes were probably not freed in England until 1834, when slavery was abolished throughout the empire. But incredible as it sounds white people in the British Isles were still held in actual slavery after the blacks were freed. These were the Scotch colliers. See Eden, F. M., History of Laboring Classes in England, pp. 7-11. 1797. Miller, H., My School and Schoolmasters, pp. 303-305. 1857.) These colliers had been freed in 1775, but the masters ignored the law. They were not freed until 1842. And, of course, we recall that the Russians were freed from slavery only in 1861.

It still has them in twenty-eight states, being one of the only three countries in which such marriages are outlawed. The others are South Africa, and Australia.

In South Africa, such unions were one legal in Cape Colony and Natal but it is a crime now. In Transvaal and Natal the penalty is imprisonment and the lash.

A commission appointed in 1938 by the South African government to inquire whether interracial marriages "are sufficiently numerous to be seriously detrimental" to the future of the white race recommended that "legislation on the model of the Transvaal laws should be passed prohibiting marriages between Europeans and non-Europeans."[a] As for illicit intercourse between white and black in any part of South Africa that is as serious an offense as beastiality. The penalty, according to a law of March 26, 1927 is five years' imprisonment.[b] This law has had no more success than similar ones in the United States, and "the colored population increases year after year."[c]

Nazi Germany

In Nazi Germany the Nuremberg law of 1935 provided: "Whoever ministers or tries to administer to the debasement or disturbance of German blood purity by uniting or aiding a union with members of the Jewish race or other colored races shall be found guilty of race treachery and sent to prison.

"Racial treason is committed even when sexual relations are effected with the use of prevenceptives."

In determining who are of mixed blood this law was retroactive to the year 1800. If one had a Jewish or a Negro ancestor in that year he was not an "Aryan." In 1938 a farmer, son of a German professor, was designated by his uncle to inherit his farm under the hereditary farmer's act as the nearest male relative. On investigating the prospective heir's ancestry it was discovered, however, that his great-grandmother had been a mulatto, born in 1805 of a white father and a black mother, and he was disinherited. The court ruled that the requirements of blood purity are so imperative that although only "Aryan" strain was visible in him it did not count. The rich estate went to the Reich, that is, the Nazis.[4]

2 Haldane, J. B. S., Heredity and Politics, p. 140. 1938.
3a Race Relations News. No. 15, Sept. 1939. Most of the mixed marriages in South Africa between Negroes and whites from 1927-36 were between whites and mulattoes—698 white men to mulatto women; and 137 white women to mulatto men. (Ibid. Jan. 1939). See also: Sex and Race, Vol. 1, pp. 131-141,
3b Statutes of S. Africa, Vol. 1, p. 14. 1927.
3c Ziervogel, C., Brown South Africa, p. 19. 1938.
4 New York Post, Aug. 10, 1938, as reported by the Reich Food Laws.

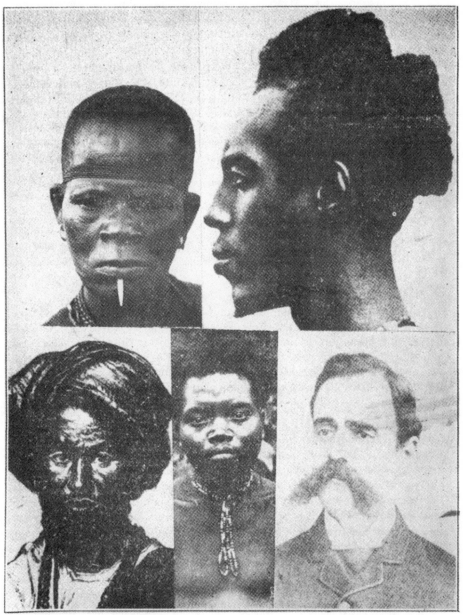

V. Upper left to right: Woman of Central Africa, a Negro; and a Batusti, of East Africa, who though black-skinner and wooly-haired is not classed a Negro. Below: Native of Mauritania, Africa, coal-black and frizzly-haired, but also, "not a Negro." Centre: Black-skinned, frizzly-haired Malayan, also "not a Negro." Right: Peyton M. DeWitt, noted horticulturist, born in the United States and with a distant African ancestor. He "is a Negro."

According to strict "Aryan" requirements, most white Americans, even some of the most racially proud, would be considered undesirable partners for Nazis. The German ideal of a woman is "a blonde Aryan with blue, wide-open eyes, a pink and white complexion, a narrow nose, a small mouth, and by all means, a virgin." This type, says *Das Wissen der Nation,* should by no means marry one of the darker European peoples, as blondness is the highest sign of racial superiority. Also that no "blond, blue-eyed" Aryan man should marry a brunette, or a woman with "short legs, or black hair, or hooked nose, or full lips and large mouth, or an inclination to plumpness." White persons with full lips and other facial features that appear Negroid are also barred. "The Aryan hero must marry only his equal Aryan woman."[5]

Anti-Marriage Laws of the United States

In the United States twenty-seven and a half states have laws against so-called mixed marriages; seventeen make no mention of them, thus making them legal; while one, Michigan, expressly provides that the marriage of white and black is legal.

The anti-miscegenation laws of the twenty-seven and a half states, when viewed nationally, as say the marriage laws of France, England, or any of the other countries of the New World, present a pattern so confused that it is fantastic. It is no exaggeration to say that in their freakishness and the mix-ups they have caused, especially in the inheritance of property, they could very well have been composed by a congress of prize lunatics in the heart of a madhouse at the craziest season of the year.

Hardly any two of these states agree on what degree of Negro strain constitutes a bar to marriage. Certain of them as Arkansas, California, Delaware, Idaho, Kentucky, and Louisiana declare marriage between a white person and a "mulatto" illegal. Now in strict ethnology a mulatto is the offspring of an unmixed white and an unmixed black. But in America, one with only one-sixty-fourth Negro strain, is sometimes called a mulatto. The result is that the definition of "mulatto" can be twisted to suit every wind of prejudice. In Louisiana, for instance, the state with the greatest percentage of Negro strain in the white population, one in whom the Negro strain is no longer visible, can be adjudged a mulatto. In 1938, a Louisiana court annulled the marriage of a white man to a woman whose great-great-grandmother was a Negro. In fact, if a white person in some way has associated long enough with Negroes as to become known as one, he is likely to run afoul of the marriage law if he marries a white person. R. W. Woolley

5 Quoted in Schuman, F., The Nazi Dictatorship, p. 383. 1939.

reported such a case from New Orleans when the present anti-miscegenation law of Louisiana came into force in 1908. He says, "Decidedly the most perplexing case with which the district attorney of New Orleans had to deal was that of Stanhope P. Turnbull and his wife, Charity Turnbull. The man is a grandson of a former United States District Judge and a nephew of a former administrator of the city of New Orleans. The woman claims to be the daughter of a German named Gottlieb Lindermayer and to be white, although she has two colored children . . . She says that years ago she began associating with Negroes, was promptly dropped by her white friends completely and soon became known as a colored person. Her first husband was a Negro, she rides in the Negro section of the street car and a Negro preacher married her to Turnbull. Moreover, at the time of her marriage to Turnbull, the Reconstruction law permitting white and colored persons to wed had not been repealed."[6] This elderly couple went to Mississippi, probably either to escape the publicity or because they were ordered out of the state, but they were sent to prison and the marriage annulled. Mrs. Turnbull, by all accounts, looked as white as her husband. One of her sons was at the time one of the most highly respected lawyers of the city.

In Oregon, a citizen with less than a fourth Negro strain in a direct white line was adjudged white and could marry a white person but could not marry a quadroon or a mulatto. In Alabama, Florida, Indiana, Maryland, Mississippi, Missouri, Nebraska, North Carolina, North Dakota, Tennessee, and Texas the bar is against those with an eighth or more Negro strain. In Georgia, Montana, Oklahoma, and Virginia the prohibition is absolute. Negro strain, however remote, is barred. The Virginia law provides that if there is any "ascertainable" Negro strain, the marriage is illegal. That is to say, if certain cousins of Queen Elizabeth II, were to migrate to Virginia, husbands and wives would have to separate or run afoul of the law. These cousins are members of the Mountbatten family. The present head of this family, David Francis, third Marquess of Milford Haven, is a grandson of the Countess Torby, who is a descendant of Pushkin, whose Negro strain is very much "ascertainable."[7]

The matter becomes still more ridiculous when one remembers that next to Louisiana and South Carolina, Virginia has, perhaps, the greatest amount of Negro strain in its white population. Miscegenation started in Virginia in 1630. Virginia's marriage law is as fantastic as the distorting mirror of a dime museum. Numbers of Virginians have had to change their

---

6 The South's Fight for Race Purity. Pearson's Maga. January, 1910.

7 Ruvigny, Titled Nobility of Europe, pp. 307, 1450. 1914. Burke's Peerage, Vol. 2, p. 1773. 1939. Lord Milford Haven is a nephew of Lord Louis Mountbatten, famous Commando, and Commander-in-Chief of Allied Forces in the Far East.

"racial" status not less than three times since 1866. In 1866, those with less than a quarter Negro or Indian strain, were white; in 1910 the proportion was raised to a sixteenth; in 1924, the law provided that there must be "no trace whatsoever" of other blood than Caucasian. Feeling that even this was not strong enough the law in 1930 was finally made to read that if there were any "ascertainable" Negro strain, that is, if one could dig back a thousand years and find a Negro in any white American's ancestry that white man became a Negro. Thus, as I said, Virginians who were white in 1866, ceased to be so in 1910; those who remained white in 1910, were no longer so in 1924; and so on to 1932, because the law was again tinkered with in that year. The penalty on mixed marriages is now one to five years' imprisonment.[8]

As for the Indian, the process has been much the same. Intermarriage with one in any degree is barred. The law declares that if one has a fourth or more Indian strain and less than a sixteenth Negro, he is legally an Indian provided he remains on the reservation. If an "Indian" leaves the reservation, however, he becomes a Negro. The real Indian has ceased to exist, by law, in Virginia.

In Georgia, the law as to who constitutes a Negro has also been changed in similar manner, with the result that there are complications from time to time in the inheritance of property. In May 1943, one Mrs. Irish, a white woman, claimed the $10,000 estate of her cousin, Mrs. Jones, a Negro woman, almost white and married to a Negro, on the ground that when Mrs. Jones was married she was legally a white person. The law making one of her ancestry a Negro was not passed until 1927.[9]

In Oklahoma, marriage between white and Indian is legal while that between Negro and Indian is illegal. The Osage or Oklahoma Indians are wealthy. There are several oil millionaires among them. But the Osage is

---

[8] Guild, J. P., Black Laws of Virginia, pp. 34-6. 1936. For examples of legal and domestic complications see Mangum, C. S., The Legal Status of the Negro, pp. 236-73. Also chapter, "Who Is a Negro?" pp. 1-17.

[9] Carey McWilliams says, "That many persons of non-Negroid blood are frequently caught in these absurd regulations is clearly indicated by the increasing number of libel and slander actions that have been successfully prosecuted in southern courts. As the percentage of persons of pure Negro extraction decreases (as it is doing) the classification upon which Jim-Crow statutes are based are becoming increasingly unreasonable. I am convinced that many statutes are for this reason alone clearly unconstitutional. A Louisiana appellate court recently held invalid a marriage between a white man and a woman whose great-great-grandmother was a Negress. How can such classification be upheld as reasonable? A few years ago a woman in Arizona, who was part Negro and part white, challenged the constitutionality of a miscegenation statute on the ground that the way the law was worded she could not contract a legal marriage with either a Negro or a white man." (Antioch Review, 1942, p. 638).

much more Negro than anything else.[10] The rule is that if such live on the reservation they are Indian, no matter what they are. Thus while a Negro who is an "Indian" may marry a white person on the reservation he'd go to prison if he married a Negro from the city, should the law be strictly enforced.

In Louisiana too, a Negro and an Indian may not cohabit or marry, although the real Indian of that state disappeared centuries ago into the Caucasian and Negro groups, principally the later. In North Carolina, Negroes and Indians (there are really no Indians) may marry, provided the "Indians" do not come from Robison County. Georgia includes natives of the West Indies in its prohibition.

For freakishness, Colorado takes the cake. While mixed marriages are legal in the southern part of the state, they are punishable with two years' imprisonment in the northern part.[11] The southern part of the state was settled by Spain and was permitted by the state constitution to keep its marriage laws. The northern part was settled by the Anglo-Saxons.

As Vernier says in his analysis of these laws, "There are several points of variation and conflict in the statutes prohibiting miscegenetic marriages. Those prohibiting marriages between whites and Negroes differ widely in their definition of "Negro." Fourteen, in general terms prohibit inter-marriage between a white person and a "Negro" or "mulatto," or persons African descent; five apply the prohibition to the descendants of Negroes "to the third generation inclusive"; while six apply it to those having one-eighth or more Negro blood; one to those having one-fourth or more of Negro blood; and one to persons having one-sixteenth or more Negro blood. Two states includes "mestizoes" (the offspring of an Indian, or a Negro and a European or person of European stock); four states extend the prohibition to Indians; and in two, marriage between Indians and Negroes is prohibited. . . .

"The general rule adopted by statute in twenty-six states seems to be that prohibited interracial marriages are null and void from the beginning. The language used in some of the statutes might, however conceivably be construed to render such marriage merely voidable. But such terms "null and void," "illegal and void," "utterly null and void," seem clear declarations of complete nullity especially in the light of the fact that in almost all of these states miscegenation is a crime, often a felony. Only one states, West

10 See Sex and Race, Vol. 2, p. 358, for more detail.
11 General Laws of Colorado, Chap. 63, 1736, sec. 2, and 1737, sec. 3. 1877. For extract from this law see, Rogers, J. A., 100 Amazing Facts About the Negro, 19th ed., pp. 18-19.

Virginia, directly provides that such marriages should be "void from the time they are so declared by a decree of divorce or nullity." Three states have no statutory statement upon the problem."[12]

Couples who have been living happily for years and with grown children in good positions are liable to find their entire lives upset. Believing themselves white they have sometimes discovered, or some enemy has discovered it for them, that unknown to them, a law had been passed changing the racial status of one of them. Once legally white, they are now legally colored. Others not dreaming they had a Negro strain have contracted marriages in good faith only to discover that they were really outside the pale, with sometimes great tragedy resulting. Research into ancestry is frequently resorted to in order to win divorce, or for personal vengeance and blackmail.

In short, the situation as to the marriage of citizens in twenty-six and a half states of the union is so tangled as to make the famous Gordian knot a veritable poem of simplicity by comparison. The constitution of no less than six of these states rules that a Negro is one thing while the state laws declare him to be something else. Thus if such laws are strictly interpreted there are citizens who can marry neither colored nor white. If they remain in those states their only hope of getting a partner is to import an Eskimo, or some other racial group not named in the law.

Woolley tells of the chaos that the Louisiana miscegenation law of 1908 created as soon as it was passed. The district attorney, he says, was "stumped" when he found in the town of Lee "that among the truck gardeners, fishermen and other classes of people that the color line had been ignored for years. The accused white men swore they were Negroes and their neighbors backed them up. There were no birth records to disprove the stories—only the absence of the slightest kink in the hair and the absence of blonds."[13] He relates further how "the very first arrest" for miscegenation "took the state by the ears and gave Dame Gossip the center of the stage. At select gatherings family skeletons were trotted out wholesale." Among the number was the brother of a United States senator who had married an octoroon in the days when such marriages were permissible, and who, as a consequence was now thrown into the social discard. One man, seeking revenge on a neighbor, went to dig in the parish records, hoping to prove him of Negro

---

[12] Vernier, C. G., American Family Laws, Vol. 1, sec. 44, pp. 204-09. Also 1938 Suppl. pp. 24-5. The states are: Alabama, Arizona, Arkansas, California, Colorado, Delaware, Florida, Georgia, Idaho, Indiana, Kentucky, Louisiana, Maryland, Mississippi, Missouri, Montana, Nebraska, Nevada, North Carolina, North Dakota, Oklahoma, Oregon, South Carolina, South Dakota, Tennessee, Texas, Utah, Virginia, West Virginia, Wyoming. Oregon and California have since annulled this law.

[13] See also Sex and Race, Vol. 2, p. 325. 1942.

VI. Marie Alexandrovna Bykova (nee Pushkin), daughter of Pushkin's oldest son, and direct descendant of the great poet (Chatwood Hall photo). In Virginia, Mme. Bykova would be a Negro. Her Negro ancestry "is ascertainable."

ancestry, when he discovered that he, himself, had a Negro grandfather, on which he sold his property and left the state. One leading New Orleans banker was similarly discovered to be colored, and his name and that of his family were struck off "the calling lists" of the best people. He left for New York and became "a big figure in Wall Street." Still another case, that of two brothers and sister, "bearer of one of the foremost names" were discovered from the parish records to be colored. One brother became "a raving maniac" and was sent to an asylum; the other brother remained on his estate but was cut off from "the very people who have known him longest and esteem him most"; while the sister went to Europe.[14]

In other states with similar laws, a mixed couple legally married in one state, say in Pennsylvania, if they cross the line into Virginia or Maryland even for a day and remain together are criminals, liablbe to imprisonment and fine. Be it noted, too, that to these fantastic laws the like of which an Adolf Hitler in his craziest moments had never been able to concoct, the United States Supreme Court has repeatedly given its approval. In 1883 it held in the case of State versus Jackson that the privileges and immunities of the Fourteenth Amendment do not include the right to marry outside of one's own "race"![15]

Worst of all, these anti-marriage laws leave the door wide open to concubinage and interracial fornication. There are, of course, laws against these but they are observed nowhere, except in the case of white women and Negro men. Louisiana, whose law against illicit intercourse of white and black is one of the most stringent, is one of the worst offenders. In short, the laws of the twenty-nine and a half states above-mentioned are a direct inducement to sexual promiscuity—an inducement that mankind has never needed.

With the fall of Hitler, his Nuremberg law met the fate of similar freak laws of the Middle Ages, like that of Avignon, against the Jews.

Anti-marriage laws are a reflection of the greed of their makers and the crooked social vision of their approvers. But one ought to expect noth-

---

[14] For another very tragic case related in greater detail see Sex and Race, Vol. 2, p. 376. 1942.

[15] Mangum, C. S., has cited many cases ruled on by the U. S. Supreme Court, pp. 239-40.

[16] See Communique issued by the Tripartite Conference of Berlin (the Potsdam Conference), Aug. 2, 1945. Sec. 3, A, 4, which provides for the abolition of all discrimination "on grounds of race," etc. in Germany. Equally fantastic laws in the United States, South Africa, and Australia remain untouched, however.

ing better, at least he will not, if he remembers that it is usually the slickster and the opportunist—men whose mission it is to prove that "fair is foul and foul is fair" who dominate in law-making of this kind.

In 444 B.C., Rome, a pagan nation, passed a law abolishing the statute prohibiting marriage between certain of her citizens because of caste. Christian America, more than two thousand years later, has not yet caught up with her in this respect, has not yet seen fit to legalize the union of citizens who have been mixing illegally for more than three centuries.

ADDITIONAL BIBLIOGRAPHY

Hoernlé, R. F. A., South African Native Policy, pp. 39, 42, 55. 1939.

Negro Year Book, 1921-22, pp. 178-181.

Legal Status of Negro-White Amalgamation, Amer. Jour. of Sociol., Vol. 9, pp. 666-78. 1915-16.

Stephenson, G. T., Race Distinctions in American Law. 1910.

Styles, F. L., Negroes and the Law. 1937.

Woodson, C. G., Fifty Years of Negro Citizenship as Viewed by the U. S. Supreme Court. 1921.

Gilligan, F. J., Morality of the Color Line. 1928.

Turner, H. M., The Black Man's Doom (Decision of the U. S. Supreme Court on the Civil Rights' Act for Negroes. 1896).

Chapter Three

MIXED MARRIAGES AS SEEN BY THE WHITE SCIENTIST

*"In the accumulation of knowledge there has been great progress.
In the psychology of the scientific observer there has been no
fundamental change since the Reindeer Age. In point of scientific
ethics the last hundred years mark a retrogression." Lowie. "Are
We Civilized?"*

P RIOR to the popularizing of the so-called science of anthropology by
Blumenbach in the early years of the last century, the favorite instrument for proving the doctrine of inequality or equality within the human
race was the Bible. St. Augustine held that no true believer in God could
assert that an Ethiopian was not the equal of a white man. Mohamet, too,
preached the equality of all "races," and told his followers that even if a
Negro slave with pepper-corn hair had become their ruler they should obey
him.* Spain, Portugal and Italy actually practiced this equality.

The fight both for and against slavery in the United States was waged
first along scriptural lines.† The pro-slavery faction even asserted at times
that the Negro was descended not from Adam but from a pre-Adamite group
from which it was said Cain took a wife while the anti-slavery faction was
as firm in proving from the Bible that "of one blood" God had made all the
races of the earth. There was also the theory of the descent from Ham
which attained great vogue and still does in certain quarters.

With the superseding of religion by science the battle of inequality
shifted from a scriptural wording to a scientific one. Now it was no longer
practical. Now it was up to the equalitarians to prove that science was
wrong, though, be it noted that the first scientists, like Blumenbach and
Lamarck, held to the equality of the human race. In other words, the pro-
slavery faction and the anti-slavery one had entered the stage in new costumes. Underneath were the same bodies.

In this chapter and the three that follow I have given, therefore, an
anthology of what has been said in modern times on mixed marriages.

---

* "Hear and obey although a Negro slave whose head is like a dried grape be
appointed to rule over you." (Al Hadis Chap. 2, para. 108. trans. Fazul Karim.
Book 1, p. 231. 1938.) The text says "Ethiopian slave,' which is correctly translated "Negro" because of the kind of hair mentioned. For slaves who rose to be
rulers in Islam see pp. 221-2. Also Volume 1 of Sex and Race, Chaps. 10 and 11.
† For a list of these works see Work, M., Bibliography of the Negro, under
the headings, "Slavery and the Bible,' and "Slavery and the Church." 1928.

26

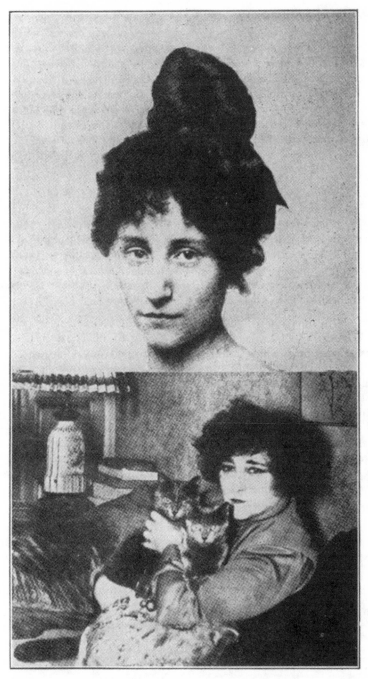

VII. Colette (Gabrielle Sidonie), France's leading female novelist. In most Southern states she would not be legally white. (See p. viii).

Some of these opinions are from world-famed scientists, one or two of whom are Nobel prize winners; others from biologists working in great laboratories; or doctors of philosophy from great universities; or able writers, as well as mere scribblers and the man in the street. However, no matter what the degree of knowledge, there will be seen again the spirit of the ardent upholder of slavery; or that of the milder advocate of it; or the sincere Christian; or the opportunist. The language has changed; the psychology of the respective contenders has not. Note the racialism or the lack of it in the case of the Negroes, too.

Scientific Opinions

Paul Broca, foremost French anthropologist of his day: "The union of the Negro with a white woman is frequently sterile while that of a white man with a Negress is perfectly fecund. This might tend to establish between the two races a species of hybridity analagous to that existing between goats and sheep which we have termed unilateral hybridity." He adds that Professor Serres "fully alive to the gravity of the fact has given the following explanation," namely, the length of the Negro male genital as compared with that of the Caucasian vagina.[1]

Dr. Franz Boas, noted anthropologist of Columbia University: "There is absolutely no biological evidence which would countenance the assumption that race intermixture of itself would have unfavorable results, that the children of white fathers and of mulatto or quadroon mothers would be inferior to their Negro ancestors. It would seem, therefore, to be in the interest of society to permit rather than restrain marriages between white men and Negro women. It would be futile to expect that our people would tolerate inter-marriage in the opposite direction although no scientific reason can be given that would prove them detrimental to the individual. Intermixture between white males and Negro females has been common ever since Negroes were brought to our continent, and the efficacy of the modern attempt to repress this intermingling is open to grave doubt.

"Thus it seems that man being what he is the Negro problem will not disappear in America until the Negro blood has been so much diluted that it will no longer be recognized just as anti-Semitism will not disappear until the last vestige of a Jew, as a Jew, has disappeared."[2]

* * * * *

"I do not doubt that notwithstanding all legislation, intermixture between Negroes and whites will continue.

1 Phenomena of Hybridity in the Genus Homo, p. 28. 1864.
2 Yale Review, Jan. 1921. p. 395.

"I do not think there is any danger of deterioration of American manhood and destruction of American civilization involved . . .

"I do not think that the Negro is inherently inferior to the white. There may be reasons to think that the Negro may be slightly different when we consider the average of the two types, but there is no doubt that there are a great many family strains among the Negroes that are superior to many white strains . . .

"Amelioration of the race problem can be obtained by making it clear to people there is no instinctive feeling of one race against another, and by emphasizing that instinctive race feeling is merely an automatic reaction which is brought about by impressing upon the mind of children and young people the consciousness of the incompatibility of races."[3]

"If we were to select the most intelligent, imaginative, energetic and emotionally stable third of mankind, all races would be represented. The mere fact that a person is a healthy European, or a blond European would not be proof that he would belong to his élite. Nobody has ever given proof that the mixed descendants of such a select group would be inferior . . .

"Those who fear miscegenation which I, personally, do not consider in any way dangerous . . . not for the white race or for the Negro, or for mankind . . . may console themselves with the belief in a race consciousness, which would manifest itself in selective mating. Then matters would remain as they are."[4]

Fay-Cooper Cole, professor of anthropology, University of Chicago: "There is sufficient reason to believe that the Negro and Caucasian races in the United States will ultimately amalgamate. This is going on to-day, has, in fact, gone so far that pure-blooded Negroes are in the minority, while a very high percentage of our Negro population is predominantly white. It should be noted that this is chiefly due to the white men seeking Negro women, and not to the union of Negro men and white women.

"Do I think race amalgamation would lead to a deterioration of American civilization? I DO NOT . . .

"My chief objection to race amalgamation as relating to black and white is in behalf of the half-breed. He has to struggle against such odds that SUCCESS can be attained only by a man of unusual ability and tenacity of purpose.

"I am not satisfied that the Negro is inherently inferior to the Caucasian. He is different — different physically. In his homeland he is different and has an entirely different background — social, economic and mental — while

---

[3] Symposium on Race-Mixing conducted by T. Dabney in Baltimore Afro-American, February-April, 1925.
[4] Anthropology and Modern Life, pp. 75-6.

his life here in America has not been such as to give him the same outlook as his white neighbor.

"He has had no opportunity as a race to show whether or not he is capable of assimilating our civilization. Given the same background and opportunities I think it is quite probable that he will show himself the equal of the white. At the present time one of my best graduating students is a Negress.

"Give the Negro equal opportunities with the whites. Give more equipped schools and opportunities to advance as he shows ability; recognize merit regardless of color. See that the Negro population is decently housed, not pushed off to undesirable portions of the city.

"Assist the colored man to become a self-respecting member of our society; recognize his worthwhile qualities, and encourage him to become a loyal forward-looking American, rather than a member of a resentful, half-educated group which may easily be used by selfish leaders."[5]

Dr. Charles B. Davenport, noted eugenist and biologist: "Already the South is full of persons of one-eighth Negro blood whose (illegitimate) children may legally marry descendants of blacks . . . Many a child arises in the third or later generations that by no test shows evidence of 'African' descent. How unjust the Missouri law that provides that the proportion of Negro blood is to be determined by the jury from the appearance of the person! The South, indeed, has a problem in its huge 'feeble-minded' colored population: but the problem is of the same order as that in the North and in England and the solution is: Forget unessentials like skin-color and focus attention on socially important defects. Then by sterilization or segregation prevent the reproduction of the socially inadequate. Thus will the mentally incompetent strains be eliminated and the good physical traits of some of the black races be added, as a valued heritage to enhance the physical manhood of the South.

"I feel sure that if law will take lessons from biology many of the disasters that have been feared may be averted."[6a]

Dr. Davenport suggests the following law: "No person having one-half or more Negro blood shall be permitted to take a white person as spouse. Any person having less than one-eighth part of Negro blood shall not be given a license to marry a white person without a certificate from the state."[6b]

Dr. George A. Dorsey, late curator of anthropology, Field Museum, Chicago: "Nature is not so prejudiced as we are. She says that there is a human race, that all human beings are of the same genus Homo, species

---

[5] See No. 3.

[6a] Report Inter. Congress of Eugenics, London, 1912, p. 155.

[6b] Eugenics Record, Bull. Eugenics Record Office, 1913.

sapiens. She draws no color line in the human or in any other species. Black and white dogs mix as readily as do blacks and whites when the sex impulse is not outlawed, and are equally fertile."[7]

Edward M. East, late professor of genetics, Harvard University: "The Negro as a social group has produced but one man who would be placed among the first 15,000 or 20,000 Great Ones of the Earth. This is Alexandre Dumas . . .

"The obvious conclusion . . . is that the gene-packets of African origin are not valuable supplements to the gene-packets of European origin. It is the white germ-plasm that counts. This is further shown by the fact that the first generation hybrids, have hardly ever had distinctive achievements to their credit. It is when re-combination of the genes occurs, bearing with it the possibility of additional white endowments that men of merit appear.

"We can find no probability, that the Negro will contribute hereditary factors of value to the white race yet the pure Negro will gradually die out and the remaining members of our population will vary imperceptibly from black to white. In the social sense the black race will be absorbed. In the genetic sense the black germ plasm will remain because the inheritance of genes is alternative. What are we going to do about it?

"It seems to me that we must make the best of the situation. The Negro cannot be deported or sterilized. He must be treated decently, educated up to his intelligence level and made a part of our political system when qualified I can see no reasonable excuse for oppression and discrimination on a colour-line basis."[8]

F. H. Hankins, professor of sociology, Smith University: "We think it can be shown that race-crossing is a factor in the production of talented men, and hazard the guess that most of the superior men of European history have been of mixed racial ancestry . . . Since the crossing of sound strains of different races is biologically sound we contend that well-endowed Italians, Hebrews, Chinese, and Negroes are better material out of which to forge a nation than average, or below average, Nordics.

"A second biological principle is that crossing of strains increase variability. This is highly important as a factor in evolution because it gives natural selection a wide range of individuality to choose from.

"Even as regards Negro-white crosses one can see no sound biological argument against them . . . Since the crossing of the races occurs primarily between white males and Negro females it may also be argued that miscegenation is a factor in race elevation. Such crossing usurps the reproductive

[7] **Why We Behave Like Human Beings**, p. 44. 1926.
[8] **Heredity and Human Affairs**, pp. 199-200. 1927.

capacities of the Negro race without affecting the fertility of the white stock. In so far, therefore, as the actual white fathers might be assumed to be superior to the possible Negro fathers an assumption not always correct the offspring will be better endowed.

"Arguments against the crossing of white and Negro must therefore be purely sociological."[9]

Dr. Frederick Hoffman, statistician, Prudential Life Insurance Company: "I have never found an inter-mixed or inter-married white-Negro couple where the stamp of social inferiority was not plainly traceable as the result . . .

"Intermarriages between whites and blacks, just as much as wrongful sexual relations without marriage, are essentially anti-social tendencies and therefore opposed to the teachings of sound eugenics in the light of the best knowledge available to both races at the present time . . .

"The conclusion would seem warranted that the crossing of the Negro race with the white has been detrimental to its true progress and has contributed more than anything else to the excessive and increasing rate of mortality from the most fatal diseases as well as to its consequent inferior social efficiency and diminishing power as a force in American natural life.[10] (Hoffman believes that it is only degenerate white women who marry Negroes and cites a number of instances.)

Earnest G. Hooton, professor of anthropology, Harvard University: "Amalgamation between whites and Negroes will go on, as it always has gone on. But the process is a slow one, because of the fact that few primary crosses occur and because the whites so largely outnumber the Negroes.

"Ultimately we might expect the entire population to show signs of Negro admixture in the same way that practically all of the people of India show more or less traces of the Dravidian admixture. But this process would take a very long time in this country, because of the preponderance of whites and because of their reinforcement by immigration.

"I see no reason why one should anticipate disaster as a result of such slow and almost imperceptible amalgamation as must necessarily take place under the circumstances.

"I neither oppose nor advocate it (amalgamation). After we have studied the results of race mixtures between whites and Negroes, I shall be in a position to decide upon its advantages or disadvantages.

"Anthropologically, the Negro displays rather more features which may be considered primitive than do white races, but in many physical

9 Racial Basis of Civilization, pp. ix, 330, 347. 1926.

10 Eugenics in Race and State Report. Sec. Inter. Cong. of Eugenics, Vol. II, p. 187.

VIII. Left to right: John Archer, photographer of Negro-Irish parentage, who way Mayor of Battersea, one of London's largest boroughs; Andrew Bogle, (See Sex and Race, Vol. I, p. 204, 2nd ed.) and (lower right) Thomas Tallis (1515-1585) "The Father of English Cathedral Music."

features the Negro is more advanced than the white. I do not feel that there exists any satisfactory method of appraising the comparative mental abilities of different races. I am unwilling to express opinions as to racial superiority or inferiority until some real basis of knowledge has been laid down.

"From the scientific point of view the prime desideratum is an anthropological study of the Negro in the United States and a study of the results of race mixture. But I am not at all certain that anything scientists can learn would have great efficacy in settling the race problem.

"If it were discovered that race mixture with Negroes produced undesirable types many whites would be pleased and most Negroes would not accept the conclusions.

"If on the contrary certain mixtures were demonstrated to be superior many Negroes would be pleased and most whites would be unwilling to accept the demonstration. In either event discontent and dissatisfaction would result. Democracies will always be swayed by ignorant prejudices rather than led by scientific principles or by ethical ideals."[11]

Dr. Ales Hrdlicka, late curator of anthropology, Smithsonian Institution, in reply to the question: "Do you think white and black will amalgamate? replied, "Yes." Asked: Would amalgamation lead to the destruction of civilization? he replied, "No." He opposed race-mixing, however, so far as white and black are concerned because "the differences are too great and the results could not be an advantage."[12]

Ellsworth Huntington, Yale University: "The army mental tests showed that 86 per cent of the southern Negroes possess inferior intelligence. Other evidence shows that almost the only Negroes who have accomplished much of importance have been partly white. The blending of white and black has produced something more competent than the pure black but less competent than the pure white. It has often made a most dysgenic blend, creating a white man's ambition in a black man's lethargic body. A certain group of scientists maintain that within a few hundred years there will be no more pure blacks in America. If that were to happen the mentality of the nation would be materially lowered."[13]

H. S. Jennings, professor of zoology, and Director of the Zoological Laboratory in John Hopkins University, says: "No incompatibility of chromosomes is to be observed among the different races of man. The Negro and the white man each have 24 pairs of chromosomes. These work perfectly together both in forming vigorous offspring, and in the much more

11 See No. 3.
12 See No. 3.
13 Builders of America, p. 82. 1927.

delicate tests of later uniting to form germ cells in those offspring . . . With respect to the main features of physical structures of functions, and of physiology, the offspring of parents belonging to diverse races are as perfect and vigorous and efficient as the offspring of members of the same race."[14]

Algernon Lee, Director, Rand School of Social Science: "Ever since the first Negroes were brought to this country, mixture of Caucasian and Negro blood has been going on, chiefly through intercourse of white men with colored women.

"I see no reason to doubt that this process will continue.

"I do not know of any way in which I could oppose or check this historic process.

"Anthropological research gives no support to the theory that any one race or variety, of mankind is inherently superior to another.

"The solution of the race problem is to be found in social justice. It is essentially not a race problem."[15]

Prof. Jacques Loeb, former head of the Department of Experimental Biology in the Rockefeller Institute for Medical Research: "It has been stated that the mixtures between white and black are an inferior breed; that the pure breeds—the pure black and the pure white breed—are superior to the mixed race. As a matter of fact biology has nothing in support of that position, but we have some definite facts which show that in certain cases the hybrid is superior to both parent races . . .

"It would be wrong to say that in each case the result of a mixture of races is better than the pure breed. That is true in some cases, in other cases the opposite is true. But the fact that in a number of cases the mixture yields results that are superior to both parent breeds is enough to show the absurdity of the sweeping statement that the intermixing of races should be considered a felony."[16]

William McDougall, professor of psychology, Duke University: "I hold that eventual complete amalgamation of the Negroes and whites is almost certain to occur in the United States of America, if the matter is left to nature.

"In my opinion, miscegenation must be regarded as a dangerous experiment which the white race can ill afford to make. It is impossible to forecast what the white stock would suffer in quality through absorbing the 100 per cent of Negro blood present in the population.

14 Biological Basis of Human Nature, p. 278. 1930.
15 See No. 3.
16 Crisis Maga., Dec. 1914.

"I am opposed to amalgamation . . .

"I do consider that in spite of much that is amiable in the Negro the race is inferior to the white race, i.e., is less high cultured, more childlike in various ways."[17]

Henry Fairfield Osborn, paleontologist, American Museum of Natural History: "My personal opinion is strongly against race mixture of any kind. I believe each race which has been produced by nature should try to develop its best qualities along its own natural lines."[18]

Dr. Robert W. Shufeldt (1850-1933), Major, U.S.A., head of the Army Medical Museum, and one of America's foremost scientists and naturalists: "Any number of people can be found in this country to-day who will stoutly deny, and they believe what they say, too, that there is any interbreeding going on at all between the blacks and the whites, and that the numerous mulattoes are due to climate. Such people are, of course, absolutely blind as to what is going on about them; they are ignorant and do not care to see. Take the city of Washington, for instance, I can remember thirty-five years ago when the mulattoes in the streets of that place were comparatively the rare exception, while they are to be seen there now simply in scores upon scores. Some are wonderfully handsome creatures with superb figures but handsome and fine-physiqued only in the sense that our American skunk is likewise a beautiful creature. It is also a *black animal* with more or less of a *white stripe in it* that is given to stealing chickens and can when irritated elevate its tail and raise the most outrageous stink, which is quite sufficient to check the progress of any Anglo-Saxon, however robust and civilised he may be . . .

"These half-breed Negroes in the United States, or in fact all that class of people having any Negro blood in them at all, are extremely objectionable factors in our civilization. They often, indeed, in a large proportion of instances are worse than the typical Negroes themselves. They are dangerous from whatever point of view man may elect to view them . . .

"Mulattoes, too, have better opportunities to contract white alliances in marriage and thus insidiously pass the savage Ethiopian blood into the veins of the Anglo-Saxon or American. This is most deplorable for I have frequently remarked the Negro has absolutely nothing in his organization that can be added to our own with slightest value while on the other hand nearly everything about him, mentally, morally, and physically is undesirable to the highest degree . . . Personally, I have found them equally superstitious, treacherous, mendacious, and unreliable . . .

[17] See No. 3.
[18] See No. 3.

"It would doubtless be a capital thing, if it could be done, to emasculate the entire Negro race and all of its descendants in this country and effectually stop the breed right now and thus prevent any further dangers from them and the horrors of the crossing continuously with the Anglo-Saxon stock . . .

"I have presented enough I think . . . to illustrate what an intensely sensuous and lascivious race the Negro race is—utterly lacking in sexual chastity . . ."[19]

William Benjamin Smith, late professor of philosophy, Tulane University: "At no time have two such distinct races each numbered by the millions, the one representing the highest stage of civilization and advancement, the other practically but a day removed from savagery and cannibalism, been thrown together in the same geographical region and not separated by any natural barriers. And our glorious Anglo-Saxon blood—the flower of the human race—is being polluted by the African taint, beastialized by 'gorilla damnifications.' This is a terrible thought to him who reveres the mortality of his ancestors, and prizes above earthly possessions the unblemished caste distinction of a thousand years of Europe's best culture."[20]

Sir Harry Johnston, noted colonial administrator, traveller, and authority on the Negro: "He (the Negro) has certainly been endowed by nature with a degree of race fertility probably far surpassing that of the European, Asiatic, and American Indian living under conditions similarly unfavorable to the struggle for existence. Those few scientific men in Britain, Germany, France, the United States and Brazil, who have striven to understand the anthropology of the Negro and to compare it with the white man are rather inclined than otherwise to argue now that the Negro and the Negroids have contributed in the past and still more may contribute in the future, a very important quota to the whole sum of humanity—an element of soundness and stability in physical development and certain mental qualities which the perfect man of, let us say, twenty or twenty-two centuries after Christ, cannot afford to do without."[21]

Dr. J. B. Lacerda, Director, National Museum of Rio de Janeiro, Brazil: "Galton's deduction in regard to hybridity in animals cannot be wholly applied to human half-breeds. In the case of man there is an inheritance of moral and intellectual qualities that follows no fixed and absolute rules. Under the influence of agencies of which we do not know the nature, the intellectual qualities, often reach in the mixed progeny of the white and black a degree

19 The Negro: A Menace to American Civilization, pp. 99-130.
21 Interracial Papers (G. Spiller), p. 333. 1911.
20 The Color Line, p. 7. 1905.

of superiority which cannot be explained in terms of heredity either remote or proximate. Some unknown force gives rise in them to an intelligence that is capable of developing to a pitch neither of the parents could reach. It is, in fact common to find as the offspring of a white of very mediocre intelligence mated with a Negress of the lowest grade of culture an individual of considerable intellectual powers; just as if one of the effects of crossing in the case of man was precisely to improve the intelligence, or the moral and reflective qualities which distinguish individuals of the two races crossed."[22]

J. W. Gregory, British anthropologist : "The extreme view of some American writers that 'no race has maintained its civilization when tainted even slightly with African blood,' need not be accepted; but in view of the debt that the world owes to the northern section of the white race—its dilution to the extent that would take place in the United States by the absorption of all its Negroes would be a disaster to humanity, yet this occurrence is probable. Although I recognize that nothing seems to rouse more intense indignation among some Americans than the idea that racial intermixture is taking place in their country to any serious extent, the evidence seems to me to be overwhelming to support those who like Prof. Bowman (1924, p. 17) report that the intermixture of the races goes on with increasing momentum."[23]

H. B. Fantham, professor of zoology, University of Witwatersrand, South Africa, "Intermarriage between white and black seems invariably to induce degeneration. The white becomes more animal-like, less energetic, more careless . . .

"White society long ago instinctively reached the conclusion that inter-marriage between white and black must be banned."[24]

Otto Klineberg, professor of psychology, Columbia University: "Little can be said with any definiteness either in favor of or against race mixture . . . Miscegenation as such is biologically neither good nor bad; its effects depend entirely upon the health and vigor of the individuals, who enter into the mixture. The observed effects of race crossing appear to depend very much more on social than on biological factors." He also says, "Miscegenation between all racial groups has been going on since the beginning of history."[25] Luther Burbank, plant wizard (1849-1926), holding that "Nature does not approve of crosses" between races as have in "the ages grown widely

22 Interracial Papers (G. Spiller, p. 380. 1911.
23 Menace of Color, p. 89. 1925.
24 South African Assn. for the Advanc. of Science Jour., Vol. 23, pp. 410-11. 1925.
25 Race Differences, p. 219. 1935.

apart" from the white as the Negro and the Mongolian, says: "No permanent results have been generally achieved, for example, through the commingling of Mongolians and Aryan blood, or of Aryan and Negro. I have said before and I say it again, that part of America's greatness and part of our country's possibilities for influence and leadership in the world are due to the crossing of races—the mixing of blood. But . . . there is a limit in the crossing of diverse strains beyond which it is not politic to go."[26]

M. F. Ashley Montagu, Department of Anatomy, Hahnemann Medical School and Hospital: "One of the most strongly entrenched of popular superstitions is that interbreeding, or crossing between "races" results in inferior offspring, and that the greater part of such crossings leads to degeneration of the stock. The commonly employed stereotype has it that the half-caste inherits all the bad and none of the good qualities of the parent stocks. These bad qualities the half-breed is said to transmit to his offspring so that there is produced a very gradual and a very definite mental and physical deterioration within the group, finally resulting in complete infertility . . .

"As is the case with most of the evils which have been attributed to so-called miscegenation, or race mixture, there is not one particle of truth in any of these statements. Such facts as they may have reference to, are in practically every case due to purely social factors . . .

"There can be little doubt that those who deliver themselves of unfavorable judgments concerning race-crossing are merely expressing their prejudices. For in the framework which encloses the half-caste we are dealing with a conspicuous example of the action of socially depressing factors and not the effects of biological ones. The truth seems to be that far from being deleterious to the resulting offspring and the generations following them, interbreeding between different ethnic groups is from the biological standpoint highly advantageous to mankind."[27]

Charles Richet, professor of physiology, Faculty of Medicine, University of Paris, and Nobel Prize winner: "A white woman should by no means marry a Negro. Even if the signs of his ethnic inferiority is little apparent, they will appear in the children . . . All mixture of race is detestable . . ."[28a]

"I would gladly let my sons marry an Italian, Spanish, German, or English woman, or a Jewess but I would be very much pained if they married a Chinese or a Negro woman . . . Prejudice, perhaps, but I readily believe

26 Partner of Nature, p. 117-18. 1929.
27 Man's Most Dangerous Myth: The Fallacy of Race, pp. 97-99. 1942.
28a For the source of this as well as a French symposium on race-mixing see: Sex and Race, Vol. 1, p. 231. 1941.

that this prejudice would be shared by all the whites even those who criticize me most strongly."[28b]

Lancelot Hogben, mathematician and biologist: "As an experimental scientist I know of only one way of finding out whether mixed marriages are advisable. That is to encourage them where we can assure the offspring the same cultural advantages as children whose parents belong to the same ethnic group."[29]

[28b] Revue gén. de sciences pures, etc., Vol. 16, p. 891. 1906.
[29] Dangerous Thoughts, p. 48. 1940.

Chapter Four

MIXED MARRIAGES AS SEEN BY THE POLITICIANS[1]

"Politicians think that by stopping up the chimney they can stop it from smoking. They try the experiment; they drive the smoke back and there is more smoke than ever." Borne.

A BRAHAM LINCOLN: "There is a natural disgust in the minds of nearly all white people at the idea of an indiscriminate amalgamation of the white and black races, and Judge Douglas evidently is basing his chief hope upon the chances of his being able to appropriate the benefit of the disgust for himself . . .

"I am not, nor ever have been, in favor of bringing about in any way the social and political equality of the white and black races—that I am not, nor ever have been, in favor of making voters or jurors of Negroes, nor of qualifying them to intermarry with white people and I wish to say in addition to this that there is a physical difference between the white and black races which, I believe, will forever forbid the two races living together on terms of political and social equality. And inasmuch as they cannot so live while they remain together there must be the position of superior and I as much as any other man am in favor of having the superior position assigned to the white race."[2]

Senator Thomas J. Heflin of Alabama on the marriage of Phil Edwards, Negro athlete, to a white girl: "The far-reaching harm and danger of marriage between whites and Negroes to the great white race that God intended should rule the world is apparent to all intelligent students of history; such mixtures have always resulted in weakening, degrading, and dragging down the superior to the level of the inferior race. God had a purpose in making four separate and distinct races. The white, the red, the yellow, the black. God intended that each of the four races should preserve its blood free from mixture with other races and preserve race integrity and prove itself true to the purpose that God had in mind fo reach of them when he brought them into being.

---

[1] The number of quotations in this chapter are limited to a few since because though they abound in the Congressional Record and in Nazi writings they are all based on unquestioned belief and sound very much alike.

[2] Speeches and Letters of Abraham Lincoln, pp. 231, 369. 1920. Nicolay and Hay, 2 vols. This is a very favorite quotation by Southern politicians, and appears often in the Congressional Record. It is also much used by anti-Negro writers as Dixon, Pickett, Shufeldt.

"The great white race is the climax and crowning glory of God's creation. God in His Infinite wisdom has clothed the white man with the elements and the fitness of dominion and rulership, and the history of the human race shows that wherever he has planted his foot and unfurled the flag of his authority he has continued to rule. No true member of the great white race in America is going to approve of or permit, if he can prevent it, the marriage between whites and Negroes.

"The desire and purpose on the part of the great white race in America to keep its blood strain pure and to prevent marriage between whites and Negroes can better be designed as 'the call of the blood.' It has come down to us through the centuries. White women rather than become the wives of black men, whenever the issue was presented, fought and died, if necessary to remain true 'to the call of the blood.' "[3]

Senator Theodore Bilbo of Mississippi on the marriage of Mary B. Dawes, relative of Vice-President Dawes, to Julian D. Steele, Harvard graduate and a Negro, "She appears to be sustained in her mad insane determination to mingle blood impregnated with the highest genetic values of the Caucasian with the blood of an African whose racial strains have dwelt for six thousand years or more in the jungles of a continent." He pictures Mary Dawes as "entwining her arms around the frightful product of barbarism she envisions and presses tenderly and sympathetically the black burry head of the Ethiopian upon a bosom white and stainless as the snow."[4a]

"Scientific research has successfully established three propositions beyond all controversy.

"First, the white race has founded, developed and maintained every civilization known to the human race.

"Second, the white race, having founded, developed and maintained a civilization has never been known in all history to lose that civilization so long as the race was kept white.

"Third, the white man has never kept unimpaired the civilization he has founded and developed after its blood stream has been adulterated by the blood stream of another, more especially another race, so widely diverse as the black race."[4b]

Ex-Kaiser Wilhelm II: "The laws concerning the hygiene of races are fundamental. They must be obeyed or else the human species will destroy

---

[3] Congressional Record, Feb. 6, 1930.
[4a] Congressional Record, May 24, 1938. Also several dates in June, 1944.
[4b] Ibid, April 24, 1939, p. 4654. Bilbo flays the "miscegenationists" and uses Thomas Jefferson to support his arguments. Jefferson, however, not only declared that race-mixing appeared to be a "great provision made by nature," but practiced it much himself. Jefferson's statement quoted in Sex and Race, Vol. 2, p. 186.

itself. Races of different colors must never mix because they are fundamentally different and each race is governed by its own law of growth. I observe with dismay in France the decline of feeling that it is the imperious duty of the white race to avoid miscegenation."[5]

Mussolini, warning Americans to oppose race-mixing said that if this was not done, "We shall encounter an Africanized America in which the white race by the inexorable law of numbers will end by being suffocated by the fertile grandsons of Uncle Tom . . . Are we to see within a century a Negro in the White House?"[6]

On February 8, 1934, Hein Schroeder, Nazi eugenic authority, demanded the immediate sterilization of all children in Germany that had been born of German mothers and Senegalese fathers during the French occupation of the Rhineland.

[5] From an interview given to George Sylvester Viereck at Doorn, Holland in 1928. (Viereck had asked the ex-Kaiser what he thought about the French policy of race-blending in order to avoid race conflicts.) **New York Sunday American**, about April 23, 1928.

[6] About 1934. The exact date has been mislaid.

Chapter Five

MIXED MARRIAGES AS SEEN BY THE CLERGY AND THE LAITY

"A weak mind is like a microscope which magnifies trifling things but cannot receive great ones." Lord Chesterfield.

WENDELL PHILIPS: "Amalgamation! Remember this, the youngest of you: that on the 4th day of July, 1863, you heard a man say that in all the light of history, in virtue of every page he has read that he was an amalgamationist to the utmost extent. (Applause.) I have no hope for the future as this country has no past and Europe has no past, but in that sublime mingling of races which is God's own method of civilizing and elevating the world. (Loud Applause.)"[1]

The World (New York) registered its disapproval of Eugene O'Neill's play, "All God's Chillun Got Wings," in which a Negro marries a white woman, and urged the Board of Aldermen to stop it, holding that:

"An act which is illegal in more than half the nation and is disapproved in the entire country is to be represented in a manner indicating approval in a public theatre."[2]

Ruth S. Keen (letter of rebuttal to Arthur Brisbane): "Many white men are bullies and braggarts, but there is one group over which they have no control—their white women.

"From the beginning of time, at first stealthily and subtly but now quite openly and shamelessly, white women have always had what they wanted (you see, we share our lord's rapaciousness) and they have always given themselves to men whom they admired and preferred quite regardless of class, creed, race, color or previous condition of servitude.

"So—Mr. Brisbane, I have the honor to inform you that, if white girls admire and prefer men of other races, neither bluster, bragging nor bombs will stop them from doing so for they not only trust their own convictions in such matters but have the courage to carry them out."[3]

Letter of an educated white woman to a Negro writer. ". . . When the better class of white women get freed from this color psychosis you (black men) are going to be the kings of the earth. We will try to make up to you

---

[1] Quoted from D. G. Croly, Miscegenation, p. 66. 1864. On p. 67 is an equally strong endorsement by Theodore Tilton, another abolition leader.

[2] Editorial, March 4, 1924.

[3] Reprinted from the Los Angeles Times in Pittsburgh Courier, March 8, 1930.

for some of the things you haven't had. I take a great delight in performing the most menial tasks for all my dark men friends. It sort of evens things up . . . and I am quite open and shameless. Being in the fatal forties my gestures are not misunderstood and I have a warm maternal feeling for the boys and girls which they respond to easily as they know it to be sincere."[4]

Albert Stowe Leecraft of Houston, Texas, on the mulatto: "In animal life crossing of breeds produces what is called "a Mule . . .""

"A Mule-Nigger is the aftermath or fruitage of the clandestine visits of a low-down, depraved, degenerate white scallawag who by day lives in the midst of social refinement in the white communities of this Christian world and frequents the colored settlements under the cover of darkness of the night and plants his seed of iniquity secretly, with only the eyes of the recording angel watching his footsteps, and those human skunks well know the inevitable birth of their progenies brings disgrace to decent humanity.

"A child brought into life through such a union of mixed bloods of 'strange flesh' is neither a white child or a Nigger; he is not white and he is not black, and the offspring of social error does not inherit the spiritual blessing of God or the fellowship of man . . . He is a social outcast of society, a living monument in the walks of life, visualizing the abortion of the plans of God Almighty and picturing the perfidy of immoral humanity . . .

"The laws of nature do not permit the cross-breeding of foreign seeds of life . . . A coating of tar will not make an ink-spot white, and a million years of evolution will never bring forth a clean, pure, spotless-skin white child after the ancestral blood has been polluted with blood of Negroid taint . . .

"The big, burly, flat-footed, thick-lipped, spread-nose, black-skin, kinky-haired 'Nigger' of this age are all of the blood of Cain, the man God made black."[5]

Father Gillis, Catholic priest of New York: "There are those who maintain that as much as one-third of the whole population of the United States has some strain of colored blood. Be that statement accurate or exaggerated the unquestionable fact remains that however much man, both white man and black man, may revolt from miscegenation, Nature does not abhor the union of the races. If Nature does not, God does not for the laws of Nature are the laws of God. And the Church takes her cue from the laws of God rather than from the feelings and prejudices of man. The Church will baptize a mulatto, ordain him a priest, or consecrate him bishop. She

---

[4] Letter in author's possession.
[5] The Devil's Inkwell, p. 33, Houston, Tex. 1923.

has done so here in the United States. She does not consider the offspring of a Negro and a white a monster.

"Enough! man is man, be he black or white."[6]

Dr. J. H. Oldham, English writer: "Those who hold with Dr. Stoddard that 'it is clean, virile, genius-bearing blood streaming down through the unerring action of heredity' that is going to 'solve our problem and sweep us on to higher and nobler destinies' ought, if they are consistent, to welcome such blood wherever they find it. But if they refuse to do this and instead of keeping to the question of strains, which exhibit the highest mental and moral qualities begin to talk of 'race which includes bad as well as good strains, the bottom falls out of their argument. The argument from heredity, whatever may be its force, is concerned with particular strains or lines of descent and warrants no conclusion in regard to races as a whole.' "[7]

Putnam Weale, English writer: "Where the white man has not absolutely cleared the ground of his colored rival he may be bred down to a position of inferiority . . . The whites of the Southern States when they do everything they can to prevent all mixing of blood are simply obeying natural laws, which if they had ignored, would quickly lead to their own undoing. In the Southern States miscegenation is rightly held to be an offense far worse than manslaughter . . . The position of the whites would speedily become intolerable from an interbreeding which would perforce drag down all to the mixed white level of certain parts of South America, notably Brazil—where the black man has bred not only with white but with Indians thus producing dreadful hybrids . . . the black man is something apart . . . something untouchable."[8]

Lord Olivier, Colonial Administrator, and former Secretary of State for India, says of the union of the black man and the white woman: "There is no correspondingly strong instinctive aversion nor is there so strong an ostensible objection to a white man's marrying a woman of mixed descent. The latter kind of union is much more likely to occur than the former. There is good biological reason for the distinction. Whatever the potentialities of the African stock as a vehicle for human manifestations, and, I, myself, believe them to be like those of the Russian people, exceedingly important and valuable—a matrix of emotional and spiritual energies that have yet to find their human expression in suitably adapted forms—the white races are now, in fact, by far, the further advanced in intellectual human development and it would be expedient on this account alone that their maternity should be economised to the utmost. A woman may be the mother of a limited

6 Catholic Worker, Jan. 1935.
7 Christianity and the Race Problem, p. 60. 1924.
8 Conflict of Color, p. 231. 1910.

number of children, and our notion of the number advisable is contracting, and it is bad natural economy to breed backward from her."[9]

Mason Dixon, white Southerner, denouncing the verdict in the Rhinelander case said the marriage "should have been annulled as soon as it was established that there was colored blood in her veins. Down South we know how to handle such affairs. If the couple feel that they must live together that is their affair. But no civilized state should sanction marriage between white and black. New York and other states have no law against mixed marriages. Until they adopt such laws these states will be a disgrace to the nation."[10]

Rev. W. A. Cotton, missionary in South Africa: "During four hundred years Europeans *as a race* . . . have continuously, and confessedly do still lack, the gift of continence in their relations with colored peoples whom they have brought under their sway.

"Consequently the prohibition of marriage is very gravely to be reprobated . . .

"I must confess a very special drawing to me of delighted affection towards children who show in their faces not only their African origin but also the clear evidences of their derivation from people of my kin."[11]

Peter Nielsen, South African student of native life: "The familiar cry that once white blood is diluted with black it is "all up" with our civilization is not convincing when we remember that the groundwork of this civilization was built up by races that were not 'pure' white. Civilization during the dark ages sank to a very low level through no dilution of African blood, and that it was a mixed race, the Moors, who brought back to Europe the lost principles of Aristotelian science in which the crumbling structure of European culture was rebuilt . . . So far from being a deterrent to mental growth it would seem that an infusion of African blood in a white family is often associated with marked intellectual ability."[12]

White woman married to a Negro in a letter to the Philadelphia Tribune: "No doubt my problem is not a new one, but I may present it in a different angle. It is that of intermarriage.

"Until I met the man who became my husband, I had thought that it was only the people of the white race who held such decided prejudices. But since, I find that the people of the colored race hold them also.

"Only within the last few days I overheard a conversation concerning

9 White Capital and Coloured Labour, p. 37. In the 1928 edition this passage is omitted.

10 Collier's Weekly, Jan. 29, 1926, p. 410.

11 Race Problem in South Africa, p. 103. 1926.

12 The Black Man's Place in South Africa, p. 127-8. 1922.

my marriage in which this remark was made, 'Only a white woman out of the gutter would marry a colored man.' That seems such an unfair accusation, not only to the white woman, but to the colored man. To assert that he could only marry a woman of a low type seems to cast a reflection on the whole Negro race. If a Negro is honest, upright, a God-fearing citizen, why can't he command the respect and admiration of anyone? Should it follow that because a white woman learns also to love him, that she is indecent?

"I sacrificed a great deal to become the wife of a Negro. But nothing that I gave up could ever compensate for the great happiness that we have together. Every day that I know him gives me greater respect for him, greater faith in everyone.

"The majority of people do not or pretend that they do not believe in intermarriage among the races. That is for each individual to decide for himself or herself. But why, I ask you, cannot two people who sincerely love each other spend their lives in married decency without people of both races trying to put stumbling blocks in their way and making it so humiliatingly hard for them?

"In this land which was founded on freedom, liberty, and equality, is it fair that only some should receive these blessings, their right to the pursuit of happiness? Is the Constitution of the United States only a mockery?

"I do not regret my marriage. A thousand times 'No.' I think I care for my husband as much as any woman has ever cared for a man. I only ask of my country the right for us to be able to find our own happiness and to gain our livelihood by our own exertions. This though seems an almost impossible favor to ask. I wish that you, through your paper, could help to make your people see that there COULD be harmony between men and women of different races and there must be if we are to hope for any prosperous future."

Gilbert Haven, Methodist Episcopal bishop (1821-1880), predicting that some day America will think as highly of a human being in a black skin as it now "loathes" one: "The grand ladies of the South may yet be the mixed bloods of that region and many a white and fastidious wealthy Solomon will solicit the duskier, yet none the less loving and lovely daughter of Pharaoh, to give his house her perpetual blessing . . .

"The hour is not far off when the white-hued husband shall boast of the dusky beauty of his wife and the Caucasian wife shall admire the sun-kissed countenance of her husband as deeply and as unconscious of the present ruling abhorrence as is his admiration of her lighter tint . . .

"The Song of Songs will have a more literal fulfillment than it has

IX. Left: Alexander Dumas, pere, as a young man. Right: First known portrait of Charles Dickens. Dickens was in all probability white but note a certain resemblance to Dumas, whose Negro ancestry is certain. Inset: Pierre Laval, former Premier of France.

ever confessedly had in America; and the long existing divinely-implanted admiration of Caucasians for black but comely maidens, be the proudly acknowledged and honorably gratified life of Northern and Southern gentlemen."[13]

Mrs. Eleanor Roosevelt: "A great many people believe that there should be no intermingling of races. Hitler has proved with bloody massacres that he holds this belief. Nevertheless, down through the ages, it has been proved over and over again that this is one of the questions which people settle for themslves, and no amount of legislation will keep them from doing so.

"We would not have so many different shades of color in this country today if this were not so. This is a question, therefore, that I think we have to leave to individuals, not only all over the United States, but all over the world, to handle.

"There is no more reason to expect that there will be more intermarriage if the four fundamental basic rights of citizens are granted to tell people in this country than there will be if they are withheld. In fact, I think it probable that there would be less."[14]

When apparently taken to task for the above, she wrote: "Some people have written to ask me if I was advocating mixed marriages and I would like to make it clear that I would never advocate this. It seems to me that in the mixing of racial strains the difficulties which always exist in any marriage are greatly enhanced. Races will mix, however. Even in this country we see the evidences of this mixture. Whether it has occurred in wedlock or not makes little difference from the biologist's standpoint, because over the centuries a strong racial strain will probably obliterate a weaker one."[14]

A Southern white man, writing to the Chicago Defender: "I have been living with a colored woman whom I love dearly for several years. We have five children, but were not married because the laws of this state do not permit intermarriage and because I had not given the matter of marrying much thought. However, after reading the Defender, I realized that I owe it to my children to give them a legal standing so that they can carry my name as well as inherit my property, of which I have considerable."

[13] National Sermons, pp. 356, 626, 624. 1869. Bishop Haven was one of the greatest spokesmen for the oneness of mankind in American history. Like Wendell Phillips, he indulged in none of the hedging so common among American leaders today. He once refused pastorship of a church in the South because Negroes would not be admitted to it on equality with white people.

[14a] New Threshold Magazine, August, 1943.

[14b] N. Y. World-Telegram, July 29, 1943. ("My Day.")

According to his letter, he slipped away from Louisiana, brought the colored concubine to Chicago, married her and then went back to his Louisiana plantation. His white neighbors resented what he had done but dared not interfere because of the property he controlled. He concludes, "We are happy now. My hope is that other white men who are faced with the same situation that faced me will solve the problem as I solved it."

Rev. John LaFarge, S.J., "No scientific proof appears to be available as to the deleterious effects from a *purely biological standpoint,* of the union between different races of mankind. Were such proof forthcoming it would fare hard with most of the civilized inhabitants of the earth as few of them, least of all, of European descent can claim any purity of stock. The evidence of Pitcairn Island or of the Russian-Aleut half-breeds of Alaska is against any theory of inherent deterioration due to the cross-breeding of ethnic groups. Some of the groups in the United States who are most vociferous in their insistence on 'white racial integrity'—although a fair number of such have a dash of Negro ancestry without knowing it—take special pride in claiming Indian blood in their veins . . .

"Quite independently of any dubious biological considerations there are *grave reasons* against any general practice of intermarriage between members of different racial groups. These reasons, where clearly certified, amount to a moral prohibition of such a practice . . .

"Racial intermarriage naturally produces a tension in family relations not unlike that tension which is produced by a mixed marriage in the field of religion . . ."[15a]

Writing six years later, Father LaFarge says, "If interracial justice brings intermarriage then any other form of contact between the races is fraught with the same danger. If intermarriage will grow out of such remote causes as admitting Negroes to trade unions or employing Negro stenographers, or allowing Negroes to vote or a voice in the expenditure of public funds, or educating those who possess natural talents then it will come out of tolerating their presence in the country at all or from baptizing Negro children or from admitting Negro converts to the Faith. Such an argument proves everything and nothing."[15b]

New Republic (October 18, 1943): "The bugaboo of intermarriage, which lurks in even the most civilized white minds, could as well be forgotten. People are going to mate with whom they please as they have in the past and laws to prevent it are futile . . . There have been many mixed couples legally married in the Northern states, whose lives would put to

15a Interracial Justice, pp. 143-6. 1937.
15b The Race Question and the Negro, p. 198. 1943.

shame the clandestine carnality of the white men who have created the generations of mixed blood Negro—to whom they have repudiated all obligations of parenthood . . .

—"It is ironic that those who cry loudest against social equality by which they mean "intermarriage," hail from the states, counties and townships where white blood, regardless of the law, flowed in the heaviest volume in Negro veins. These protestants should know, if anyone should, that people mate with whom they please; it is a very personal and private decision."

Walter A. Maier, "Lutheran Hour, Bringing Christ to the Nations" (letter to Baltimore Afro-American, Nov. 20, 1943): "In hesitating to advocate the intermarriage of colored and white people I follow the same principle in speaking against mixed marriages for Jews and Gentiles, Protestants and Catholics, and Lutherans and Reformed.

"I feel that young people who enter upon married life without being able to worship at the same altar are under a definite handicap.

"Answering the question, "Isn't marriage better than the race mixing we have now without benefit of clergy? If two people like each other haven't they the right and obligation to marry rather than engage in the kind of illicit intercourse which has changed the color of the colored race in America from black to brown?

"This certainly is not in any sense the exclusive alternative. The fact I do not advocate mixed marriages does not mean that I espouse the cause of illicit intercourse."

Chapter Six

MIXED MARRIAGES AS SEEN BY NEGROES

"Prejudice, like the spider, makes everywhere its home, and lives where there seems nothing to live on." Thomas Paine.

B OOKER T. WASHINGTON, founder of Tuskegee Institute: "I have never looked upon amalgamation as offering a solution to the so-called race problem and I know very few Negroes who favor it or even think of it for that matter.

"What those whom I have heard discuss the matter do object to are laws which enable the father to escape his responsibility or prevent him from accepting, or exercising it when he had children by colored women . . .

"Those who are fighting race distinction are doing so not because they want to intermingle socially with white people but because they have been led to believe that where race discrimination exist they pave the way for discriminations which are needlessly humiliating and injurious to the weaker race.

"Let me add that I do not wholly share this view myself. While there may be some serious disadvantage in racial distinctions, there are certainly real advantages to my race at least."[1]

Bishop A. Walters: "These laws forbidding intermarriage of the races and the injustices resulting therefrom are crimes which are calling aloud to Almighty God for vengeance and we are compelled to suffer as a nation until such ways are righted.

"None but Almighty God and the women of the Negro race know the baneful effects which colored women have to suffer by such prohibitory laws. Speaking with a colored woman not long ago, she said there is nothing so grinding, so crushing as to look in the face of a white woman and have her say by a sarcastic and withering look, 'You're nothing but a thing to be used by our men.' I say again that prohibitory marriage laws such as I have mentioned above are a sad blot on the escutcheon of our land."[2]

About 1928, the Baltimore Afro-American carried a serial "Brown Love," in which mixed marriages were approved, and asked its readers to express their opinion. The following are excerpts from some of the letters it received:

"I can stand all the interracial love stories you are able to publish.

"I live down South where I haven't a chance to learn what is going on."

1 Amer. Jour. of Social., Vol. 21, p. 672. 1915-16
2 Quoted in Holm, J. J., Race Assimilation, p. 488. 1910.

"There is no disgrace about a colored man marrying a white woman and vice-versa. We need to bury the hatchet and shake hands."

"I really enjoyed reading the story. I don't see any harm in printing those stories. I am engaged to a very refined, cultured, white girl, who is a college graduate and also a graduate nurse of a refined family, and I am made welcome in her family. I do not have to sneak or hide to see her. We love each other and will be married in December.

"I think Mr. and Mrs. Saunders of Columbus, Ohio, are wrong in their statement when they say that this is contrary to the holy command of God that races should ever be together, when God made of one blood all mankind.

"No race can consider itself above another. May you continue to print such stories, regardless of the narrow-minded ones."

"There are interracial loves, interracial marriages, interracial dances, interracial penthouses, half-white and half-colored children, men and women, so why can't we have interracial love stories?

"Here in the city of Camden, the above is quite true. Since it is, there must be interracial love stories, so please let us have them."

"I love to read interracial love stories, but down here where I live, no colored man makes love to a white woman; and probably won't for a long time."

"If we discuss interracial love affairs from now until a hen learns to chant the Greek alphabet backward, will someone please tell me in what way it is going to help get jobs for our scores of boys and girls graduating in a few weeks?"

"Interracial love, romance and marriage. The most thrilling type of romance and love obtainable. The delicious blending of the attractions that opposites in sex and color have for each other.

"My husband is sealskin brown and I am an ash blond of English extraction. We have an adorable daughter, a picture in pale bronze which only emphasizes our contention that black-white marriages produce the best children possible of any union.

"I adore my husband and child and pity the ignorant and prejudiced members of both races—who do anything to hinder the sweet mating of black and white."

"This note represents an even dozen white girl members of the Vanilla-Chocolate Social Club of lower Harlem—who are all constant readers of the

AFRO, and who needless to say are enthusiastic advocates of interracial romance and marriage. This club has three blonde southern girls among its members, who admit the ridiculous and malicious prejudice of certain sections of the South and make every effort in their power to atone for the blindness of some members of their race.

"Our little club we feel is a practical demonstration of the fun and thrill and genuine good of interracial social association and for not a few of our members wedding bells are ahead.

"Interracial love and marriage should be subtly advertised for eventual national harmony—and among young couples at least is noticeably on the up-swing. Any social gathering in or near Harlem will show that."

"My wife, who is colored, has just showed me the last two copies of the AFRO containing mixed love fiction, and I intend to buy the AFRO as long as you use that type of story.

"The country needs more interracial love and marriage for the best interests of all concerned. The happiness of the couples involved and the true brotherhood of man in general."

"I am very anxious to get my vote in and counted on the 'yes' side of the editorial policy dealing with black-and-white love and sex stories.

"The extent of such affairs in real life is much greater than the average man or woman realizes—and I cannot for one instant think why stories and articles dealing with this situation should not be published. While these mixed matches often result in marriage, many thousands of mutually agreeable love episodes are carried on "behind the scenes," and deserve to be brought to the attention of any modern and up-to-date section of your reading public. Perhaps a few 'bandanna' sundowners may object, but I am sure a large portion of your younger and more modern subscribers will enjoy at least one such story or article each week.

"Personally, I have enjoyed being the principal and confidant, on many more than one occasion, in such matters and have enjoyed the society of some very lovely and gracious ladies."

"I have been married for five years to one of the finest gentlemen that ever lived, even though you would classify him as colored. We live in a very fine neighborhood. I think it is real nonsense to think one race is better than another. God made all of one blood."

The Afro-American said as regards the letters it had received, "Readers who have written in overwhelmingly requesting interracial as well as intra-racial love stories, based their opinion on what is going on around them.

"Last week in Philadelphia, a white U. S. marine officer chose a brown mate. This week two white women in Washington tell how they happened to choose colored husbands.

"If we could put all the bigots, ignoramuses and damphools on the race question in a garbage can with a tight cover for a few years, intermarriage of races would be about as uneventful as mating between a white hen and a black rooster, a white bull and a black cow.

"After all there are only two parties to a marriage and when it's unanimous, with them, who else has anything to do with it?"

The Amsterdam News of New York, a Negro weekly, once told of the Penguin Club, an organization formed by mixed couples in New York, to combat ostracism by both whites and Negroes. As a result of this news article, it reported: "Following the publication of a recent story in The Amsterdam News, telling of the announced purpose of the organization of intermarried couples, the club has been swamped with applications for membership, officials revealed yesterday. So great was the press of applications, that the officers were unable to decide the question at the last business meeting.

"As a result, the Penguin Club has called a special meeting for next month. All persons who sent applications to the club at 56 East 112th Street will be invited to the April meeting where their request for membership will be acted upon. New applications are being received there.

"In forming the club, members pointed out that they were going to make an attempt to provide the social life for themselves and their children with both races. Negro and white, usually deny persons who cross racial lines to seek their life mates."

The Afro-American which also reported the story about the Penguin Club carried a letter about it from two white girls of which the following are excerpts: "We are two real 'cornsilk'—and, to be frank, 'cornfed'— blondes, recently arrived in New York City, both single and both very much in favor of the principles and aims of the club.

"However, we find that, because since, we are not eligible to become affiliated, and hence would like to suggest that the club organize an auxiliary for single persons of both races who desire to associate. This will, we are sure, augment the club greatly in the future by marrying.

"As Mr. Cabot of the club is quoted as saying, regarding the thousands of men and women of both races who, if given their choice would marry their opposite in color, we are two of the latter and hope our suggestion may find favor with the club officials.

X. Upper row: Two Negroid Jews of Berlin (Guenther). Negroid Bedouin (Guenther).
Centre: Turkish mulatto (Guenther). George A. P. Bridgetower, celebrated pianist, and accompanist of Beethoven, who was born in Poland. Polish mulatto Jew (Fishberg). Lower row: Egyptian mulatto (Guenther). The Emir Saud of Arabia. John IV, King of Portugal (Bibliotheque Nationale).

"Please keep up this good work, which will eventually ameliorate the sad and unnecessary barriers which now exist between colored and white girls and boys who otherwise would freely carry out Nature's true law— 'opposites attract' by meeting and marrying."

The Chicago Defender, Negro weekly, attacking a Superior Court judge for his stand on intermarriage: "We do not oppose intermarriage; we believe intermarriage is far preferable to the sort of intermixing as is done in the South. We believe, also, that the blood which white people have poured into our veins for 300 years has a definite right to go back into the veins of those who started it, if it chooses that direction.

"We have no patience with white men, North or South, who go about preaching their views under the cloak of what 'better class of Negroes think.' We are articulate, and quite capable of speaking for ourselves about what we think. Judge Carpenter would be a better judge if he confined his efforts to learning the laws and discussing them as they pertain to his duties. Had he been wanted as a law-maker he would have been sent to that position instead of the one he holds. But finally whether we do or do not want intermarriage is beside the question. We want exactly what is every man's and every woman's right—the right to select who we shall marry, and love knows no color, creed, or religion."[3]

A Defender correspondent taking issue with the above said: "A white woman never has, nor ever will marry a poor Negro. If you must write of it, give it what it deserves by saying: 'Two fools met. One white and one black.'

"Judge Carpenter was right. The best Negroes are against intermarriage and any one who says they are not tells a falsehood. It is unfair and misleading and gives the world the wrong opinion of the Negro. Only two classes of people believe in intermarriage, namely, people possessing less than one per cent of race pride, and people possessing less than one per cent of intelligence. Why can not we be as proud of what we are as the other group? It is a coward who would like to don the uniform of the enemy and cross to the winning side. If your race is not what you want it, stay and help make it."[4]

Another Defender correspondent wrote on miscegenation. "I am for it. I think it is unavoidable and will redound to the benefit of the country and of the world at large. Yet, what chance has a sincere white person to meet a decent colored person? Where are there places, if there are any,

3 Editorial, March 22, 1930.
4 Editorial page, May 3, 1930.

where white and colored can meet on purely social basis without getting drunk or indulging in other dissipations? Why don't you publish the locations of these places where, for instance, the races meet for discussions of a political, artistic and other subjects of universal interest? Keep on publishing those places. See to it that really representative members of your race frequent those places and that the rowdies are kept away from them, and you will see after a while you will get results. Nobody in France draws the color line. Why should they here? It is true we have in this country a vast number of the brutal, stuck-up and conceited Nordics—Dutchmen, Scandinavians, etc. Don't mind them, their influence on this country's psychic is not as large as the one your colored race is going to exert."[5]

In January 1939 a young white man "madly in love" with a colored girl wrote Dr. W. E. B. DuBois, sociologist, then editor of the *Crisis*, asking him whether he thought it advisable to marry her. DuBois, in turn, asked his readers what they thought of it and received many replies, among which was the following (from a Negro married to a white woman): "Although during a lifetime I have favored interracial marriages I feel very kindly disposed toward those who disapprove. Years ago I once wrote a strong letter of protest to a friend who had it in view because he was a man of parts and so near the boundary between the so-called races that my fear was that his genius would be lost to the colored race if he took this step. Whether influenced by my letter I know not, but he did not, and now has three children identified with the colored race through an intraracial match.

"The value of intermarriage is that it tends to increase the bond of fellowship between races, destroys prejudices and often produces clever and beautiful offspring. Consider the Eurasians and other vital stocks produced by the racial mixing. Of the last there are countless illustrations. There comes to mind a family of Greater New York in which the husband and wife, white and black, are very ordinary people by human standards. But their three children are clever and beautiful beyond description. My own marriage, though childless, is happy. My wife is of solid English stock, with a long range of accomplishments and a granite character."

Another letter read: "Such a marriage union would set an example for the 100 per cent white gentlemen in the Southland who are ever ready to disgrace young colored girls and who by such illicit unions are filling the country over with mulattoes, quadroons and octoroons. These unions as the world knows, take place in sections below the Potomac without the sanction of the church or of the state, in face of the fact that in these sections laws are made to prevent colored and white persons marrying into each

[5] Editorial page, March 15, 1930.

others' families. The white man is instrumental in defeating his own laws; he is opposed to the black man marrying his daughter and yet, he makes possible these illicit unions. A young brown-skin man was walking on the street with his wife, a woman of fair hair and complexion and a decided Anglo-Saxon appearance. He was asked by his employer the next morning on going to work: "Did you marry a white woman?' 'No, I married a white man's daughter," he answered."[6]

Dr. W. E. B. DuBois himself said: "A man named Lawton writing to the Independent says that the N.A.A.C.P. 'expressly advocates intermarriage' of whites and blacks. It does nothing of the sort. It simply declares that if white folk will have sexual commerce with blacks, this must take place under the legal restrictions; that prohibition of such legal marriage is a direct bid for bastards and prostitutes and removes all civilized protection from colored girls and women, and finally that if healthy persons wish to marry that that is their business and neither Mr. Lawton's nor ours. This is a long way from advocating such marriages. In spite of everything we still maintain that English dukes should have the right to marry Americans. But we do not 'advocate' it. We have too much respect for Americans.

"If any white person does not want to marry a colored person no one is going to compel him. If he is asked he has simply to say no."[7]

Earl Finch, late professor anthropology, Wilberforce University: "Race blending, especially in the rare instances where it occurs under favorable circumstances, produces a type superior in fertility, vitality, and cultural worth to one or both of the parent stocks."[8]

Gilbert H. Jones, former president of Wilberforce University: "Race admixture is as undesirable on the part of the best colored people as it is on the part of the best whites . . .

". . . Legislation (on race-mixing) is one-sided and is based on the presumption that Negroes want to mix with whites while whites do not want to mix with Negroes; a thing which is absolutely untrue.

"Futhermore, it gives the Negro woman no method of defense in her fight for right living and the protecting of her womanhood, such as every woman ought to have. It breaks down all the restraint of white men and outrages Negro women, and their offspring born under such conditions have no opportunity in law to take on the name of those responsible for their living. If the white men would leave the Negro women alone there would be no such problem from their angle.

"Human sentiment and artificial barriers may delay the intermarriage

---

6 Crisis Maga., March. 1930.
7 Crisis Maga., Jan. 1927, p. 128; Feb. 1928, p. 108.
8 Inter-Racial Papers, G Spiller, p. 108. 1911.

XI. His Highness, the Kizlar-Aghassi. (See "The Negro in Turkey," Sex and Race, Vol. I, Appendix).

and amalgamation of the races, but if the laws of biology, holding sway in the whole gamut of living things, tell man anything, it preaches profoundly the fact that racial amalgamation through intermarriage is the ultimate end the whole gamut of living things, tell man anything, it preaches profoundly of racial contact in the United States.

"As a biological principle, I am not opposed to race amalgamation for nowhere is there evidence that nature took any precautions to prevent it or prohibit it. Personally I am opposed to it as a matter of race pride."[9]

A black Garveyite, in all probability, a West Indian, on the topics: "As to Mulatto Leaders."

"It blunts the finer sensibilities to think that conspicuous among the so-called leaders are the mulatto element. Think of having these bastards, offspring of commercialized Negro women, to be assuming to represent the race. Men who knew no father and therefore have no name. Dogs because their mothers were, and they have developed all the instincts of the lower animals. Coming into the world without pre-natal affection and dying without knowing whence they came."[10]

Kelly Miller, late Dean of Howard University: "The Negro resents the reputation that he is over-eager to marry into the white race. Every time a Negro marries a white person, a white person marries a Negro."[11]

Alain Locke, professor of philosophy, Howard University: "It is my opinion that race amalgamation proceeds much more rapidly where races are socially and economically unequal, and that it is this kind of miscegenation that is from both Negro and Caucasian points of view undesirable.

"Considering that the considerable amount of race intermixture has up until recently been the outcome of such exploitation of the economically and socially weaker group, we must, I think, conclude that any degree of amalgamation in the future could not produce deterioration of physical stock or of the standard of living in this country, since it has not done so thus far.

"Theoretically, then no unbiased mind can be opposed to the principle of race amalgamation. On the whole, nature has answered that question affirmatively."[12]

Arthur Hale, in letter to Baltimore Afro-American August 9, 1941): "As you know, my wife is white. We never lose an opportunity to let the world know that I am colored and that what we have accomplished represents colored.

9 See No. 3, chapter 2.
10 Negro World, Dec. 25, 1922.
11 Release to Negro Press, Jan. 1930.
12 See No. 3, Chapter 2.

"Better still, we thus drive home to the whites the fact that a colored and white couple can love, marry and live in a normal, successful, happy life together. Thus we destroy, in a small way, another of their pet theories.

"We often go about with white couples. I always find some way to let others know what I am. I feel proud to do so. When traveling abroad foreigners never think for a moment that we are what are called American colored people.

"It is always our delight to let the world know what we represent. You would be amazed at the worlds of thought that this opens up for the foreigners. And they are glad to learn of us."

Negro Youth, a magazine in the interests of the unmixed Negroes as against the mulattoes: "Where a black man marries a mulatto or half breed he strikes a greater blow than white people could ever strike for the degradation, dishonor, and enslavement of the black race . . .

"Mulatto women are the greatest saboteurs and fifth-columnists among our race. They corrupt and debauch the moral character of black men . . . White men use mulatto women as concubines and for the worst forms of sex perversion . . ." (April 1941).

One article in the same issue is entitled, "Mulattoes—An Insult to Black People," and denounces the mulatto as a "damnable" mixture.[13]

In its issue of November 20, 1943, the Baltimore Afro-American asked the question, "When a white man marries a colored woman or vice versa, do you think they love each other, or is it merely a sexual attraction.?" Among the answers received were:

"When two people marry they marry for love in most cases. I think that mixed couples marry for love and it doesn't matter what color the parties are."

"They marry for sexual reasons. If there is any love I think that it is on the man's side. A white woman couldn't love a colored man and if a colored woman married a white man it would only be for what he could give her materially."

"Races shouldn't intermarry. My experience has been that mixed marriages aren't as happy as others."

"I don't think that true love exists there, because love is based upon understanding and there is very little of that between the races."

---

[13] The editor of this magazine is Samuel W. Daniels. For further pronouncements of his see J. R. Carlson's Under Cover, p. 157, 1943.

Chapter Seven

THE "FOUR LAWS" OF RACE-MIXING

"Men are like bricks alike, but placed high or low by chance."
Webster.

H AVING seen arguments in great variety of pro and con offered by whites and Negroes of all classes, we shall now proceed to examine the subject in its more intimate detail.

As a basis for this, I can think of nothing better than the so-called four laws of race-mixing laid down by Lester F. Ward (1841-1913), the Father of American sociology, when discussing the rape of white women by black men as the supposed reason for lynching. Ward, it is true, wrote some fifty years ago but his view is still held not only by the masses but, I have reason to believe, by most of the white sociologists and certainly most Southern politicians and racial agitators. Since, therefore, it is popular opinion we are dealing with here, we shall examine these four "laws."

They are:

1. "The women of any race will freely accept the men of a race which they regard as higher than their own."

2. "The women of any race will vehemently reject the men of a race which they regard as lower than their own."

3. "The men of any race will greatly prefer the women of a race which they regard higher than their own."

4. "The men of any race, in default of women of a higher race, will be content with women of a lower race."[1]

Roughly adapted they read:

1. "Negro women will freely accept white men."

2. "White women will vehemently reject Negro men."

3. "Negro men will greatly prefer white women."

4. "Negro men, unable to get white women, will be content with Negro women."

Do Negro Women Freely Accept White Men?

Taking the first law I suggest for concurrent consideration another "law" which I will as broadly state:

[1] Ward, L. F., Pure Sociology, pp. 358-60. 1911.

The women of any social status will freely accept the men of a status which they regard as higher than their own, that is, lower-class white women will freely accept upper-class white men[2]; and lower-class Negro women will freely accept upper-class Negro men; and so on with Chinese, Africans, Jews and other peoples. In all countries, primitive and civilized, wealth and social position are powerful factors in deciding a woman's choice of husband or lover. As Byron says:

"Maidens, like moths, are ever caught by glare

And Mammon wins his way where seraphs might despair."

In Europe and Asia, the beautiful untitled girl, rich or poor, if ambitious, dreams of marrying a lord. It is the old story of Cinderella and the prince. Sir Harry Johnston tells of the craze that existed among English girls of the lower middle class to marry into the African nobility, as Zulu princes and Ashanti noblemen.[3] The white peasant woman thinks highly of an illegitimate child got by a lord or famous man and one suspects that the American 400 would not regard with too unmoral an eye a child got by one of its debutantes by a certain prince of the "royal" blood, when the latter visited America in the 1930's.

The daughter of a lord, if ambitious, looks forward to carrying the son of a duke or prince; the daughter of a kinglet, as say one of the many little monarchies that used to exist in Germany looked forward to capturing a Prince of Wales, and so on.

There are, I believe, few dyed-in-the-wool Americans, who, however much they may turn up their noses, do not feel a certain elevation in being in the company of a titled person, even though he is bogus. Many are attracted to titles as a Solomon Islander to five-and-ten-cent jewelry, as note the slobbering of the American press over titled visitors.

Two notorious instances of American plutocrats being bamboozled by bogus lords come to mind; that of a stableman of the Emperor Franz Joseph II, who, posing as "Count Gregory of Austria," ruled the American *beau monde* for ten years, extracting millions of dollars from it; and of a French cook, Edouard Rousselot, who, as a "marquis," fleeced the elite of New York and Washington of large sums.[4] "A smile from a lord," says the old proverb, "is a breakfast for a fool."

Now what titles or social positions are in Europe, Asia and other parts

[2] For good treatment of caste within the white "race" itself see Prof. E. A. Ross, "Caste and Class," American Jour. of Sociology, Vol. 22, pp. 467-76; 594-608; 747-760).

[3] Johnston, H. H., Negro In The New World, pp. 462n. 1910.

[4] For how one Negro potato-peeler, posing as a prince, fooled the American 400, see Sex and Race, Vol. II, pp. 359-62. 1942.

of the world, that is, the standard of social value, irrespective of mental or moral worth—the aristocrat may be a diseased rogue and yet be considered the superior of many an honest, healthy and intelligent man of the people— even so, in every respect, is a "white" or almost unpigmented epidermis in the United States of America. As rank in Europe is generally a passport to superior opportunities, so is a white epidermis in America. As in Europe the commoner is forced to look up to the lord, so in the United States, the majority of Negroes are forced in various ways to look up to, or to bow, to white. In short, "white" ideas predominate as in Europe titular ones do.

In Europe there are few noblemen who do not feel hurt if mistaken for a commoner; and few commoners in Europe or America who would not be pleased if mistaken for a lord. Again, there are few mistresses in a household who would not feel insulted if mistaken for the maid—a reason why many prefer Negro maids—and few maids who would not be pleased if taken for the mistress.

Similarly in the United States few white persons would not be incensed if taken for a Negro. In Virginia, Louisiana, South Carolina, Georgia, and all those states where centuries of race-mixing give color to the allegation, to question a white man's color is like questioning a woman's chastity. In the first three states and in Oklahoma, it is a libel, according to the Supreme Court of these states, to call one presumably white, a Negro, as in Nazi Germany it was a gross libel to call an "Aryan" a Jew. In 1929, Professor Fuenfkircker of the University of Budapest sued editors of the Budapest "Who's Who" for listing him as a Jew, and the judge in awarding him the verdict, ordered confiscated 6,700 copies of the book.

Furthermore, in Europe, the one who works hard is said to toil "like a peasant"; in America, "like a nigger." The Negro who has a good position will boast that he has "a white man's job," quite mindless of the fact that the wages of most white men doing the same kind of work is higher than his and that the United States with its highest paid workers contains but a sixth of the white race.

The result of all this is to create a powerful bias in the mind of the female, white or black, in favor of the white man. Of course, we're speaking only of present conditions and not of slavery days when white prestige among Negroes was much higher than now.

To pursue the comparison: As in Europe certain commoners wish to enter lordly society, and those in that group are doing all they can to bar them because they believe them inferior; as certain rich in the United States are doing their best to enter aristocratic American circles, as say buying boxes in the Golden Horse Shoe, and getting into certain clubs, and those in that

XII. The Rev. George Grenfell, who had a Negro wife. (See Sex and Race, Vol. I Chap. 14).

circle are fighting to keep them out because they deem them inferior; even so are the more aspiring Negroes trying to get certain advantages from a dominant group, incidentally white, and that group is doing its best to bar them, because it believes them inferior. It is in this sense that Ward's first law of racial intermixture is true—a law, which, in its final sense is, as was said, an economic one. In short, it is but a matter of human beings, regardless of so-called race, shunning what they have been taught to consider disadvantageous, and seeking that which they are taught to consider advantageous.

In the above analysis, however, it is seen that false values can be set above real ones; that a diseased and inferior white man, provided he belongs to a "good" family may, in Europe, be set above a healthy and intelligent white man who comes from a humble one; that, in America, a diseased social parasite, who, perhaps never did a useful thing in his life may have advantages that a healthy working-man may not; and that the most vicious ex-criminal, provided he has a white skin, will be permitted advantages as entrance to certain hotels, parks, libraries, bathing beaches, trade unions, railway cars, from which the most intelligent and worthy citizen would be barred if he had a "colored" skin.

A social value is not necessarily a biological one. Values created by man may be in direct opposition to natural ones—values such as are conducive to the health and happiness of the human race. The deduction, therefore, is that there is no real difference between a woman, incidentally white, who surrenders herself to a white man she has been taught to believe is of a higher social order; and that of a woman, incidentally colored, who surrenders herself to a man of a group she has been taught to believe superior. Both are identical cases of love dazzled by economic advantage. As Dr. Jacobus X says, "The love of the Negro woman for the white man, though it is flattering to her pride, is rather an affection of the head than of the heart."[5]

A large number of Christianized Negro women would prefer a white man as husband or lover, especially the former. This will be strongly denied in the United States, but it is true of the West Indies and South America where weakness of the color bar makes such marriages possible.

Hannibal Thomas, a Negro who served in the Civil War, tells how the Negro women, who had all along been going with white Southerners, flocked to the camps of the Union soldiery for infamous riot with white Northerners.[6]

Will one say that there is any fundamental difference between the

---

[5] For additional confirmation of this, see Sex and Race, Vol. 2, p. 403, 1942, especially what Lady Dorothy Mills says.
[6] For the exact quotation and additional instances, see Sex and Race, Vol. II, pp. 260-62. 1942.

colored woman south of the Rio Grande, and the one north of it; indeed, that there is any well-defined psychic difference between women of the different varieties of the human race? The colonel's lady and Judy O'Grady, no matter what their color are forever sisters under the skin. The sole difference I have been able to discover between white American women and colored ones, for example, is that the latter usually have an inferiority complex, while the former have a superiority complex.

As was said, the majority of Negro women, whenever their group comes into competitive contact with the whites, consciously and unconsciously, prefer a white man, because of the better advantages to be gained for themselves and their offspring, that is, it is a matter of protective coloration as among the so-called lower animals.

A large number of colored women, and the number is increasing rapidly, believe that in order for their children to be of any consequence, they must be light-skinned and flossy-haired. At any rate, they will find it easier to love them if they are. That is to say, if they had their choice they would have preferred the child's father to be white or near-white.

I once heard a full-blood Negro preacher tell an outdoor audience composed almost wholly of his own color, "Any time a woman of your color have a child for you she sho' does love you." The crowd applauded.

A black man of social standing rarely, if ever, marries a woman of his own complexion. In the West Indies one who does so would be charged with having done nothing to elevate his race. The slogan there is: Raise the color. In New York I once heard a prominent colored woman blame the black West Indians there for continuing to have so many black children.

The bias of the Aframerican woman is decidedly toward having light-colored children with straight hair. Negro hair is quite popularly described as "bad" hair, and is disappearing, at least to outward appearance, under a flood of anti-kink preparations. Black children, in orphan asylums, stand a better chance of adoption by white women than by colored women. The latter select the lightest babies, which they will wheel down the street with great pride.

It is important to note, however, that had these women been reared in Africa, their selection would have been just the reverse; it would have been progressively toward black, that being the color of the chiefs.

Shooter wrote of the black of Natal, South Africa, in 1857, when they had much less contact with the whites than now. "Dark complexions as being most common are naturally held in high esteem. To be told that he is light-colored or like a white man would be deemed a poor compliment to a

Kafir."[7] Certain ethnologists class the Ethiopians as white, that also would be considered no compliment. Indeed, I knew Ethiopians who would be as highly insulted if called a *natch*, or white man, as there are white Southerners who would be if called a "nigger."

Henry M. Stanley, the famous explorer, said that he found at the court of the noted King Mtesa of Uganda that the light-colored women were not specially favored. Of three of the most comely of the twenty beauties he saw there, he said, "They had the complexions of quadroons, were straight-nosed and thin-lipped with large lustrous eyes. In the other graces of a beautiful form they excelled and Hafiz might have said with poetic rapture that they were 'straight as palm trees and beautiful as moons.' The only drawback was their hair—the short, crisp hair of the Negro race—but in all other points they might be exhibited as the perfection of beauty which Central Africa can produce." The king, however, said Stanley, did not think these three girls any more beautiful, or "superior, or even equal" to his other flat-nosed, black wives and that one day when he pointed them out to the king as being especially beautiful the king "even regarded them with a sneer."[8]

In Negro Africa, the married women shun a white man "like the devil," roundly abusing those who make advances to them, fearing visible proof of unfaithfulness. On the other hand, in America, it is no uncommon sight to see a married woman with a child very much lighter than herself or her husband.

[7] Kafirs of Natal, p. 1. 1857.
[8] Through the Dark Continent, Vol. 1, p. 308. 1878.

Chapter Eight

THE MIXING OF NEAR-WHITE AND BLACK

I N refutation of what was said about the preference of some colored women for white men, so far as having children is concerned, it might justly be objected that throughout the United States the tendency of the "light" women is to marry, or to be seen in public with men considerably darker in color than themselves. In the case of Negro couples seen on the street in perhaps seven cases out of ten the woman is lighter in color than the man, so much so that one is led to think that Negro females have a tendency to be born "light,"[1] or that black women must go unmated. Whenever a prominent black man marries it is hardly necessary to ask what color the bride is. In many cases the wife is so white that some of the white people are almost as white as she is.

The reply is that, in this case, we have to deal with that important characteristic of the feminine mind discussed in the last chapter: The desire for masculine appreciation and support. The "light" girl, like the daughter of the well-to-do white man, is often no more endowed by Nature for earning her own livelihood than the black one, and as men, regardless of race, have the superior economic position, it is they who generally do the selecting. In most parts of the world, a man buys his wives directly. In Christian countries the same thing is done but in a "respectable" manner.

In the West Indies, where colored women are free to marry white men, a fair colored girl no more thinks of marrying a black man than a white Southern woman does. Indeed, I think the latter is the less prejudiced of the two if I am to judge by the number of white Southern women I have seen married to, or living with, very dark men. Wealthy West Indian girls prefer a white man, even if he is poor to a colored one, even as the rich American girl, at least of a generation ago, was so eager to marry some moth-eaten count or duke in preference to a rich countryman of theirs. But in the United States where intermarriage is unpopular light girls will marry dark men. As was said, whiteness is a standard of social value, and certain

---

1 Often these women are not so fair as they seem. An ordinary observer will note that their faces are sometimes several shades lighter than their arms or neck. due to powder and bleaching compounds. This fact was strikingly brought out in the Rhinelander case. Alice Rhinelander's body, when she stripped for the jury, was found to be much darker than her face. The reverse would be true of a white woman.

71

black men, feeling greatly the handicap of color, desire to identify themselves with white, and failing that, as near to white as possible. Besides, to be seen with such a woman makes them the envy of certain other Negroes.

Wishing to give their children a better start in life than they themselves had is another reason for selecting such women and in order to get them, they are willing to give more, that is, more appreciation, gifts, and all those little flatteries dear to a woman's heart, than a light-colored man would be inclined to give. Black men, in short, win "light" women for the same reason that plain men are usually more successful suitors than handsome ones. The former, in endeavoring to atone for what they consider a defect, are less proud and more considerate. I have this statement direct from the lips of many of these "light" women themselves. One of them told me that there is hardly anything black men will not do for her. Another who "passes for white" told me that she was prompted to accept her husband not because she really loved him but because he was so very attentive. "Kindness," she said, "goes a long way toward winning a woman."

The color prejudice of some Negroes against other Negroes is sometimes stronger than that of some whites against Negroes. There are white men who would more readily marry a black woman than would some mulattoes. There are also unmixed blacks who do not like to see other unmixed blacks about. I have seen the same thing among Jews. One of their "own" is too strong a reminder of their affliction. Thus those Caucasians who are prejudiced against Negroes might be reminded that if they consider having color prejudice a smart thing, they may find people they would look down on who can beat them doing the same thing. For instance, in New York cafeterias and automats, white men and women will sometimes sit at a table at which there is already a black man or woman. That, however, you'd rarely see in the West Indies in the case of a light mulatto and a black person. Newly-arrived Europeans in the West Indies are far less prejudiced than the mulattoes and near-whites. While the European, in his native land, shows little or no prejudice for unmixed blacks, the West Indian mulatto in Europe shows much.

The pursuit of the light-colored woman in the United States by the black man has sometimes an adverse psychological effect on the light woman. It is not only responsible for a large number of women becoming haughty, spoilt, and so engrossed in their looks and their complexion that they are intellectually dwarfed, but it is also responsible for wifely infidelity. Women who are led into marriage through any other cause except love, usually regret the bargain. Nothing — gifts, flattery, adoration — can compensate for long. The novelty soon palls, the men finding that mere color of skin is a poor substitute for wifely qualities, in the same way that the American heiress

XIII. "The African Prince." An old English print. (Coll. Richard B. Moore).

73

who marries a European title may learn that she wants something more than rank in a husband; or that the titled husband may find that he wants something more in a wife than money.

Moreover, some of these light women have had their fling, and are "marked down" just as a certain type among the whites. It is thus easy to understand why many colored women take so much pains to lighten their faces.

It is quite possible that certain physical reasons may enter into the union of black men and light women, but many such matches are rather "an affection of the head than of the heart." It is to be remembered that these women do pride themselves on their white ancestry.

The implication here, however, is not that mulatto-black marriages are a failure. There are many couples, who, because of spiritual affinity, which is the real cement of any marriage, interracial or otherwise, seem well-mated; nevertheless, there are many such unions which may be regarded as a *marriage for color*. In this case it is usually the men who are the first to be disillusioned. An educated Negro, after reading a printed statement of mine to this effect, told me that he had tolerated his wife all these years simply because of her very light skin. "Had she been my color, I would have given her the air long ago," he said.[2]

Many black men (Negro-Americans and West Indians in the United States, especially) can see absolutely no beauty in a black woman. I have often heard them so express themselves. In the good old vaudeville days in the Negro theater a black woman was usually the butt of the jokes while the "yaller" woman was the prize.

A not unlike condition exists among the white men. A beautiful wife will be forgiven much; a plain one, little. White men who marry merely on physical attraction have the same trouble. Even as the beautiful woman among the white is much more likely to be lower in sex morals than the plain one, so the light-colored girl, particularly in the Northern cities, is likely to be on a lower moral plane than many of the whites and the blacks. Courted most assiduously by black, white and parti-colored men, they not infrequently become the mistress of the last two and finally the wife of the first.

The black man-mulatto woman marriage serves a good purpose, however. It effectively prevents the rise of a mulatto caste as in the British West

---

[2] A West Indian Negro long resident in Europe once told me that he preferred a white woman to a black because in moments d'amour he could see some color in her face while that of the black woman remained like "a blank wall."

Indies. To have Negroes divided is just what the white exploiters wish. Many white writers, consciously or by inference, are attempting to herd the mulattoes into a superior caste. I predict that when the retreating force of white supremacy in the South shall have been driven from its front line trench it will endeavor to take refuge in the second line: the mulatto caste, precisely as it did in the West Indies and might in South Africa. Already in certain Southern states a "Negro" who is more than seven-eighths white is legally white.

Up to the present, the mulatto caste, though fairly strong in certain centers, as Washington, D. C.; Richmond, Virginia; New Orleans, and Charleston, South Carolina, is a negligible factor as the mere fact of the black-mulatto marriages prove. Closed castes are possible only where the women are not free to marry men of another caste. Still, it is strong enough to distress a good many dark Negroes. A correspondent wrote me: "Another thing that has caused me a great deal of distress is the status of the darker woman in the United States. Being of the darker type myself, I am in a position to feel the mild and in some cases, the deep contempt, colored people have for a dark complexion."

Mulatto Men and Black Women

And what is the attitude of the light-colored man toward a union with the black woman? As may be inferred, he is not any too eager for it. But masculine vanity also plays its part. Most men are egotistic in love, and as the dark woman is inclined to idolize her light husband in the same manner as the dark man is to idolize the light wife, it is possible that there are more such marriages than are commonly seen.

The sex relations of the "light" man and the black woman tends, as in the case of her and the white man, toward concubinage. At least I have noticed that the number of male parasites is greater among light men than dark. A rascal, whose only claim to distinction is the very squalid one of lightness of skin and slickness of hair, will have some black woman wearing herself out to keep him loafing. However, some black men are formidable "sweet-backs."

Another important factor is that the "light" girls, conscious of their unique position, demand too much, thus driving many of the light men to seek the company of black women or white ones. On the other hand, white "Negroes" who decided to remain in the Negro camp not infrequently marry women considerably darker than themselves. I have known several such who even had black wives.

It is evident that the desire of certain Negro women to marry or to consort with white men, like that of certain black women to seek mulatto men, is artificial rather than natural, and arises out of the abnormalities of the color situation. Had these women remained in Africa, their selection would have been blackness, not fairness of skin, as was said.

"Women," says Weininger, "seeks to create as much personal value for herself and so she adheres to the man who can give her the most of it." The value may take the form of wealth; empty flattery; accomplishment, intellectual or physical; and social or racial position, all of which are directly related to economic advantage.

If the Negroes in America had the same wealth per capita as the whites, it would be much more difficult for white men to get Negro women than at present. The Negro women are reacting more and more to the attitude created by color prejudice and discrimination. Moreover, as I have proved in Volume Two, the Negro has no inherent desire to mate with white people. Such as there is of this has been cultivated or induced by the environment.

I will go further and say that under the same present conditions of prejudice if the blacks were wealthier than the mulattoes, they, too, would be inclined to have a closed caste. As I showed in Volume One, the mulatto child of the black mother in certain parts of West and South Africa is practically an outcast. This treatment of the part-white child is a reflex of the treatment of the blacks themselves by the whites. That is, they want no part of the whites. The Garvey movement was distinctly pro-black. I also showed that in certain parts of the West Indies and West Africa there is a sort of quadroon caste in old families into which it is hard, not only for blacks, but for whites, to enter.

Ward's first law may thus be amended to read: The women of any race, social status, nation, clan or tribe, will freely accept the men of any race or any other group which they regard as higher than their own. In short, they do the very common thing of accepting what they consider most advantageous. Thus Ward, in a certain sociological sense, is right. The economic factor is the principal agent in bringing about amalgamation where the will of the Negro is concerned. The result is that sociologically the process of race-mixing is "a levelling-up and not a levelling-down," as Ward says.

However, Ward is away off when he introduces race, the biological factor, into it, as he does in pages 358 to 360 of his Pure Sociology. To accept this view one must first accept the dogma of "superior" races and "inferior" races, which has yet to be proved. And it is going to be increasingly difficult to do that as the darker groups advance. It could not be proved even when the Negro was a slave.

Chapter Nine

IS VEHEMENT REJECTION OF THE NEGRO MAN BY THE WHITE WOMAN SINCERE?

The lady doth protest too much, methinks." **Shakespeare.**

Ward gives as his second law racial intermixture the following: The women of a superior race will vehemently reject the man of a race they regard lower than their own. To this we will add: The women of a superior status, regardless of race, will, as a rule, reject the men of a status they regard lower than their own, as coachman, waiters, ditch-diggers.

By merely referring to the many cases of marriage and sex relations between Negroes and white women[1] as well as what some white psychologists have said on the desire of the white woman for the black man[2] it is possible to refute this law. Also, one Southern state, at least does not believe that white women will invariably reject Negroes—Maryland. The law of that state specially penalizes a white woman who shall suffer herself to be got with child by a Negro.[3]

Dollard, a painstaking investigator, also says, "There is a form of evidence that white women are interested in the matter of Negro sexuality which is quite impressive to me." He gives his reasons. He also quotes Dr. Helena Deutsch, "The fact that the white men believe so readily the hysterical and masochistic phantasies and lies of the white women who claim they have been assaulted and raped by Negroes is related to the fact that they (the men) sense the unconscious wishes of the women, the psychic reality of these declarations and react emotionally to them as if they were real. The social situation permits them to discharge this emotion upon the Negroes."[4]

Dr. Owen Berkeley-Hill, medical superintendent of a mental hospital for Europeans in India, has some very frank words on the subject. After relating certain traditions dealing with the cause of the fear of some white people for black people, he says, "Following the precepts of psychoanalysis we must not forget when studying an emotion to be on the lookout for a close association with its opposite in type, especially when the emotion we are in-

[1] See Sex and Race, Vol. 2, Chaps. 24-25. 1942.
[2] See Sex and Race, Vol. 1, pp. 180-190, 206-213, 230-35, 261-62. 1941.
[3] Mangum, C. S. Legal Status of the Negro, p. 266. 1940.
[4] Dollard, J. Caste and Class In A Southern Town, pp. 168-170. 1937.

vestigating is hate, for we are nearly aways certain to find its opposite, love, lurking somewhere around.

"By applying this principle we find there is another side to the relations between colored and non-colored races, namely, the very subtle and powerful attraction sometimes exercised on the less pigmented races by the more pigmented races, especially the Negro races. It is a purely sexual attraction. It is a form of sexual perversion. Also there is nothing new in it as anyone who recollects the first chapter of 'The Thousand Nights And a Night,' will recognize. The story relates how a certain king returning unexpectedly from a journey found his wives enjoying themselves with the Negro men servants. The king takes council with a neighboring chief and the latter tells him no woman can be trusted to remain chaste if a Negro is accessible to her. The first chapter of 'The Thousand Nights And a Night' contains in the guise of fiction a solid piece of fact, namely, the occasional development in women of an overpowering attraction for men of a more racially primitive type. Both in ancient and modern literature many references to this phenomenon are to be found.

"Lucius Seneca in his 'Letters to Lucilius' mentions that numbers of Negroes of both sexes were introduced into Rome at that time for the purposes of prostitution."

After citing other instances in Europe and America and especially in South Africa where an investigation by the government on alleged charges of rape on white women in which "the commission was confronted with some very astonishing evidence," he adds, "In my opinion, the phenomenon of lynch law against the Negro can only be explained by supposing the idea of sexual intercourse between his women kind and a Negro stirs in the depths of the white man's mind a fury that is the entire product of sexual jealousy. It is a general belief that the Negro not only possesses a larger penis than men of other races but is capable of maintaining it in a state of erection for a longer period than is possible for a male of any other race. Thus sexual jealousy of the Negro potency drives the white man temporarily mad to the end that he inflicts the most horrible retribution on his unfortunate rival."[5]

Freyre says similarly: "Perhaps the real basis for this belief in the physical superiority of the Negro male should be sought in the added pleasure given by the strange, the bizarre even, and in the sexual interest which the white woman takes in the mulatto, and even the Negro. This belief, however, is an old one. For the very first chapter of the *Arabian Nights* (as Owen Berkeley Hill reminded us a few years ago in *The Spectator*) gives

[5] The Color Question from a Psycho-Analytic Standpoint. Psycho-Analytic Review, Vol. 11, p. 250. 1924.

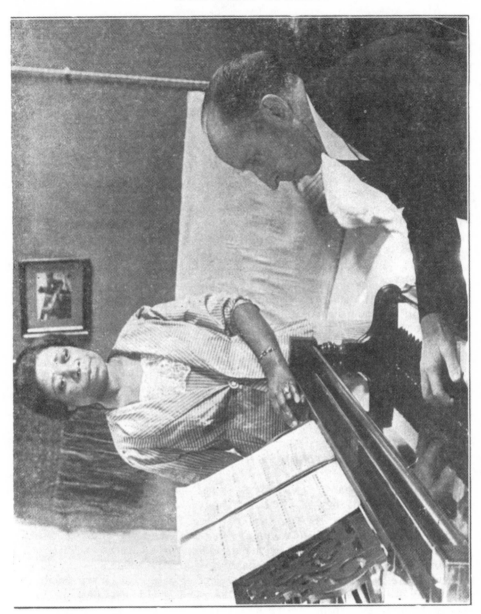

XIV. Professor Boris Titz, Moscow Conservatory of, Music, and his American Negro wife Coretti Arle Titz, (Chatwood Hall Photo). See Sex and Race, Vol. I.

us a clear-cut picture of the sexual charm which a man of a primitive and darker race exercises over a refined white woman. And Lieutenant Colonel Berkeley Hill has also noted the fact that the Negro, perhaps because of his more elementary nervous reactions and his greater physical vigor as well as the fascination which individuals of a darker race exercise over the lighter, plays a prominent role in the sexual life of the Turks, Persians, Hindus and Parisians."

Citing how the ancient Romans of both sexes were fond of Negro men and women—the Venus fusca—Freyre adds: "It appears evident to Berkeley Hill that the men as well as the women, but especially the refined white woman, the female of what he calls 'a racially superior type,' is especially susceptible to the much stronger sexual attraction exercised by individuals of a racially more primitive type. Whence the furious jealousy or sexual envy which the male of the higher race exhibits toward such sexual unions; and which should explain when coupled with the economic motive, certain types of race hatred, especially that of the white man against the man of color. In his attempt to discount the charm which a Negro man exercises over a white woman, the civilized white man has had to resort to a campaign of ridicule and defamation against the black man and his primitivism; and to embellish this campaign of antipathy, he repeats the same charge against the mulatto. He accuses the mulatto of fickleness and inconstancy in love, of his inability to equal the white man in real gentlemanlikeness and authentic masculine elegance; and this takes no account of the white man's intelligence, his nobler sentiments, his more solid qualities of stability, discernment, and powers of concentraton, which are according to the critics of *mulatismo,* rarely attained by the mixed-bloods or the pure blacks."[6]

The Psychology of "Vehemence"

Moreover, as regards "vehemence" would not that of itself be the strongest argument against Ward's second law. It is not necessary to go to Freud to prove that for these women to reject Negroes *vehemently,* they must have been thinking about a union with them.[7] And why think of that if they have no inclination that way? For instance, if I have no inclination to marry say, a Japanese girl, why I simply do not think about it at all. But suppose I had and there were social restrictions against it, as on the Pacific Coast, and there were those who would use my inclination to hurt me in society, business, etc., then, of course, I would very likely deny it. And I

[6] Freyre, G. Sobrados e Mucambos, pp. 338-40. 1936.

[7] See illustrative story from real life, Sex and Race, Vol. 2, pp. 320-322. 1942.

would speak up forcefully, hoping by strenuousness to drive home the "truth," as Peter so vehemently denied any relationship with Christ.

Dr. Andre Tridon tells of a white woman patient of his who was so hysterical in her hatred of Negroes that she wanted to have them lynched. But this, he discovered, was only her way of trying to overcome her desire for them. At nights she would dream of Negro men and one day when the Negro janitor came into her apartment she said she had to take a firm grip on herself to keep from making advances to him. Dr. Tridon wonders how many Negro-obsessed white women like this have caused lynchings.[8]

Wulf Sachs, a white man, who saw deeply into the psychology of the more primitive South African natives, gives an even more striking instance of this Negro complex in a white woman—an instance which, if it happened in a civilized land as France would be viewed as far more comic than tragic.

The white woman in question was an elderly South African spinster, quite unattractive, whose "phobia" was that some day a Negro would rape her. She continually complained of this to the manager of the hotel in which she lived. Well, one day her longed for opportunity came. It appears that she was going to the bathroom wearing only a Kimona. A Negro was coming behind her when the kimona "accidentally" slipped off her body leaving her quite nude. The Negro picked up the kimona, handed it to her, and went on his way. But soon the hotel was resounding to her cries of attempted rape. The Negro, she asserted, had been following her for that purpose.

Now, this Negro, as psycho-analyzed by Wulf Sachs, had as much aversion for sexual contact with a white woman as a born lesbian has for a man. In fact, he was so masculine that even after he cohabited with black women, he felt that a void had come into his life. Thus, when the spinster accused him of rape, he took it nonchalantly and declared that she should be allowed to enjoy her moment of publicity. Why, said he, she is a hen that was "past laying." Not only was she old but she was white, he said.

However, his fellow-blacks were not so calm about it. The spinster's charge was equivalent to a long term at hard labor for him, and they advised him to flee. "Yes," said one of the blacks, "she may be a hen that's past laying, but that's the kind that cackles the loudest."[9]

The white men and women least likely to mate with Negroes are not the vehement objectors but the indifferent and neutral ones. The psychology of the white woman who violently rejects the mere suggestion of a union with

[8] Psychonanalysis and Love, p. 79. 1922.
[9] Black Hamlet: The mind of an African native revealed by psychoanalysis, pp. 71-76. 1937.

Negroes, and that of most woman-haters, white or black, is identical. The latter, even with their strong sex antagonism, find themselves attracted to certain women, or to one woman, in spite of themselves and so by screaming against all women, they try to delude themselves. Schopenhauer, Strindberg, Nietzsche, Tolstoi, and the early Fathers of the Church, are examples. In thundering against women they were really thundering against their own desires.

The white woman who violently rejects Negroes might dislike them as a group, chiefly because of their low social and economic standing, but from time to time she meets certain Negroes·who appeal powerfully to her, which makes her angry both with herself and the Negro. However prejudiced a white person may be, he or she is likely to meet some time at least one attractive Negro. In Europe, a woman of this type would indulge, if possible but in America she must bow to custom, and in attempting to kill her desires she utters violent protest and denunciation. It is the old story of the fox and the grapes.

The interest of the white people in the race question generally takes a sexual turn. Almost invariably in their discussions of race the question of intermarriage comes up. Negroes, on the other hand, are almost always more interested in the ethical and the economic sides. They think of better jobs, better homes, more money, and greater freedom to enter public places. They will generally deny that they wish "social equality," a Southern idiom meaning association with white people, and most of such were never more sincere.

A great deal of the hate for Negroes really is a reflex of the desire for sexual contact with them. As William Archer, an English writer, says, "Much of the injustice and cruelty to which the Negro is subjected in the South is a revenge not so much for sexual crime on the Negro's part as for an uneasy conscience or consciousness on the part of the whites. It is because the black race inevitably appeals to one order of low instincts in the white that it suffers from the sympathetic stimulation of another order of low instincts."[10]

Dr. Carl Jung, noted Swiss psychologist, is of the same opinion. The Negro, he says, "fascinates the inferior layer of our (the white) psyche." "Since," he says, "the Negro lives in your cities and even within your homes. he also lives within your skin, subconsciously."[11]

Virey tells how mistresses in America who used to cohabit with their

[10] Through Afro-America, p. 216. 1910.
[11] Your Negroid and Indian Behavior. Forum Magazine, April, 1930.

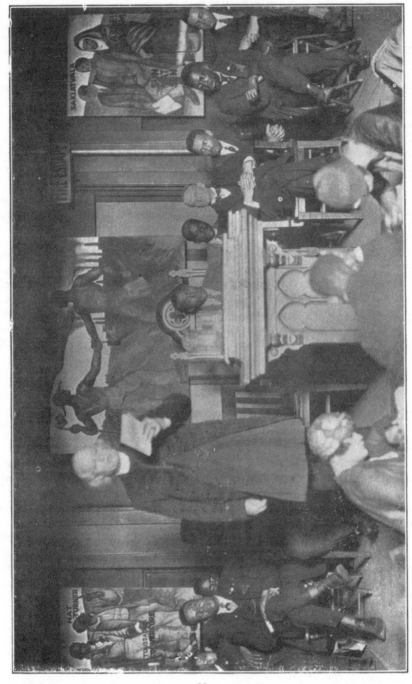

XV. Bishop William Montgomery Brown of Arkansas denouncing race prejudice at a Negro Labor Congress (Chicago Defender Photo).

Negro slaves and then have then whipped. The first was to satisfy their pleasure; the second their pride.

D. G. Croly was quoted on the attraction of the white mistresses by their slaves. It is possible to prove by a simple deduction that Croly was right. These women were the descendants of men with a strong desire for Negroes, and it is a well-known fact that a child often inherits the tastes and tendencies of its parents.

Some Negro women have always thought it an honor to bear light-colored children, hence the latter are in evidence; most white women think otherwise and have borne few mulattoes. The comparative fewness of mulatto children by white women is not due to lack of association with Negroes, just as the fewness of mulatto children by colored women in large Northern cities is not due to lack of association with white men.

In the Northern states a large number of Negroes have had some association with white women, prostitutes or otherwise. And this illicit intercourse goes on a good deal in the South, except that there greater secrecy is necessary. The writer has visited many towns in America with Negro inhabitants and cannot recall any in which some form of miscegenation was not practiced. As in the days of slavery when nude little black boys played with the children of their masters, and in the sex play that goes on among children of all "races" and classes of mankind initiated their young mistresses in the so-called mysteries of sex, so it is in the South today.

The number of white women who elope from the South with colored men is on the increase. In short, the whites have had no more success in maintaining a closed caste than royal families, aristocrats, Brahmins, or any other group in history.

Perhaps the greater number of white women experience no inherent attraction toward Negroes, and would in all probability shun contact with them. But propinquity and personality are powerful enemies of social barriers and prejudices; hence the segregation law, which it must be pointed out, operates chiefly in keeping the middle-class of Negroes and whites apart. Sex attraction is no respecter of color, creed, or biological value as it exists in the brain of some "scientific" writers. Juvenal, Martial, Tacitus, and the early Fathers of Church tell of the infatuation of the patrician Roman women for slaves and gladiators, and human nature has remained the same. Siki, and Jack Johnson, modern gladiators, were lionized by this same type of woman.

So far as friendliness toward Negroes is concerned white women may be divided into three classes: those who are sexually attracted (it is possible for some of these to have a strong feeling against Negroes as a group;)

those with a sublimated interest, as those who go to the South to teach Negro children and are students of Negro folk-lore, songs, etc.; and those who believe that all human beings belong first of all to humanity. It is quite possible that the last type may feel no attraction for Negroes as Negroes. But it must not be forgotten that there is likely to be a sex motive for everything a woman does. As a keen female thinker once said to me:

"Desire for more sex was the real motive behind the demand for woman suffrage. When women do not get enough sex they just mould in resentment; when they do they sing about the house."

Persons, however opposed to any one thing, can never tell what will be their final view regarding it. Prejudice is often enthusiasm barking up the wrong tree. Given a new set of ideas—a new light as it were—and there may be a violent change of opinion. Saul of Tarsus in a classic example.

Another was Dr. William Montgomery Brown, Bishop of Arkansas. Bishop Brown in his "Crucial Race Question," strongly defended color prejudice calling it "God-ordained." Then he was converted to Communism, and in another book, "Communism and Christianism" as well as in his other writings and at his trial, strongly denounced it as a capitalistic device. Communists, too, have sometimes become the strongest anti-Communists.

A great deal of American color prejudice, too, is mere deceit. As the Prussian soldiers of ex-Kaiser Wilhelm II would stiffen themselves at the sight of an officer and from a smiling human being become an automation so do many white associates of Negroes when in public.

In private life most of the blatant Negrophobes show no prejudice, and are usually well-liked by the Negroes who know them well. Sometimes such go out of the way to aid Negroes, as Cole Blease. The latter, when governor of South Carolina turned out Negro convicts by the thousands saying that they had been put in there unjustly. One of the most violent attackers of the Negro in Congress and on the political stump of his own state had a Negro family. The Negro housekeeper was the real boss of his mansion, and the white wife almost a nonentity.

Of course, no right-thinking person will admire individuals of this type. They are that detestable combination of opportunist and hypocrite. Personally, I prefer the outright Negrophobe. He is at least sincere. The other is a snake.

Chapter Ten

DO NEGRO MEN GREATLY PREFER WHITE WOMEN TO NEGRO ONES?

"THE men of any race," according to Ward's third law, " greatly prefer the women of a race they regard as higher than their own."

As was seen the primitive Africans, while having great respect for the white man's power, generally shun a union with white women.[1] Do the descendants of Africans, who have come into long contact with white people and are even biologically mixed with them, do the same?

Once in a Chicago restaurant I overheard a Negro veteran of the Spanish-American war complaining to a colored waitress that no colored Red Cross nurses were being taken to France to care for the colored soldiers. The waitress listened to his story with an ominous calm until unable to stand any longer what she considered a deception said, with a flash of scorn, "Now don't tell me that. If you would rather have a colored woman to wait on you than a white one, believe me you're an exception." His companion, also a veteran, took up the cudgels on his behalf: "I'll tell you why," was his retort. "When we were in the hospital, the white woman would come around with an apple or an orange, while the colored woman would come around with blood in her eye thinking somebody was trying to take away her man."

On another occasion a well-known Negro writer said to me: "We do

---

[1] See Sex and Race, Vol. 2, 402-04. 1942. I may add here that my own impression of such of the different peoples I met in Africa is that they were not eager to marry even those not of their own tribe. These peoples had no more love for their neighbors than any European nation has for its neighbor. Each believed that its own people were the bravest and best of the blacks, and their own women the most generally desirable. I noticed, too, that the blacks in the villages of the interior had the same opinion of the blacks who lived in the towns, and especially the mulattoes, as the whites of a village in America's Bible belt have for a New Yorker, that they believed they were degenerates headed straight for perdition. The only thing that tied the blacks together and that went too even for the native whites of North Africa was their common dislike for the European, who, during the centuries has, on the whole, made a very bad name for himself in Africa. I have heard blacks in Africa say repeatedly that while they wanted the white man's inventions and manufactures they wanted none of his color or his philosophy, that is, they wanted to remain black. Blacks are quite as chauvinistic as whites. I would even say more so because their lives have been more circumscribed. The European in Europe is decidedly more broadminded about color than the African Negro.

not extend our quarrel with the white race to the women: we leave that to our women." The fact is, that the men of opposing group are not, as a rule, hostile to the women of the other. If so, there would perhaps never be any hope for reconciliation among hostile peoples on this earth.

Oppenheimer, in his study of the development of the State shows the important part that "the exchange of women" has always played in "the peaceable integration of tribes."[2] Among primitive peoples the chief would often offer his favorite wife to the guest for the night as proof of his friendship.

The hostility is strongest between the same sexes of the opposing groups. In attacks on tribes or nations in older days, the younger women were usually spared. Sexual attraction plays its part it is true. But it must be noted that in the case of warfare between Europeans and primitive Africans, the African women probably because of their little sexual desire for European men, were even more vindictive and cruel in their treatment of the white captives than the African men. This was especially true of the older women. Correspondingly those European and white American women who liked colored men generally dislike colored women.

The men of the undeveloped races, as a rule, have no aspiration for the women of developed races. In their simple ways they much prefer their own women.

This is equally true when there is no sharp economic exploitation, or race persecution. In the West Indies the blacks seem to have little or no desire to produce children lighter in color than themselves. I have heard several times West Indians in New York being blamed because they persisted in having black children.

In the West Indies as in Europe freedom from having to earn a living is considered the hall-mark of gentility. Ambitious black and colored men there may rise out of their environment to association with whites and near-whites, while there are no laws, or iron-clad convention against their marrying a white woman. The well-defined class differences which prevail in the region South of the Rio Grande, and which tend to place one in his fitter sphere are the strongest factor in the preservation of color harmony there. When a rising generation is not taught to regard any color as inferior it accepts that color as normally as other animals accept differences of color in their own kind. I saw, as I said, little or no color prejudice among Europeans in Europe.

The color question south of the Rio Grande is not acute except in those

2 The State, pp. 132-36. 1922.

parts of Cuba, the Canal Zone, and Central America where American influence is strong. In the British West Indies color topics in conversation are as
infrequent as in the United States they are frequent.

In the mountain regions of Manchester, Jamaica, there are a number of
"pure" whites who were of no higher status than the blacks. There was little
or no attempt on the part of the black men to associate with these white
women although they came into daily contact with them. In fact, most of the
black peasants showed a contempt for these humble whites, calling them
"white labor" in contrast to the "Buckra," or upper-whites. The American
equivalent of this is the Negro term "po' white trash."

The Barbadian black exhibits an amused contempt for the poor whites,
who are in the main, descendants of white slaves and overseers.

But what has been said of the African and West Indian Negro as
regards white women is not altogether true of the American Negro and the
West Indian living in the United States. There may be three causes of this:
First, the large number of whites of no higher social status or intrinsic worth
than an equally large, or much larger number of Negroes; second, the United
States is professedly a democracy where all are said to be equal; and third, the
anti-marriage laws and other race restrictions.

In the first cause it will be noted that there is an actual equality between black and white, which the second confirms, but which the third
denies.

Furthermore, it is human nature to believe that what is out of one's reach
is more desirable than what is. In the Hebrew myth of the Creation, Eve was
incited to desire the apple because Jehovah had aroused her curiosity by prohibition. Life is a perpetual striving after the desirable. Since much is done to
place white women out of the reach of Negroes and since whiteness is, at the
same time, associated with better advantages, many ambitious Negroes seek
white wives or sweethearts, often placing upon the mere color of these women,
a value out of all proportion to the worth of the latter.

When such Negroes marry white women or as near to white as possible
they are thus merely striving, ofttimes quite unconsciously, to attain that color
which the dominant group decrees they must have in order to enjoy the rights
of ordinary human beings. Face-bleaching and hair-straightening are still
more palpable evidences of this.

Some Negroes in default of white women pick the lightest colored ones
they can find. A certain Negro rich and quite black, who visited Europe with
such a wife, caused many white Americans to gnash their teeth in rage at the
idea of a "nigger with a white woman." To make matters worse he stopped

XVI. Three mulattoes of Soviet Georgia. Note the Turkish-Armenian cast of features. (See Appendix of this volume). Sov-foto.

at hotels patronized by them, and quite enjoyed their rage. In fact, he wanted them to believe that she was white.

These white "colored" wives serve a double purpose. When it is known that they are "colored" the feelings of both Negroes and hostile whites are soothed; and at the same time it gives the Negroes a chance to strut with "a white woman."

Mere curiosity is also a powerful factor and prompts many colored men to seek white women. On the occasion of Negro excursions to the North from the South, white prostitutes reap a rich harvest. Similarly white men who go South from states like Nebraska and Minnesota where colored women are scarce look forward to meeting them, and will ask Pullman porters to introduce them. During Mardi Gras and fraternity conventions in the South colored prostitutes do a thriving trade with Northern white men.

A still more powerful factor is revenge. Many Negroes seek white women, and sometimes treat them very badly hoping to get even with white men. A great deal could be said on this subject. It is this feeling also that inspires many assaults on white women.

On the other hand some American Negroes seem to manifest a total lack of desire for white women, a fact especially true of the Garveyites and those Negro groups who call themselves "Ethiopians" and "Africans." I recall the case of one Southern Negro who attended the American Legion convention in Paris in 1927. Taken by his comrades to a *maison de joie* he shrank back as he saw all the women were white but was finally induced to take one. He walked off with her looking as if he was going to his execution and returned with her a few minutes later untouched, saying that he was too much unused to her racially to have any desire for her. He wanted to know where he could find some women of his own color.

In a large city on the North Pacific Coast I once went to a Manasseh ball, that is a dance where all the women were white, and the men colored. The girls, most of whom were waitresses and shop-girls, were fairly attractive. Three or four of the men stood around listlessly, whereupon the madame, a full-blooded Negro woman, asked one of them why he wasn't dancing. "Give me my own color," he replied. "God bless you, honey," was her heartfelt response.

As to the great masses of Negroes in the rural districts of the South, most of all of those who come in little contact with whites, it is safe to say, they do not generally wish association with white women. Like the African black they seem to retain their primitive traits in this respect. It is different with the average Northern Negro who is often eager for such adventures.

XVII. Left: Native Negro woman of Georgia (Soviet Caucasus). The others are white (Sov-Foto).

I have heard West Indian blacks in England indignantly scorn the idea that they would marry a white woman, asserting that they went around with them only because there were no black women. The Africans were, on the whole, even more emphatic, especially the Moslems.

This lack of desire on the part of some colored Americans may be due to the timidity that is ingrained in them by the attitude of white men. Many Negroes are positively afraid when approached by a white woman. As to being seen in public with one they simply would not do it.

A friend of mine who was approached by a white woman in San Antonio, Texas, said that her doing so caused the cold sweat to come out all over his body. In the Northern States this fear manifests itself in the dread of losing their jobs, or of being ostracised by others of their own group when it is known that they have a white wife, and to a certain extent, a white sweetheart. In this matter Negroes are not as bold as white persons. White women sometimes have no hesitancy even in making their wishes known, a fact sometimes disturbing to Negro bell-boys in Southern hotels.

The reason why the primitive African has no desire for white women while the American Negro has to a considerable extent is because the latter finds himself a member of a white society with the same economic urges and training as white Americans. At the same time the white woman is set up as grand prize by the ruling class, which indeed she is, if exploitation on the ground of whiteness, is to survive.

In the hope of making the Negro distasteful to the white women the ruling class uses such methods as lynching, propaganda by press and by religious, political and scientific leaders; and talk about venereal disease, crime, and rape.

Some white men generally do all in their power to frighten away the white woman from Negroes. What tales were not told to French women about the American Negro soldiers in the last war One effective remedy is left untried however: white men leaving colored women alone.

I recall in reading a book in which a white woman relates her amours with a Negro. She confessed that her desire for black men had been first aroused by what she knew of the affairs of white men and Negro women.

The truth is that much of the propaganda against the Negro helps to excite the curiosity of white women, who, otherwise might have not have thought much on the matter.

I am convinced that but for the advertisement given to Negroes by racial segregation in America there would be less zest in interracial mating for both whites and blacks. I recall the case of one American Negro who went into a European brothel noted for its young and very pretty girls. Of these there were some twenty, clad only in their shoes. All this Negro had to do was beckon to one of them and she would have come. But instead of being pleased he was disappointed. "Ah, no," he said, "this is too easy. Give me the states where white women and sex are bootlegged."

MacCrone very rightly says, "The attempt to prohibit such intercourse so far from discouraging it, or protecting the individual against himself, might, for some individuals merely serve to increase the temptation on the principle that forbidden fruits are sweetest."

Criswell, in a study of children in two New York schools, found that both the white and colored children when they reached a certain age, tended to prefer the girls and boys in their own racial group, regardless of what their preferences might have been in the earlier years. He says, "Race and color preference are present in inter-sexual choice even in the primary grades. Colored boys prefer white girls in the first two grades then shift to light (colored) girls. Colored girls prefer light (colored) boys until grade four then medium (colored) boys. White boys and girls prefer their own race but choose Negroes as late as grade six or seven. By grade eight interracial choice has almost completely disappeared."[3]

Most Negroes in America approach a white woman with hesitancy and if she makes no advance she will in the majority of cases be left alone. Black men, too, have had to fly from the attentions of white women, instances of which I have given in the two preceding volumes.

The inference from the foregoing seems to be this: *The black man desires the white woman not for what she is, but rather for what she represents, that is, better social and economic opportunity, while the white man desires the black woman not for what she represents but for what she is.* The urge of the former is sociologic; of the latter biologic. The black as a rule, seeks gain or prestige; the white sensual, or sensuous, love, which, perhaps, would be a less selfish motive of the whites did not generally insist on concubinage as the refusal to marry has as its motive the maintaining of social prestige, which is largely economic. True love risks all.

Since the Negro male is already in possession of those qualities in the Negro female which are apparently deemed so desirable by some white men he would hardly be likely to seek them in the white woman otherwise. One may safely say that but for the glamour arising from "the color line" the American, like the African, Negro, would wish little contact with white

[3] A Sociometric Study of Race Cleavage in the Classroom. (Archives of Psychology, No. 235. Jan., 1939).

women. As Sir Harry Johnston very rightly says, "The mass of the race, if left free to choose, would prefer to mate with women of its own."

An important concluding detail: It was pointed out that the whites took the first step in mixing, even to bringing the Negroes from their native land, and still lead in the initiative. The investigation of Ward's four laws was conducted without any special awareness of this, yet the facts as presented, pro and con, have substantiated this.

The Negro male, however, is rapidly learning the lesson set him by the white man. If segregation and color prejudice continue we may expect an increasing number of affairs between Negroes and white women.

Chapter Eleven

WHICH ATTRACTS THE OTHER MORE STRONGLY, WHITE OR BLACK?

"Miscegenation is not a peculiarity of modern times. It has occurred all through human history and we may well believe that it took place between Mousterian man and Homo sapiens in the days of the mammoth and the cave bear."

George L. Collie, "The Aurignacians and Their Culture," p. 30.

Iwan Bloch, noted sexologist, thinks that the desire of the blacks to mate with the whites is much greater than that of the whites to mate with the blacks. So, too, does William Archer. In fact, this is a general belief. Bloch says, "But much greater is the alluring force exercised by the white upon the black; more especially among the civilized Negroes does the white woman play the part of a fetish. This is the explanation of the frequent rape or attempted rape of white girls on the part of Negroes—one of the principal causes of the Southern lynchings."[1]

The question prompted by this statement is: Has the primitive aversion of the black for mating with the white been entirely bred out by centuries of white environment? Do such Negroes who seek white women prefer them in their hearts to their own women?

To what I said in the last chapter I may add this: Individuals reveal their true natures and desires in many small ways, and especially in informal conversation. I have listened to many conversations by white men on sleeping cars, in clubs, hotels, and other places and have noted that sex is an abundant topic. Similarly, I have listened to conversation by Negroes, and they speak most often of "brown-skinned," "golden-brown," "seal-skin-brown," "tantalizin' brown," "high-yellow," and the like. Not many of their conversations centre on white women.

Might not the inference be that the majority of Negroes really put their own women first? This seems natural as the desire for white has been acquired, second, there is the coolness caused by prejudice; and third the uncertainty, and even the risk, of meeting white women. Comparative lack of talk about white women is not due to reticence as Negroes are inclined to boast of their amours with white women even as white men of theirs with colored women.

---

[1] Sexual Life Of Our Times, p. 614.

Again the term, Negro, in America wrongly includes all mixed-bloods, some of whom are more white than black. If there is any truth in the doctrine of heredity might not the desire of some Negroes for white mates be explained on the ground of natural inheritance, the call of the "white" blood, if you will?

A desire for the society of white women by most other Negroes would be acquired, and its strength, as was said, would depend entirely upon the degree of restriction in the environment. Bloch's statement may be true in two cases, namely, that of certain educated and ambitious Negroes; and of the rapist.

Let us look into these:

The life-long training of many Negroes fit them only for white environment. In Africa they are out of place, and the natives very rightly call them by a term meaning "white man." That is they acted like white persons.

Many Negroes have been reared on tales about snow-white skins, raven tresses, beautiful golden locks; their fairy heroes are white and so are their social "superiors," their God, Christ and movie heroes.

On the other hand the evils they are taught to shun are described as black. Caught young and filled with this like a mother-bird cramming food down the gullet of her young what wonder, therefore, that they think "white?" What else could they think? Idolize black at the expense of white and the effect would be exactly the same. In Ethiopia, the lower classes call the white man "natch," equivalent of the white term of contempt, "nigger." Thus, there are many American Negroes, quite black, with a strong white complex. To them other Negroes do not exist so far as mating is concerned. This is true even as regards members of their "race" who are indistinguishable from white. It is clear, therefore, that such individuals are interested in a white skin, not biologically, but socially, that is, what it stands for in prestige. Thus with social motives so strongly mixed in, it is impossible to tell just how strong would be what Ward calls "the biological imperative."

With the Negro away from Africa for three centuries and so impermeated not only with "white" blood but with the "white" outlook and education it is the height of nonsense to talk of a "Negro" psychology. The white mountaineer of the South has mannerisms and speech that set him off from the city whites of the South, does that make of him a separate white race? Also, the rural Negro of the South, talks and acts differently from the city Negro, especially of the North, does that make of him a different Negro race? We insist that the mannerisms of the white mountaineer are no more distinctive than those of the Southern rural Negro.

XVIII. "An Unpleasant Discovery" by Hogarth. See Notes on the Illustrations No. 53, Sex and Race, Appendix, Vol. I.
(Coll. Richard B. Moore)

The Negro of each West India island has a certain different psychology. It is like that of the nation which colonized it. The French Negro is essentially French; the Spanish Negro, Spanish, and so on. As for the American Negro and the African there is "a hopeless gap" between them psychologically, to use a phrase of Dr. Carl Jung's. Indeed, even so far as facial resemblance is concerned, one has little difficulty in discerning most West Indian Negroes from American Negroes, especially new arrivals. In Europe I could pick nine times out of ten an American Negro from an African, West Indian, or Egyptian.

Europeans who make a living by catering to tourists easily spot American Negroes and accost them in English, even though they are entirely clad in European clothes.

Peoples who live together, and think together grow to have a certain resemblance in spite of so-called race. And in the matter of psychology, one can safely say that the Afro-American is more American than the Euro-American. Since 1810, the percentage of black aliens entering the United States has been very small while that of white aliens has been very large. Moreover, most of the Negroes lived in the south where the whites were more native to America than those of the North. The 1900 census showed only 20,336 foreign-born Negroes in the United States; that of 1930 only, 98, 620, a figure which in 1940 fell to 83,941. In 1940 there were 11,419,138 foreign-born whites, or nearly 17 per cent of the total white population. Another large percentage was that of whites born of foreign parents. The groups most native to America are the Negroes, the white mountaineers, and certain communities in New England.

What nonsense, therefore, to talk of a "Negro" psychology. There are of course, certain Negro mannerisms but the uneducated Negro differs from the educated white only in the respect that, being the less privileged he has generally an inferiority complex, while the white being the stronger, generally has a superiority complex. What really exists, as I have said before, is an American people shading from white to black with all its intermediate tints.

Being then so thoroughly American, and so strongly imbued with the national sentiments that wonder is there that the environment makes some Negroes prefer white to black?

Again there is the Negro who is attracted to white women because of some intellectual or psychic affinity, just as a white man would be to them. It happens, moreover, that the cultural level of the Negro women is below that of the Negro men. For instance, of the 100 Negroes listed in "Who's

Who in America" in 1934-5, only two were women, or one in 50; while there were 1953 white women to 31,081 white men, or about 1 in 17.

Some white women use Negroes as a sort of experience school. They flirt with them chiefly to test out or cultivate their powers of attraction, preparatory to tackling bigger game, and the men sometimes mistake this as well as other courtesies for an invitation. This, however, holds true of men in general, who not infrequently mistake a woman's interest for something else.

Not a few white women believe that any colored man would be glad to get them. But they are mistaken. Once on a sleeping-car I overheard a white woman telling some passengers that while she would marry a Chinese, a Japanese or an Indian, she would not a Negro. She was past the marrying age, however, and as I observed her rather crabbed and discouraged appearance I could not help thinking that she would have been lucky to get any sort of man.

Within the past fifteen years or so I notice that the type of whites and Negroes who are associating is very much higher than it was in the 1900's. At interracial dances, say at the Savoy in New York, held by the National Association for the Advancement of Colored People, as well as at other gatherings, are to be seen whites and Negroes of the finest social calibre. At dances and dinners given by certain unions, whites and Negroes also meet in apparent equality.

Negroes are thought to be more eager for interracial sex affairs because the custom is to place the principal blame for such mating on them. If there is an intimacy between a white man and a colored woman, then the woman is blamed. Take the case of Jack Johnson. The impression the newspapers gave was that Johnson was running after white women, while the truth was, as I personally know, that he had to do far more running from them than toward them. White women of all grades of society used to pester him, as the fair Parisiennes used to pursue Siki, Senegalese boxer.

The American whites usually blame the Negroes for race-mixing in much the same way that men, regardless of "race" usually blame women for love affairs, in which more often than not the men had taken the initiative. Adam blamed Eve; Nordics blame Negroes. One Southerner, in blaming the blacks, said "Tell the Blacks to not mingle or marry the whites, which makes the Higher Whites so angry."[2] But are not the whites strongly intrenched behind their color-line? If they stayed there would the Negroes be able to reach them?

The tendency is to regard as depravity all liasons or friendships be-

2 Crisis Maga. March, 1923.

tween white women and anyone not belonging to the white caste. And markedly is this so in the case of the black man. White men who have colored concubines, and consider it quite the regular thing boil with anger at the sight of a black man and a white woman together. The woman of the "inferior" race, they think, has no morals to lose while their so-called own must be guarded sacredly. This is the view of most English and Americans, and particularly South African whites and near-whites. But I fail to find any justification for the charge of depravity, after coming into intimate contact with mixed couples in England, France, Canada, the West Indies, the United States and elsewhere. I have found their home life not a bit different from that of white and white, or black and black, or Japanese and Japanese, African and African. There were even the usual marital squabbles.

Where and Why Negroes Attack White Women

In this matter of the attacks on white women by black men there are two important factors: First, as was seen, the native African not only shunned association with white women, but according to Sir Harry Johnston returned them unharmed when captured; and second, that this kind of rape, is almost solely a product of the United States. In the British West Indies, Hayti, San Domingo and Africa, where black outnumbers white: in Panama, in Cuba, Puerto Rico, Brazil and other Latin-American countries where colored and white are equal or nearly equal in numbers attacks on white women by black men are practically unknown. This fact is even more strikingly true of Egypt, Tunis and Morocco where whites and blacks have been living together for thousands of years.

Lord Olivier says, "In the British West Indies assaults by black or colored men on white women are practically altogether unknown. No apprehension of them whatever troubles society. I say this as an administrator familiar with the judicial statistics. . . . Whatever may be the cause it is the indisputable fact that Jamaica or any other West India island is as safe for white women to go about in, if not safer, than any other European country with which I am acquainted. . . . If then, there is a special ground for fearing assaults of this character by colored on white in America, is clearly cannot be due to any necessary or special propensity of race."[3]

Sir Harry Johnson, in quoting this passage says: "The statement may be applied with equal truth to all parts of Negro Africa." He adds: "I was informed by every resident or official whom I questioned that cases of Negro assaults on white women were practically unknown in Cuba. . . .

3 White Capital and Colored Labour, p. 49. 1906.

"It is scarcely too sweeping an assertion to say that there has been no case in Jamaica or other British West Indies, of rape or indecent assault or annoyance (to a white women) since the Emancipation."[4]

Huntington Adams, commenting on articles by Robert Herrick says, "What reliable evidence is there that assault upon white women by Negroes has ever occurred or been at all attempted on a scale sufficient so that it might be considered as a likely danger? Certainly the say-so of those who have been implicated in group-murders called lynchings, a say-so which is not given under oath, and not subject to the analysis of cross examination by legal counsel is not sufficiently convincing.

"Can it be that the "usual crime" does not exist and has not existed?"

The same writer adds that in a discussion with Hon. E. St. John Branch who has been attorney-general for Jamaica and other islands, the latter said that during his seventeen years of office, he could remember no case of assault or attempted assault of a white woman or girl by a Negro had occurred in the courts.[5]

Paul Morand, writing from the West Indies says," I was struck to see how indifferent the blacks were to white women. At no time did they ever appear to me as the satyrs and gorillas the American newspapers make the Negro out to be."[6]

It is important to remember that in the countries mentioned rape among the blacks themselves, goes on just as rape among the whites. Inter-racial rape seems undoubtedly to be confined to the United States.

John Temple Graves paints this picture of the mental attitude of the white South: "The terror of the twilight deepens with the darkness, and in the rural regions every farmer leaves his home with apprehension in the morning and thanks God when he comes from the fields at evening to find all well with the woman of his home." If this typifies the Southern state of mind why have not white people living among Negroes in other parts of the world a similar fear? Why, also, were the white women safe during the Civil War? "Rape," says Calhoun, "was practically unknown in war days when Negroes were left as guardians of white women and children."[7]

There are two chief causes of rape of this kind: first, the action of segregation (already dealt with) and its effect on Negroes of defective mentality; second, merely incidental as when a feeble-minded Negro comes into close contact with a white woman, in which case the result would have been the same were she colored. This second might also be true of normal men, black or white, under stress or rare circumstances, as in war.

[4] Negro In The New World, p. 279. 1910.
[5] Nation (N. Y.), July 23, 1924.
[6] Hiver Caraibe, p. 113. 1929.
[7] Social History of the American Family, Vol. 2, p. 307. 1917.

Defective mentality is the chief cause of rape. The impulse of most healthy men is to capture the woman, to seize her bodily; it is also that of the woman to be so taken. But civilization restrains the crudity of this primitive instinct and wooing is restorted to. The rapist, like the shouting, shrieking religious enthusiast, is merely a helpless instrument in the grip of a blind impulse. Lynching, therefore, does not help as rational human beings do not commit rape.

In the list of mental defectives must be included, at least the man who attempts rape under the influence of drugs or drink.

Another very important consideration: "Black rape" is exaggerated. White women are often frightened in advance by hearing of Negro rapists so extensively advertised by the yellow press.

Ray Stannard Baker has cited several instances of this sort in his "Following the Color Line." There is no doubt whatever that many innocent Negroes have been lynched on this account. Some hysterical white woman meets a Negro in a lonely spot. She screams. The mob gathers. The Negro, or a Negro, is caught and to confirm her story she "identifies" him. Hot irons are applied to the black man's body, and to gain temporary relief he "confesses."

Once in the New York Public Library an incident happened that had I been in the South, might have cost me my life. I had just stepped off the elevator on the first floor, and was going toward the Fifth Avenue side. As I turned a corner, I came abruptly face to face with a white woman, who screamed as loudly as if she had been struck. Yet I was a foot away from her, and neither of us had expected to see the other.

Another important fact; Suppressed sexuality sometimes causes hysterical women to imagine that they are being pursued by men. Spinsters in delirium generally rave that men are watching or pursuing them. The wish projects itself, as it were, into reality. This would be particularly true in the case of a white woman with a Negro complex, that is, an ungratified desire for intimacy wth Negroes.

Again some attacks have been invited. White women, surprised with Negro lovers, have shouted rape, which, it will be admitted, is easily possible. Had Joseph surrendered to the wiles of Potiphar's wife and been caught she could easily have made a case against him: as it was she did get him into prison on a charge of attempted rape.

A well to-do-colored woman, who for the greater part of her life, had passed for white" tells me the following story: A white woman, a great friend of hers, had a secret that had been troubling her for years. This secret

XIX. White wife of Ingida, Ethiopian painter, by himself (See Sex and Race, Vol. I, Chap. 14).

was that while living in Lexington, Kentucky, there was a Negro stableman, named Joe, who used to come to her home while her husband, a travelling salesman, was away. Joe would creep through the bushes around the house and climb in through a bedroom window. One night while she and Joe were in bed, her husband returned unexpectedly at which Joe leaped through the window and ran off through the bushes. Her husband had heard the noise, however, and had caught a glimpse of the Negro running away. To save herself, she had screamed, and claimed that rape had been attempted on her. Soon the mob was in pursuit.

The wife, however, was never able to learn just what had happened to the Negro. Some said he had been lynched; others that he had caught a train going North. For years, the wife continued to worry. Finally she confided in a colored woman who was "passing" and the latter advised her to put an ad in the Illinois Conservator, a Negro paper, whereupon to her great relief, she did get a reply from Joe who was in Chicago.

On matters of sex, women are not expected to tell the truth, hence cases of rape on grown women should be thoroughly investigated. I have heard some of these cases in New York police courts, some of which were white women who accused Negroes of attacking them, and in nearly every case it turned out that both had been lovers, and that the woman was trying to be revenged on the man. Herodotus, who apparently had an opportunity of studying the capture of women at first hand, said that if they do not wish to be carried off it is a very hard thing to do so. Rabelais tells of a man who was brought into court, accused of rape. The judge ordered the accused to give the woman a piece of money, then to follow her as she left the court and take it away. But she fought off the man so successfully that the judge called them both back and dismissed the case. It will at least be admitted that cases of rape should not be heard with the mob as judge and jury.

Dr. William J. Robinson says: "I repeat the injunction that I have given so many, many times. Be very, very careful before giving any credence to any accusation of rape. At least ninety of every hundred cases of accusations of assaults on females are false. In some instances the accusers are hysterical and believe their dreams and vicious unrealities.[8]

Humane persons will sympathize fully with those white women who are the bonafide victims of rape, by any kind of color of men; they will also be horrified to think of the innocent persons who have been burned alive on the wrong complaint of hysterical women.

[8] Medical Journal & Guide, Feb., 1922. Also Ovid's Amatoria, Lib. I.

To return to Bloch's assertion, it is likely that the difficulty experienced by timid Negroes in meeting white women magnifies the attraction for them but when one considers that the Negro has been taught to look up to the Caucasian while the latter has been trained to look down on Negroes, it can be truly said, that in view of how certain even very noted white men have sought out the black woman his statement even in the case of the transplanted African is open to doubt. Indeed one may paraphrase Ward's third law to read:

Certain men of the "superior" race while considering their women higher do indicate by their actions that they prefer women of the 'inferior' race."

These facts and others already given controvert those writers who maintain that the white man's seeking of the colored woman is mere "lust" and has no other significance. If "lust and not racial difference were the motive these men could find any number of white girls, and often with less trouble.

When it is remembered that a sexual union, is preponderantly the motive of love, and that a man's association with a woman when it has naught of love in it, is essentially the same as male companionship, it becomes evident that the racial lure is the thing and that were there no color barrier such men would marry black women in preference to white ones. One thing is sure; when a white man has a Negro sweetheart he really has greater love of the heart for her than his white wife, just as the morganatic wife of a prince is his real love.

Chapter Twelve

THE REAL PURPOSE BEHIND ANTI-MISCEGENATION LAWS

"Cunnus belli teterrima causa." Latin proverb.

B UT the real answer to Bloch's statement that the alluring force exercised by white upon black is greater than by black upon white may be found in a consideration of the real purpose of the laws against intermarriage.

Against whom are such laws chiefly designed, white or black?

The majority of both white and black will say that it is the black man for instance, the epidemic of bills that followed the Jack Johnson marriage. But since the whites have the superior economic and social position, and as such have the stronger option of refusal, against whom can such laws be directed but themselves. To prevent mixed unions all that would be necessary is to say, No. Laws against intermixing differ in spirit not a whit from those of Colonial days. Those, as was shown, were directed against the whites, the blacks then being slaves.

In reality, however, they are directed not against white men, not against black men, nor yet against Negro women but only against white women. The Maryland law makes this clear. It provides that any white woman who suffers herself to be got with child by a Negro or a mulatto is a criminal. Nothing is said against the Negro woman being got with child by a white man. The reason for this agitation against the white woman is that whiteness in America and South Africa is a system for the exploitation of the black and this system can be continued only by having the white woman breed white. If she breeds mulattoes that smashes up the system. So-called race purity is capitalistic.

On the other hand when the black woman breeds mulattoes she produces only more victims to be exploited.

In the South only white men and colored women enjoy sexual freedom. Such objections as there are to the mixing of white men and black women are only a pretense at being impartial. Some of the lawmakers of the South are themselves the worst violators of the anti-miscegenation law. Objections to the mixing of the black man and the white woman are real and deep, however.

As early as 1860, while the Negro was still a slave, the Democratic

XX. Upper left to right: Kamehameha the Great, and Kamehameha II, Kings of Hawaii. Lower, Tawhaio, Maori King, and Sir Mauri Pomare, K.B.E. (1876-1930), New Zealand state-man, also a native Maori.

party, fearing emancipation, had as its slogan, "Should you like to see your daughter marry a big, buck nigger." At that time, Negro women were being forced to have children by white men. Today, whenever there is an argument over the citizenship rights of the Negro, one of the first questions to be asked is usually, "Would you have your sister marry a nigger?"

Many Southern whites are afraid to have their daughters come North lest they meet a Negro at some social affair and fall in love with him. This is one of the reasons why certain Southern writers and newspapers rage against "social equality" in the North. According to the Winston-Salem (N. C.) Journal, the pastor of a white Baptist Church of that city said in a sermon:

> "With the present movement northward of the Negroes, and in the absence of a race prejudice that has protected the Southerners, there is the greatest possible danger of the mingling of the races, so that in the future it may come to pass that you will send your daughter to the North for culture, and she will come back *with a little Negro.*"

This reverend Southerner was running true to form. Harriett Martineau writing in 1837 says:

> "Yet the planters who sell their own offspring to fill their purses dare to raise the cry of 'amalgamation' against the abolitionists of the North, not one of whom has, as far as evidence can show, conceived the idea of mixture of the races. It is from the South where this mixture is hourly encouraged that the canting and groundless reproach has come."[1]

This attitude shows not only an absolute lack of faith in the white woman, but it points strongly to something else. Knowing only too well the attraction of the colored women on themselves, the white masters saw the collapse of their system of exploitation as based in skin color. There has been no talk of "your son's marrying a black woman," a relation far more likely to occur—illegally.

It is not too much to say that had the initiative in mixing been left to the blacks there would have been very few mixed progeny in America today.

Another thing I noticed in Europe was that the colored American men there were always anxious to meet visiting colored American women. The latter, in spite of the abundance and easy availability of white women, need never have been lonesome. One or two men I knew actually left the white women for the Negro ones. In Europe where social restrictions were not based entirely on color, some ambitious Negroes did precisely what some white Americans did: they sought association with titled women.

[1] Society in America, Vol. 2, p. 81. 1842.

XXI. Royal Family of Hawaii. Upper: King Kalakaua and Queen Liliuokalani. Below: Leleiohoku, brother of the king; King Lunalilo, and Mrs. Dominis, sister of the king, who married the American governor of Oahu, John Dominis.

American color prejudice, though fundamentally economic, has been so skillfully wrapped up in sex, the home life, and the perpetuation of "good Americanism" by the exploiters of labor that some of the bitterest opponents of capitalism, even with their loud declarations that it is economic, cannot throw it off. With all their protests, they hang on to it because it feeds their ego.

Ward's Fourth Law

From the facts so far brought forward it will hardly be necessary to discuss this. It reads: "The men of any race in default of women of a higher race will be content with women of a lower race." This means that Negro men are satisfied with Negro women only because they cannot get white ones.

Furthermore, not only would men of a so-called higher race be glad to get women of any race but the women of a so-called higher race in default of men of a so-called higher race would be glad to get men of any race. It is certainty that if there were no white men about, or an insufficient number of them, white women would be glad to find mates among men of any other race that was available.

In Europe, as in every other long settled land, there is a shortage of males, and men of any kind, are nearly aways welcome. In France, for instance, there was Landru, a worse than Bluebeard, a bald-headed, little and most unprepossessing man, who was able to captivate so many women. Again in certain lands, as Rapa in the South Seas, the men are treated as gods because they are so few in proportion to the women. The law of supply and demand operates with as much force in sex as it does in salt or any other need of humankind.

Another important factor as regards future race-mixing in America: The white woman is about to lose the glittering position she has held all along—glittering in comparison with that of the white woman in any European land. Less in number than the white man, due to the fact that more white men than white women had been coming in from Europe all along, she has, with the cutting down of immigration, now outnumbered him. In 1910 she was 6 percent less than the white man; in 1930, she was only 2.7 less and in 1940 only seven-tenths of 1 percent. And, according to the census report of 1942 the women exceeded the men by 644,196. This means there will be greater competition among the women for the men. Thus we may expect in about the next thirty years that the unmarried white woman, like her sister in Europe, will be more ready than ever to find a mate where she can.

As for the Negro women in America they have been outnumbering the Negro men for more than a century, to be exact since 1840. The 1940 census showed a surplus of 1,240,529 Negro women over Negro men in the South. With the white men, however, it was the other way about. They had a surplus of 308,576 over the white women.[2] This meant that a certain degree of race-mixing in the South was inevitable even had there been no predilection of certain white men to seek out Negro women, that is, the surplus of white men would have sought mates among the available women, in this case, the Negro ones.

[2] A part of this male surplus was due to the foreign-born white men who exceeded the foreign-born white women by 51,824.

Chapter Thirteen

WHICH IS MORE BEAUTIFUL, A WHITE SKIN OR A BLACK SKIN?

"Aristippus: Do you mean, then, that the same things can be both beautiful and ugly?
"Socrates: Of course I do, and good and bad, too. Everything is good and beautiful for whatever purpose it serves; but bad and ugly for what it does not."—Xenophon's Memorabilia.

HINTON ROWAN HELPER in his book "Nojoque," went into long and minute detail trying to prove that a white skin was more beautiful than a black one. He enumerated almost everything he could think of including the color of buildings, a white building being more lovely than a black one, he said. Thomas Jefferson spoke, too, of "the eternal monotony" of a black skin, while many American writers and Southern politicians go into ecstasies over whiteness. Of course, the English and the Americans would include the brunet whites, but Hitler and his scientists excluded them.[1] Heinrich Driesmans, German sociologist, held that one sure proof that members of the Catholic priesthood were of an inferior race was that they are all "dark-skinned" and that "a blond Catholic priest is an abnormality— a white crow."

This kind of reasoning cannot help but bring a wry smile from thinking people. It seems almost below one's intellectual dignity to discuss it at all but alas, it is still too alive and too widespread to be ignored. The teachings of slave days have created a very active color complex in the psychology of the majority of the inhabitants of North and South America.

Those who have read the romantic writers as Sir Walter Scott, Bulwer Lytton, Charlotte Bronte, Dorothy Dix and Laura Jean Libby will recall the admiration showered on flowing, flaxen tresses; creamy, snow-white skins; and azure eyes. There is no doubt that they were right provided we'll admit that an East Indian, or a Negro poet is equally right when he praises dark-skinned women.

The white group, due to the greater number of "races" that has con-

[1] Of course we have a tinge of this in the United States where one hears so much over the radio and elsewhere about making "a date with a blonde," never with a brunette.

112

LE RÊVE DE LA RACE BLANCHE

XXII.   French Satire on the Craze for a Dark Skin. (Translation: The Dream of the
White Race).   Le Journal, Paris. Aug. 21, 1932.

RETOURS

--- *Si nous avions pu revenir bronzées comme ça.*
-- *Demande lui donc à quelle plage il était,*

XXIII. French Satire on the Craze for a Dark Skin. (The scene is on a train returning from a bathang-beach. ...The girls are envying the Negro's color, thinking he got it at the beach. "If only we could have returned bronzed like that," they are saying). Le Journal, Paris.

tributed to its composition, is, without a doubt, less monotonous in appearance than an all-black audience would be. A white American audience, with its blonds and brunets, presents more chromatic variety than one composed of West African Negroes. But as regards these Negroes and an audience in Northern Scandinavia where nearly everyone is blond and flaxen-haired I think Jefferson, himself, would have to admit a certain "eternal monotony" there also.

If variety of color in a gathering is pleasing, as it is in a bouquet or a picture, then a gathering of Northern Negroes where one sees the whole gamut of coloring from black to blond would be more pleasing than a white gathering of only blonds and brunets.

This is, of course, highly argumentative. However, nature has so arranged matters that one human coloring that is pleasing to some is unattractive to others. The reason is that sexual selection, which is usually very active in the consciousness (but is at times too deep in the subconscious to be recognized as such) decides for us what color, or colors, are the most pleasing or the most repellent. I have found, in general, that the whites are much more likely to think a dark-colored skin beautiful than dark-skinned people, especially those who have had little contact with white people, are likely to think a white skin desirable.

Bishop Heber, on seeing some almost black boatmen in India, said: "Two observations struck me most forcibly: first that the deep bronze tint is more naturally agreeable to the human eye than the fair skins of Europe since we are not displeased with it even in the first instance, while it is a well-known fact that to them a fair complexion gives the idea of ill-health and that sort of deformity which in our eyes belong to an albino."[2]

Maurice Evans says of the South African Negro: "When thoroughly washed and duly anointed there is a peculiar richness about his color that makes the somewhat anemic color of town-bred Europeans sickly by comparison."[3]

Dudley Kidd says, "No one who has seen a white man bathing alongside a black man can for a moment help feeling that the natural color of the skin is dark and that the white man has a bleached skin which must therefore be covered up in sheer decency."[4]

Peter Nielsen, a white ethnologist, who lived many years among the blacks of South Africa, says similarly: "I have often heard white men who have kept native women say that they found the black or deep-brown colour

2 Narrative of a Journey, etc., Vol. I, p 43. 1829.
3 Black and White in South Africa, p. 27. 1911.
4 Savage Childhood, p 29. 1906.

of the Native woman far more beautiful than the dead-white skin of the white woman, and I have also heard white women of culture and refinement admit that the black or dark-brown torso and tints of the African man have seemed to them a more pleasing sight than the stark white limbs of the European male."[5] He adds that the white men call the women "Black Velvet," and that those whites who have not been taught to have color prejudice find a black skin "very pleasing" and "more pleasant to the touch" than a white one.

Fortie, another European who lived in Africa, says of his Negro wife, "Her smooth skin had the satin luster of a rifle barrel. Rather than black, it was of a deep warm bronze that attracted me ever after, that made the white skin of my race seem sickly and cold.

"There were no white women in town and my graceful Zahabu seemed peerless to me. One day I saw in a bazaar a sickly being in outlandish flounces and feathers: the wife of a British missionary. The flaxen hair; pale, blue eyes; thin, waxy face chilled me. I fled to my Galla bride, to the warm bronze of her firm, healthy body."[6]

Furthermore, white men who have had long and continuous contact with blacks might even experience a certain aversion to a white skin—a state of mind to which Henry M. Stanley, the explorer, confessed. Stanley says, when he saw some dark-skinned white merchants, "The sight of the Embomma merchants gave me the slightest suspicion of an involuntary shiver. The pale color, after so long gazing on rich black and richer bronze had something of an unaccountable ghastliness. I could not divest myself of the feeling that they must be sick."[7]

Many white persons, however broadminded they would like to be, find it impossible to overcome their aversion to a black skin because as children they were taught to regard it as inferior, or because black men were used as "bogies."[8] Precisely the same holds true of the African. Primitive African mothers, says Dudley Kidd, in his "Savage Childhood," frighten their babies with white men. Livingstone says the African mothers tell their children: "Be good or I shall call the white man to bite you." He adds: "Most whites believe the blacks to be savages: nearly all blacks believe the whites to be cannibals. The nursery hob-goblins of the one is black, of the other white."

Rhin-Chen Lha-Mo, a Tibetan lady, says that in her native land the

5 The Colour Bar, pp. 18-19. 1938.
6 Black and Beautiful, p. 9. 1938.
7 Through the Dark Continent, Vol. 2, p. 462-3. 1878.
8 For a psycho-traditional study of this see: The Color Question from a Psycho-Analytic Standpoint by Dr. Owen Berkeley-Hill in Psycho-Analytic Review, Vol. 11, 1924.

white man is still "held up as a bogey to frighten naughty children much as I understand some of you hold the black man" in America. She relates how as a child she would "run away in panic" at the sight of a white man.[9]

Naturally such children grow up with an ever-active dislike for black or white persons as the case may be. On the other hand Kidd tells how a Kafir had become very much attached to him because one of his earliest memories was a white man's riding him on his knee, and permitting him to search for candy in his pocket.

Rin-Chen Lha Mo, in spite of her early fright, married an English official.

Furthermore, white children who have been reared in Negro families, if well-treated by them, have sometimes an aversion to other white people. I recall one case in particular that of a white girl of about eighteen whose white mother left the South with a Negro and was married to him in Chicago. At school her playmates were Negroes, she goes to Negro dances, churches, etc., and shuns white men. As for her mannerisms and accent they are entirely those of the class of Negroes with whom she grew up.

African children, too, who have been reared in Europe, and kindly treated often dread the thought of being sent back to their own people.

Other things beside color can also arouse aversion in the infantine mind, whether of children or grown-ups. I recall the case of a white baby friendly alike to whites and blacks, who screamed aloud when a bearded man attempted to take her. She had been seeing only beardless men.

I remember seeing once, too, in West Indies, a number of children at play. One of them leaving the group, took some reddish-brown berries and stained her face. When she returned her three-year old sister ran away screaming. She was not calmed until the sister washed her face.

At bottom there is thus really no such thing as a fixed color aversion. A white baby will take as readily to a black breast as a black baby to a white one. Southerners who boast of their black mammies know this only to well. Children of different colors who grow up together have no color prejudice unless taught, although in certain lands they later drift apart for the same

9 We, Tibetans, p. 107. 1926. She says as regards Europeans, "We consider your noses too big, often they stick out like kettle-spouts; your ears too large, like pigs' ears; your eyes blue like children's marbles; your eye-sockets too deep; and eye-brows too prominent, too simian." (P. 31).

Pearl Buck, in "The Good Earth," gives this impression of a Chinese who saw a white man, a missionary, for the first time: "This man had eyes as blue as ice and a hairy face and when he gave the paper to Wang Lung it was seen that his hands were also hairy and red-skinned. He had, moreover, a great nose projecting beyond his cheeks like a prow beyond the sides of a ship and Wang Lung although frightened to take anything from his hand, was more frightened to refuse, seeing the man's strange eyes and fearful face." (P. 109. 1935).

reason that the rich white boy usually shuns his poor white chum later. In Northern orphanages I have seen white children and black ones romping together in utter ignorance of the doctrine of instinctive repugnance of certain white sociologists. White Americans in the North, because of their less contact with Negroes and the bad things they read of them in the press, are, like the primitive blacks, more likely than Southern whites, to have a genuine color aversion.

A well-known Negro educator told me of his visiting Houston, Mississippi, many years ago. At that time he said white and colored got along excellently there. On one occasion he said that he visited the town late at night, and soaked with the rain, he called at the home of the leading farmer. Arriving there he was taken through a large room where the white girls were sleeping. They had been picking cotton that day and tired had thrown themselves on the floor, clothes and all.

In another room were the white men, also asleep. To cross these rooms he had to step over the sleepers. The farmer received him most courteously, and finally led him into the room where the farmer's mother was asleep with his children. Here the old lady gave him one of her gowns to sleep in while his own clothes were being dried.

Years later, he said, he had occasion to revisit Houston but conditions had changed. The railroad had penetrated there and with it the great racial agitator, Senator Vardaman. It was only then that the whites of Houston had discovered that they were white people, he said.

What the average Southerner detests is not the black skin—so many do confess that they love it—but the thought that under it lies the possibility of progress, which, in time will inevitably take its owner away from doing his dirty, ill-paid labor. Color and economics are thus hopelessly scrambled in many a white Southerner's brain.

There are those who will tell you that the Negro is a plague but offer to relieve them of him and they will at once be alarmed, as in the case of Negro migration in the last war. In addition to needing the Negro as the stomach needs the hand, they need him as a shot in the arm for their ego.

The story is told of a little poor-white Southern girl, who had been complaining to a Northern visitor of the Negroes, but when the Northerner promised to take them all away, she begged him pathetically not to for said she: "I would have no one to better than."

Olmsted in his "Slave States," says: "When the Negro is definitely a slave it would seem that the alleged natural antipathy of the white race to associate with him is lost."

Color prejudice, too, is sometimes a collective, not an individual thing

Get a rabid, fire-eating Negro-hater off by himself and you'll find a courteous gentleman. Such was my experience with two of Virginia's great Negrophobes, Ernest Sevier Cox and John Powell, with whom I once talked for hours in Cox's home. Most of the professed Negrophobes of the South are Jekyll and Hydes.

Another remarkable thing about this "instinctive" color prejudice is that it sometimes does not know when to be instinctive. Prejudiced white people can be quite happy in the company of people of Negro or Jewish ancestry until they know them to be such.

Take the case of the Jew who is sometimes fairer in complexion than some American whites. How often have I not met persons, friendly to Negroes, who simply detest Jews. How often I have heard them say: "Anything else but a Jew goes." I once knew a European, a native of Bohemia, who is very fond of Negroes, but who told me that the very sight of a Jew troubled him, and he would no sooner think of touching "the prettiest Jewish girl than he would a rat." Yet I once saw him quite friendly with a girl he did not know was Jewish.

Any Pullman porter can tell of requests made to him by Gentile passengers not to place Jews near them on sleeping-cars. Once on a sleeping-car a clean-cut American lad on seeing a Jewish girl of remarkable beauty told me in the most shocking language how he would have liked to rape her "just for spite." In Europe I found much prejudice against Jews, and I could understand the dislike for them only because I understood a similar unreasoned animosity for Negroes in America.

As regards those white persons who are positive that their dislike for Negroes is inborn and who will aver, (indicating the region of the heart), "Say what you will but I can feel it right here," had persons with this kind of one-track psychology been reared in say a Jewish, Christian, Islamic, Shinto, or other faith, they would feel the same towards others who are not of their faith. It is their emotions, not their intellect, that is at work.

Among the Mohammedans religion is a far stronger bond than race. Between the Arabs and the Ethiopians, both of whom are of Negro strain, there existed fierce wars of over a thousand years. Today there are still differences between the Coptic Ethiopian and the Islamic one, as also between the Christian West African and the Islamic one, both of whom are black. There were also wars between them. In America, too, certain Negro Baptists and Negro Episcopalians will show greater ill-feeling towards one another than they almost will to a lyncher.

In Europe, too, the visible bond of color has been totally displaced by the invisible one of economic and national interest. Certain European nations hate one another as bitterly as a lyncher hates a Negro. In fact, the hate between white and black, is almost nothing in comparison with the hate that has existed in Europe between white and white. Since the first Punic War of 264 B.C., the whites have had 2,200 years of almost continuous wars among themselves— a fact that those who talk about the "inherent incompatibility" between white and black have ignored entirely.

I have met Frenchmen, and Belgians, and even Englishmen, who prefer the blackest Congolese to the whitest German. In Ireland, too, the partisans of the Orange and the Shamrock are far less friendly to one another than Southern whites and Negroes. The atrocities committed on both sides in Ireland immediately before the first world war showed how very strongly white people of the same general appearance can hate one another.

The true Communist, too, has a much stronger feeling against capitalism than against color. I recall one evening at a dance given by white radicals in New York at which there were many Negroes, I overheard one of the latter telling a white woman how he had been to a Tammany Hall dance a few nights before. This Negro was known as a "radical," and the white woman, quite shocked, wanted to know how a "radical" could conscientiously go to a capitalist dance. Soon after another Negro asked her to dance and she readily consented.

As I listened to the conversation I could imagine this same woman with a religious, or racial, or a political bias, saying instead: "I wouldn't dance with sinners, and I don't see how any good Christian could," "Or, I wouldn't dance with Negroes, or Germans, or Frenchmen, or Jews, or Republicans, as the case may be." That man Jesus, said the Pharisees, can't be a good Jew. He dines with publicans, sinners, Samaritans, and Gentiles.

White people have even been known to divide themselves into colors and then set out to butcher one another. Once the people of Florence divided themselves into Whites and Blacks (Bianchi and Neri), and assassinations were common. Dante and eight other Bianchi, as will be recalled, were sentenced to be burnt alive by the Neri. There was also the struggle between the Whites and the Reds (the Wars of the Roses) which lasted in England for thirty years. And it may be set down that whenever a Red heard a White mentioned his "instinctive repugnance" sprang into action just as effectively as when some white American hears mention of a black. This applies with equal force to a Red Russian and a White one.

Again, many light-complexioned Negroes have an aversion for darker Negroes that is fully as strong as that of the average white American, as in the West Indies and even in the United States.

In this pre-disposition toward white on the part of certain blacks and

XXIV. Dutch Lady With Her Negro Page—By Jan van Noordt (1620-1675).

mulattoes, white Christianity also plays its part. Originally, the black man's god was black. The Bantu God, Unkunkulu, is pictured as the deepest shade of black while his Devil and evil spirits are white. So it was among the Ethiopians before the coming of the white missionary. Antonius Fernandez wrote four centuries ago, "They paint Christ, the Blessed Virgin, and other saints in black form, and devils and wicked men in white. So they paint Christ and the apostles at the Maundy, black, and Judas, white; Christ in his passion, black, and Annas, Caiphas, Pilate, Herod, and the Jews, white; Michael, black and the Devil, white."[10]

Among the white people, white is a sign of purity. God, Christ and the angels are pictured as white people dressed in long white robes. The Devil, of course, is black.

Each people creates its own God, that is, its super-representative and protector, in its own image. The yellow man's God is yellow, the Japanese God is a Japanese; the German God has Teutonic features, and what good American ever pictures his god as having Turkish features, or as a composite of mankind? To most white Americans, God is a white man, a la Uncle Sam of the cartoons, and with all the American virtues and aversions. Hence Negroes are unwelcome in most white churches.

The American and the West Indian Negro with no traditions of their own have a white God. Sometimes when a Negro of the humbler class goes to the mourner's bench during a revival meeting, his fellows will ask him, "What do you see there?" He will reply, "A little white man with long hair, walking in a garden," (meaning Christ.) Then will come the cry, "Hallelujah! Now you're saved." To get into heaven, the Christian black man must, of course, be changed to white, hence he sings, "Now wash me and I shall be whiter than snow." An old slave song ran, "Half-way to glory is a white-washin' station."

Related to this species of inferiority complex is that which I saw among the English lower classes as late as 1937. I recall the case of an African, very dark, living in a small English town, who used to wear his top-hat and frock-coat of a Sunday to the great outraging of his white neighbors. Finally, one day a barkeeper stopped him and asked him why he dressed like that. Dress-suits, said the bartender, were only for gentlemen, adding, "Why, I, myself, am not a gentleman!"

Many Negroes feel ashamed of their color when in white gatherings, especially in prejudiced lands. But if the whites were an unprivileged minority in a black man's land they would feel the same about their color. David Livingstone, great missionary, when he saw in Africa black men all about

10 Quoted in M. Russell: Nubia and Syria, p. 275. 1833.

him and he, the lone white, wrote: "One feels ashamed of the white skin; it seems unnatural like blanched celery or white mice."[11] And Livingstone was, on the whole, well treated by the blacks.

Those Negroes in America who feel that they must change their color in order to be in style have their counterpart in any numbers of whites. I recall how once on the French Reviera a prize was offered for the bather who at the end of the season showed the blackest skin, genuine blacks barred, of course. One young woman who was burnt as black as a Oklahoma Indian won first prize. The London Daily Mirror wrote the same year as regards the bathers at Brighton."

"Poets will have to reverse their similies in writing of women. Marble brow, snowy shoulders, milk-white arms are no longer good. Holidays in Africa or where the sun burns brownest are sought. Very soon a mere tan color will seem tame. The ideal will be that of the Song of Solomon: 'Black but comely'."

In Germany I was told that the German ideal was "a tall, broad-shouldered man with a brown skin." Everywhere I went over Germany one summer I saw the pre-Hitlerites doing their best to change their color from that of "the noble blond" to "the ignoble black."

During the Paris Exposition of 1931 I saw white women made up to look like Africans. I recall the case of one who had been to the Riviera and who had had her hair so kinked that the only thing that gave her away were the white streaks left by the shoulder straps of her bathing suit.

Another white woman created a sensation by staining her skin with iodine and kinking her blonde hair. But she could not tint her blue eyes, The result was that she presented a most curious spectacle, and had everyone wondering what "race" she really was. One white writer who saw her white." It is from the blackest Congo that light is coming to us."

Of course, there are Negroes in Africa who paint their bodies white but this is chiefly for mourning. Being born in the mourning color used by the whites they had nothing else to do but to change themselves to white. So-called savage peoples, who wear little or no clothes, stain their bodies for ornament or for rituals. The ancient Britons, said Pliny, stained their skins until they rivalled "the swarthy color of the Ethiopians."

Victor Hugo seems to have thought that the most beautiful color was of the mulatto variety. In his novel, Bug-Jargal he makes the black hero say to the white heroine: "Thou art white and I am black but day must join with night in order to bring forth the dawn and the twilight which are more beautiful than they." Leigh Hunt expresses the same thought in his Wishing-

11 Quoted by W. I. Thomas in Amer. Jour. of Sociology, Vol. 9, p. 608. 1903-04.

Cap Papers when he gives preference to a "loving Quadroon" over a white
or a black woman.

But the truth is that no human coloring is really beautiful, that is, if the
coloring of fishes like the Rainbow Trout, the Dania Rerio, and the Hemi-
chromous Bimaculatus; of butterflies like the Morpho Menelaus, with its
glistening, chatoyant tints of mauve; and even the common earth-worm
with its rich iridescence, are. Few animals, but have a more beautiful coloring than man. The latter atones for this defect with art. Lovers in their
flattery are compelled to borrow comparisons from the plants as the rose,
the peach, the apple, the violet.

Aversion, whether it be to a particular kind of skin color, or nationality,
religion, politics, food, or to anything else which our everyday neighbors find
quite normal, is all of the same pattern. When this aversion becomes too
vocal then it is intolerance.

Color prejudice is such sweet, convenient wrath. It can be made to
serve either as a meal-ticket, a scapegoat, or a mental cigarette. But to all
sane people skin color, no matter what it is, will be *comme il faut*. A white
skin and a black one evolved, so far as we know, from an identical natural
cause: environment. Thus neither can be better than the other, a fact equally
true of all the intermediate shades.

In short, there is color prejudice only where economic interests are involved. European kings, queens and nobles from the days of ancient Rome
and Athens down to the late nineteenth century loved to have black men
and women about them, as I have shown elsewhere. The same was true of
African rulers. White men who visited black kingdoms sometimes found
themselves virtual prisoners, the king wishing to keep them for show. Win-
wood Reade, the explorer, wrote, "All African kings like to keep a white
man at their courts as a human curiosity just as they like to keep dwarfs,
hunchbacks, and albinos."[12]

North American Indians when seeing a wooly-haired black man for the
first time would regard him as some kind of extraordinary creature. York, a
Negro, who accompanied Lewis and Clark on their expedition to the North-
West was regarded as "a very god" by the Indians and "the greatest kind of
great medicine." Raphael Pumpelly, the explorer, tells how in Yesso, Japan,
the natives who had never seen a black man before regarded his Negro
servant, Trusty, as the most important person in the expedition because of
his color and made him the lowest obeisance even though he had ridden in
the rear.[13]

12 African Sketch Book, Vol. 1, p. 267. 1873.
13 Reminiscences of Raphael Pumpelly, p. 313. 1918.

As regards beauty there are always those who will prefer a shade of skin different from their own.[14] Beauty lies in the lover's eyes. This is nature's way. As regards the moral qualities inherent in any particular kind of human coloring what Shakespeare said about there being nothing good or bad but thinking makes it so, fits this case exactly.

The most eminently sensible pronouncement on this vexing question of color is, I think, that of Abdul Baha, great religious leader, who says: "Colors are accidental in nature. That which is essential is the humanitarian aspect. And that is the manifestation of Divine Virtues and the Merciful Bestowals.

"Therefore let it be known that color is no importance in Man, who is the image and likeness of God . . . whatever be his color. Man is not to be pronounced Man simply because of his physical attributes. Difference of color in the human kingdom is similar to the difference of the flowers, the variegated flowers in a garden. If you enter a garden you will see yellow flowers, white flowers, dark variegated flowers, the utmost delicacy and beauty, radiant, and each one through difference lends a charm to the other.

"This diversity increaseth their charm and addeth unto their beauty. How unpleasing to the eye if all the flowers and plants, the leaves and blossoms, the fruits, the branches and the trees of that garden were all of the same shape and color! Diversity of hues, form and shape, enricheth and adorneth the garden and heighteneth the effect thereof.

"Therefore Baha u' allah has said that of the various colors of human kind, one is white, one is black, one is yellow—this sort of differences lends a harmony of color and beauty to the whole. Therefore all must associate with one another even as flowers consort harmoniously in a given garden."

14 For a remarkable discussion on the different kinds of skin-colors, etc., especially white versus black, see: The Man of Al-Yaman and His Six Slave Girls in Burton's Arabian Nights (unexpurgated edition).

Chapter Fourteen

COLOR ATTRACTION AND HOMOSEXUALITY

"*. . .women did change the natural use into that which is against nature.*

"*And likewise also the men, leaving the natural use of the woman, burned in their lust one toward another; men with men working that which is unseemly.*"—St. Paul: Romans, 1:27,28.

"*In brief, I tell thee, that all these were clerks*
Men of great learning and no less renown
By one same sin polluted in this world."

—*Dante's Inferno, XV, 106-108*

The most striking proof that there is a law of attraction of white by black is to be found, as I said, in the homosexual relation. Here is a relation where reproduction is not the motive but where the affinity moves on its very own.

Interracial homosexuality probably goes back to Ancient Greece and Rome and may be traced here and there through European history. According to some translators. Martial's Epigram VII, 87 "*Fruitur Tristi Canius Aethiope*" (Canius delights in a black Ethiopian), has a homosexual connotation. The story of Angelo Solliman, Negro, and his relations with Prince de Lichtenstein certainly sounds homosexual.[1] Today there are white men who want only Negro males, the blacker the better. Dr. George W. Henry in his monumental work, "Sex Variants," has given several cases of this in the United States.[2] There are also Negroes who wish only white men, instances of which are also given by Dr. Henry. The superior technique of the white

[1] Bauer, W. A. Angelo Solliman Der Hochsfurstliche Mohr. Wien 1932. Until the First World War, unmixed blacks were fairly common in the homes of the German and Austrian upper-class. They were kept as pages, and not necessarily for immoral purposes, nevertheless there were a few scandals. The Austrian nobles, like the Russian ones, had these blacks dressed up in gaudy livery for how in their palaces. I knew very well one of these Negroes, a West Indian, who served in this manner but who had to leave because his master suspected him of relations with his wife. Later, in Germany, he posed as a prince but was interned as a British subject in 1914. See also Chap. 17, Sex and Race, Vol. 1.

[2] Sex Variants. 1941. See especially, Vol. 1, pp. 53, 56, 141, 197, 270, 275-290, 283, 325, 350-370, 484. Some of these interracial attractions were very strong, and some of the white men cultured.

XXV.   Hans Lehari of The New Casanova, Berlin. Photo, W. Fleischer, Berlin.

homosexual also influences the Negro, while both prefer a mixed relation thinking it makes for more secrecy.

Homosexuality is a product of civilization.[3] It is probably latent in all human beings and would very likely not show itself were there no segregation of the sexes. The habit once formed in youth often becomes fixed, and is very erroneously believed to exist only among cultured individuals, probably because it was so rampant in ancient Greece and Rome. Plato in his Symposium (Pausanius) speaks of the love of grown men for boys as if it were a common thing. Some of the Roman rulers as Julius Caesar, Nero, and Tiberius were notorious in this respect. Homosexuality is now common in India, China, Java,[4] and Islamic North Africa. Homosexuality is undoubtedly one of Nature's expedients for checking population growth while not withholding pleasure.

Germany, England, France and the United States, especially the first three have a large number of homosexuals, many of whom are artists, writers, singers, preachers, musicians, and idle sons and daughters of the rich.

Germany has long been known for its homosexuality. In 1907 and 1908 there was a terrific scandal of this kind at the Kaiser's court involving Prince Phillip Eulenburg, Counts Hohenhau and Lynar and others. "Real Gods of War," says Wittels, "were then revealed and caressing and giving sweet names to each other." Dr. Magnus Hirschfeld has written a book on homosexuality in Berlin.[5]

Hitler, too, had a number of sex perverts in his entourage. Among them was his bosom friend, Roehm, whose killing and that of others in the blood-purge of 1935, he justified by accusing them of this. charging that they had been surprised in bed with male prostitutes. Hitler, himself, if one believes several of his most intimate friends as well as one of his doctors, is, or was, a homosexual.[6] Earlier, too, Hitler had created a scandal by the arrest and imprisonment of a number of Catholic priests charged with the vice. The few black men who lived in Berlin were always being pursued by the Aryan homosexuals.

In 1931, I visited one Berlin club, the New Casanova, where I saw what I took at first to be handsomely gowned women in low neck, but who were all men. Some Africans who went to this club one night were made very

[3] Lacroix. P. History of Prostitution. 1926. See index of this work.

[4] Hirschfeld, M. Man and Woman, 1935, treats of this subject in the Far East.

[5] Les Homosexuels de Berlin. 1908. I once saw a more recent work on this in Le Crapouillot of Paris about 1937 but neglected to keep it. Hirschfeld placed the number of homosexuals in Berlin then at 50,000, and says that there were both male and female prostitutes of this kind, also.

[6] Krueger, K. I Was Hitler's Doctor. 1942. Schuman, F. The Naxi Dictatorship, pp. 440, 445. 1939.

welcome and the "fairies" ran their hands over the kinkly pates of the blacks, evidently getting quite a thrill out of it. On Friedrichstrasse, which had the greatest parade of prostitutes, perhaps in the world, day and night, were males who dressed as women and solicited men, regardless of color. In France, where there were many more Negroes I saw and heard of much the same thing.

In England I saw Negroes who sold themselves to white men, some of the latter being from the best families. I recall one case in particular, a mulatto of about twenty-eight, who I saw sitting in Hyde Park, and to whom I spoke. At the time he was down-and-out. Three weeks later, however, I met him again and he was well-dressed and well supplied with money. When I asked him the cause of his good luck, he said that he had met the son of a certain rich English nobleman. As coincidence had it I had met the latter, he, having accosted me on a London bus one evening. He insisted on my accompanying him, saying that he had several Negro friends, when he served in the first world war, where he says he had been only a private, a fact of which he seemed proud. I followed him to a very finely furnished apartment, owned by a wholesale tailor, which I later discovered was a homosexual retreat for the rich. There were some eight or ten of the latter there. One of his homosexual friends held such a high position that were his name to be called it would not be believed. Also, one of the finest and most cultured Englishmen, wealthy and very well-known in artistic circles, I discovered on my second meeting with him was homosexual.

An Englishman of fine family and good education confesses in the Modern Psychologist (November 1936) to his great fondness for "strongly masculine young men as soldiers, sailors, and Negroes." He also says, "One thing I have discovered in the course of my experience has been the enormous extent of inversion and perversion. Many of the most noted names in England are homosexual." Dr. Henry tells of one Negro, now living in America, who was adopted by a rich Englishman, and how the latter had homosexual relations with him.

I spoke of having once lived in a garrison seaport in the West Indies, so fond were the English sailors of black boys that whenever the fleet came on its annual visit, the local pharmacists had to lay in an extra supply of unguents.

The United States

Homosexuality is common in America, too. Dr. William Lee Howard wrote, "The number of sexual perverts is astonishing to one acquainted with this important branch of neuropathic studies. As I said, they belong to the intellectual classes and are found in the pupit, at the editorial desk, and in the studies, as well as before the bar and the bedside. They exist in both male and female societies and clubs."[7]

While a police court reporter in New York, I listened to several such cases, among them that of a wealthy Italian olive oil importer with offices on Fifth Avenue, who had been arrested with a Negro porter in a subway toilet at 125th Street and Lenox Avenue, which was a rendezvous for the "fairies." A son of one of New York's richest men, a name that once dominated in Wall Street, I, personally knew to be a pronounced homosexual. One day an automobile accident case in which his chauffer was involved and of which a friend of mine was an eyewitness, brought this rich young white man to my friend's house while I was there. Present was a young Negro and the white socialite was so persistent in his attentions to him that the young Negro had to leave the house to escape him.

There are a number of cultured male Aframericans, some of them graduates of America's top white universities, who are homosexuals and who prefer white men. One of the latter has been twice to the workhouse for this. Another who made a promising debut as a writer, has become a veritable jail-bird because of his incurable fondness for and pursuit of white boys.

Up to a few years ago, when it was forbidden by the police, the Hamilton Lodge of Harlem used to have an annual or semi-annual ball patronized by white and Negro "fairies" that was the talk of New York. The New York-Amsterdam News (April 3, 1931) describing one of these balls said:

"Depravity, Nudity, and Sensual Dancing Feature Hamilton Lodge's

---

[7] Jour. of Dermatology and Urinary Diseases, Jan., 1904. Some of the world's greatest men and women have been perverts. Bloch names among others Michael Angelo, Tchaikowsky, Duquesnoy, and Rosa Bonheur; Carpenter names Shakespeare, Marlowe, Alexander the Great, Julius Caesar, Christina of Sweden, and Sappho. McCabe says that six of the Popes were sodomites. Chevalier names Henry III of France, Pope Leo X, Le Grand Conde. Catherine the Great in her later days, Madame de Maintenon, James I of England, and Archbishop Jean de la Casa. Some are bisexual as Julius Caesar. If Shakespeare were a pervert he also must have been bisexual as he had three children.

It might be that sex perversion is inherent in certain individuals. As nature gives freakish sex organs to some individuals sometimes mixing the male organ with the female organ (see H. H. Young, Genital Abnormalities, 1937), so to some persons she gives sex instincts that are out of the normal and consequently homoexuality is acquired through living in a milieu where the sexes are segregated as in prisons, etc. Others, too, tired of the heterosexual relation might take to it for variety. The question is a vast and complicated one. See also: Schienfeld, You and Heredity, pp. 317-24. 1939.

Masquerade—Several thousand white and colored persons pay $1.50 each to witness and take part in Harlem's most sordid dance." It adds:

"Many of the persons who paid the $1.50 general admission fee have attended the ball for years. But even these registered disgust at this spectacular exhibition, the sixty-third one to be given by the lodge . . .

"More white than colored persons were "in drag." The white ones made excellent female impersonators, for they were carefully selected types; their facial features were softer; their physique more nearly resembled those of women, and their costumes were more elaborate and varied than those of the colored masqueraders. They exercised care in applying make-up to their bodies and faces, and they were not unmindful of the arrangement of their coiffures . . .

"The occasion seemed to have its own license for everything—it made no difference to a white pleasure-seeker whether he did the Lindy-Hop or some fanciful waltz-step with a white or colored man or woman. After all, it was hard to tell in many instances, which was which and who was who . . .

"The elite at the ball included physicians, lawyers, politicians, musicians, artists, writers, and teachers."

Lesbianism

The same is true of the women. The number of lesbians among white actresses is said to be large, some of whom have the reputation of being particularly fond of black women.

France, it seemed to me, had an unusually large number of lesbians who could be principally at cafes as The Dome, the Dingo, The Select and at dance-halls. Some men would have fun going to ask these masculine women to dance and watch them turn up their noses. Two men, these latter felt, did not dance. Some of these white women would "proposition" the colored women from the colonies. I knew personally one little American Negro girl, twelve years old, who had made a big name for herself in vaudeville in the leading European countries, and who lost out entirely after she had fallen under the spell of the white lesbians. In Berlin, too, lesbianism was so open that one of the famous clubs was a lesbian one. Men were religiously barred, but one Negro writer succeeded in getting an invitation to visit it, at least so he told me.

In America, too, there is much lesbianism between white women and Negro ones, high-school girls, college girls and grown women, some of them married. Dr. Henry gives the case history of an Englishwoman of noble ancestry who courted assiduously a Negro singer, finally won her, and now lives with her in a Negro neighborhood. Another is of a mulatto woman entertainer who won considerable social prominence in Europe, even in royal circles, and was once fairly wealthy who has had several affairs with white women. Just as in the normal relations where some Negroes of both sexes care only for white people so there are Negro lesbians who do not care for others of their "race" but wish only white women, giving as a reason that the white women are more refined and accomplished in the art. This, of course, is not always the real reason. Henry cites the case of a vaudeville artiste, a dark woman, who admitted that she was most attracted by white women, less so by mulatto ones, and not at all by women of her color.[8]

In penal institutions in the North there is said to be lesbianism between the white women and the Negro ones. Some of the former, however, would, but for their confinement, have undoubtedly preferred Negro males.

J.L. Moreno tells of one New York reform institution where the black girls attracted the white ones. He says, "It is different and without a parallel in a normal environment when white girls have crushes on colored girls not only as individuals but *en masse*. This form of crush greatly outdoes in intensity, variability of attitudes and effect upon conduct the fancy of a white girl for another white girl. It is a paradoxical phenomenon. This form of bizarre behavior we have rarely found to be mutual. It is a onesided attraction of the white girl for the colored. The white girl goes through all the gestures of courtship, send notes, makes dates . . ."

"The colored girl," he says, "plays a different role in this game. She is the subject adored and rarely the wooer. She frequently takes a pride in the onstorm of attentions and in this pride is mingled the satisfaction of a more subdued race which makes a 'conquest.' While overtly she responds with affection she almost invariably ridicules the courtship. She gets fun out of it showing the notes and gifts to her colored friends. . . . It appears that the blacker the Negro, the more she is pursued and that blacker she is the more she despises the courtship."[9]

In native Africa there is very little or no homosexuality though cunnilinguis and other forms of perversion have been introduced there by Europeans. Auguste Forel charges that it is white men who are largely responsible for such perversion as is now to be found among primitive peoples and he is very likely right. I found on investigation among the black prostitutes of the East African coast towns catering to Negroes that they knew nothing at all about sex perversion. "The free Negro," says Dr. Jacobus X "is neither a sodomite nor a pederast. Besides the action of the hand on the circumcised gland would take a longer time than the natural act."

Of the African woman, he says: "She is not a Lesbian . . . nor a

8 See: Sex Variants, Vol. 2, pp. 563-70, 720-728, 776-783. 908; 1941, for this and other similar cases.
9 Who Shall Survive, pp. 229-31. 1934.

sodomite, having a profound aversion for this depraved taste."[10] Schapera, who studied the sex life of the Kgatlas, a South African tribe, describes it at being on the whole, unperverted.[11] The African calls homosexuality the white man's way."[12]

In North Africa and Egypt, on the other hand, pederasty seems to be very common, due possibly to polygamy. One man will have so many women that there will be a shortage for other men, especially those who are poor. Some of these asked about it will say, "What can we do? We must take what we can get." The Germans, it is said, had a particular preference for these lands because of the ease with which black boys could be had.

On the other hand, an over-abundance of women also breeds homosexuality, as we find it in Germany, France, England, and other lands with a great excess of women. The men, it would appear, are "fed up" with women.

Much more could be said on this subject, historically and currently, but it is not within the scope of this work. I mentioned homosexuality merely to show how deep is the interpenetration of color attraction.

[10] L'Art d'Aimer aux Colonies, pp. 255-6. 1927. (The correct name of this author is either Louis Jacolliot or Jacobus Sutor, according to card index N. Y. Academy of Medicine Library).

[11] Schapera, L. Married Life in an African Tribe, p. 183. 1941.

[12] Forel says, "One thing may be regarded as universal, viz: that the sexual depravity of savages most often arises from the influence of civilized people, who immigrate among them and systematically introduce immorality and debauchery. It is the white colonists who appropriate the women of savage races and train them in the worst forms of prostitution . . ." Sir John Harris in "Dawn in Darkest Africa," mentions similar conditions in the Belgian Congo.

Chapter Fifteen

WHICH IS MORE SEXUALLY COMPETENT, WHITE OR BLACK? ANCIENT BACKGROUND OF THE QUESTION

THE answer to this question like others of its kind can be traced to the most primitive memories of the human race. Color being so obvious must have played its role in human sexual selection as it did among the animals. There is not only a rivalry between black and white in mating but between brunet white and fair white. The Nazi doctrine glorified the blonds over the brunet whites of France, Spain and Italy. Nazi writers frequently referred to the latter as "Negroid," while the Russians are called "Mongoloid."

In the Museum of the University of Pennsylvania is a tablet 4400 years old, which, according to its translator, Professor Stephen H. Langdon, tells of Nintu, a black-haired Sumerian goddess, who created "dark-skinned creatures because of her aversion to blonds" and the quarrel with the other gods that resulted. Gerald Massey, noted Egyptologist, tells of the rivalry between the blacks from Ethiopia and the lighter-colored Egyptians in Ancient Egypt. He says, "On the Egyptian monuments the dark people are commonly called 'the evil race of Kush,' but when the Ethiopian element dominates the dark people retort by calling the light complexions the pale degraded race of Arvad."

He finds the same in ancient Wales which was once inhabited by blacks and whites: "And in the ancient poem called 'Gwadd Lludd y Mawr' the detestation of the dark race for the light break out in a similar manner[1]."

In ancient Egypt with its sex worship and cohabitation as a rite there was undoubtedly some rivalry in the clash of cultures; whether "black" sex from the south was more magical than "lighter-color" sex from Lower Egypt. Phallism, or the worship of the god with the eternally erect genital, was undoubtedly the first direct step among all peoples to the worship of the One God, including the Jews, Greeks and Romans. The phallic god, later called Priapus by the Greeks, was black like the earliest gods. The first of these gods seems to have been Min, the fertility God of the Egyptians of about 5500 B.C., who like the earliest Egyptian gods, originated, so far as we know, in the Sudan. In any case Budge and others have said these gods came

---

[1] A Book of The Beginnings, Vol. p. 454. 1881.

XXVI. Left to right: Isis with the infant, Horus; centre: Diana of Ephesus, Greek, also known as the Goddess Multimammia, or Many-Breasted. Inset, enlarged, to show Negroid face. Right, another conception of Isis and Horus. Below, Mylitta, greatest of the Assyrian goddesses. (See Notes on the Illustrations).

down the Nile from Nubia, or Ethiopia. Xenophanes, Greek writer of 550 B.C. says that the Ethiopian gods were "black and flat-nosed" and Homer who lived much earlier tells how the Greek gods used to go to feast in Ethiopia, their ancestral home. Aristotle (384-322 B. C.) says that both the Ethiopians and Egyptians were black and wooly-haired.

The Egyptian ruler, Seti the Creator, who is described by Rawlinson as "thoroughly African" with prognathous features, "depressed nose, thick lips and heavy chin," and whose mummy is coal-black, is shown several times in the temple of Karnak, Upper Egypt, with a formidably erect organ.[2] Needless to say there was no prudery in those days. Seti was worshipped as the God, Amen, that is, Father. When Christians say Amen in their prayers they are imitating the ancients.

These ancient phallic emblems some of them as tall as trees may still be seen in Ethiopia, the Nubia of the Egyptians. Ireland, too, has its famous Phallic, or Round Tower.

With the coming of Egyptian civilization into Europe and Western Asia, also came the worship of Priapus. The Greeks took Priapus to Rome and Rome took it to France, Germany, and England.[3] Later, too, came the worship of the black Venus for the female organ was worshipped, too, but to a less degree. Originally Isis, she later became the black Madonna.

Rendell Harris in his "Origin of the Cult of Aphrodite," shows how the Black Aphrodite, later the Black Venus of the Romans and the Black Madonna of the Christians, was worshipped for her "magical" powers in ancient Greece.[4]

With the rise of Christianity the gods of the old religion became as usual, the devils of the new. The old, now outlawed, became witchcraft. It is absolutely impossible to root out entirely any old custom or belief, unless the children as soon as they are born, are transported to an environment where they have no chance of hearing of the old. Paganism had roots so enormously older and deeper than Christianity, that the early Fathers of the Church to

---

[2] For reproductions of Seti in this manner see Wall, O. A., Sex and Sex Worship, pp. 392, 413, 447. 1922. For sources on the African origin of Egyptian religion see Sex and Race, Chapter 3. Vol. 1, 1941.

[3] Des Divinites generatrices, p. 153. 1825. See also C. W. Olliver, "An Analysis of Magic and Witchcraft," chap. on Phallic Worship. 1928. Westropp, H. W. Phallism in Ancient Worship, 1875. Phallic Objects and Remains, 1889. Archaic Rock Inscriptions, 1891. Forlong, J. G. R., Faiths of Man. 1906. See PALA. For pictures of ancient phallic monuments in Ethiopia see: Encyc. Brit. Vol. I, p. 304. 1942.

[4] John Rylands Memorial Library. Quar. Bull, Vol. 3. 1916-17, p. 16-17. This black goddess was also known as Melaina, "The Black Lady," and was believed to be the mother of Delphos. founder of the Delphic Oracle, the greatest shrine of the Greeks. The coins of Delphos show him a Negro. (see Sex and Race, Vol. 1, p. 81, 1941, and p. 80 for sources.) Melanin, or the black pigment, in the human skin is derived from the name of this goddess (Greek: melos—anos, black).

get a hearing at all had to graft much of it on the new religion as Grant Showerman has shown in his "Eternal Rome." Today Christian missionaries in Africa and the South Seas to make any headway have often to use "heathen" terms to get the natives to understand the new religion. And occasionally they run face to face against some very ancient custom as the Holy Sacrament, where the flesh and the blood of the Saviour are eaten and drunk. So much is this so that the missionaries have thought it best not to give the sacrament to cannibals converted to Christianity because with the logic of primitive man they would ask, "Did you not tell us that it was wrong to eat and drink human flesh and blood?"

Even Christ, himself, identified God and the Devil as one, as in the Lord's' Prayer, where God is asked not to lead us into temptation, which function, explain it as the theologians will, is clearly that of the Devil.

With the advance of white civilization in Europe there came also the struggle—largely unconscious because whites and blacks as individuals got along well together—to replace memories of "black" with "white." The black goddess, Isis, which had been transformed into the Christian, Black Madonna, became the white Virgin and "black" worship became "black" art, or necromancy, more correctly, negromancie. Sin and evil became black.[4a]

Favoring this was an already powerful factor. Night, with its fear of wild beasts and other dangers, was black. Nearly all the white peoples, as far east as Russia, had black gods. "The Slavs," says Frazer, "had a white god and a black god but paid adoration to the last alone, having as they supposed nothing to apprehend from the beneficience of the first, or white deity.[5]" Some writers think that this black god was symbolic of night; others say it was a relic of the times when the blacks dominated in that part of Europe. In any case we find that while in Central Africa the color of the white man was an object of fear, in Europe it was both one of fear and worship.

Thus, it was very difficult for the Christian church in Europe to displace "black" symbolism with "white." For instance, Scotland's most cherished emblem was black—the Black Rood, or Holy Rood, a crucifix which was said to have been made from the cross of Christ, which was "black." The British House of Lords still has as its most honored emblem, The Black Rod, which is surmounted by a lion. This lion shows, incidentally, the penetration of Egyptian culture into Britain because the lion is indigenous neither to England nor Normandy. Black, too, was retained in heraldry as a symbol of constancy, prudence, and wisdom. Milton says of Casseiopeia, black queen

---

[4a] Rudwin(M., The Devil in Legend and Literature, p. 45. 1931. The same was true of cats. Worshipped in Ancient Egypt, they became a symbol of evil under Christianity (p. 41).

[5] Golden Bough, Vol. 9, p. 92. 1936.

of Ethiopia, "O'erlaid with black staid Wisdom's hue." In art, however, black was used to symbolize evil, falsehood and death. And as I said earlier, all of this symbolism, white or black, arose originally out of sex worship.

Sex was of such great importance then because offspring was next to food, primitive man's greatest desire. Children meant protection and wealth. They could even be sold as slaves. As late as the seventh century A.D., we find the Christian Archbishop of Canterbury writing into the laws of England the right of a father to sell his son into slavery (Theodorus P. 19:28. Ecg. c.27). Progeny was also a necessity for defense or war, thus in our times, Hitler and Mussolini gave premiums to mothers to bear children so that they could be used as cannon-fodder.

Since, therefore ,progeny was so desirable, and the symbol of this was the male genitals, or Priapus, the Fathers of the Church found it impossible to abolish the worship of Priapus so they made him a saint. J. A. Dulaure says, "Priapus, metamorphosed into saint, was honorably placed in the churches and invoked by sterile Christian women, who made him offerings in the hope of being heard." Priapus, he said, was now known variously as St. Foutin, St. Rene, and St. Guignole.

Of course, he was now clothed but his emblems were carved into the Christian cathedrals and were even made into drinking fountains, the most notable of which is that in a public square in Tarn, France, where the water spouts from the organs of three male figures; or in Brussels, Belgium, where a more polite form exists in the celebrated Mannikin-Pisse.

As what was called paganism evolved into Christianity so the worship of "black" sex in Europe evolved into that of "white" sex, which was natural because now the worshippers were white and the further north Christianity journeyed the more likely was this to be. Therefore the Negro phallus, which was once used as a charm by the women,[6] found its way into folk-lore and the depths of the subconscious mind. Numbers of white women now saw themselves cohabiting with black men in their thoughts and dreams. Margaret Murray in her "Witch Cult in Western Europe" gives any number of cases in which these women tell of having intercourse with the Devil in the form of a black man. But this Devil, she points out, was to these women "not a bad man but God manifest and incarnate." That is, he was the old god, which in the new order, was now a devil. The women adored him "on their knees" and were "much content with him," she says.

The desire of some of these women for black men was so evident that it found its way into an English proverb, "A black man is a jewel in a fair

---

6 See sources in Sex and Race, Vol. I, p. 293. 1941 ed. See also, Paul Nettl, "Traces of the Negroid, Etc.," Phylon, 2nd Quar. 1944.

woman's eye."[7] Shakespeare used it thus." Black men are pearls in beauteous ladies' eyes." It is asserted by certain anthropologists that "black man" here means "evil man," but in these tales you read of "the black man on a black horse."[8] Does that also mean a "bad" horse, or an actual black horse? And if the horse is really black why not the man also? Besides there is frequent mention of black cats, black dogs, black clothes, etc.

It was not necessary, moreover, for the women to draw on imagination alone because there seems to be no time in history when black men were not to be found in the countries of northwestern Europe. In England, for instance, there were the Silures, or Western Britons, found there by Julius Caesar and mentioned by Tacitus, who were black, or nearly black. The Romans, udoubtedly had Negroes in their armies there during the four centuries they ruled the island—John Oakesmith mentions one African tribe at Moresby;[9] and the Crusaders brought Negroes with them when they returned from Palestine. As for Shakespeare's day, they were fairly common, too, and he must have been struck by the affection showered on black men by some of the white women (even as I was centuries later) hence his creation of Othello and Aaron the Moor.

As for the art of healing which was then wrapped up in religion it continued for a long time to have more of the "black," or Oriental, in it than the "white" or European. Imhotep of Ancient Egypt, the first recorded physician, was black. Gerald Massey, noted English poet, and student of ancient lore, especially that of Egypt, shows the evolution of Imhotep, the healer, into Christ, the healer. "The child-Christ," he says, "remained a starrily-bejewelled blackamoor as the typical healer in Rome."[10]

In Europe, and especially in England (as I said in Volume One) I was struck with the superstitions that still remained there about black in luck, as at the races, and in cures. Black doctors were favored in England because the women, especially, associated them, it seems with the folk-lore of the black god, the black witch-doctor, who could cure magically even though some

---

[7] Bohn, H. G., Handbook of Proverbs, p. 282. 1867. Another English proverb given by Bohn reads, "A black woman hath turpentine in her."

[8] Murray M., Witch Cult of Western Europe, pp. 29, 34, etc. 1921.

[9] Race and Nationality, p. 96. 1919.

[10] Ancient Egypt: The Light of The World, p. 754. 1907. Garry, T. G. Egypt: The Home of the Occult Sciences with special reference to Imhotep, The Mysterious Wise Man and Egyptian God of Medicine. 1931. Osler, Sir Wm., The Evolution of Modern Medicine, p. 10. 1921. In connection with this subject of magic and Ancient Egypt one may also see: Goodwin, C. W. Fragment of a Graeco-Egyptian Work Upon Magic. 1852; Iamblichus, Mysteries of the Egyptians, Chaldeans and Assyrians. 1821; and other related works in the New York Public Library.

of the Negro physicians were honor graduates of the best English universities.[11]

It would take much more space to go deeply into this history of "white" sex versus "black" sex than I could devote in this book. But so far as I have gone let me say that I claim no infallibility for my theory. It is largely an attempt to introduce some calmer thinking on the subject. This much I will say for it, however, it is based on recorded history, on matter that has been taken from the researches of painstaking scholars, and not what emotional minds, ignorant and scientific, feel it ought to be. I go further, I am ready to listen to any other, provided that also is based on recorded history.

Before I go on to the present day aspects of the question I should also like to make a few observations which I consider pertinent. First, I am convinced that the problem, whatever it might have been, was peaceably solved by the ancients, even in northern Europe. It is therefore odd to find it revived many centuries later in the United States and South Africa and to see it such a source of irritation and even of mob murder.

So charged with emotion is it in these two lands that it is no uncommon thing to find some of the apparently most objective, most scientific minds losing their equilibrium over it and go tearing off into the wilds of prejudice like a badly frightened horse.

But the emotions of more reasonable folk can be calmed if they will stop long enough to remember that the American race question is fundamentally economic. It began absolutely as such. Did the colonists of Virginia buy the first slaves and send for more because they wanted to mate with them? Absolutely not. They wanted their labor. Moreover, the first slaves were men. The race-mixing that began eleven years later was Nature's idea. Having caused an instalment of white people to come to the New World the forces behind the running of the universe—what St. Paul calls "the invisible things of Him from the creation of the world"—also caused an instalment of Negroes to come, too, to be mixed in with them following a process that had been going on for hundreds of thousands of years. Imagine a man going on a journey and making provision for it, and then think of the unconscious forces of Nature (unconscious, of course, only to us) doing

---

11 For the amazing success—and fall—of a black doctor in France, he was really a faith-healer—see the account of Le Docteur Noir (The Black Doctor) in L'Intermediare de Chercheur at des Curieux, Vol. 37, pp. 5, 414-15.

One finds still much of witchcraft, or folk-lore in the belief about cures in the more backward regions of the civilized lands as Russia, Spain, Portugal, the Balkans, and the more primitive Negroes and whites of the United States. Frazer, in his "Golden Bough" devotes more than 400 pages to the use of "black" art in healing. As for the United States as regards both white and black, the Journal of American Folk-Lore, gives abundant evidence.

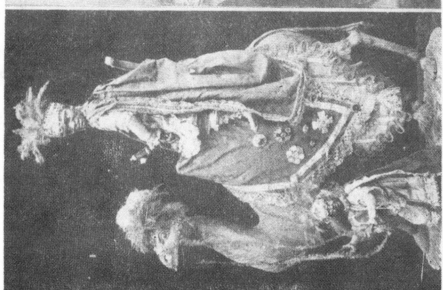

XXVII. Left to right: Balthasar, one of the Three Wise Men (Christmas Crib, Oberammergau, Germany). Black Christ of the Philippines. Black Madonna of Alt-Otting, Bavaria.

the same thing. The religious man call such forces, God. Race-mixing, then, was God's idea. The scientist who prefers the term, Nature, or something else, might admit that some power, older than Science, also ordained the so-called mixed-blood. As for South Africa, the whites planted their own race question there. The blacks had been living there for centuries before Christ, without one.

Nature, too, is never so clumsy as the politicians and the right-wing anthropologists and sociologists make her out to be. Having created a certain "race" she is interested in preserving it for a certain length of time, therefore she places in the minds of most of the members of that group a preference for themselves, that is, having grown up together they get more accustomed to one another than to outsiders. The child usually wishes to be like its father. In the vast majority of cases, the men and women of any given group will give sexual preference to their own group. This is true of whites and of Negroes. In fact, this feeling is, or was, even stronger among the blacks, as I have shown in Volume Two; the primitive blacks had so little desire for association with white people that they regarded them as ghosts and hobgoblins and took to the woods at the sight of them.

With then such powerful reins on race-mixing, the process in America would have taken place gradually. Nature would have eased gently some Negro strain into the white one without friction as she had been doing for thousands of years in Europe and the lands that are now Islamic. But this gentle and decent process would have meant recognition of the mixed-blood, and that did not fit in with the economic program of the slave-master, the more so as he found he could eat his cake and have it, too, because although he had brought the Negro with no intention of amalgamating with him when the black woman arrived he found her good to look upon and sometimes preferred her to his wife. Being the master he could outlaw race mixture on the books for others but as for himself was he not the law?

The outlawry had one important effect that the master had been too greedy to see. Whatever is forbidden, most of all sex and drink, becomes at once a great temptation, a joy that we feel others would snatch from us. What was there in "black" sex? Was it something that the masters had found so good that they wanted it all for themselves? And so curiosity was aroused until "black" sex became an obsession. So much so is it now that I believe if one were to propose an expedition to Mars composed of white and Negro scientists there would be those who would at once foresee its leading up to some white woman in the arms of a black man.

Even as early as the 1770's the opposers of slavery had to face the argument that if the Negro was freed he'd be marrying white women. In 1860, as was said, while the majority of Negroes were still slaves, the Democratic party had as its slogan, "Would you like your sister to marry a big, buck nigger?"

Whenever, today, the question comes up of giving the Negro his citizenship rights there are always those who immediately sniff approaching nuptials, or to be more precise, vision the double-backed animal with which Roderigo frightened Brabantio in Othello. Such have a foresight that would simply have ruined Shakespeare's plot for him. The wife of a New England college professor who used to give a weekly soiree to students was once asked by one of her guests whether he could bring a fellow-student, a Negro prize-winning poet. Embarrassed, she replied that so far as she was concerned the Negro was welcome but she was afraid that one of the white girl students might fall in love with him and she would get the blame. Another instance is that of H. O. Tanner, great American painter. Tanner, while his pictures were on exhibition at the Chicago Art Institute, was made a visiting member of the Cliff-Dwellers, the city's leading artistic, musical, and literary club. Tanner used to have his meals there. One evening, however, when he came to dinner, it was ladies' night on which a certain miniature painter growled on seeing him, "Why didn't he stay away? Didn't he know there would be ladies present?" The ludicrous thing about this is that Tanner looked more like a Southern Italian than an Aframerican—he is about three-fourths white —and in France was received in the homes of the beau monde.

Some Negroes, too, are equally narrow. One wealthy Negro woman refused to entertain the members of an interracial committee at her home. "Those white women," she said, "are only coming there to meet our men and might take away my husband." Thus in spite of all the jim-crow laws and social fortifications and the oft-repeated assurance that it is only the dregs of both "races" that mix, each side continues to be as suspicious of the other as two gamblers who are certain that the other will cheat at the first opportunity.

In short, the fear of race-mixing is a bugaboo created by the shrewd exploiters of labor for silly people. We shall proceed further to chase that myth into the open and see just what there is in it which has caused it to have so powerful an effect on American politics and social life for the past three centuries. When a horse shies from a strange object he can be cured by leading him up to it and letting him see that there is no danger of his being eaten by it. Human beings are supposed to be more intelligent than horses.

Chapter Sixteen

WHICH IS MORE SEXUALLY COMPETENT, WHITE OR BLACK? THE QUESTION TODAY

THE ancient belief that "black" sex is more virile than "white" sex has emerged in our day from folk-lore to be also a subject for humor. Innumerable are the jokes told about the black man in this respect and in none of them is he ever described as incompetent. One of the first I heard was that of an Irish woman who had a Negro husband relating her experiences to another Irish woman. These jokes may be heard even in Europe. The belief in dark-skinned potency persists. It is to be found even in the case of dark whites, and is perhaps an evolution of the "black" sex belief. Most people still believe that brunets are more passionate than blonds. The great lovers of romance are dark. One hears "tall, dark, and handsome," not tall, blond, and handsome. Had Rudolph Valentino been flaxen-haired and fair-skinned, he would hardly have attained the preeminence he did in feminine hearts; Casanova, too, the world's greatest lover. Casanova was very dark, almost black.

Havelock Ellis says, "This association of pigmentation and sexual aptitudes has been recognized in the popular lore of some peoples. Thus the Sicilians, who admire brown skins and have no liking either for a fair skin or light hair, believe that a white woman is incapable of responding to love. It is the brown woman who feels love; as it is said in Sicilian dialect: *Fimmina scura; fimmina amurusa.*" (A dark woman is a passionate woman).[1]

As I have shown elsewhere the Negro phallus was used as a charm by white women in ancient times while in the Arabian Nights' Entertainment Negroes are shown as the very model of sexual competence.[2] I also cited Brantome, a sixteenth century chronicler, who tells of a grand dame of Naples who had a Negro lover "the ugliest man in the world" but who was noted for his *avitallement*.[3]

In Cuba, Brazil, Haiti, and other parts of Latin America it is the mulatto who is sometimes given the palm. Freyre ascribes the alleged greater sexual attractiveness of the mulatto to the environment: the women could not hope

1 Studies in the Psychology of Sex, p. 193. 1910.
2 Sex and Race, vol. 1, pp. 101-105, 293. 1941.
3 Oeuvres. Vol. 1, pp. 703-4 (Lalanne). Paris. 1873.

XXVIII. "An Englishman of Barbadoes Sells His Concubine." (See Sex and Race, Vol. 2, p. 89).
Coll. Richard B. Moore.

to get ahead except through their eroticism and they cultivated that. Much the same was said of the Louisiana mixed-bloods, examples of which were given in Volume Two. In Brazil, the mulatto men were thought to be more attractive because of the difference of "race" and the supposed greater size of the genitalia as compared with the European. Again, there are writers who say that the blacks are more frigid than either the whites or the mulattoes and they use this to explain the erotic nature of most African dances, which are needed, so they say, to stir up desire in the primitive blacks. Crawley and Havelock Ellis are among the subscribers to this theory. On the other hand, Dr. Jacobus X who lived in West Africa describes the blacks as being very competent sexually and Schapera, who studied one African tribe gives the impression that sex intercourse plays a great role in its daily life.

But what is the truth? Here is one belief that seems quite impossible of scientific proof. Hence I shall merely give what has been said upon it by certain travellers, scientists, and novelists, some of whom refer to the Negro phallus; others to the depth of the Negro vagina; others to Negro sexuality. All are white.

External Genitalia

Mantegassa says: "Sono ancora molto scarse le osservazioni sulla forma diversa e le diverse dimensioni degli organi genitali nelle diverse razze; ma é pero dimostrato come i negri in generale abbiano un membro virile molto piú voluminoso che gli altri popoli, ed io stesso, esercitando la medicina per parecchi anni nell'America meridionale, ho potuto verificare questo fatto coi miei propri occhi. A questo maggior volumne dei genitali del maschio corrisponde anche una maggior ampiezza della vagina nelle negre. Il Falkenstein ha trovato che i negri di Loango hanno il pene molto grosso e le loro donne si accontentano male del nostro amplesso, rinfacciandoci l'esiguità del nostro strumento. Lo stesso autore combatte l'idea singolare del Topinard, che il maggior volume del membrio dei negri non si verifica che nello stato di flaccidità, mentre il pene dei negri sarebbe piú piccolo, quando è in erezione. Falkenstein ha pure osservato che presso le negre di Loango come presso di noi la comparsa della menstruazione presenta grandi differenze indivaduali, verificandosi dal dodicesimo al diciassettesimo e fin al ventesimo anno."[4]

Ales Hrdlicka of the Smithsonian Institution, "The penis (of the Negro boy) is longer than that of the corresponding white boy."[5]

---

[4] Gli Amori degli Uomini (Lalanne). 1873. Larousse (Dictionnaire Universel de 19e siecle) agrees with this. It says, "Les organes genitaux volumineux." (See NEGRES). Vacher de Lapouge, however, says that the genital organs of the white woman are like those of the long-headed black races and the South Sea Negroes. (L'Aryen, p. 30, 1899).

[5] "Physical Differences Between White and Colored Children," Amer. Assn. for the Advanc. of Science, Vol. 47, p. 476. 1898.

Sir Harry Johnston: "In both sexes the development of the external sexual organs is large—larger than in the European (white) race, more considerable than among the Mongoloid yellow races of Asia, America, and the Pacific."[6]

Sir Richard Burton is of the same opinion. He says, "I measured one man in Somaliland, who, when quiescent, numbered nearly six inches. This is a characteristic of the Negro race and of African animals, e.g. the horse; whereas the pure Arab, man and beast, is below the average of Europe; one of the best proofs, by the by, that the Egyptian is not an Asiatic but a Negro partially white-washed. Moreover these imposing parts do not increase proportionally during erection; consequently the deed of kind takes a much longer time and adds greatly to the woman's enjoyment."[7]

Serres: "One of the characters of the Ethiopian race consists in the length of the virile organ as compared with that of the Caucasian race. This dimension coincides with the length of the uterine canal in the Ethiopian female and both have their cause in the form of the pelvis in the Negro race. There results from this physical disposition that the union of the Caucasian man with an Ethiopian woman is easy and without inconvenience for the latter. The case is different in the union of the Ethiopian with a Caucasian woman who suffers in the act. The neck of the uterus is pressed against the sacrum, so that the act of reproduction is not merely painful, but non productive."[8]

J. Campbell quotes Soemerring: "There are no essential differences in the organs of generation; their construction and functions are the same in various races of mankind. The Negroes, indeed, have generally been celbrated for the size of a principal member of this apparatus. 'Nigritas mentulatiores esse vulgo ferter (Sic) (fertur). Respondet sane huic asserto insignis appartus genitalium Aethiopis, quem in suppelectill (sic!) (supellectili) et mea anatomica servi. Num vero constants sit haec praerogative et nationi propria, nescio.' Two specimens in the College Museum strongly confirm the common opinion, which is also corroborated by Mr. White, both from dissection and observation of living Negroes."[9]

Blumenbach: "It is generally said that the penis in the Negro is very

6 British Central Africa, p. 399. 1898.

7 Arabian Nights, Entertainment, Vol. 1, p. 6 (unexpurg. ed.). Tale of the Ensorcelled Prince.

8 Quoted by Broca, P., in Phenomena of Hybridity in the Genus Homo, p. 28. 1864.

9 Negro Mania, p. 124 1851.

large. And the assertion is so far borne out by the remarkable genitory apparatus of an Ethiopian which I have in my anatomical collection."[10]

Duckworth: "The relatively greater size of the penis in Negroes has long been recognized . . . The vagina in the black races is said to be longer than in women of white races."[11]

Love and Davenport seem to think that the Negro is less liable to imperfect sex development than the Caucasian. They say . . .
"Mississippi, and Arkansas, all states characterized b ya high percentage of Negro population in which these defects are relatively uncommon . . . The high percentage of cases in New Jersey and in Massachusetts is very likely racial as the population of recent immigrants from South-Eastern Europe showed a relatively high percentage of the defects."[12]

James Joyce, speaking of Lily Langtry's supposed affair with the Prince of Wales (later Edward VII) said, (*Molly Bloom's soliloquy*) "he's like the first man going the roads only for the name of a king they're all made the same way only a black man's . . ."[13]

Sexuality

J. J. Virey: "Negresses display no common proficiency in the art of exciting the passions and gaining an unlimited power over individuals of a different sex. Their African blood carries them into the greatest excesses."[14]

"The percentage of this defect is indeed small in Louisiana, Alabama . . ."

Sir Harry Johnston: "Nature has probably endowed him (the Negro) with more than the usual genesic faculty . . . Yet, the Negro is very rarely knowingly indecent or addicted to lubricity. In this land of nudity which I have known for seven years I do not remember once having seen an indecent gesture on the part of either man or woman . . . "[15]

Havelock Ellis: "I am informed that the sexual power of Negroes and slower ejaculation are the cause of the favor with which they are viewed by some white women of strong sexual passions in America and by many prostitutes. At one time there was a special house in New York City to which white women resorted for these "buck lovers." The women came heavily veiled and would inspect the penises of the men before making the selection."[16]

---

10 Anthropological Treatises, p. 249. 1865.
11 Morphology and Anthropology. pp. 377-8. 1904. Dr. Julian Lewis cites the first half of this in his ::Biology of the Negro," p. 77. 1942.
12 Physical Examin. of the First Million Draft Recruits, p. 107.
13 Ulysses, p. 737. Modern Library ed. 1942.
14 Natural History of the Negro Race, p. 113. 1837.
15 British Central Africa, p. 408. 1898.
16 Studies in the Psychology of Sex, Vol. 3, p. 238. 1913.

XXIX. Upper Left: Malay Negro, and Henry Pu-Yi, Emperor of Manchukuo, last of the Manchus, who once ruled China. Lower, Batavian woman, and His Highness, Syed Alwi, Rajah of Perlis, Malaya. An evident Negro strain runs through all four. The Emperor Pu-Yi has, in the upper part of his face, the white strain of the North and in the lower part of it the Negro Strain of the South. All four types may be found among Americans.

J. Richardson Parke: "They (the Negroes) are uxorious; but the sexual instinct is far feebler than with the white race generally."[17]

Remy de Gourmont, noted French author and esthete, who probably spoke from experience: "One knows that a cat's tongue is rough; so is the tongue and all the other mucous surfaces of Negroes. This roughness of surface notably augments the genital pleasure as men who have known Negro women testify."[18]

I. Schapera tells of African men who "sometimes have coitus six or seven times in succession" in one night.[19] Dr. Jacobus X. confirms this. He says, "Il est certain qui'un Negro bien nourri et circoncis peut besogner une femme pendant presque une nuit en n'ejaculant que cinq ou six fois." Such an exploit he says would render a white man dizzy.[20]

John Dollard: "If Negro women are represented as sexually desirable in the folk imagination of the whites, Negro men are viewed as specially virile and capable in this sphere . . . There is a widespread belief that the genitals of the Negro males are larger than those of whites, this was repeatedly stated by whites . . ." Dollard gives illustrations from his informants, one of them a doctor for the draft examination of 1917.[21]

Shufeldt quotes Dr. William Lee Howard: "Nature has endowed him (the Negro) with several ethnic characteristics which must be recognized as ineffaceable by man . . . especially the large but flexible sex organ which adapts itself to the peculiar sex organs of the female Negro and her demands . . .

"These ethnic traits call for a large sexual area in the cortex of the Negro brain which soon after puberty works night and day . . .

"The chief, the controlling *primal* instinct in the African is the sexual."[22a]

Shufeldt, himself says: "In the Negro all the passions, emotions, and ambitions are almost wholly subservient to the sexual instinct . . .

Negroes are grossly animal . . . and as a rule equipped far above the average man for unlawful indulgence."[22]

---

[17] Human Sexuality, pp. 352-6. 1909. On page 364, he reports a remarkable case of vaginismus, involving a rich white girl daughter of a brewer, and a Negro in an Atlantic City hotel, necessitating an amputation. An old resident of that town tells me it is a fact.
[18] Natural Philosophy of Love, p. 60. 1931.
[19] Married Life in an African Tribe, p. 185. 1941.
[20] L'Art D'Aimer aux Colonies, pp. 149-150. 1927.
[21] Caste and Class in a Southern Town, p. 160. 1937.
[22a] America's Greatest Problem: The Negro, pp. 99-100. 1915. 22b. p. 145.

Gilberto Freyre: "One supposed defect of the African race, its eroticism, lewdness, and sexual depravity, was communicated to the Brazilian.
Yet it has been proved that the Negro peoples of Africa, like primitives in
general, are much more moderate in their sexual desires than Europeans.
Negro African sexuality is such that it needs strong outside stimulation in
order to be aroused, erotic dances, orgies, the phallic cult; the sexual appetite in the civilized, on the other hand, is easily aroused, without outside
stimuli, upon the slightest provocation. Crawley attributes the popular belief
in sexual excess in the Negro to the expansive temperament of the race and
the orgiastic nature of its festivals, which create the illusion of an unbridled
sensuality. But this very fact "proves just the contrary" because it demonstrates
Negro need for 'artificial stimulation.' Havelock Ellis puts the Negro woman
among the more frigid rather than passionate women; among those 'indifferent
to the refinements of love.' He also agrees with Ploss that the sexual organs of
primitive people are often comparatively undeveloped."[23a]

"The mulata, on the basis, it seems, of the hurried findings of the im-
mature science of genetics, is regarded as a continual "super-sexual excitant," which would make of her an abnormity; and from the point of view
of European Catholic morality a dangerous corruption. Certain things
about her are supposed to be highly suggestive sexually: her eyes, her walk,
her smile; and, according to some, even her feet, which are supposed to
be much more sensitive than those of white and Negro women. Her fingers
are supposed to be much more skillful in wanton play and the stroking of
the head; her sex is generally believed to be tighter; and they say the odor
of her flesh has a special attraction. In fact, two very level-headed Brazilians, Nina Rodriques and José Verissimo, give credence to these beliefs.
Even common sense, so often wise in its happy intuitions, but at times guilty
of profound untruths, that the earth is flat and fixed, for instance, continues
to believe in the diabolical, super-excited *mulata* as a creature of nature and
not as a product of her social environment. Social circumstances stimulate
her to adventures of physical love from which the better protected, and the
socially better situated women of the pure and more stable race are shielded.

"The same aura [as that which surrounds the *mulata*] surrounds the
mulato: the *cabra sarado* of folklore, the *mulato bamba*, the *mulato escovado*,
the *mulato sacudido*, the *mulato bicho-cacau*. Popular report credits him
as well as the Negro with physical superiority to the pure blond white in

---

[23a] Casa Grande & Senzala, 3rd. ed. p. 229. 1938. 23b. Sobrados e Mucambos,
pp. 336-38. 1936. These Brazilian terms are almost untranslatable in connotation,
but literally they mean: **cabra sarado**, brave goat (Cabra or goat is a Brazilian-
ism for mulatto), **mulato bamba**, valiant mulatto; **mulato escovado**, clever mulatto,
mulato sacudido, elegant mulatto, **mulato bich-cacau**, cacao-worm mulatto.

the act of love. His superiority is stated in much more specific terms than those priapean qualities attributed to the *mulata* when she is being compared with the supposedly much more frigid and refined white woman."[23b]

Paul Morand: "Fleuve a l'estuaire profond comme un vagin de nègresse." (the comparison is with the Mississippi). "On eut dit la peau nue et sans poil des nègresses, toujours profonds et fraiche, comme une cave; il eut chaud a la nuque."

Petion Savain: "Il pense au pays lá-haut, a son pays couché entre deux grandes cuisses de montagnes. Comme un sexe de belle nègresse. Le sexe de la maitresse de l'eau."

Lawrence Durrell: "Always I find myself turning from the pages of Geography, of flora and fauna, of geological surveys, to these studies in ethos. The creeds and mores of a continent, clothed in an iridescent tunic of oil. It turns always to those rivers running between black thighs forever and forever. A cathartic Zambesi which never freezes over, fighting its way through, but flowing as chastely as if it were clothed in an indescent tunic of oil. I turn always to those exquisite horrors, the mutilations and deformations, which cobble the history of the dark continent in little ulcers of madness. Strange streaks here and there you will find: hair trigger insanities, barely showing, like flaws in ice, but running in a steady, heavy river, the endless tributary of sex. They feed those fecundating rivers of seed which flow between the cool thighs of the Nubian, stiffen in his arteries, and escape in steaming laughter down his sleeve. Look, if you dare, and see the plate-mouthed women of the Congo basin, more delectable than the pelican. Vaginas turning blue and exploding in dark flowers. The penis slit like a ripe banana. Seed spurting like a million comets. The menstrual catharsis swerving down from the loins, dyeing the black carpets of flesh in the sweet smell, the urao rich of blood. The world of sensation that hums, dynamically, behind the walls of the belly. The slit lips of the female opening like a whale for the Jonahs of civilization. The vegetable rites. The prepucophagous family man: the foreskin eater. All this lives in the wool of Miss Smith, plainly visible, but dying."

Again: "That focus which attracts us all so much is centered like a cyclone, over sex. You may think you are looking at her [Miss Smith, the Negress], looking at the idea of her, but really, seeking under her cheap European dress, you are looking at her fertility. The potential stirring of something alive, palpitating, under her dress. The strange stream of sex which beats in the heavy arteries, faster and faster, until the world is shaken to pieces about one's ears, and you are left with an indeterminate vision of the warm African fissure, opened as tenderly as surgery, a red-lipped coon grin . . . to swallow all the white races and their enervate creeds, their arks, their olive-branches."[24]

Henry Miller: "She wanted to know if there wasn't anyone in the place good enough for us except this Negress. I told her bluntly NO. And it was so—the Negress was the queen of the harem. You had only to look at her to get . . . her eyes seemed to be swimming in . . . She was drunk with all the demands made upon her. She couldn't walk straight any more . . . at least it seemed that way to me. Going up the narrow, winding stairs behind her I could not resist the temptation to . . . ; we continued up the stairs that way, she looking back at me with a cheerful smile and wiggling . . . a bit when it tickled her too much."[25]

Dr. Albert Chapotin: "Cffest ainsi que nègres, dont plusieurs Francaises sans scruples ont eprouvé les caresses, sont prodigieusement doués, non pour accomplir des prouesses numeriques, mais pour prolonger, une nuit entière, leur aptitude amoureuse."[26]

Iwan Bloch: "Ein Negerbordell. Ein Lüstling bringt stets in das Bordell der Juliette zwei Negerinnen mit, weil der Kontrast zwischen weissen und schwarzen Menschen ihm besondere Befriedigung vrschafft (Juliette VI, 152). Neger und Negerinnen spielen auch bei dem anthrophagischen Diner in Venedig eine Rolle (Juliette VI, 204). In dem Schlosse des Cardoville bei Grenoble wohin Justine als ein Opfer der Lüste dieses Wüstlings geführt wird, sind wei Neger als Helfershelfer bei diesen Orgien tätig (Justine IV, 331). Im dritten Band von, Aline et Valcourt 'findet sich auf Seite 200 ein schönes Bild, drei nackte Weiber darstellend und einen Mann, der die Genitalien des einen Weibes berührt, wahrend von vier dabei stehenden Negern zwei mit wildem Ausdruck Keulen schwingen.

Die Neger sind auch keine Erfindung Sade's! Es existierte schon vor 1790 in Paris ein Negerbordell! Dies befand sich im Hause einer Mlle. Isabeu früher rue neuve de Montmorency später rue Xaintonge welches letztere Haus einem gewissen Marchand gehörte. In diesem Bordell waren Negerinnen, Mestizen und Mulattinnen vorrätig. Es gab keine festen Preise sondern die Insassinnen wurde verkaufft, wie man die Sklavinnen einer Karawane verkauft."

Fraxi meint dass der Geschmack für schwarze Frauen vielleicht den Franzosen eigentümlich sei. Jedenfalls findet man noch heute in mehreren

---

24 The Black Book, a novel. Paris. The Obelisk Press, pp. 127-8.
25 The Tropic of Cancer, a novel. Paris. The Obelisk Press, pp. 236-7. I have omitted eight words from the quotation.
26 See Sex and Race, Vol. 2, p. 405 for the source of this and others in a similar vein.

Bordellen von Paris und in den Provinzen ständig Exemplare dieser schwarzen Schönheiten."[27]

Geoffrey Gorer, an Englishman, who travelled much in Africa with Benga, an African, (who once danced at the Folies-Bergere in Paris) says that because Benga "was a Negro and a dancer everybody considered that they had a right, if not a duty to make sexual advances to him." This was in Europe.

He adds that in certain Parisian circles it was "definitely chic" to have a Negro lover. "This, a successful Negro explained to me, was due to their greater development and also to the fact that a Negro when stimulated can continue almost indefinitely. The same informant told me that white women were not exciting. They were so amorously incompetent. He should know what he was talking about for he earned his living by exploiting his talents."

Gorer says also: "It is very questionable if puberty is earlier with them (the Africans) than with Europeans, and I certainly do not think that their sexual desires are stronger. They are on the contrary very much more difficult to stimulate than we are, and the pre-erotic states which can be so easily produced in us by contact, kissing, dancing, reading and spectacles, particularly films, can only be produced in the Negro by far more violent measures which seem to us indecent."[28]

E. Fortie, a European, who lived in Africa, and who had a black wife, whom he adored, tells how he was wounded to the depths when he overheard her one day discussing their sex relations with another black woman and saying how much she preferred "big-fleshed" black men to him.[29]

As for my own observations on this subject they are many and varied. For instance, I lived for nearly four years in a garrison town in Jamaica, West Indies, where there was much talk and no end of jokes about inter-racial sex. In this garrison were two companies of white soldiers—English, Irish, Scotch—and two companies of native Negro ones, a total of about 230 whites and the same number of blacks. Most of the men went in swimming daily in a fenced-in pool in the sea. There were very few white women and these, as a rule, would scorn going with soldiers, regardless of color. The white men, therefore, went with Negro women. In the various cities of America and Europe I gathered also much information on this subject, however, I am withholding these observations as I do not think they would in any way give a final answer to this question of sexual competence.

[27] Der Marquis de Sade und Seine Zeit, pp. 133-4. 1900.
[28] Africa Dances, pp. 3, 14, 245. 1935.
[29] Black and Beautiful, p. 94. 1938.

XXX.   Left: Two Negro heads, Perdrizet). Left, below: Queen Mut (Cairo Museum).
Right: Bust of Queen (Courtesy Metrop. Museum). Centre: A Pharaoh (British Museum).
Below: Head from the Old Empire (Louvre).

Sexual competence, it seems to me, depends primarily upon the degree and quality of nourishment; lack of preoccupation with nerve-consuming work, principally athletic and commercial; and natural inheritance. Some individuals are more highly sexed than others. Athletes and men with financial worries are reputed to be notoriously incompetent. Brigham Young, Mormon leader of Utah, for instance, was a formidable lover. He had eleven wives and forty-seven children, eleven of whom were daughters by eight different wives. But had he been some big business executive with a host of worries (instead of a host of wives, whom thanks to his leisure, he was able to satisfy), he would, with all his huge amorous endowment, have been one of the great sexual flops of history. Worse, his life would have been a hell on earth.

Ill-fed African tribes are weak sexually, while well-fed ones with easily obtainable food are not. I believe this to be true of all individuals and peoples regardless of race, Boccaccio, in his Tenth Story (Third Day), very rightly makes the monk, Rustico, a beaten out man sexually because of his diet of roots and herbs. Oddly enough, one complaint against the American soldiers in England, according to one correspondent, is that they are over-sexed. If they are stronger sexed than English men it is because they are better fed.

As regards a white man and a black one living in the same civilization, and equally well-nourished, the tradition of the Negro's greater alleged sexuality, will probably always cause a difference of opinion, which, so far as I can see, cannot be solved. Some writers say that the Negro has a blunter nervous system, among them Sir Richard Burton and Dr. Jacobus X. The Negro generally has a large organ, too, it is true, but this also is no positive proof of superior competence any more than bigger biceps always mean greater strength.

Another assertion sometimes made is that larger genitalia means a smaller brain; while a smaller one is indicative of higher intellectual and spiritual endowment. This was a Nazi belief. Otto Hauser, Nazi scientist, says that "the smaller external genitals" of the Nordics, male and female, is proof of their superiority, of their greater "spirituality," and that the admixture of foreign blood can always be told from the size of these organs.

If there is any lack of sexual competence in the white man it has not prevented his sowing his children among the darker primitive peoples from the forests of the Congo to the frozen wilds of Alaska. There is not a single "race" on earth that does not bear his stamp.

Are White Women Colder Than Colored Ones?

The popular belief regarding white women versus colored women is, in my opinion, not true, or not possible of proof. The women of the darker races, being in the lower social position and generally less educated, are inclined to give themselves more freely and spontaneously than white women, generally, and this together with the attraction of a difference of "race" has served to create a bias in favor of the darker woman. Another attraction for the white man in Africa or Oceania, is that the colored woman is by tribal training, more submissive, and far less inclined to nag. But whatever be the truth of this matter I do not know. I believe it too dependent upon the individual senses to be capable of a correct answer.

That white women, especially blonds, are inherently cold in love, is not true if one judges by some of the cases told in the scientific books and periodicals. For instance, the American Journal of Psychiatry (Nov. 1940) gives cases of white women who were very highly sexed. It says of one of them, a university student of good family, "She collected men as others would collect stamps or autographs and she kept a list of some eighty-five individuals with whom she had contact. On one occasion, during the football season, she journeyed to a distant city and cohabited with at least ten of the football squad on the night before the game. (The team lost the next day)." In Volume Two, I mentioned a white woman who collects Negro celebrities in the same way. It would be interesting to know which group, white or black, furnishes the higher percentage of nymphomaniacs. My guess would be the former.

Finally, individuals of both sexes, who are cold to members of their own "race" are sometimes very passionate with those of another "race."

In English-speaking lands, sexual vigor, though privately admired, is something to be ashamed of otherwise. However, is it not possible that great manifestations of genius, especially in music and art, might be largely sublimations of sex, and that no individual is more mentally virile than he is sexually virile, though this latter power is sometimes latent? Plato went so far as to say that thought, itself, was a sexual manifestation while Walt Whitman expressed it thus:

"Sex contains all. Bodies, souls, meanings, proofs, purities, delicacies, results, promulgations. Songs, commands, health, pride, the maternal mystery, the seminal milk: All hope, benefactions, bestowals. All the passions, loves, beauties, delights of the earth; All the governments, judges, gods, followed persons of the earth—These are contained in sex as parts of itself, and justifications of itself."[30]

30 **A Woman Waits for Me.**

And Coleridge:

"All thoughts, all passions, all delights.

Whatever stirs this mortal frame.

Are all but ministers of love

And feed his sacred flame."

I attribute the animalistic, appealing style of modern woman's dress, with its increasing leg and hip display to the waning genesic powers of the leading civilized groups. Compare the styles of today with those prior to the war of 1914. The efforts of the fair sex in this respect remind one of the chef who arranges his dishes in a manner to stir the jaded appetite of the bloated gourmand, or of the female firefly who lights up and goes in search of the male.

Every line of modern woman's dress is designed to allure. Is it by chance that each detail is so nicely worked out—bust so arranged as to show its fullness—sometimes artificial—skirt and overcoat so fitted as to bring the region of the hips into striking relief, and exquisitely stockinged calves? Compare the dress of a nun, or a Chinese or Japanese woman with that of the American woman.

It may be objected that it is men who have designed these dresses but the women enter so fully into the spirit of wearing them, that one may say that the designers are simply their tools.

Consider also the flood of magazines, revues and plays with nude, or nearly nude women, all of which are intended to whip up the sex instinct of the men. Let anyone who has observed civilized men and boys absorbed in such sights imagine a native African looking at them for the same reason Imagine a Zulu Ziegfeld building a theatre for the exhibition of nude women. To get any patronage he would have to dress them. On the other hand, white men who live in such parts of Africa, are continually excited by looking at the nude young girls—a reason why the missionary is so anxious to get clothes on them. That civilized man is more sex conscious than primitive man is indisputable.

Another result of over-developed intellectuality and civilization, in general, is sexual impotence. Dr. William J. Robinson speaking as I have reason to believe, chiefly of white people says "My impression, startling as it may seem, is that at least fifty per cent of the adult population of any civilized community suffer with sexual impotence, or some other sexual disorder.

"A careful man does not form his impressions out of thin air and my impression certainly has a definite foundation. I know so many men who

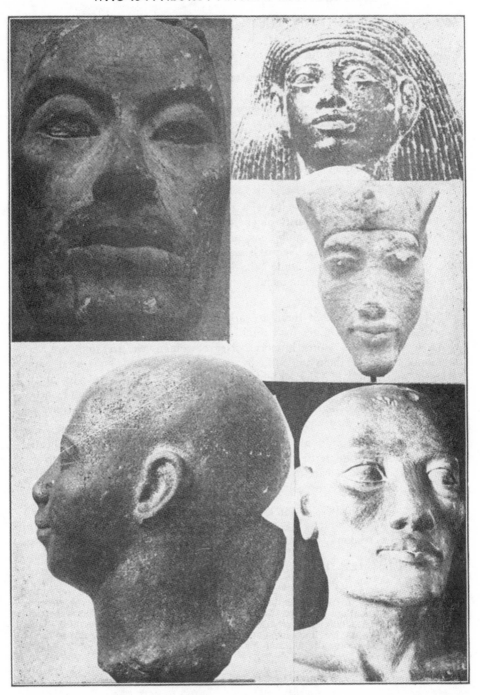

XXXI. Left upper: Ay, father of Queen Tiyi (Berlin Museum). Lower: Bust of Egyptian (Louvre3. Right (top): Senmut, architect of Queen Hatshepsut, and builder of the Temple of Deir-al-Bahri, Luxor (British Museum). Centre: Akhenaton—Amenophis IV (Courtesy, Metrop. Museum, New York). Below: The Scribe (Louvre).

are considered by everybody, including their family physicians, perfect specimens of manhood and who are to my knowledge sexually crippled that
I do not pay much attention to a man's exterior."[31]

This belief in the Negro's greater sexuality is undoubtedly responsible
for the charge that he is more immoral than white people. Conditions that
existed during slavery when the Negro woman's body was not her own; and
when marriage between slaves was not allowed, though sexual intercourse
between them was very much encouraged, have strengthened this belief. "An
intensely sensuous and lascivious race," says Shufeldt "A strong sex instinct
without corresponding self-control," says Davenport. And so on, with any
number of others.

However, here again we have a popular belief that is not capable of
proof. I believe that similarity of environment, training, and education will
create similarity of sexual inhibitions, or "morality" in any people, regardless
of color. The upper-class Negro is as secretive about his sex relations as
the upper-class Caucasian, while "the lower-classes," regardless of color, are
less so. In fact, the lower financial standing of the latter leaves them more
open to the public gaze.

I do not believe that there are any people more inherently moral than
others. As there are whites who think all Negroes immoral so there are Negroes who think all whites immoral. Negro women, we are told, are very
immoral. Some of them undoubtedly are. Nevertheless, I have seen white
women, apparently of "the better class" leaving on a journey, who at the
moment of the train's departure had to be torn out of their husband's arms,
and who, the same night had to be torn by the Pullman porter from the
arms of strangers they had met on the train.[32]

What Shufeldt said about Negro immorality can easily be duplicated
by what other white writers have said about white immorality. Ruth M.
Martin, who made a careful study of three old New England communities,
all white, says of the townspeople:

"Their sex appetite is appeased from adolescence and early in life they
are learned in this lore. They are not especially immoral but markedly unmoral. They respond to their sex desires which are noticeably unsup-

[31] Sexual Impotence (15th ed.), p. 396. 1930.

[32] Bureau of the Census, Prisoners, 1923, says in comparing the morality of
the different groups of women. "There were eight offenses for which the native
white females had higher percentages than the foreign-born whites or Negroes,
as follows: Fornication and prostitution, vagrancy, violating drug laws, keeping
house of ill-fame, adultry . . . " On this matter of immorality see also Havelock Ellis' Studies in the Psychology of Sex, Vol. 3, pp. 224-227 & Appendix B,
as well as the Report of the Chicago Vice Commission, 1911, or that of Baltimore,
or San Francisco.

pressed as naturally and freely as any animal. Physicians who attend them grant sex activity is for the community, as a whole, one of their few interests. Save for a few who seem exceptionally over-sexed, exceptionally erotic they do not appear to take an indecent attitude toward this part of their lives."[33] This is generally true not only of New Englanders but of humanity in general.

I lived, as I said, among the Negroes of Jamaica, West Indies, where the standard of morality was very low. Sometimes the illegitimacy rate was more than 70 per cent of the births, yet except at the capital, there was no commercialized vice or perversions as in Europe, and America.

The simple truth is that no people, no matter what its color, race, class, or religion, is any more moral than circumstances force it to be. Nature sees to that. All normal individuals experience sex hunger and the gratification of such depends chiefly upon opportunity.

Another statement often met with, even in scientific books, is that white women are attracted to Negro men principally because of the size of the organs of the latter. Now I have no means of knowing what really animated these women, yet one is led to ask, what in that case, attracts white men to Negro women, which is even more in evidence. Dr. Jacobus X and others relate how Negro women sometimes use astringents to accommodate white men[34]—a fact, incidentally true of some European women in cases where the muscles of the vagina have been weakened from childbirth or other causes. Might not the explanation for this interracial attraction be that certain individuals played out from long contact with the members of their own group, even as certain married couples are from a strictly monogamic regime, find sex contact with those radically different in "race" a whipper-up of the sex instinct—a psychic aphrodisiac, so to speak. Lester F. Ward rightly says that "the charm of sexual novelty" in this respect is a "product of the biological imperative."

Works of art and great accomplishments are blossoms of sex. No individual, however originally gifted, who expends his energies too freely in sex intercourse ever rose above the level of mediocrity. The most advanced members of the white group were forced into activities that gave them less time and thought for sex, hence their intellectual development. The group that does not draft most of its sex energy into useful, constructive channels, no matter what its "race," has no future.

---

[33] Intermarriage of Blood Relatives in Three Old New England Communities in Eugenics, Genetics and the Family. Internat. Eugen. Congress I, pp. 278-284. 1923.
[34] L'Art D'Aimer aux Colonies, p. 146. 1927.

At the bottom of the American race question is sex. Any number of white men, educated and otherwise, believe that the alleged sexual superiority of the Negro makes him more desirable to white women than themselves. Now there is a positive cure for this belief namely: Give the Negro better opportunities; load him with responsibility and make him use up his sexual powers that way. Very busy Negroes are no better lovers than very busy white men.

Finally, to put too much importance upon any single part of the human body—to adore it, to make a fetish of it whether it be genitalia, shape of nose, color of skin, or hair—is to reveal a wretchedly poor mentality. To do this is to ignore the profound truth that in the final analysis we like people best for their mental qualities, such qualities as make it agreeable for us to be in their company. And even in the case of those who make a fetish of any part of the body there will come a time when that, too, palls, and they will prefer those who are spiritually agreeable.

Chapter Seventeen

SEX: ITS COSMIC PURPOSE AND FUNCTION

"Like leaves on trees the race of man is found—
Now green in youth, now withering on the ground;
Another race the following spring supplies;
They fall successive and successive rise."
                                        —Homer—The Iliad

EVEN the most casual observer of Nature cannot help but be struck by the infinite variations in form and color, taste and sound, through which it manifests itself. No two individuals are alike, or no two nations, or two sides of one's face, or two fingerprints, or two handwritings, or two blades of grass, or grains of dust, or even two atoms. Everything in the world is different from everything else. Nature abhors duplication. This applies also to things even as they appear in time, as the very earth on which we live is different at this moment from what it was the preceding moment. Thousands who were alive as this is being read are now no longer so; while thousands of others have been born. One may in this way realize how very important is the role of variety in the life of man, the planet, the universe.

Variation in the inanimate is brought about in many ways—by the winds, the tides, the rotation of the earth, earthquakes, the northward drift of the sun's heat; the seasons. For the animate, however, there is a force for creating variety which is not to be found in the inanimate—a force that is more direct and rapid, namely, Sex.

Of course it is true that many of the lowest forms of life are asexual, that is, sexless. To reproduce themselves a segment of the creature detaches itself from the main body and grows. Imagine a sausage breaking away from the link, and growing into a link itself. But all these protozoa will, according to their kind, be found to be as nearly alike as it is possible for any two living things to be.

Higher in the scale and possessing a greater degree of variation are organisms that are hermaphrodite, so to speak, that is, each combines male and female. But highest in the scale and with a still greater degree of variation are those animals and plants in which the sexes are separated. The presence of the asexual or sexless seems to indicate that sex reproduction is not an absolute necessity for the continuance of life; hence sex reproduction must have some greater function and that is *Variation.*

Think of the fine exactitude with which the man eyes the woman and she, him. Eyes, nose, hair, teeth, size, color, each important, and often some minor part of the body being carefully appraised. Argument upon argument could be advanced to prove that mere satisfaction of the sexual appetite will not satisfy mankind. Who has not felt the pangs of jealousy, for instance?

The counter-argument of prostitution might be offered. For instance, I have seen soldiers and others standing in line to get into a house of prostitution both in Europe and America. But is this not a perversion of nature arising out of civilization, in which almost everything is commercialized? Was there a man among those waiting who would not have preferred a woman of his own choice?

An open example of sex selection even in prostitution is recorded by Herodotus. Each Babylonian woman, he says, was compelled to go to the temple of Venus Mylitta once in her life and there to consort with a stranger. Seated in rows the women waited, tin-cups in hand, while the men walked up and down the lines appraising them, and selecting the ones that pleased them by dropping a coin in the cup. A virgin so selected could refuse no one. Those with symmetry and beauty, says Herodotus, were often set free in a day, while the plain ones had sometimes to wait for "four years," because having once entered the temple no woman could leave until she had paid tribute to Venus, or rather her priests.[1] Even in houses of prostitution today men do make a choice.

Of all land animals, man is the one that has withstood Time with the least degree of physical change. All the others as the mammoth, mastodon, sabre-tooth tiger, the giant rhea, the tyrannosaurus, and giant armadillo, have either totally disappeared; have been replaced; or been modified greatly by such existing species as the elephant, the ostrich, the tiger.

Perhaps man's survival may be explained thus—: "Whenever he was forced into an unfavorable climate his superior intelligence came to the

1 Herodotus. Book 1, chap. 199 (Rawlinson).

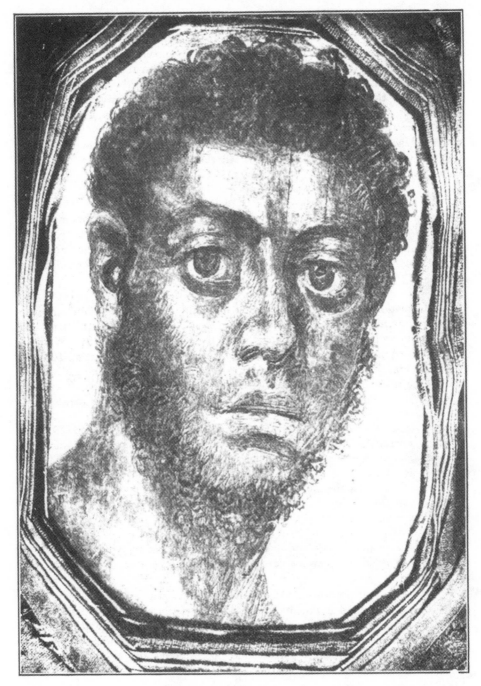

XXXII. Mulatto of Graeco—Roman Period (Moeller).

rescue. For while his physical body was dominated by the environment like that of the other animals, and was modified to a certain extent by it, he could, with his brain, create an artificial environment that offered a sufficiently strong resistance to the first. The result was that while the lower animals often perished, a new variety of mankind with changed ideas—caused by the new struggle—came into existence. These varieties in the course of time overflowed into other environments and by cross-breeding (exogamy) transmitted these qualities and experiences to still others. Of course, each variety selected from others only those ideas it deemed necessary for survival in its own environment. In the clash for supremacy there was always a conflict of ideas.

This theory is strengthened by a realization of the very important part that food plays in one's development. The difference between the energy of the new-born child and that of the grown man is almost solely the result of food that he has eaten. Food, in its turn, is the quintessence of common earth, as distilled by vegetable life, whose growth is yet more dependent on climate.

Climate is all pervading, affecting mankind in the minutest detail, even in the sound of the voice. The Easterner, Westerner, Northerner, and Southerner of the United States, have their respective accents. What is known as "race" is merely the genus, Man, manifesting itself in the form in which climatic environment has moulded him. Spengler was eminently right when he said that one's skeleton was but a part of the landscape. The body is, as it were, but the same clay in the hands of different climatic artists.

This fact is indisputable: The assimilation of variety in food, knowledge, contacts, is necessary for a high-grade of development individual or racial, moral or economic. The contrary, that monotony stultifies and stagnates—is equally true. Variety is the foul water that by running becomes pure; monotony is the pure water that by standing still, stagnates. Variety is the wise man who changes his mind; Monotony is the hide-bound fool that never does.

Home-keeping races and nations, like home-keeping youths, have ever homely wits. No one is ever greater than his contacts.

A very great portion of the advance the European has made over other varieties of mankind is due to his world-wide contacts. Where did William Jenny, inventor of the sky-scraper get his idea? From seeing the bamboo buildings of the Filipinos. The English people—the most widely travelled—leads or led all the white groups, having absorbed the culture and ideas

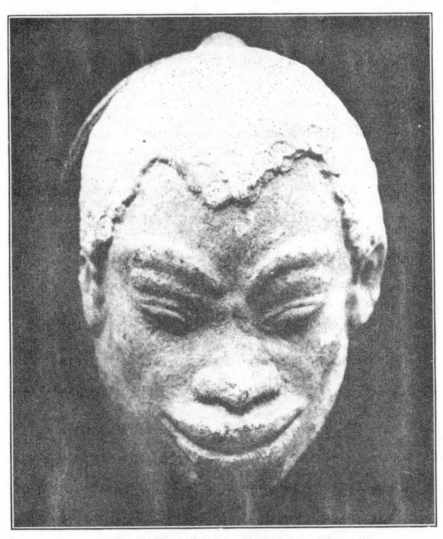

XXXIII.   Negro mask from Ancient Sicily (Greek).

of all other varieties. English, the most comprehensive language on earth, is a hodge-podge of the rest.

Mongrel Races The Best

As it is with languages so it is with peoples. The most advanced are the so-called mongrel or "impure" races. These have the greater proportion of human totality, that is, in their veins flow a greater variety of climatic accretion. The leading peoples of the world, today, are the mixed ones as the English, the French, the Americans and the Japanese. The English are a mixture of the ancient Mediterranean variety (the same stock from which it is said sprang Negros): Celts, Phoenicians, Africans, Asiatics, Romans, Jutes, Saxons, Normans, Gascons, and some twenty or thirty others.[2]

It happens to be that the most backward races of mankind are the purest, that is, those with the least variety of strains, as the Ainus of Japan, the Veddahs of Ceylon, the Andaman Islanders, the Bushmen of South Africa and Australia, and the Eskimos.

In America the purest "Anglo-Saxon stock" found in some of the New England States, as Aristook County, Maine; Windham County, Connecticut; in Clinton and Franklin Counties, New York; in Kentucky, Tennessee, Georgia, and North Carolina, is the most backward of all. In parts of the South it is a common sight to see young white girls with wash-board chests, instead of the flowing bosoms and well-developed breasts of adolescence; constricted pelves, unfit for bearing robust children; razor-backed men, whose vertebrae stand out like the beads on a Chinaman's abacus; stork-like necks with huge Adam's apples; skeleton-like arms, without biceps or triceps; and straight, thin legs without calves.

The same holds true of the poor whites of the West Indies of "pure" stock, as the "Red Legs" of Barbadoes; the "Cha Cha's" of St. Kitts and Tortola; and the "Poor Buckras" of Jamaica. These are chiefly the descendants of prisoners captured by the Roundheads, or those of the regicides sold into slavery by Cromwell and Charles II.

Insanity Among The Best New England Families

Upper-class whites who mate only among themselves also have a tendency towards degeneracy. Two noted psychiatrists, Dr. Abraham Myerson and Rosalie Boyle, have reported much mental instability among the "best" New England families.

2 Oakesmith, J. Race and Nationality, pp. 94-101. 1919.

Their findings are based on a study of the century-old case records in McLean Hospital, Belmont, Mass., one of the leading private hospitals of the country to which these aristocratic families have been sending their sick.

In only five years (1934-1938) they found 315 cases of insanity of which 235 were maniac-depressive and 80 of schizophrenia, or split personality in this hospital. "A study of distinguished American families," they say, "reveals a great deal of mental diseases if the term family is extended to include cousins to the third and fourth degree, uncles, aunts, grand-parents and great-grandparents."

Represented in the McLean Hospital were families who had furnished "several governors of Massachusetts. There have been a great many federal judges, including justices of the Supreme Court, numerous members of the Constitutional Congress and of the Senate and House of Representatives, which succeeded these bodies; Secretaries of State; ambassadors to great foreign powers; great and significant lawyers" as well as "founders of colleges. churches, business houses . . . the people of these families have built railroads, financed and carried through in important measure all of the great United States enterprises . . ."

Members of these families had also furnished "presidents of the United States, philosophers of international importance, writers who have founded schools of literature, scientists in every field from astronomy to chemistry, medical men galore . . ."

Interbreeding is thought by these two scientists as being the cause of the high percentage of insanity among these rich people. Such families marry among themselves to conserve their family wealth and power and "to build up dynasties which shall increase in power and in influence through what is believed to be proper mating and perhaps more relevantly the amalgamation of family fortunes." The rich, they point out, are suspicious, when it comes to contracting marriage, of the motives of those who are not rich. Therefore even cousins and double-cousins among them will intermarry.

Myerson and Boyle further pointed out significantly, "It is interesting to note how misleading the genealogies of these important families are so far as the incidence of mental disease is concerned. One can read the elaborate records collected in any genealogical study of a family and not find a single case of mental disease recorded despite the fact that a dozen or more branches of the family tree from time to time reposed within hospitals for mental disease. It may be stated without fear of contradiction that genealogies, as a whole, stress only assets, and very conspicuously and no doubt purposely neglect liabilities."[3]

Mental Defects Among Humbler New Englanders

Among New Englanders of humbler stock even worse conditions seem to exist. Ruth M. Martin, who investigated three old New England communities, which she calls X, Y, and Z, reports how in town Y marriage to anyone not belonging to the town was opposed. The first idea, she says, was "to keep property," such as old silverware and other heirlooms. People who married outside the town had things "made so miserable for them that they left the town in time." She adds, "No doubt Y is hopeless. It will in time accomplish its own extermination. Yet the town is a menace to the country for it is true that annually a few of the "prettier" girls or less feeble-minded boys do drift out into the surrounding towns and marry. Wherever they go their traits hold true and the menace is especially great in instances where a reasonably eugenic New England man sets aside his feeling about Y and marries a pretty Y girl. This girl practically always bears the man a large family of children and in a few instances are they other than true descendants of Y, feeble mentally, moron at most."

Similar conditions existed in the other two towns of one of which she says, "The pauper list . . . has as far back as record goes been unbelievable for the size of the population; in surrounding towns a by-word for genera-

---

[3] Amer. Jour. of Psychiatry, Vol. 98, No. 1. July, 1941, pp. 11-21. Also Woods, F. A. The Conification of Social Groups: Evidence from New England Families. First Internat. Eugenics Congress, pp. 312-328.

This neglecting of liabilities is very likely what happens in the classical comparison made between the Adamses of Massachusetts and the Jukes—the first furnishing so many distinguished individuals; the latter so many criminals and good-for-nothings. There is, without a doubt, a goodly number of mental defectives among the Adamses, not to mention those who wound up in prisons and police courts, but in their case their prestige and power fully permitted them to cover up, while the poverty of the Jukes left them open to the public gaze. In the case of the Adamses it would never have done to say anything bad about them. The papers would not have printed it.

An unbiased study of any family tree will show a certain percentage of delinquents and jail-birds. European jails hold more than a few descendants of royalty, one of whom, a Bourbon prince was sentenced in France for forgery about 1933. I could name a dozen kings of England, as Richard III or Henry VIII, who had they been private individuals, would have been hanged for their crimes. America, too, holds, more than one scion of royalty in her prisons.

The Adamses were more fortunate than the Jukes, that's all. Life started the former in the right groove; the latter in the wrong one. The money and the prestige of the Adamses served not only to keep them in respectable paths but as a cover-up. Incidentally "Jukes" was not the name of this family, thus persons with that name may not be related to it at all.

tions."[4] X-town, she says, is known as "suicide town." I have quoted else-where what this writer said of the great sexual immorality that prevailed in these old Anglo-Saxon towns.

Degenerates of Other States

Dozens of similar unfortunate white communities exist in the United States, not to mention families as the Jukes and Nams of New York, and the Kallikaks of New Jersey, which have furnished such a number of crim-inals and degenerates that they have become a marvel to eugenists. For in-stance, there are the Ishmaelites, as well as those in one Kentucky mountain town, which was studied by W. S. Anderson of the University of Kentucky. Dr. Estabrook of the Carnegie Institution, who studied the Ishmaelites, or Tribe of Ishmael, as they call themselves, says that they are descended from John Ishmael, a "diseased" white man, who went to Marion County, In-diana, in 1825 and married a half-breed Indian woman. It appears, also, that in the County were other cacogenic whites, who had drifted west after the Revolutionary War, and these all amalgamated with the descendants of Ishmael, who married among themselves until they numbered probably tens of thousands. In 1885, there were 6,000 of them. They have since spread into Kentucky, Illinois, Ohio, Michigan, Iowa, and Kansas.

Estabrook quotes McCulloch on one Ishmael family in the 1880's, "Since 1840, this family has had a pauper record. They have been in the almshouse, the House of Refuge, the Woman's Reformatory, the penitentiaries, and have received continuous aid from the township. They are intermarried with the other members of the group and with 250 other families. In this family history are murders, a large number of illegitimacies and of prostitutes. They are generally diseased. The children die young. They live by petty stealing, begging, ash-gathering. In summer they "gypsy," or travel in wagons, east or west."

Of the present Ishmaelites, Estabrook says, "There are three outstand-ing characteristics of the Tribe: pauperism, licentiousness, and gypsying . . . at one time the greater proportion of the women keeping houses of prosti-tution belonging to the Tribe. Several of these houses were famous in this region of the State (Indiana) . . . The Ishmaelites often used members of their own family as inmates of these houses. In one a woman and her two grand-daughters, while in several cases a woman and her daughters com-posed the personnel of the bagnio." "The Ishmaelites," he says "are con-tinuing to mate like to like and reproducing their kind . . . About 90

4 Intermarriage of Blood Relatives in Three Old New England Communities. First International Eugenics Congress, I, pp. 278-284. 1923.

per cent of the total group and even more are what we would call socially inadequate. The Ishmaels have been more or less under the public eye to a certain extent for about forty years specially in the cities and we do not find many among them who have reached the average class." Only about "2 or 3 per cent" reaches the standard set by the United States draft classification.[5]

As regards the Kentucky mountaineers above-mentioned Anderson says, "The in-and-in marriages, due in part to voluntary isolation and in part to the inability of the young people to find marriage partners outside their own relatives, have resulted in concentrating in their germ plasm the factors for chorea, ungovernable tempers, imbecility, violence, and general anti-social disposition." He adds, "Their sex appetite is their ruling passion." Their neighbors blame them for their degeneracy, says Anderson, but he "believes it is as natural as their uniform physical appearance of blue eyes and light hair and certain facial features."[6]

Mental And Physical Defectives In European Royalty

Inbreeding among civilized peoples seems to run true to form in both high and low society. In the supreme upper-crust we find like degeneracy. European royalty, the supposed cream of the cream not only of the white "race" but all humanity, is particularly noted for its mental and physical defectives—a fact especially true of the Hapsburgs, Bourbons, and the British royal family.

Queen Victoria of England, for instance, passed on the germs of severe haemophilia to one of her sons and two of her granddaughters, the Queen of Spain and the Czarina of Russia. Count Covadonga, son and heir of Alphonso XIII of Spain, died from the effects of this dread disease; while Alexis, son and heir of the Nicholas II of Russia, who was later killed by the Bolsheviks, was an invalid from it.[7]

---

5 The Tribe of Ishmael. First International Eugenics Congress, pp. 398-412. 1923.

6 The Effect of The Germ Plasm of Isolation in a Mountain Section—First International Eugenics Congress, L. 297-302. 1923.

7 Schienfeld, A. You and Heredity, p. 131. 1939; Haldane, J. B. S. Heredity and Politics, p. 88. 1938. Schienfeld shows in a startling, but very logical manner that but for this bad gene in Queen Victoria there might not have been a Russian revolution and the lives of the Czar and his family would have been saved. But for her son's illness, he says, the Czarina would have had no occasion to fall under the influence of Rasputin. Blood, it is said, will tell. And how it sometimes does. Queen Victoria was the highest of the high socially, the blue-blood of all the blue-bloods, but suppose Count Covadonga, instead of having had her as a great-grandmother, had had some healthy peasant woman instead, even a black one from the depths of Central Africa, would he not have been better off? The same holds true of the Czar Nicholas II, the illness of whose son, through this inherited disease, brought calamity on all his family.

XXXIV. Left to right: Peuhl girl of West Africa (the Peuhls are of Jewish Ancestry); Native woman of Timbuctoo; The King of Mossi, French West Africa, from a painting by Nivelk (note the resemblance to Mussolini); and centre lower, General A. Dodds, Senegalese quadroon, who rose to be commander-in-chief of the French Army, and was a member of the Supreme War Council (1914-1918).

Royalty, more than ony other group, has been forced through political and social interests, to marry within its own ranks. Almost every member of European royalty is at least a cousin of some degree to one another. Thomas Jefferson, speaking on "the habit of breeding kings," said: "While in Europe I often amused myself with contemplating the character of the reigning kings of Europe—Louis XVI was a fool of my own knowledge, and in despite of the answers made for him at his trial. The King of Spain was a fool, and of Naples the same. The King of Sardinia was a fool. All these were Bourbons. The Queen of Portugal, a Braganza, was an idiot by nature. And so was the King of Denmark. The King of Prussia, successor to the great Frederick, was a mere hog in body as in mind. Gustavus of Sweden and Joseph of Austria were really crazy and George of England, as you know, was in a straight jacket."[8]

Speaking of homosexuals among royalty, Havelock Ellis says. "Various kings and potentates have been mentioned in this connection including the Sultan Baber, Henri III of France; Edward II, William II, James I, and William III of England, and perhaps Queen Anne; George III, Frederick the Great, and his brother, Heinrich; Popes Paul III, Sixtus IV, and Jules II; Ludwig of Bavaria and others. Kings, indeed, seem peculiarly inclined to homosexuality."[9]

In royalty, one has, if anything as pure a race as it is possible to get. It is society's recognized highest, and would in all probability be something like what the right-wing eugenists would breed were they permitted a free hand.

Jews And Monotony In Environment

Another but much less glaring example of the result of much restricted environment and inbreeding in reflected in the mental instability of many Jews. According to the Medical Record[10] of 7,000 cases examined at the Clearing House for Mental Defectives in New York City, the Jews alone furnished 2,198, or only 834 less than such groups as the Anglo-Saxons, Celts, Teutons, Latins and Slavs combined. Even assuming that the Jews constituted a fourth of the city's population, thus outnumbering any two of the above-mentioned groups, the ratio for them in regard to the total population would still be very high.

---

8 Writings, etc., Vol. 5, p. 515. 1853. For later instances of this kind of mating among royalty see Princess Radziwill's The Royal Marriage Market of Europe. 1915. Such mating was stopped only by the last war. See also: Woods, F. A., Heredity in Royalty, 1906.

9 Studies in the Psychology of Sex, Vol. 2, p. 35. 1901.

10 February 16, 1918. Analysis by Dr. M. G. Schlapp and Alice E. Paulsen, pp. 269-275.

According to Fishberg, mental diseases occur more frequently among Jews than among the non-Jews." He attributes a high percentage of this "to marriage of near-kin" and to "identity of environment."

"Finally," says R. N. Salaman," it must be remembered that the Jewish community is a closed one. That is, it takes little or nothing from outside and is inbreeding." He adds "Jews certainly suffer from the same forms of nervous complaint to a much greater extent than others; neurasthenia, hysteria, and melancholia are the more common troubles." Salaman attributes it largely "to strain and tension induced by the constant fight to achieve success in a partly alien and almost wholly hostile atmosphere."[11]

Smalldon found that Jewish women had a much higher rate of puerpal mental illness than other women and adds, "This lack of mental stability rendering Jewish women to be particularly prone to be upset by the stress of pregnancy and childbirth is explained by A. Myerson as due to the gradual narrowing of the sphere of the Jew's activities by the hostile attitude of society, this leading to the development of an urban, sedentary and cerebral character at the expense of the body."[12]

Myerson, admitting that there is no question but that Jews have a higher percentage of mental diseases than others, says that as a Jew "familiar with the life and history of his people," he finds that it is due not to biological heredity but to persecution and the peculiar conditions under which Jews have been forced to live.[13] Under the American environment, he says, the Jew is changing mentally for the better, even though the dissolution of Jewish life in America is creating other problems.

But it might be asked whether the basis of this trouble is really only mental? The Negroes in America are much more repressed than the Jews and were quite as subject to pogroms and massacres as the Jews were in Poland and Russia. In America the Jew belongs to the white caste and enjoys all the privileges denied the Negro. The Negro, on the other hand, has less insanity and mental instability not only than the Jews but every other white American group, including the white Southerner, who according to Hoffman, exceeds him by four to one. And here I advance a theory import-

---

[11] Second International Eugenics Congress, p. 141. 1923.

[12] Psychoses in Pregnancy and Childbirth. Amer. Jour. of Psychiatry, July, 1940, p. 86.

[13] The 'Nervousness' of the Jew. Mental Hygiene (Quar.), Vol. 4, Jan., 1920. pp. 65-72. Klineberg apparently denies that Jews have a higher rate of mental diseases. He says that in 1917, the Jews, who were 25.8 per cent of the population of New York City had only 16.5 per cent psychopathic cases in the hospitals in 1918, and 14.5 in 1919. As for the whole state they had in 1917, 16 per cent of the population and only 11.6 of the total admissions He notes, however, the disinclination of the better off Jews to send their mentally unfit to public hospitals.

ant to my thesis, namely, that the Negro being nearer to the primitive, has in so far as it is possible to weigh group against group, a biologically fitter organism, which gives him a greater elasticity to stand up against adversity and persecution. As Joseph W. Burtt says the Negro "appears to be an enduring world race. His physical vitality, ready emotionalism, and joy in life show a vital youth as the hopelessness, lack of fecundity and joyless pursuit of materialism point to the declining age of more advanced nations."[14]

This seems to be true: In those diseases that are sociologic, that is, those caused by ignorance and bad living conditions, as tuberculosis, syphilis, and heart disease the Negro leads; in those that are metabolic, that is, those that show a general crack-up of the organism, as insanity, suicide, cancer, and infantile paralysis, the whites lead.[15]

In the case of the American Jew the question, therefore, is: Does the latter take more to heart the much fewer disadvantages he has in America as compared with those the Negro suffers than does the Negro his handicaps? If the answer is yes, only then can the greater mental derangement of the

14 Spiller, G. Interracial Papers, p. 323. 1911.
15 It is difficult to get mortality statistics that are nationally representative of whites and blacks. City, State, and U. S. census reports usually give deaths and hospital reports but many of those with these diseases may die of something else or do not go to public hospitals, etc. The most nearly representative report I know of is that furnished by U. S. Army statistics of the draft of 1917-18 However, even here any comparison made will be largely arbitrary since about 70 per cent of the Negroes have from an eighth to three-fourths or more white strain.

Love and Davenport, compilers of the statistics, found the Negroes exceeded the whites in the following diseases: Tuberculosis of the lungs, 2½ times; pneumonia 2⅕ to 4½; syphilis 4; and gonorrhea 2½ times. The venereal rate, in general, for Negroes in the last ten years was "a little less than double the rate for the whites." On the other hand, the whites had 3 times as much neurasthenia; 3 times as much mental derangement; twice as much alcoholism; and twice as much diabetes. The report adds that the uninfected Negro "has more stable nerves, better eyes, and metabolizes better. Thus, in many respects the uninfected colored troops show themselves to be constitutionally better physiological machines than the white man." (A Comparison of White and Colored Troops in Respect to Incidence of Disease. National Acad. of Sciences, Proceed, Vol. 5, 1919, pp. 58-67.) It will be interesting to know what the draft of World War II will reveal. Figures so far released show the Negroes still greatly ahead in venereal disease. (Britannica Year Book, 1943, p. 732.)

As regards suicide the white rate has always been higher than the Negro one. Hoffman, from figures furnished him by the Bureau of Census, reported for the 5-year period, 1921-25, white: 12. per 100,000; Negro 4.6 per 100,000. In 1924 the rate was white 13; Negro 3.6.

On the other hand, the American Negro rate is about three times that of the Negro in Jamaica, West Indies. Hoffman says, "In the island of Jamaica in 1926, in a total population of 930,000 there occurred only 10 suicides, or at a rate of 1 per 100,000. The population is almost entirely black except for about 10,000 whites. In the city of Kingston in a population of 66,000 there occurred one suicide during the year." (Suicide Problems, p. 15. 1927).
See also Notes on Chapter 17 in the Appendix.

XXXV. Senegalese Sharpshooters Parading in France. Numbers of these Africans had children by French women. (See Sex and Race, Vol. I. Chap. 19).

Jew be charged to mentality induced by persecution rather than to inbreeding and city life.

In any case inbreeding undoubtedly has the same effect on a group as it has on the individual, but that in the group it takes longer to make itself felt. Long continued mating among members of the same group, especially if it is a small group becomes in time a sort of third cousin to incest as the "race," nation, or tribe is but the individual expanded. Some African and Australian tribes to prevent this compel their young men to marry outside the tribe.

"Pureness" of blood and inbreeding are not of themselves, apparently a cause of degeneracy however. The Pitcairn Islanders, a people of white and black ancestry, are inbred and by all accounts are healthy. An inbred people who live in primitive surroundings with good air' and food seem to be able to perpetuate themselves for centuries. But civilized man with the bad air of cities, artificial food, drinks of high alcoholic content, over-work and over-study and late hours, degenerates no matter what his "race."[16]

Individuals with a tendency to neurosis as the result of over-civilization if shifted while still very young to a more natural and healthful environment, like the Canadian Rockies, or the mountain regions of the West Indies, would very likely develop normally. In any case the cause of their neuroses, outwardly, at least, would be removed. As for their children they certainly would be an improvement. In the 1920's when the Jews abounded more than now in the neighborhood of 110th Street and Fifth Avenue, New York City, I used to walk into Central Park where they were sitting on the benches to observe them. Rarely ever had I seen poorer specimens of humanity. They showed the effect of all the centuries of persecution in Europe. How different are the younger generation of Jews one sees nowadays in New York City? A freer, more healthful life in America seems to have done wonders for them. I have also strong reason to believe that the figures and the statements I have just cited on Jewish insanity do not apply to the younger generation but to the older Jews who migrated here from the Old World.

---

16 Health is more natural to man than disease. Given the proper food, rest, and altitude, illness will be rare and health plentiful. I once lived in a mountain region of Jamaica of about 4,000 feet altitude. Scattered about this region were some 80,000 persons, and the general health was so good that the single doctor in the area had to move to the nearest town 18 miles away. There was but a single drug store, and midwives, who were sometimes illiterate, took care of all births. The soil was very fertile and little work was necessary to produce food. The thermometer never fell below 70; the days were agreeable with no humidity; and woolen clothing was unnecessary. Nearly everyone was in bed by nine o'clock. Not one in a hundred wore shoes. Whites and blacks were about equally healthy.

Man is inherently nomadic. He is "a ranging animal." He must have change—change that replenishes the chemicals in his blood—change that stimulates thought. Like the corpuscles in his blood, he must circulate if he is to keep mentally and physically fit. Solitary confinement is the deadliest form of punishment in prisons and sometimes drives its victims insane.

Agitation for race purity is really agitation for isolation and stagnation. which led one cynic to remark that he certainly hoped the Southern whites would really get the race purity for which some are clamoring. The group that agitates for isolation, social or racial, is mentally the same as the individual who seeks isolation from his own group.

The finest specimens of wheat, flowers, orchids, pigs, horses, bees, have been produced by crossing. The hybrid Italian bee is very much superior to both its pure Italian and its black parents.

Luther Burbank, the great botanist, held that the hybrid was the most efficient of human types. In his chapter on "The Mingling of the Races" he declared that there was an advantage in merging an "absolutely wild strain with one that long over-civilized has lost its virility,"[17] and that among the descendants of such are likely to be some who are stronger and better than either parent.

Nietzsche, himself, whom the Hitlerites were very fond of quoting, says, "Where races are mingled we find the sources of all great civilizations. Maxim: Have nothing to do with anyone who participates in the preposterous race-humbug."

The lowest humans, like the lowest animals, are those in which the desire for variety and the capacity for receiving sensations are weakest. The recognized highest are those in which these factors are so strong, so universal in scope that their possessors, as Shakespeare, Leonardo de Vinci, and Victor Hugo are capable of expressing the sensations of a vast number of individuals regardless of "race" or environment.

Effects of Monotony on the Social Life of the Individual

Nor is the urge for variety confined to the sex relation. In every other phase of life it is manifest. Give any one his heart's desire and that alone for a sufficiently long period and he will get to hate it like poison. Bliss, paradise, itself, soon becomes a bore when there is nothing else. That is why popular songs soon become as much avoided as they were once enjoyed. Excess of pleasure cloys and straightway becomes pain.

---

17 Training of the Human Plant, p. 9. 1907. Burbank excludes the Negro and the Mongolian. His prejudice, however, does not invalidate this important truth. I have discussed this elsewhere.

Humanity has evolved through pleasure and pain. Nature inflicts pain on us and when the environment becomes so improved that there is a minimum of pain we create tragedies to inflict it vicariously. At a performance of Quo Vadis I saw some women weeping and evidently suffering, yet they stayed on. At an aviation meet in Chicago, I noticed that there was general disappointment because no one fell, yet the members of that crowd might not have been in the least cruel or unsympathetic. They were merely craving excitement.

Still another example of the necessity for variety is the case of the very rich with a poor grade of mentality. Having almost everything that wealth can command, almost without effort, but barred by their limited intellect from ascending into that realm of diversity to be found in those pursuits that are mental rather than physical they suffer terribly from boredom and as Schopenhauer says flit from country to country seeking relief as a beggar goes from door to door seeking alms. Sometimes they kill themselves from sheer satiety, or because they are denied something money cannot get.

Many rich women are like sitting-hens that set up a shrill squawk at the approach of anyone. The King, in Ecclesiastes, having sounded all the pleasures of life found them vanity and a vexation of the spirit. Even variety in time is boring. Man is the dissatisfied animal, par excellance. He is not happy and nothing can make him so for long. He will interrupt his moments of supremest happiness to build himself castles of doubt and fear.

With this exposition of the part that variety plays in the affairs of the individual and the race the path has been prepared to answer the question why many Caucasians desire a union with the Negro. It is necessary to bear in mind what was said of the more primitive natural endowment of the Negro.

White Mankind, An Evolution Of Brown One

The Caucasian, as was said, is now thought by most of the leading anthropologists, to have been brown-skinned, having been bleached by his environment after the manner of green plants when placed in a cellar. Chlorophyll in plant is really analagous to pigment in man. Every known color is a product of sunlight plus, of course, some indefinable quality within us. Without sunlight, man and plant grow pale.

That the Caucasian was also different in facial contour seems to be proved by the bio-genetic law, that is, in the nine-months' period of gestation there is a full recapitulation of the process that once took perhaps billions of years to accomplish, in such the same manner as by the telephone, the printing press, or the airship, we can accomplish in one minute what it took our ancestors thousands of years to build up painfully. Or again, how after having learnt our alphabet with difficulty we can later scan the whole page of a book with less effort than it took us to master a single letter; or how after a very difficult book has been once written and set up in type, millions of copies can be reproduced from the mold without effort. Once any process is established the rest is routine.

Evolutional Process in the Womb

Beginning as an egg the child at stages of its development resembles a worm, a serpent, a fish, a dog and an ape, respectively. A good deal of the time it has a tail, which has even been known to remain after birth, and into adult life. A two-inch tail has been known, says Dorsey. This process is regarded as proof that man passed along the main trunk of evolution, on which the so-called lower animals remain only as branches. The newly-born child is really earliest man, symbolically as well as actually. For instance, he goes at first on all fours like an animal, and little by little assumes the upright pose.

It is sometimes impossible to tell by the features of the newly-born child whether it is Caucasian, Negro or Mongolian. No matter how acquiline its nose may be later, at birth it is as flat as the ape's; however thick its lips may be later, at birth it is as thin as the ape's. As regards hair, all babies, when born with hair on their heads, have straight hair, the kink in the Negro's developing later. Nor is there much difference as to color, the black or the white coloring as the case may be, coming with the years, which is perhaps proof that earliest man was neither black nor white, but something more of a mulatto color, and that a black skin and a white one are later evolutions.

In cold countries whiteness of skin develops faster in the infant; while blackness develops slower there; and the converse in warm lands. "It appears" says Davenport, "that the proportion of black in the skin increases to about the age of ten or twelve years and then slowly diminishes."[18]

The new-born child, as earliest man, will, in the course of the years then go through that other evolutionary process, a very minor one, called "race" which was evolved through his particular progenitors having lived for hundreds of thousands of years in some one environment. That is, if the parents are Negro, it will acquire full lips and spiral hair, or other Negroid characteristics; if Caucasian, the infant will acquire Caucasian characteristics.

[18] **Heredity of Skin-Color in Negro-White Crosses**, p. 7. Carnegie Instit. Pub. No. 188.

Chapter Eighteen

THE UNIVERSAL DECAY OF EMPIRES—
FUNCTION OF THE UNDERMAN

"The most civilized people are as near to barbarism as the most polished steel to rust. Nations have only a superficial brilliancy."—Rivarol.

"The ultimate tendancy of civilization is towards barbarism."—Hare

"The economic man has replaced the spiritual man. Everything is cracking."—Lin Yu Tang.

WHAT was said of the individual's passing away and the infant (symbolically primitive man) taking his place, is also true of the race. That peoples who start on the road to civilization are headed for eventual decay had already been recognized by Lucretius, Roman Poet of the century before Christ. He says in De Rerum Natura: "They procured huts and skins and the woman united to the man came to dwell in the same place with him and when the pure and pleasing connexions of indiveded love were known and they saw a progeny spring from themselves then first the human race began to be softened and civilized. For fire now rendered their bodies less able to endure the cold under the canopy of heaven and love diminished their strength."[1]

Oswald Spengler, German philosopher, has developed this thought of Lucretius in his "Decline of the West." He shows how civilizations follow the same natural process as the individuals of which they are composed. "Every Culture." he says, "passes through the age-phases of the individual man. Each has its childhood, youth, manhood, and age." Some of the ancient civilizations, he says, as Egypt, India, and Islam, continue to show signs of life but they are like "worn-out giants of the primeval forest still thrusting their decaying branches to the sky."

He pictures poetically and beautifully the life process of Cultures thus:

"Over the expanse of the water passes the endless wave—train of the generations. Here and there bright shafts of light broaden out, everywhere dancing flashes confuse and disturb the clear mirror, changing, sparkling, vanishing. These are what we call the clans, tribes, peoples, races which unify a series of generations within this or that limited area of the historical sur-

[1] De Rerum Natura, Book V, 1010-1017.

XXXVI. Negro Athletes of Paris, France.

face. As widely as these differ in creative power, so widely do the images that they create vary in duration and plasticity, and when the creative power dies out, the physiognomic, linguistic and spiritual identification marks vanish also and the phenomenon subsides again into the ruck of the generations. Aryans, Mongols, Germans, Kelts, Parthians, Franks, Carthaginians, Berbers, Bantus are names by which we specify some very heterogeneous images of this order.

"But over the surface, too, the great Cultures accomplish their majestic wave-cycles. They appear suddenly, swell in splendid lines, flatten again and vanish, and the face of the waters is once more a sleeping waste."[2] He predicts the final downfall of Western civilization in the twenty-first century.

Why Do Civilizations Decline?

The question is: Why is it that civilized groups, in spite of their superior knowledge for the preservation of life seem even less able than primitive groups to perpetuate themselves?

Here are a few of the civilizations, racial, religious, national, that have passed away or declined:

In Africa: Egypt, Ethiopia, Meroe, Thebes, Zymbabwe, Carthage, Songhoi, Mellistine, Morocco, Bornu.

In Asia: Accadia, Assyria, Babylonia, Scythia, Phoenicia, Medo-Persia, Judea, Mohammedan, Sassanid, Punjab, Dravidian, Aryan, Cambodia.

In Europe: Mycenae, Macedonia, Greece, Sparta, Rome, Byzantium, The Golden Horde, Moroccan Spain, Spain, Portugal, Netherlands, Turkey in Europe, with the British and the French Empires, probably the next to go.

In America: Mexico, Guatemala, Yucatan, Peru.

In Oceania: Java, Sri-Vishaya, and Majapahit.

To all of these add a host of minor ones as Etruria, Khotan, Khmer, Venice, Vizyana-ghar, and those other probable thousands that lie unexplored in Asia and Africa, or are buried under the floors of the Atlantic, the Pacific, and the Indian Oceans.

Here were civilizations that were as haughty in their day as the great ones of our time.

This law of decadence becomes more strikingly apparent when we recall that it is usually the most civilized, that is, the most developed portion of any civilization, that is the first to decay, and that its place is usually taken by the lower class which has been gradually working its way upward like oil

---

[2] Decline of the West, p. 106. 1932. See also Briffault, R., Decline and Fall of the British Empire. 1938; Nitti, F., The Decadence of Europe; and Volney's Ruins of Empires.

from the bottom of a well. Plato might have had this in mind when he said that every king could count slaves among his ancestors and every slave could also count kings among his, that is, the descendants of the slaves had become kings, and those of the kings had become slaves.[3]

Lester F. Ward expresses much the same when he says, "The history of social classes furnishes to the philosophical student of society, the most convincing proof that the lower grades of mankind have never occupied these positions on account of any inherent incapacity to occupy higher ones. Throughout antiquity and well down through the Middle Ages the great mass of mankind were slaves. A little later they were serfs bound to the soil. Finally with the abolition of slavery, the fall of the feudal system and the establishment of the industrial system, this great mass took the form of a proletariat, the fourth estate, considered of so little consequence that they are seldom mentioned by the great historians of Europe. Even at the close of the eighteenth century when the greatest of all political revolutions occurred it was only the third estate that was at all in evidence—the business class, bourgeoisie or social mesoderm. This class has been looked down upon and considered inferior and only the lords spiritual and temporal were regarded as capable of controlling social and national affairs. This class is now at the top. It has furnished the world's brains for two centuries, and if there is any intellectual inferiority, it is to be found in the poor remnant that still calls itself the nobility in some countries."[4]

Wherein lies the principle for the universal decay and passing of empires, so eloquently depicted by Count Volney?

War, absorption and economic pressure are the answer for most of them. But as regards the most powerful ones, as Rome, that lasted for more than a thousand years, the cause is also to be found in the only link between earliest man and the people of today—the power to procreate, especially under civilized conditions.

All human organizations have a core, and begin usually as an idea in one man's brain, recent examples being Mussolini and Hitler. This core gathers other individuals around it until it becomes a power. But the individuals of which that power is composed die, and if the power itself is to continue and to grow stronger, it must be continually reinforced by new individuals until it becomes, perhaps, a mighty empire. To retain its power the core (or mother country) must remain virile and like the heart it is, it

---

3 Plato says in *Theatetus*, "Every man has had countless myriads of forefathers among whom in every case are found rich and poor, kings and slaves, both Greeks and Barbarians, recurring again and again." May I also call attention to what I said on this in Sex and Race, Vol. 1, p. 14. 1941.

4 Applied Sociology, p. 97. 1906.

must be strong enough to pump blood to all parts of the empire. But the moment it weakens, it begins to lose its influence in its colonies.

And the core inevitably weakens. Old nations, like old families and old persons lose the power and the desire to procreate. They become decadent, their power declines and they die. Perhaps it is, at bottom, but a manifestation of the law of gravity, whose tendency is to pull everything to the bosom of the earth and make it one with that. Whatever goes up will come down.

The same is true of localities within the mother country itself, examples of which can be found in even a new country like the United States. Virginia, the oldest and once the most powerful of the states, was superseded by New England, which later yielded to New York, New Jersey and Pennsylvania. Now intellectual and industrial energy seem to be shifting westward, at least that is the opinion of J. McKeen Cattell who says, "The situation in New England is ominous for the future. Every state has lost and it appears that the rural population is becoming intellectually sterile . . . Analagous conditions obtain in all the New England States and southward along the Atlantic. The losses of New York and New Jersey and Maryland in spite of, or it may be, because of their enormous increase in wealth are startling. Pennsylvania and Delaware are almost stationary."[5] Chicago which is less than a century old, is already the second largest city in the union. With the richness of the Middle West to draw from and its Great Lake ports together with the growing importance of the airplane, it may yet be America's largest city.

Whoever reflects however little on life cannot help but be struck with the tremendous conflict that reigns within Nature, and even in his own breast where he first becomes conscious of it. Life is precious to everything that moves: nerves of beasts, as those of mankind, are most delicate and susceptible to pain, yet throughout animate Nature there are forms of life, like the tiger, lion, wolf, eagle, so constructed that they can exist only by eating others like the deer, the giraffe, the rabbit, the dove. In the sea, the stronger fishes eat the weaker who are just as fond of life as they. The weaker insects are eaten by the stronger ones, who in turn are eaten by the birds, and so on and on. At the base of all is the mineral, from which the vegetable derives its nutriment. And let it not be thought that the mineral is lifeless. Certain minerals like mercury, molten metal, and nitro-glycerin are more sensitive than the most sensitive nerve. Small wonder that Schopenhauer when he pondered on this universal rending of the tissues of the weak by the strong cried out in bitterness; "A God that could have created a world such as this must have been tormented by the devil."

5 American Men of Science, p. 1123. 4th ed. 1927.

That this conflict is universal and not merely confined to this planet is evident. It inheres in the very nature of things for in the beginning human life was not so abundant as now, hence death could not have arisen as the result of over-crowding. Whatever it be one fact is evident; this conflict rages throughout Nature. The herb lives on the earth; the herbivora devours the herb; the carnivora preys on the herbivora, and man preys on all, for food, clothing, and shelter.

But man also is subject to the natural law; he is as much a part of Nature as the earth he treads on. Hence, as there is no form of life higher than man, stronger man preys on weaker man. And going still further one side of one's personality dominates the other. It has been said that one man is another man's devil. Far truer is it to say that each man is his own devil. "I, myself, am heaven and hell," said Omar Khyyam. Man wars with himself and with other men to preserve the eternal duality.

The deadliest form of the conflict and process of extermination within a civilization lies in the conflict between the two creative forces—Sex and Intellect.

Let us consider some of the more important phases of this conflict.

First, the antagonism between the sexes. Man represents what may be called the intellectual principle, and woman the sexual principle. Among the world's great thinkers are to be found few, if any of the world's great lovers. Kant, one of the greatest, ignored women all his life. Others, already cited, have spoken out openly against them, or have found them, like Shakespeare and Baudelaire, a pestiferous necessity at best.

Throughout Asia and even in the greater part of Europe woman occupies a position of inferiority, in all the world for that matter. There is no tribe, however degraded, in which woman is not exploited and even scorned as Lady Morgan charged. In China, girl babies were thrown into the canal in the same manner, and for precisely the same reason, that the Occidental drowns female puppies and kittens. Man has a certain antagonism for woman and but for his sexual needs, all but the most man-like females would soon be crowded out of existence. This is why woman are best treated in those countries in which they are in the minority. Men, even of the most primitive groups, have retreats to which no woman can penetrate. Civilized man has his monasteries, as that of Mt. Athos. As for the female retreats, as nunneries, they were probably originated by men, too. In short, this evidence of sex antagonism is to be found to a greater or less extent among all peoples and in all ages.

This, however, is but a milder phase of the conflict, for when the protagonists of either sex have said their last word it will be found that the sexes must get along somehow. Far worse is the havoc that the intellectual development plays with these qualities developed within the race when it had to put up its strongest battles against the mighty forces of Nature and the wild beasts. It is not unlikely, as Lucretius said, this softening process began when man first used fire to help keep his blood warm.

Intellectual development and Sex are forked streams, originating in the same reservoir of energy. Hence, whenever one of the streams increases in volume, the other, except in rare individuals, becomes correspondingly weaker.

Sex perpetuates animate Nature in the same manner that food sustains the individual. Intellect, the lesser creative force, draws from sex the greater. Great, prolonged effort, physical or intellectual, weakens the sexual powers. Professional athletes are all but emasculated. Intellectual effort, being creative, satisfies some individuals. The sexual powers of Sir Isaac Newton, St. Thomas Aquinas, Swedenborg, Kant and Carlyle, for instance, were completely drained by their great intellect, and sublimated into knowledge.

Intellectual creations may be described as imitations of Nature, while pictures and beautiful poems to Nature, are but flatteries, that is, they are non-creative so far as the actual reproduction of life is concerned. In short, art is a process of eating the food out of the pantry and then replacing it with pictures, carvings, or descriptions of it. All substantial creations come from the womb; the mother is really the only genuine artist.

The above is a generalized view of the conflict between Sex and Intellect. Let us now consider it in its application to the every day life of the civilized individual.

As intellect develops, self-consciousness increases. This means a heightening of individuality, and a lessening of the herd instinct. Most intellectuals are individualists, while the majority of mobs and reform movements are composed of the unthnking masses who flock together to get what they think they want.

The individualist aims to live for himself rather than the group or the future generation. With him it is after me the deluge. The result is, that sex among other things, becomes for him solely an instrument of pleasure. that is, contraception, or what is popularly known as birth control is resorted to. Added to this also is that which is still more decadent: intellect, the lesser creative force, now uses sex as a medium of expression with a result that sex is stimulated by means of stories, plays, pictures, music, dances, drugs, and styles of dress. All of this is intended solely for pleasure of the individual. Lust, to use an old fashioned term becomes, in short, the sole motive of the sex expression.

"Lust" to my thinking, lies not so much in frequency, as in the desire to prevent conception. The desire to procreate and the desire to produce works of art are at bottom the same, particularly as the former applies to woman.

 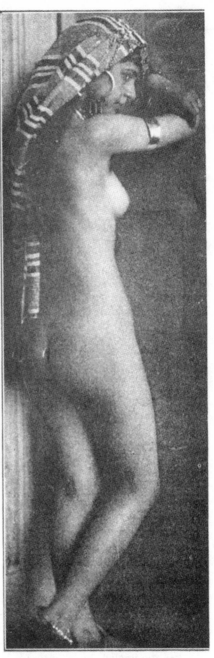

XXXVII. African Girl of Shapely Physique (Frobenius). Quadroon girl of Algeria.

The young genius restrained from producing children of the brain chafes and frets in the same manner as the motherly woman checked in bringing forth those of the womb. Indulgence in either of these forms of "procreation" would mean, therefore, that energy in the respective instances, was directing itself into different channels, that is, the brain and the genitals. The amount of indulgence in either case would depend therefore upon the capacity of the individual. Even as the real glutton is not the one who eats his fill, however much it be, but rather he who disgorges to eat again—as the old Romans used to do—so "lust" lies not in the volume of sex indulgence, but in the attempt to prevent conception. This, let me say, is not an attempt to pass upon the right or wrong of contraception.

There is at bottom no real difference between a prostitute who keeps herself free from disease and that of the society dame who will not have children; the difference is an esthetic one and lies solely in the degree of privacy and in the discrimination. Your cultured New Englander or New Yorker is thus no more moral than your packing-house Pole, plantation Negro, or ghetto Jew. Here again is no attempt to prove that the latter are superior to the former; they are only more unthinking, more natural.

The lower animals with but a flicker of intellect are with the exception of monkeys in captivity and dogs but little given to sex perversion. They live for the continuance of the species.

Race Perpetuation and "Lower" Classes and "Races"

Intellectual development decreases desire for offspring. Civilized man, especially of the large industrial centres, finds children either an expense or a nuisance, sometimes both. Women shun the trouble of parturition and child-bearing, wishing to preserve their figures and their freedom. That a very large number of women have even one child is due to the compelling force of destiny—the merest fluke, as no stone was left unturned to keep back the little one.

Ignorant persons, like the lower species of animals, are the most prolific: educated ones the least. A study of primitive peoples reveals the great importance they place on child-bearing, bachelors and barren women being regarded with abhorrence.

From time immemorial it is through the less educated that the race has been carried on. College-bred men and women are noted for the fewness of their offspring.[6] Among the highly individualized types there is also the poodle, a creature which bears the same relation to the dog family as its mis-

6 See Huntington, E., Builders of America, especially Appendix, pp. 333-341. 1927.

tress does to the human one. In Europe the birthrate is greatest in the most backward parts and lowest in the most advanced.

Nor is this disinclination to breeding confined to the women. The intellectual, the artist, and the business man all have a tendency to shun the maternal woman and her simpler, often nagging ways, for the fast woman—the type with the cocktail glass, the cigarette and the abundant display of well-stockinged legs, the kind that shuns maternity. "The atttraction toward prostitutes," says Bloch, "is one of the most remarkable phenomena in the psyche of modern civilized man; it is the curse of the evolution of civilization." This is true, not only of ours but of every other civilization on record. The preference of the cultured Greeks, Hindus, and Romans for the company of the hetaira, or intellectual prostitute, is well known. Rome, Greece, Corinth, Ephesus, ended their days in a glorious outburst of licentiousness.

Homosexuality and other forms of sex perversions, very little practiced by primitive peoples, become also a marked feature of civilized peoples. The fondness of the Greeks for young boys can be matched in any great civilization today. The same holds true of the women. In many of our large cities in Europe and America, the danger of the young girl lies no longer alone in her pursuit by the Don Juans but by the Donna Juanas. In some European cities sapphic clubs exist openly.

When women entered the intellectual and industrial field her sex and her intellect also came into conflict and it was to be expected that some of them would have as their slogan. "We no longer need men." Naturally having children is the last thought of this type.

Intellect, in short, reveals to man, the apparent nullity of life, its lack of final purpose, and this terrible disclosure acting upon his emotions destroys, consciously and unconsciously, the desire to live on in his offspring. The tendency of civilized man has been at all times to look after himself and to let Nature, so far as the continuance of the species is concerned, go hang herself. The slogan is eat, drink, and be merry, for tomorrow you die to stay dead forever.

Lust, that is, prevention of conception, is to Nature at large what alcohol is to the stomach of the individual. Both are not only powerless to sustain life but are injurious. Sex perversion (and in that term is included all the many forms that man uses to gratify the sexual impulse except the normal one) pleases the individual but it is to Nature what morphine or opium is to the individual—pleasing to the nerves but adding nothing to their sustenance.

Another phase of this conflict by no means to be overlooked—since its action is more direct—is industrialization, the drawing off of population from primitive and rural surroundngs, whence comes all of our food, except fish.

From 1900 to 1910 alone the urban population of the United States increased three times that of the rural. In 1910 the urban exceeded the rural population by 2,098,586. In 1940 the urban excess was 17,178,129 or 56.5 per cent of the whole, an increase of 7.2 over 1930. More than 90 per cent of New Englanders are town-dwellers, while the majority of the people of New York live in New York City. Western Europe is even more urbanized than the United States, a tendency greatly increased in both areas by the second world war.

Industrialization, with its crowding in cities, and its low wages, is also responsible for the production of the mentally and physically defectives, who, with the aid of modern medicine and hospitalization, are enabled to propagate their kind, thus inoculating the coming generations, and progressively weakening them. Man was made to live in the woods and wilds, not in dove-cotes, called flats.

Still another phase is the tendency of the woman to leave the home for the factory and the office; and the aversion of the salaried and the intellectual woman for marriage. In countries with a low degree of culture it is a disgrace not to be married, and a worse one to be childless. One doesn't have to be old to remember when this was true of the leading civilizations.

So-called feminism is yet another. Under its influence woman is becoming increasingly masculine. As women sometimes grow a beard and become more masculine in their features after their child-bearing days are over, so do young women age in their outlook on life in the case of the advanced nations. One may commonly see girls with bobbed hair and hard man-like faces, grim with signs of commercial struggle, in any large city. In fact some are female only so far as the primary sexual characters are concerned. So far as the continuance of the race is concerned the woman who never bore a child is, so far as this function is concerned, a man.

The above are some of the principal and inevitable causes that make for decadence. Others could be named, as the impoverishment of the soil by long continued usage, but enough has been said, I think, to show that civilization means not only a drawing off from the reservoir of Nature but also a hostility and an inability to return anything to the reservoir. Consequently as the reservoir must be fed by new streams, if it is not to go dry, even so must the civilization be reinforced by a new human supply, possessing not only a primitive and unperverted sexual vigor, but with a weak degree of individualism and intellectual forethought, and still possessing the primitive desire for offspring. Such primitive peoples are in a sense related to developed peoples as the children of a community are to their elders.

That the most advanced European nations have been declining for some time in spite of their superior medical knowledge, and other methods for race preservation will hardly be denied. Their birth rates have fallen off greatly. They are getting weak at the core.

With a lower birth rate they could send fewer men to their colonies, which were their main support. The result is that the administration of those colonies must be left more and more to the natives.

Take the case of Great Britain which was the leading colonial power. In 1870, the birth-rate in the United Kingdom was 34.1 per 1,000. It fell steadily until 1928 when it had dropped fifty per cent. In England and Wales it fell even lower.[7]

France is the next leading colonial power. Her case is even worse. In 1929 the number of deaths in France actually exceeded the births. She had a population decrease of 70,205 that year. The first World War accentuated every tendency of failing fertility in all the countries of western civilization, with the possible exception of Italy, where the quality from lack of proper nourishment was poor. World War II, with its rationing and near starvation has lowered the physical fibre of all the European nations.

On the other hand, the birth rate of the darker peoples continues to increase. Within the past twenty-five years the rise of some of them have been phenomenal, and since white civilization is really built upon the backs of the darker races, it means that as the latter increase in strength they are going to throw off more and still more of the load. England, even before the second world war was forced to abandon extraterritoriality in China. India and most of Africa are now republics.[8]

Nature—The Eternal Cannibal

The first essential for the continuance of a civilization therefore is keeping up its birth-rate. This the most advanced portion of any civilization cannot, or will not, do. A fresher, more primitive human supply is necessary as a reinforcement.

To summarize:

Beginning with crude matter, forms of life, in ascending scale, prey

[7] Statistical Abstract United Kingdom, 1929. Also O. C. Beale's Racial Decay. 1911.

[8] In 1923 I wrote: "White Imperialism is on the decline. The European intruder in Asia will be forced out before the end of the century. World dominance, as based on whiteness of skin, reached the summit of its power on July 28, 1914. On July 29, it started slowly but surely on the down grade, back to the obscurity whence it had emerged in the 16th Century."

When that time comes we shall revert to those human values that held in ancient Egypt and Rome, and particularly under early Islam, where man, white or brown, black or yellow, if he had the innate ability, whether it was for good or evil, had equal opportunity to rise to the top.

on other forms. Stronger forms of Nature devour and digest the weaker while intellect, its most powerful manifestation, preys upon and consumes, as it were, the body of man, the next highest form.

Civilization, then, is a process of digestion. It is to Nature at large what digestion is to the individual. As the individual puts food into its stomach and digests it, even so does the omnipotent force, called Nature, place man in its stomach and digests him.

As the food in the stomach of the individual is mixed and changed, the chyle, or essence, going to the nourishing of the body while the waste is expelled, even so it is in the cosmic process. The chyle from Nature's digestion is intellectual development as seen in skyscrapers, railways, paintings, literature.

The dead, or decayed races, nations, individuals, are the excrement. By their decay nourishment is provided for future generations, who are but the old individuals and generations reappearing in a fresher variation.

Civilized peoples are the food in the stomach today. But even as the food once placed there will inevitably go through the alimentary canal, as essence and waste, so, too will they pass and have been passing.

Primitive peoples are the food of tomorrow. Some of these like the East Indians have already been through the process and are again ascending toward it even as the individual at the moment of death at once recommences the ascent toward life. The process has been one of rejuvenation by fallowing.

The mixing of races is to Nature what variety of food is to the individual.

The mixing of Negro with Caucasian is Nature's getting at her reserve food. Food, rich with the accumulated sunshine and cheeriness of the tropics is being put into a pale, urbanized and intellectualized body.

The Negro is to the Caucasian what dark wheat flour is to white flour; what raw sugar is to refined sugar. The refined product is for ever being used up. And whence comes more of the refined but from the raw?

Looked at in its narrow racial sense, intermixture is really to the benefit of the Caucasian and the detriment of the Negro, precisely as the animal that is being eaten is the sufferer. As I have shown elsewhere while the native African shunned a union with the white, the latter, to a certain considerable extent, sought a sexual union with African women. Is it the seeker or the sought, who is the needy one?

The civilization of the Caucasian and its relation to the Negro is what a stimulant is to the stomach—not always wise to take, and better off without. An inevitable dose, it seems, however!

How admirable, if heartless, is Nature's process in regulating her food supply.

And how blurred the vision of those who disdain or rail at undeveloped "races"! What do these ask? That all mankind should become civilized at once? Why not demand also that all children present and to come grow into adults at once, or that all villages should at once become cities, in short that every bit of reserve supply be put into use at once?

Everything passes—Gods, solar systems, planets, races, religions, nations, individuals, ideas. *Change alone endures.*

Chapter Nineteen

THE PSYCHOLOGIC AND COSMIC FORCES THAT LEAD WHITES TO SEEK BLACKS—EXPRESSIONS OF WHITE SCIENTISTS AND POETS

"S'il est un Dieu pourquoi fit-il des nègres
Pourquoi noircir toute une race ainsi?"—St. Aubin.

(If there is a God why did he make the Negro
Why did he darken a whole race so?)

IT was shown in the preceding chapter that variation in the individual was brought about almost entirely through sex. I shall now attempt to show the modus operandi of Nature when variation is brought about, too, through the mixing of white and black. And let me repeat I do not say by women of their own class. From the point of view of the white woman the theory is necessarily correct. I am willing to yield to anything that sounds more reasonable, only asking that such be based on natural causes and not on racial prejudice and dogmatism.

McCrone, explaining the attraction of the whites by the blacks, says: "We have already seen that the black is identified with the primitive impulses, chiefly sexual, whose repression supplies the content of the unconscious and a return to the primitive level of impulse, a regression to the greater virility and sexual potency of the black may contribute to the sexual attractiveness . . ."

The crudely sexual is often a means of escape from the constant conflict of which the civilized individual is usually a victim. Again, it is a well-known fact that many men obtain a more complete sexual satisfaction with women who belong to an inferior or lower class than themselves since with such women they can let themselves go in a way they find impossible with women of their own class.

Schopenhauer gives a more generalized, cosmic reason. In his "Metaphysics of the Love of the Sexes," he tells why "blonds prefer dark persons, or brunets, but the latter seldom prefer the former," which, he says, is due to the fact that the white race was originally dark-skinned, that its present color is almost an abnormity, and that since it is Nature's will to return always to the original after she has departed a certain distance from it, the fair white persons prefer the dark as the dark skin is nearer the original type. "Fair hair and blue eyes," he says, "are in themselves a variation

196

XXXVIII. Upper, left to right: The present Sultan of Morocco (from life, by Ivanoff); and Glaoui Pasha, Morocco's richest and most powerful figure. Below: Band of the Sultan at Rabat. None of these is classed as "Negro." They are all called Moors.

from the type, almost an abnormality, analagous to white mice, or at least to gray horses. In no part of the world, not even in the vicinity of the pole, are they indigenous, except in Europe, and are clearly of Scandinavian origin. I may here express my opinion that the white color of the skin is not natural to man but that by nature he has a black or brown skin . . . consequently, a white man has never originally sprung from the womb of nature, and that there is no such thing as a white race, much as this is talked of, but every white man is a faded or bleached one. Forced into this strange world where he exists only like an exotic plant, and like this in winter requires the hothouse, in the course of thousands of years became white . . . *Therefore in sexual love nature strives to return to dark hair and brown eyes as the primitive type.*"[1]

Instances of this desire to return to the dark-skinned primitive may commonly be seen in real life, and also be found in literature. A notable case is that of Alfred, Lord Tennyson, one of the most cultured and finely sensitive of the world's great poets, who voices his desire to have "dusky" children by a savage woman. He says in "Locksley Hall":

> "There the passions cramped no longer shall have scope and
>   breathing space
> "I will take some savage woman she shall rear my dusky race.
> "Iron jointed, supple-sinewed, they shall dive and they shall run—
> Catch the wild goat by the hair and hurl their lances in the sun."
> "Whistle back the parrot's call, and leap the rainbows of the
>   brooks.
> Not with blinded eyesight poring over miserable books."[2]

This desire to return to the primitive, especially the dark-skinned, is also to be found in many society women, who, subjected to too much refinement, long for "cavemen." Some years ago, during a sensational divorce in which a millionaire banker accused his wife of adultery with a colored

---

1 World As Will and Idea, p. 349. Ed. by Will Durant in 1 Vol. 1931.

2 Beaumont and Fletcher express this desire to return to the primitive in Philaster (Act 4, Sc. 2):

> "Oh that I had been nourished in these woods
> And then had taken me some mountain girl,
> Beaten with winds. Chaste as the hardened rocks
> Whereon she dwells; that might have strewed my bed.
> With leaves and reeds and with the skins of beasts
> Our neighbors, and have borne at her big breasts
> My large coarse issue."

Related to this is a desire for a coat of tan. Magnus Hirschfeld asks, "May not the desire of many persons to get thoroughly sunburned in summer be an atavistic trait?" (Racism, p. 79. 1938). I feel sure it is.

man, the wife admitted openly that she was tired of soft-handed men and longed for cavemen. Magnus Hirschfield, in his Sexual History of the World War tells how rich society women in Europe flocked to the embraces of Negroes recruited in Africa.[3] Some remarkable affairs of this kind have also occurred in America. And as was said the heroes of the popular love stories and motion pictures are usually dark or bronzed.[4]

Other striking evidences of the desire to return to the dark-skinned primitive was the fondness of the Roman ladies for the gladiators, some of whom were Africans, and that of the great favor shown coal-black, wooly-haired Negroes at nearly all the courts of Europe as late as the nineteenth century. These Negroes were fondled in public, were admitted to the most intimate scenes of feminine toilette, and were even the fathers of children by these noble ladies, instances of which were cited in Volume One of this work.

Louis Sebastian Mercier (1740-1814), who witnessed the manner in which these Negroes were fondled in France, wrote: "The monkey, which women doted on, allowed in their dressing-rooms and called to sit on their knees, has been relegated to the antechamber.

"The parrot, the squirrel, the Angora cat, have each in turn attained the next rank to the abbe, the magistrate, and the army officer. But these cherished beings have lost their value all at once, and women have taken to little Blackamoors. These dusky Africans arouse no fear in beauty's eyes; they are born in the bosom of slavery. But who is not a slave of beauty?

"The little Black Boy never forsakes his fond mistress; burnt by the sun he appears only the more beautiful. He clambers on the knee of some charming woman, whose regard lingers on him with complaisance. His wooly head is pressed against her bosom, his lips are laid against a rosebud mouth, and his ebony hands show up the dazzling whiteness of a snowy neck.

"The caresses of a little Negro with his white teeth, thick lips, and satin skin are better than those of a spaniel or a pussy-cat. So he is preferred; he is ever close to those charms which his childish hands unveil in wanton sport as if they were made to understand all their value." Mercier adds that while the Negro boy "vit sur les genoux des femmes passionnées pour son visage étranger, son nez aplati" and with gentle and caressing hand is pun-

[3] See quotation in Sex and Race, Vol. I, p. 262, 1941.
[4] Victor Hugo gives a striking illustration of a finely cultured woman desiring a rough man in L'Homme Qui Rit, where the Duchess Josiane, the desired of all, falls in love with the hideous, dark mountebank, Gwynplaine. When, however, she discovers he also belongs to the high aristocracy, he having been kidnapped when a boy and facially mutilated, she drives him away. Of course, no question of race is involved here. There is one, however, in which Brantome tells of a grand dame of Naples who preferred her ugly black groom to the fine men of her class.

ished very lightly for wrongdoing — a punishment soon effaced by still warmer caresses, the father of the child is toilling under the lash in the tropics growing the sugar that is in the cup—the same cup—from which the Negro and his laughing mistress are drinking together."[5]

Many white Americans of both sexes felt the same way about these blacks but due to social restrictions they could not be as frank as the European dame and had to act under cover. Affairs of society whites and Negroes of the servant class continue to be legion. They are usually strictly on the quiet but now and then one pops into the light as that of Carlton Curtis, millionaire Mayflower descendant, and Letty Brown, a Negro domestic, which was extensively aired in the New York courts. Kip Rhinelander, New York millionaire and blue-blooded Huguenot descendant, also married a Negro waitress, Alice Jones, for probably the same reason voiced by Tennyson.[6]

Such marriages are exceedingly rare, however, because social restrictions have created a second nature to oppose mother Nature. There are also those whites, who though strongly drawn toward Negroes, desist from sexual relations with them because of the resistance created in them by training.

Tennyson also voices this latter feeling. Having expressed his longing for a primitive woman, he, in the next breath stifles it when he thinks of her low social position:

> "I, to hard with narrow foreheads vacant of our glorious gains;
> Like a beast with lower pleasures, like a beast with lower pains.
> "I, the heir of all the ages, in the foremost files of time
> Match with a squalid savage what to me were time or tide?"

Note, however, that upper-class white men would feel much the same towards most white women of the lower-class. Even though they strongly desire them they would not marry them because of the second nature, or pride, that their training and position have created in them. Thus in another famous poem in which no difference of color is involved, we find the society man rejecting the girl because of her low social position. In Whittier's

---

[5] Tableau de Paris, p. 262. 1853. Also Picture of Paris, W. & E. Jackson, p. 73. 1929.

[6] This desire to return to the primitive applies also to art and music. Jazz, which is Negro in origin, has had a far-reaching effect on Caucasian music. Also, the primitive art of Africa and Oceania which less than twenty years ago was regarded as so many monstrosities perpetrated by cannibals and savages and fit only for showing their hopeless inferiority, have now become, thanks to its originality, realism, and sincerity, the re-vitalizer of conventionalized "white" art. Thomas Jefferson wrote that he had never seen even "an elementary trait of painting or sculpture" in a Negro, but whose fault was it he had never seen it? Rousseau, his contemporary, spoke highly of African art. Jefferson, here, clearly uses his lack of knowledge, as a criterion.

poem, Maud Muller, the judge is greatly drawn towards Maud, the bare-footed girl, who is raking hay. She is much more desirable to him than the silken women of his own class and he would gladly have married her, but he stifled his love for her when

> He thought of his sisters, proud and cold
> And his mother, vain of her rank and gold.

Training, in short, has created a dual attitude in marriage in both race and class. When Kip Rhinelander married a Negro waitress the shock to the New York 400, differed not a whit, psychologically, from that to Euro-pean high society when Princess Victoria, sister of ex-Kaiser Wilhelm II, and cousin of George V, married a French waiter, even though the waiter was white. Also no marriage between the highest white woman in the South and a Negro laborer could have aroused a greater hostility than did the affair between Edward VIII and Mrs. Wally Simpson in British social circles. Edward not only had to abdicate but to exile himself from England. As was said, objections voiced against miscegenation by certain individuals are not necessarily sincere. Sometimes this kind of talk is but a smoke-screen, a truth set forth by MacCrone in his study of race relations in South Africa. He says, "The object which excites repulsion will come to exercise an attraction as well, though the latter may appear in far more indirect and disguised forms owing to the greater repression. The universal belief that natives indulge their sex appetites more freely and more promiscuously than do Europeans may, or may not, have some foundation in fact, but there can be little doubt about the effect of this belief upon the attitude of the representative European towards the native. Native life, native customs and practices, and above all, the sexual life of the natives exercise a perennial fascination upon the mind of the white man and the white woman. This 'call of the wild,' this urge to return to nature, this tendency to regress to the unrestrained gratification of primitive man and woman, serves as a constant pull upon the civilized, or more strictly speaking, partially civilized man and woman 'to go native' and to throw aside the restraints of civilization. In actual life as well as in the 'wish' world of novel and drama this theme is repeated with endless varia-tions. The immense popularity during the post-war years of native, or Negroid, music and dances in America and Europe was another expression of the same phenomenon . . .

"In addition to the widespread belief that the natives enjoy a freer sexual life we also find a general belief to the effect that native women are more voluptuous and have more 'abandon' than white women. From the crudely sexual point of view it would appear that the native female as well as the native male might exercise an even greater attraction upon the white man and woman than partners of their own race — an attraction which would be still further enhanced by the lure of novelty and the very contrast in skin-color. If we add to this the fact that, in many cases, men as well as women of a socially superior class find a more complete sexual gratification in intercourse with those who belong to a socially inferior and despised class it is not surprising that the very idea of such intercourse between white and black should appear as a form of sexual perversion, therefore revolting to the normal white man and white woman.

"There is sufficient evidence on record to show that sexual intercourse between white and black, and more particularly between European men and native women is of fairly frequent occurrence in spite of the strong social disapproval which it arouses not only in the white community but among many members of the native community as well as cases in which white women have seduced native men or boys . . . This obsession with race purity is to keep sexuality in the form of a potentially superior sexual rival at bay. The idea of a white woman in the arms of a black man, especially if she is there of her own free will, is enough to give rise to the most phenomenal emotional reactions to the white man."[7] The author then goes on to psychoanalyze the color-pull of the black upon the white.

Should it ever happen that certain of those very proud of their caste cohabit with one of a caste they despise, then, steps must be taken at once to reestablish their dignity in the eyes of the despised. In the Arabian Nights one reads how noble ladies cohabited with their slaves and then had them whipped after. Virey reports the same of certain American slave mistresses.

A less classical but none the less apt account of this desire and antagonism for race-mixing in a single individual is given by Ollie Stewart in the Baltimore Afro-American (May 17, 1941). It is the case of "a little blonde" he met at an interracial party, who after she had danced with him quite willingly enough, it seems, told him that each time she danced with a Negro she "freezes up inside." She said, "I'd like to make a confession. I'd like to know how you feel about something.

---

[7] **Race Attitudes in South Africa**, pp. 300-310. 1937. MacCrone, in a symposium, asked the following: If a white man were to find a native woman sexually more attractive than a white woman could you think of any reason for such greater attractions? He received such answers as greater novelty; more primitive abandon; temptation of the nudity of the black women; white men can let themselves go with Negro women in a way they cannot with white ones.

The white women asked the same question gave among their replies: Perhaps greater physical strength; more animalistic; more primitive; greater potency; more attractive than white, and some "very beautiful." Other whites of both sexes thought a desire for black people a perversion and a lack of real sanity. (pp. 273-77).

"Every time a colored man walks up to me and holds out his hand and asks me to dance with him, I freeze up inside. It happened just now when you asked me — and it's happened at every party of this kind to which I've ever gone.

"I can't exactly describe what happens to me—it's sort of hard to put in words. But I know I get cold inside, and something seems to tighten up. You're the first person I've ever told about it. What do you think?"

"I think," I said slowly, "that you're allergic to colored men. And if you're allergic to colored men, why do you come to parties where you're bound to meet them.

"But I want to meet them!" she exclaimed. "I don't want to freeze up when a colored man takes me in his arms—I'm ashamed of it—but I can't seem to help it. So I keep coming to parties like this, hoping I'll break myself of that habit. Does that make sense?"

"In a way, yes," I told her. "But why do you want to break yourself of the habit? Couldn't you just stay away from colored men and forget the whole thing?"

"No. If I did that, I'd be a hypocrite—and I hate hypocrites. All my life I've felt that racial prejudice was a terrible thing to carry around. I hate discrimination in any form.

"I'm proud of the colored friends I have — men and women. I like to be around them. I want the men to ask me to dance with them, because I enjoy it. Now, why the hell should I freeze up?"

"I wouldn't know," I said. "But some people don't like olives—at first."

In reply she blamed it on the American system, said Stewart. To prevent color prejudice she said she would start with the children of the different racial groups, have them dancing, playing, and fighting together then when they grow up "they wouldn't have the same funny feeling I get every time—"

"Whatever else she might have said I'll probably never know. At that moment a guy darker than I and bigger than I stuck his head through the kitchen door. He didn't hold out his hand. He didn't ask.

He just said, "All right, babe, let's go. Let's cut a rug!"

"She went. She threw both arms around his neck and seemed glad to go. And if she was freezing up inside, she certainly had a beautiful way of showing it."

I have proved so far, I think, that there is a very definite pull on the whites by the blacks, therefore, I shall now endeavor to reveal the deep, inner feelings that impel it—feelings that transcend society, training, and everything artificial because it is rooted in forces so primeval and powerful that legislators might as well pass laws against sunrise and sunset as againt them.

The cause, as I see it, is this: The impulse and therefore the blind necessity of Nature is to return always to the primitive and thereby renew itself. To illustrate: The child, having been born, grows up, dies and becomes earth again, the most primitive form of Nature. As earth, he furnishes nourishment for the plant; the plant produces food; food produces blood; blood, the reproductive germs; these latter, passing into the womb produces the child again who once more progresses towards old age and death, and then to earth again. And so the process goes on ad infinitum; forever and forever the return to the primitive, to the rebirth. Now what is true as regards the whole human race, is also true as regards varieties of it. The original color of mankind being dark, therefore, in this case, too, Nature strives to return to this hue. When we understand this I think we will also know why, for instance, it was that the distinguished German gentleman mentioned by Shufeldt said that he preferred "congress with a fine, good-looking Negress than any white woman he had ever met." It was merely innermost Nature leading him *through the color lure to re-establish the brown or primitive color of mankind,* in other words, it was the same motive that led Tennyson to desire a savage woman to rear "his dusky race."

But why the brown or primitive color? The answer is that the black contains in his body chemicals that have been bleached out in the case of the white, precisely as in the simile I once used of white flour and whole wheat flour; bleached sugar and brown sugar.

We must remember here that Nature does not work through mind alone. In any case she uses matter and is visible only through it. And man is made of flesh and bones, which, in their final analyses, are chemical substances. Now, Professor J. R. Marett in his able book, "Race, Sex and Environment: A Study of Mineral Deficiency in Human Evolution," has advanced the very logical theory that Man, or rather the sub-conscious forces in Man, have led him into migrations and race-mixings because of certain mineral deficiencies in his organism. He shows that certain peoples because of a long-continued stay in one environment have stored up a super-abundance of certain chemicals—acids, alkalis, salts, etc.—while others in another environment are suffering from a deficiency of the same. Thus he pictures Nature as a consummately clever chemist who so mixes the "races" that those who have too much of this or that chemical give to those who lack.

His book shows, so far as my comprehension of it goes, how white and black have been mating since prehistoric times; how Negroid Bushman and Caucasoid Cro-Magnon mated in Europe tens of thousands of years ago to produce Neanthropic, or modern man. He says, "The moderately tall

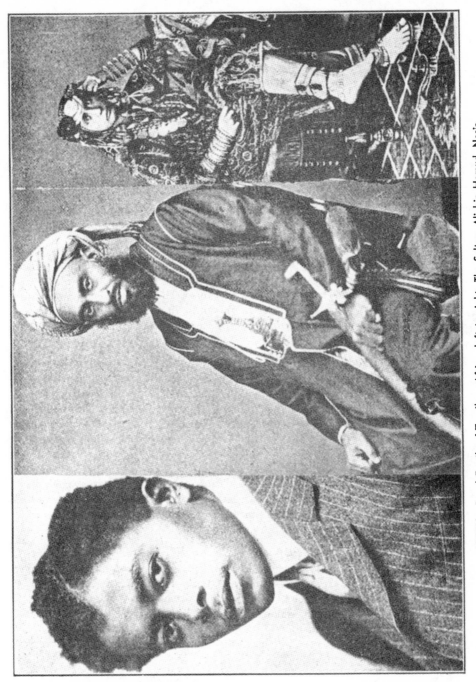

XXXIX. Royal Family of Zanzibar, Africa, left to right: The Sultan, Ali bin Hamud. Nasir bin Said, cousin of the Sultan. Princess Salamah bit Said, of Part German parentage, also cousin of the Sultan. (Reute; An Arabian Princess).

people of Africa may be considered as a Negro-Bushman cross and the Nilotic giants as a further European or Cro-Magnon cross with the taller issue of the first process."[8]

Retaining in our minds this thought about chemicals in the human body we return to what, I think, has been proved so far, namely, that primitive dark-skinned peoples have a greater aversion to mating with white people than the latter have to mating with them. I have also shown that in the United States while the race question is viewed by Negroes chiefly as an eco-nomic one—that is, better jobs, better housing, etc.—the whites view it as a sex question—intermarriage. Since, therefore, the whites have the greater thought of mating with the blacks than the blacks with them, it seems to me that in the case of the whites Nature is leading them in search of certain chemicals which they lack and which the blacks have.

On the other hand the same reasoning would indicate that the whites have few or no chemicals that the darker peoples seem to crave. And here again I find my simile of bleached foods versus unbleached ones apropos. In bleached flour, there are little or no minerals; in whole wheat flour there are; therefore one would naturally not go to a bleached product in search of minerals.

But here the question arises: Why are there white people who have no desire at all to mate with blacks? The answer as I see it is: Nature, having brought into being a particular species is interested in its preservation, and gives it love of life; but she is also interested in tearing it down since *change* is her paramount law. In the case of the individual, for instance, she gives him the instinct of self-preservation even while leading him sooner or later, to certain death. Thus those whites who have no desire to mate with blacks are the preservers of their so-called race; while those who wish to do so are those who are destined by nature to bring the inevitable change in it. In other words, there is a principle of race attraction and another of race repulsion, both of which are legitimate, provided one side does not use laws or social taboo to gain the upper hand.

Race attraction, or exogamy—marriage outside the tribe—and race repulsion, or endogamy—marriage within the tribe—have long existed among primitive peoples. In civilized communities, the two usually are found working side by side. Furthermore, our distaste for mating with individuals of another "race" is only a heightened form of our distaste for mating with certain ones of our own "race."

It is essential to remember, here, also that race-mixing alone cannot

---

8 Race, Sex, and Environment, p. 228. 1936. Also pp. 40, 98, 197, 222-3, 226-230, and Chap. XI.

improve humanity. It must be accompanied by good, healthful living. The poor and the under-privileged must not be exploited, must not be kept in a state of perpetual infantilism through insufficient or perverted education. For instance, the Jukes, the most degenerate family of which we have record, had mulatto, quadroon, and octoroon members, who were no better than the rest. One of them, Burton, a mulatto son of Bell Juke by a Negro (not named), is reported by Dugdale as being the best of the 709 members of this family, the majority of which was white. He says of Burton, "Farmer, industrious, owned property, intelligent, the best of his generation." Burton's children, however, turned out no better than the most of the Jukes, due no doubt to environment.[9]

Estabrook shows how a change of environment and better living conditions have brought a change in some of the Jukes. "In these men and women," he says, "the bad traits which have held down their brothers and sisters have become lost and they are the fountainhead of new families and good strain . . .

"Heredity, whether good or bad, has its complemental factor in environment."[10]

In short, we must bear in mind in this matter of "race" there are at work certain forces for the charge of existing types; and also certain forces at work for their preservation in the same manner and that while we are all marching to our graves we continue to make preparations for living.

Agencies working for the transformation of "races" into other types are thus doing Nature's work; so are those that are working for the continuance of existing types. Both are fulfilling their particular destiny. Both should, therefore, work harmoniously. But when arbitrary means are resorted to like the laws of certain American states; and those of Hitler and South Africa and Australia then we have a civilized barbarism. This is all the more so when the economic and the sex life of a people are being exploited for the benefit of the stronger group.

9 Dugdale, R. L. The Jukes. Chart of Bell Juke. 1877.
10 Estabrook, A. E. The Jukes in 1915, pp. 28, 85. 1916.

Chapter Twenty

WHAT ARE "THE WHITE MAN'S LANDS?" IS THE UNITED STATES ONE OF THEM

"The sun is my undoing."—Marguerite Steen.

THE white variety of mankind is now spread more or less thinly over the world but before Columbus it existed only in Europe, parts of Asiatic Russia a few degrees east of the Ural, and parts of Asiatic Turkey. In India, Persia, Egypt, North Africa were also groups of isolated whites, who were being absorbed by the dark-skinned populations. Incidentally, this process of the absorption of incoming whites in these lands had been going on since the days of the Pharaohs.

Except for the above-mentioned regions all the remainder of the world was colored.

The question, therefore, is: Are the white populations of the two Americas, Australia, and South Africa there to stay, or will Nature, in time, revert to the original?

That brings us again to the matter of chemicals in the human body. Now there is one particular combination of them—a combination visible to all—that is to be found in greater quantity in a Negro than in a white man, namely melanin, or pigment.

I said "greater quantity" because there is also pigment in a white skin, at least fifteen per cent and sometimes as high as forty, which is of the same composition as that in a black man. "Even the crudest champion of the color bar," says Professor Lionel Lyde, has "this brown pigment of primeval man" in his epidermal cells.

This is also confirmed by researches made by Drs. E. A. Edwards and S. Quimby Duntley of Harvard University and the Massachusetts Institute of Technology. They have demonstrated that the pigment in the skin of white persons and that in the darker "races"—East Indians, Chinese, Negroes, and others—are of the same universal substance. They say, "Our studies do not support the theories that the pigmentation of the skin in the dark races is not to be found in the white race, or by increase of pigments other than melanin which are normally present in small amounts in the white race." They add, "Our studies confirm the idea that the colored races owe their characteristic colors only to variations in the amount of melanin present. No pigments other than those found in the whites are encountered in the dark races and the general plan of pigment distribution is identical in the two groups."[1]

It is this melanin, acquired by the organism of the black man after thousands of centuries from the sunlight and the food of the tropics, which permits him to withstand the actinic rays of the sun. On the other hand, the white man, after thousands of centuries in cold climates, has a deficiency of melanin—he had little need for it—the question, therefore, is: What effect has the sun upon comparatively unpigmented man who migrates to the lands of the deeply pigmented?

C. B. Davenport, who did considerable research on this subject under the auspices of the Carnegie Institution, says, "The Negro basks in the sunlight which the white man finds it necessary to avoid. The concentration of black-skinned races especially in the equatorial region may very well be ascribed to the fact that their pigmentation permits them to enjoy just this region and tends to keep out unpigmented enemies. The blacks who once apparently inhabited Europe were not able to hold their own there against a lighter-skinned people and were either annihilated, or migrated to a climate that was grateful for them but malignant for their enemies."[2]

The above is supported by almost everyone who had studied the subject deeply. An English army surgeon with long experience in the tropics depicts in a remarkable article in "Nature" the very important role that pigment plays in tropical man, and how lack of it affects one in the tropics. What affects the surface nerves, he says, will in time affect the whole body in a greater or less degree because as Haeckel pointed out all the sense organs, as a whole, arose in essentially the same way, that is, as parts of the external integument, or epidermis. "Nature," he says, "having learned in ages past that pigment placed behind a transparent nerve will exalt its vibrations to the highest pitch, now proceeds upon the converse reasoning and placing the pigment in front of the endangered nerve reduces the vibration by so much as the interrupted light would have excited, a quantity which though apparently trifling would when multiplied by the whole area of body surface represent a total of nervous action that if continued would soon exhaust the individual and degrade the species.

"Thus it is that man, though so many generations have come and gone since the days of his weaponless struggles with the beasts of the forests,

[1] Pigments and Colors in Living Human Skin. Amer. Jour. of Anatomy, Vol. 65, pp. 30, 32. 1939. A substance called *carotene* is said to have been isolated in the skins of yellow people, but mulattoes of yellow color are abundant. Carotene would seem to me, therefore, only a lightened shade of melanin.

[2] The Skin Colors of Mankind, Natural History, Vol. 26, p. 49. 1926. See also W. Z. Ripley's Map of Complexions in the "Races of Europe."

still retain in its full strength that color of skin which, while it aided him materially in his early escapes is now continued because it has a more important office to fulfill in warding off the millions of vibrations a second which would otherwise be poured in an uninterrupted stream upon his exposed nerve system."

He adds that when the vertical rays of a tropical sun, and also its heat, plays upon a transparent skin as that of a white man's they produce upon the nerve endings over the entire surface intense and disadvantageous nerve vibrations. He concludes, "May it not therefore be claimed that there is much foundation for the suggestion that the black skin of the Negro is but the smoked glass through which alone his wide-spread sentient nerve endings could be enabled to regard the sun?"[3]

The chief maladies peculiar to the white man in the tropics, with the probable exception of sunstroke, are ascribed by several medical authorities to lack of pigment, as anemia, neurasthenia, and nervous irritability. C. B. Woodruff, a United States army doctor, with long service in the tropics, says that the above "is mostly due to the constant bombardment of the sun for it is worse in the blonds. They have neurasthenia even when they move to the hills.

"Those who state that white children thrive in the tropics have overlooked the appalling neurasthenia. I have many times had these pitiable neurotics pointed out to me as the manner in which white children thrive in the Philippines. Even with all the care given to white children in the tropics they begin to fade away at six or seven."

In Africa and the West Indies the whites usually settle in the hills but even there the overhead rays of the sun have their effect. For instance, one is as liable to sun-stroke there as in the plains. The old resident whites even in the highlands of Ethiopia had some of them anemia, while the later European arrivals were nearly all heavy drinkers, due probably to the irritability caused by the heat. Woodruff thought that the white man would probably not survive even in the mountains of South Africa because "from the brownness of the natives in this light country we are safe in predicting the dearth of the Boer type in time."[4]

Dan Crawford, famous missionary, who knew Africa well, says, "For the fearful fact must be faced that all things European degenerate in Central

3 Alcock, N., Why Tropical Man is Black. Nature (Lond.), Vol. 30, pp. 402-03. 1884.
4 Effects of Tropical Light on White Men, p. 233. 1905.

XL. Ethiopians. Their facial types can be found among Negroes in America. Most books on the subject will say they are not Negroes.

Africa. European provisions go to the bad. European fruits, European dogs degenerate. So, too, do European men and women."[5]

Dr. Jacobus says:

"The depressing and anemic action of the climate of Guiana on the pure white race is so great that after three or four generations the stock is completely exhausted and marriage between white Creoles become nearly sterile. It is not the same, however, when the revivifying action (in a physiological sense) of black blood is introduced."[6]

Some twenty thousand white persons sent to settle Paramaribo in Dutch Guiana nearly all perished, while the Negro taken there as a slave took firm root, even to the extent of dominating the aborigines.

When the kind-hearted Las Casas saw the Indian being crushed under the severe burdens imposed on him by the white man he recommended the Negro, who has not only displaced the Indian but the white man as well in certain places in the British West Indies, Haiti, Guiana and parts of Brazil and Central America.

When the English took Jamaica from the Spaniards in 1655 the Indian had almost disappeared. Of the large number of Indians living in the British West Indies in 1492 there remain but 105 in the islands of Antigua and Dominica, and even these are mixed with Negro.

It must be remembered, too, that the voyage from Africa was made under hardships unparalleled in the entire history of travel. Stedman said, after viewing a cargo of newly-landed slaves: "Such a resurrection of skin and bones as forcibly reminded one of the last judgment. These objects appeared to be risen from the grave, or escaped from Surgeon's Hall, and I confess I can give no better descriptions of them than by comparing them to walking skeletons covered over with a piece of leather."

So far no white group has been able to survive in the tropics on its own birth-rate even when conditions are ideal. Take the island of Jamaica, whose mountain regions have one of the finest climates of the world. In spite of constant immigration, the white population of that island, has never exceeded 5 per cent, a part even of which was of Negro ancestry.

In the British West Indies, the whites and the mulattoes are being absorbed by the blacks. In Jamaica, in only ten years, (1911-1921) the 15,605 whites had shrunk to 14,476; the 163,201 mulattoes to 157,223; while the 630,181 full-blooded Negroes had increased to 660,420. In Barbadoes the 15,613 whites had shrunk to 12,603, in the same length of time. In 1830 the Jamaican whites numbered about 30,000. The white men can survive

5 Thinking Black, p. xv. 1913.
6 L'Art d'Aimer aux Colonies, p. 132. 1927.

in the tropics only in an administrative or other exploiting capacity. Field-work of any kind is unthinkable for him. The white man farthest down is in Africa—South Africa.

Kohlbrugge says: "Until now no white race has been able to survive in the tropics unless intermixture takes place . . .

"As we cannot become acclimated we can neither take the place of the native nor do without him." The proper habitat of the white is about 45° North and 45° South of the equator.

Woodruff points out further that even the Southern South is not really white man's habitat, that the whites there have more sunlight than their degree of pigment warrants. Florida, he says, really corresponds with the African Sudan, and the Southern South in general with North Africa and the lands of other dark-skinned peoples as the Arabians and certain of the East In-dians. This means that if the Southern South had had as little white immi-gration as say Arabia, areas like Louisiana, Florida, and Southern Texas, would have the color pattern of the Arabians. Or to come nearer home, that of the Mexicans, their neighbors.

Even parts of the North at certain seasons of the year are bad for some whites. In this respect I was once much struck by an incident that happened at Williams Bay, Wisconsin. At a Y. M. C. A. summer confer-ence at which there were students of many races, mostly white but includ-ing East Indians, Chinese, Japanese, African and American Negroes, Bra-zilians and others, I noted that some of the fair whites who went in bathing were so blistered and had their skins so peeled that they really suffered and had to be dressed with cotton-batting. Some were hardly able to wear their shirts. One or two of the fair Japanese also peeled but nothing whatever happened to the darker whites, the East Indians and the Negroes. The im-portant fact was: here were some white people suffering from the sun in a far Northern climate. I could not help thinking at the time that if this had happened to the Negroes certain anthropologists would have seized on it as positive proof of "Negro inferiority."

Woodruff gives an instance not unlike the above. He tells of an Elks parade in Philadelphia in 1906 in which a multitude of white people were struck down by the sun. "Actinic shock," he says, "is much more common in blonds than in brunets, and is rare in Negroes."[7] As regards the tropics he found that in the Philippines blond soldiers suffered the most; the light

[7] Medical Ethnology, p. 136. 1915.

As regards sun-stroke which is far more deadly than sunburn, I was amazed to see in Africa how even babies are immune to this. I saw them bare-headed in the broiling sun, strapped to their mother's back, the perspiration streaming down their little faces. In such a case, a grown European might immediately have been struck down senseless.

brunets less; the dark brunets still less; while the unmixed Negro soldiers had it the best of all, and were even more comfortable than in the United States. "The Negro soldiers who went to the Philippines," he said, "found themselves so much more comfortable than at home that large numbers of them preferred to stay where their black pigmented armor was an advantage. It was curious to see the intense blackness of these Negroes, the blacker the more comfortable they were so that the majority of the colored teamsters, colored servants, saloon-keepers, and loafers were jet-black. The mulattoes did not seem to like it so well and fewer stayed."[8]

Dr. Magnus Hirschfeld, who travelled much in the East Indies and other tropical lands of the Far East and conferred with the medical societies and doctors long resident there, said similarly, "In the long run the tropics are no place for a white man. This talk of acclimatization is a fairy tale. On the contrary. This is the rule. The longer a white man lives in the tropics the lazier he feels both physically and mentally; the duller and stupider he becomes . . .

"In the tropics the family line of a white man married to a white woman scarcely ever survives three generations. It is a different matter when a white man born in the tropics has children by a native woman . . .

"European peoples should give up their right to the possession of countries to which they have no biological claim, if for no other reason that they simply cannot survive there for any length of time—at least not without intermarriage." He quotes a doctor, long resident in Java, "We, Europeans, coming as we do from countries of moderate climate, decidedly do not belong in the tropics and no European returns with unimpaired health after a prolonged residence there—I mean fifteen to twenty years."[9]

The insufficient pigment in the skin of the whites, and especially of the blonds, makes them less resistant not only to tropical heat but to certain diseases. Love and Davenport, American army scientists, who analyzed a half a million sick reports of soldiers in the first World War, said of the white men,

"In general the skin, not only on the surface of the body but also that which is unfolded to form the lining of the mouth and naso-pharynx is much more resistant to micro-organism in Negroes than whites.T he white skin seems to be a relatively degenerate skin in this respect."

They also say: "In civil life deaths from skin cancer are one-fourth

[8] Effects of Tropical Light on White Men, p. 298. 1905. See also Aldo Castellani's Climate and Acclimatization. 1931.
[9] Man and Woman, pp. 93-6. 1935.

XLI. Juan Manuel de Rosas, Argentine dictator, presenting his decree of emancipation to the Negro slaves of Buenos Aires. (See Sex and Race, Vol. 2, p. 59.) Note how white were some of the Negroes. (Pradere.)

as common in colored as white citizens. This by no means exhausts the skin differences of the two races."[10]

Thus it will be seen that skin color—the very thing that is used as the badge of Negro inferiority seems to stamp the Negro as a superior in certain respects.

Furthermore, according to the New York Times (March 20, 1943), the sea-food packers of Georgia, reported that Negroes made better handlers of shrimps than white people because the shrimp caused sores on the hands of the whites while it did not affect the Negroes. "Experiments," said the article," have shown that the acids in the shrimp have a bad reaction on the hands of white persons."

The sun takes its toll of physical and intellectual energy not only in the tropics but in temperate lands as well. For this reason in Northern American climes schools, colleges, and churches are closed in summer. Even in far northern Canada where the temperature sinks to fifty below in winter, one's activities slow down under the excessive heat of the summer, and whereas one walks very fast in the winter, he walks slowly in summer. Imagine, therefore, the effect of the heat in lands like Arabia, Central Africa, and the central portion of the New World where it is perpetually hot and even humid.

As G. W. Ellis says of Liberia, "Persons coming from abroad find Africa very slow; they have determined to do many things; they criticize everything and everybody and ask why the Africans do not move about more briskly. After having been in Africa for years they find that their plans do not materialize. In a little while they cease to criticise and later they take on the African movement. There is something in the climate that makes any kind of work extremely irksome. In West Africa the body loses its strength, the memory its retentiveness, and the will its strength."[11]

Add to this the heat and the many annoying insects, some of them almost invisible, that attack one by day and force one to sleep under mosquito nets at night. To one reared in the temperate zone a good night's sleep is rare in the tropics unless he is in the high uplands. Central Africa, that is in the historic period, has produced no civilization that is nearly comparable with that of Europe, the principal cause being the terrific heat and humidity which sap creative thought. Of course, there are others as the

---

[10] Comparison of White and Colored Troops in Respect to Incidence of Disease in Proceedings of the Nat. Acad. of Science, Vol. 5, pp. 58-67. 1919.

[11] Negro Culture in West Africa, p. 35. See also E. Huntington's Map on the Effect of Climate on Human Energy as Inferred from Work in Factories. It is true that the first great civilizations of the Old and the New World arose in tropical and near-tropical lands but they were built by slave labor.

comparative ease with which the three driving forces of society are obtained, food, shelter, and sex; and that the manpower of this region has been drawn off for thousands of years or more for the upbuilding of North Africa, Southeastern Asia; and the New World.

Of course, there are those scientists who will deny much or most of the foregoing but for myself no one would ever be able to convince me that tropical heat is not a powerful deterrent to activity. I have lived in very hot countries and very cold countries and the effect on me intellectually has been most striking. In the northern United States and Canada during the winter, I find work a pleasure. Nothing could keep me from my typewriter. But in the South and in the oppressive heat of Southern California my great desire was to put off work—*mañana*. In Ethiopia even in the mountains, except for late December and early January, I had to drag myself to do any writing. I would get up full of ambition to do a day's work but after breakfast my great urge was to go back to bed. As for Djibuti and the Anglo-Egyptian Sudan, where the sun is like an oven, I had the same urge as the animals—to loll in the shade. Mighty glad I was that I didn't have to work like the natives, some of whom were toiling in the sun, making salt, etc., all for the enrichment of white people. Had Nature intended tropical man to toil like a beast of burden she would not have given him such easily obtained food, clothing, and shelter. Work, work, eternally work is not life's chief goal. We have a right to be lazy, too.

If the whites are to survive in lands to which they are not indigenous, especially the burning tropics, they must have an admixture of the pigment of the natives. Latin America is a conspicuous example. There we see the marvelous prevision of Nature. No sooner had the white man arrived in the New World than the Negro arrived too and both started amalgamating.

In other words, Nature in causing the Caucasian to mate with the darker races is thereby restoring to him the degree of pigment not only necessary for him to live in hot lands but even in parts of the temperate zone. The Scandinavians are mostly blond, but that paleness certainly wouldn't do for the peoples of Southern Europe, therefore, from the earliest times there has always been an incoming of blacks to Europe to mate with the whites to reinforce the pigment of the latter. This principle in general holds true of the United States.

In this respect, therefore, racial intermixture is a cosmic force. One who views life as a universal whole, who observes its action in man, beast, and plant alike, might say that as the etiolated plant in the cellar stretches toward the sunlight so the Caucasian, etiolated man, in the tropics, yearns for the bottled sunlight in the skin of the black as a means of survival. Man and plant alike as Professor Moulton so profoundly summarizes it are "blossoms of the sun." Thus pigment is more significant than even some of the learned are aware of. Moreover, Mendel's Law, which is on the whole, sound shows that the *darker the color of the animal or the plant, the more dominant it is while the lighter in color it is, the more recessive it is.*

A dark-skinned race inhabited the United States for probably hundreds of thousands of years. It was almost wiped out by the white European but if it is the type best adapted physically to the soil and climate *it will eventually return no matter what artificial laws or restrictions are imposed.* Any people who must maintain themselves by force in any environment will pass out when that force weakens as it inevitably will because such force is also subject to the natural law. Whatever goes up will come down. Nature has no favorite race or nation. Moreover while she is a *mother* to the dark-skinned man in the tropics she is only a *step-mother* to the white man there even as she is to a tropical plant in a snowy land, if it is to survive, must depend on artificial aid. The Southern whites are now maintaining themselves in power by jim-crow laws but the time will inevitably come when they will no longer be strong enough to enforce such laws.

As regards the black man in the "white" regions if his living conditions are good, he thrives better than the white man in the "black" lands. But I do not think that a black race will ever thrive in Europe unless there is a return of the climatic conditions that once permitted it to live there. The Negroes who were taken in considerable numbers to European lands as England, Spain, Italy, Albania, Greece, Turkey, Southern Russia, have all or nearly been absorbed by the whites while on the other hand in Tropical America, the white, an importation, is being absorbed by the black, also an importation. To anyone, who has studied the migration and the survivals of so-called races it is difficult, if not impossible to escape, this dictum of J. G. Wilson:

"The type of man best adapted physically to the climate and soil will, in point of time, eventually prevail in spite of all restrictive legislation and man-made laws."[12]

As regards race-mixing outside of the United States: Before the end of

---

12 Popular Science, Vol. 79, p. 438. 1911. The same is also true of plants and animals. If the Middle West were to be abandoned, the few surviving buffaloes now there would once more be roaming in great herds. Australia is favorable to rabbits. Introduced there they multiplied almost like flies. Mangoes brought to the West Indies from India thrive there like weeds. The same is true of other fruits introduced from the South Seas. It was their natural habitat. Nature is true to herself everywhere.

the century, the European will probably be pushed out of Asia.[13] He will, especially the English, then be forced to concentrate on Africa, thus race-mixing on that continent will go on a vaster scale than ever with the blacks continuing to absorb the white even as they have been doing since before the Pharaohs, or as the whites have been absorbing the blacks who came to Europe either as invaders, slaves, or free workers. As for South Africa it will certainly meet the fate of Ptolemaic Egypt where the darker Egyptian absorbed the lighter Greek; or the ancient Dasyus of India absorbed the Aryan invaders; or the Japanese absorbed the Indo-Chinese. In Europe contingents of blacks will continue to arrive as they had been doing long before the Christian era to reinforce the pigment in the skins of the whites. In England, for instance, hundreds of thousands of Africans were absorbed in the 330 years of Negro slavery there. The first world war brought in thousands of Negroes who made their homes there and mixed with the whites; the second world war brought even more.

In the New World the whites of the North will continue to go southward and mix with the darker peoples there; while numbers of the darker peoples from the South will come northward and there mingle their strains with the whites. In the northern United States and Canada the whites will continue to predominate but in the tropical New World it is the Negro, the mixed-blood and the Indian, who will. It is the whites who colonized the lands of the Caribbean but it is the Negroid who is most abundant there now and will dominate it politically.

As regards our present obsession about color, that inheritance from the slave period of colonial days will pass. Men will become too enlightened to think that color makes the man. They will realize that happiness comes, not from the exterior, but from the soul, therefore, that in any well ordered system a maximum of happiness can be enjoyed under any color of skin.

Indeed, there are some who already do.

13 This was written in 1944. See what has happened since.

Chapter Twenty-one

CAN A COUPLE, APPARENTLY WHITE, HAVE A BLACK BABY?

T HE problem of the white wife giving birth to a black child, or one that is very much darker than herself or her husband, goes back to early European history.

Among the ancient writers who have dealt with it are Aristotle of 384 B. C., Plutarch, Martial, Juvenal, Calpurnius Flaccus, St. Augustine, and St. Jerome. With Negroes in considerable numbers in cities as Rome and Athens, it was inevitable that there would be white women who would consort with black men and have children by them.

For the single white woman, if she were a slave as were some of the Negroes, having a mulatto child, was probably no problem but for the married one it was very serious. Adultery was punished with death and here, if anywhere was proof of adultery because a logical mind would ask: If a single white woman has a mulatto child and we have no doubt that she had affair with a Negro, why should we give it a different cause in the case of the married woman especially since we know there are married women who are unfaithful to their husbands?

Therefore, for the defense of the married women a mystical and confusing reason was necessary—a reason whose chance of convincing depended not on facts but on oratory as happens in so many cases of law.

Two kinds of argument were used in the defense of the married woman with a mulatto child, namely, that one of the parents had a Negro ancestor three or four generations ago (it was usually four as by that time the Negro strain was no longer visible); or that the mother had been startled in some way by a black man, so-called maternal impression. Aristotle mentions the first while St. Augustine and St. Jerome did the second.

These two theories continued in vogue into the eighteenth century and are believed by probably tens of millions today. When, for instance, Marie Theresa, Queens of France, had a mulatto child, it was attributed by some to the queen's fondness of chocolate, then a novelty in Europe. Shakespeare, however, was rather more hard-headed. In his "Titus Andronicus," he attributes the Negro child borne by Tamora, Queens of the Goths, to illicit intercourse with her black lover, Aaron the Moor.

220

XLII. Upper, left to right: Placido (Gabriel Concepcion Valdes, 1809-1844) Cuba's greatest poet; and M. Morua Delgado, Secretary of Agriculture and President of the Cuban Senate. Lower left: Francisco Xavier de Luna Victoria (1695-1777), Archbishop of Peru. (Schomburg Coll.)

This theory of atavism, or a "throw-back" is accepted not only by the ignorant and the unwashed but is fostered by certain reputable scientists and writers who pass it on to the credulous to be used as a bugaboo for simple-minded white couples, one partner of which, has, or could be convinced that he has a distant Negro ancestry. Their offspring, they are told, are likely to be born coal-black with kinky hair and blubber lips.

The result is that the life of some married persons is one long fear of seeing children of their own. Daniel M. Eisenberg, noted tracer of missing persons, gives a case in point. He tells of a young couple happily married and financially comfortable, who lived in a Northern city. The wife, however, had exacted of her husband one promise: that he would never make her pregnant; but this actually happened and one day, as pregnancy advanced, the wife suddenly vanished, leaving not a trace. The husband distraught thought she had been kidnapped or some terrible accident had happened and called in a detective. To the latter he told among other things, his wife's request not to make her pregnant, which, he said he had attributed to the fact that she did not wish to lose her girlish figure. Of her family, he said, he knew little, except that it was an old Southern one.

Searching among the wife's effects, the detective found an insurance policy whose beneficiaries were a couple in Pentville, Ala. At that town, he found the old couple and to his great astonishment saw they were colored. In the house was the wife quietly sewing "on some baby clothes." Knowing her Negro ancestry and fearing that her child would be born black, she had run away, waiting to see what color it would be before she returned to her husband.[1]

Even reputable scientists endorse this superstition, as I said. For example, Major Robert Wilson Shufeldt, who was one of America's greatest naturalists, and was head of the American Army Museum gives the following case, which, he says, came under his "personal notice."

"A young American artisan of the better class and of excellent type, born of parents born in this country and with blood untainted by any mixture with African blood, meets a young and very pretty girl in Virginia, and in due course, marries her. At the end of a year a boy child is born to them, but horror of horrors, it is found to be as black as coal and with hair as kinky as the veriest young Congo that a Negress of that race ever gave birth to in Africa. Imagine the state of mind this at once threw the unhappy husband into. His poor wife pleaded with him that he was the only man on earth who had ever sexually embraced her and that the very suggestion of receiving the carnal approaches of an African were most repugnant and dis-

1 True Detective, June, 1941.

gusting to her. But the husband knew there must be cause for it as he was present in the room when the black child was delivered and quietly he went to work to investigate the wife's antecedents. After no end of trouble and expense, he finally ascertained that her great-grandmother was a plantation slave who had born several children to her master. It was in this stock, then through crossing and recrossing with other whites that this young wife saw her pedigree and her first child was simply a reversion to the black ancestry on her maternal side and had inherited the Ethiopian characters and among them the black skin and kinky hair. I have heard of several well authenticated cases of this nature, and in one, after a most heart-rending experience the couple was divorced."[2]

Since even a scientist accepts this superstition, what may we expect from a politician? Nothing less than a double dose of the same. Theodore Bilbo, UnitedStates senator from Mississippi, reports a case of twins, both coal-black, born to an apparently white couple. "I know personally," he says, "of a very sad case that happened in the State of Virginia . . . In one of the most aristocratic towns in the state, in one of the most aristocratic families there was a beautiful girl. She met one of those Puerto Rican officers on some occasion and fell in love with him, never dreaming that the Puerto Rican had a drop or strain of Negro blood as a result of the amalgamation which has been going on in Puerto Rico for a hundred years. They married and went back to Puerto Rico and returned in a year or so and the first birth was a pair of twins. A throw-back was the result. These twins were as black as the ace of spades. So when the family returned to the aristocratic home in Virginia, lo and behold, the offspring were nothing in the world but a pair of pickaninnies because of the presence of the Negro blood."[3]

John Powell, one of the heads of the Anglo-Saxon Society of Richmond, Virginia, is another. Powell, though he gives numerous cases of adulterous white women having mulatto children, repeats this fiction of the black child with approval.[4] Some years ago, also, a leading monthly magazine, had a highly dramatic version of the same in which the mother on seeing the "black" child, gasps with horror, and orders it taken away forever. Later, according to the story, the father was found to be of distant Negro ancestry.

The first proof of nature-faking in this story is that no children are ever born black, not even those of unmixed Negro parents in Central Africa. A newly-born African baby is of a darkish salmon color; while in the

2 Shufeldt, R. W. The Negro: A Menace to American Civilization, p. 95. 1907.
3 Congressional Record. May 24. 1938. p. 7352. The Senator reports two pic-aninnies. I would like to report a third ninny—just a plain one, Bilbo, himself.
4 Richmond (Va.) Times-Dispatch, Feb. 27, 1926.

United States where unmixed Negroes are usually lighter, it is often impossible to tell at birth whether the child is white or colored, unless one sees the parents. As Dr. C. B. Davenport, noted eugenist says, "It is pretty generally agreed by accoucheurs both in Africa and in the Southern states that the Negro baby is nearly white at birth." There is this exception, however, the Negro child is sometimes born with dark areas in the genital and anal regions. This is said to be generally true also of the mulatto child, but not of those, who, are say, only one-sixteenth black.

Davenport, who, with an assistant spent a year of research on race-mixing for the Carnegie Institution, says that he was unable to find a single authenticated case of an apparently white couple having a black baby. He says,

"Certainly the offspring of such an octoroon and a white person will so far as skin color goes be a white person . . . Indeed a person of one-eighth blood is, so far as skin color goes, completely 'across the line.' Married to white there is no expectation of dark-skinned offspring though the hair be curly and the lips thick.

"This brings us to a matter of great social moment to hundreds of our citizens, namely, the possibility of a reversion in the off-spring of a white-skinned descendant of a Negro to a brownskin color. There is even a current opinion that such an extracted white married to a pure-bred white person may have a 'black' child. This tradition has been used to create dramatic situations in novels and in newspaper 'stories' and the dread of this tradition hangs over many a marriage that might otherwise be quite happy. In our studies no clear case of this sort has been found and our fundamental hypothesis leads us not to expect it."[5]

East declares such a birth an "absurdity." He says that it could be possible only if both parents had a Negro strain or if there is a "fracture of the seventh commandment."[6]

It may be said with certainty that even if the child is not born "black" but mulatto in appearance and hair attributing this to a "throw-back" is nature-faking, also. For instance, Paul Rival seems to attribute the Negroid appearance of the Duke d'Alencon, son of Catherine de Medici, Queen of France, to the Negro strain in the Medici family, though neither Catherine nor her husband, Henry II, show in their portraits the slightest

[5] Heredity in Skin-Color in Negro-White Crosses, pp. 29-31. Carnegie Instit. Pub. No. 188. Also Davenport & Staggerda: Race-Mixing in Jamaica, pp. 30-31. See also Medical News, Dec. 24, 1898, where a number of doctors agree that no children are born black; and how one professor held up a newly-born Negro child to his class and asked the members of it whether it was white or black and some said its parents were white and others said they were black.

[6] Heredity and Human Affairs, p. 100. 1927.

evidence of Negro strain. He says, "A new personage came at this time (1574) to appear at the Court. He was the third son of Catherine, Francis, Duke d'Alencon, who up to then had been held in solitary castles. He was eighteen years old and had come to claim his place.

"He was a horrible little man, with woolly hair and black, a Moor, without vigor, who recalled the old story that there was Negro blood in the Medici family."[7]

The Duke was heir presumptive to the throne of France, and suitor for the hand of Elizabeth, Queen of England, who entertained him, kissed him, and might have married him had he not died.[7a]

To say that the birth of such children is due either to atavism or maternal impression seems to me like going to the moon for an explanation when a much more logical one lies right under our nose, namely the Ethiopian gentleman in the wood-pile.

American court records teem with cases of white wives of white men having mulatto children. Catterall's "Judicial Cases Concerning American Slavery and the Negro," contains many such. In these cases are seen where American juries and judges even during slavery refused to believe that a white wife could have a mulatto child unless she had had relations with a Negro, and gave a divorce to the husband. Did they not see about them single white women, who could give no such excuse as a throw-back, maternal impressions, or a virgin birth for having mulatto children? And they also saw white women married to black men having such children, as well as black women having mulatto children by white men. A Virginia judge in 1840, ruling on the case of a white wife with a white husband who had a mulatto child, declared that such was an impossibility unless the wife had had "access" to a Negro as among the hundreds of millions of whites in Europe there had been no authenticated case of a white couple having a birth of that kind.[8]

Nature never lies, and whenever a case of this kind occurs a dark, or unmixed Negro, surely is involved. For instance, in 1930 the European

---

[7] La Folle Vie de la Reine Margot, p. 42. 1930. Waldman F., says that Alencon was "extraordinarily hideous . . . with the skin of a Moor." (Biography of a Family, p. 7. 1936.).

[7a] Waldman says that when some of Elizabeth's ministers opposed her marriage to d'Alencon, "She called them to her and wept copious tears in their presence. All these years, she complained, they had begged her to marry and now that she at last found a man who suited her they had all turned against her. Had she not the right, like any other woman, to a peaceful domestic life and children?" Once when d'Alencon arrived in England, Elizabeth "made an enormous fuss over him before the onlookers, and brazenly invited him alone into her bedroom so that everybody could think the worst." (Elizabeth, pp. 271-79. 1933.)

[8] See cases cited from Catterall in Sex and Race, Vol. 2, chap. 24.

papers reported a case in Posen, Poland, that was a nine-day wonder. A white wife had had a mulatto child and there wasn't a black man for miles around. The wonder ceased, however, when it was discovered that the wife had been spending time in the south of France where there were several regiments of Senegalese troops.

Sir J. E. Alexander tells also of the white wife of a Dutch farmer who bore him a mulatto child, and for which he accounted by saying that she had been frightened by a Negro. But it happened that the wife's white sister, who was unmarried, also sustained several "frights" of the same kind. She bore several mulatto chidren.[9]

If Shufeldt's brain had not been so befuddled by his dislike of the Negro, he, an able medical man and naturalist, would have immediately attributed the birth of such a child to adultery as any jury would have done. Not only would he have seen nature-faking but he would have remembered that paternity can rarely be proved. It is a wise child that knows its own father, says the proverb. Why, there are mothers who don't even know who is the father of their child. Paternity can be absolutely certain only when the resemblance of the child to the father is strong; or if the couple were isolated on some Robinson Crusoe island.

The Germans, realists as they are, did not trust their queens, hence on the honeymoon night, officials were stationed in the royal bedroom to see that it was the ruler, or future ruler, who, himself consummated the marriage. As for the queen, herself, she was watched all her life. And there was sometimes cause for suspicion. The wife of the German-born ruler of England, George I, deceived him with the handsome Count Konigsmarck, who was stabbed to death as he was leaving her bedroom, and which, in turn, created great doubt as to the legitimacy of her son, George II of England. In short, maternal impression cannot be proved, and may be safely set down as folk superstition. If Catherine de Medici had the child described it may be safely assumed that one of the Negroes at her court, or some other court, was the father, the more so, as there were other similar ladies who had mulatto children.

DOES MENDEL'S LAW OF INHERITANCE APPLY TO HUMAN SKIN COLOR? CAN MULATTOES HAVE A BLACK CHILD?

Mendel's Law briefly stated is this: If a dark plant or animal is mated with a light one, the offspring will be intermediate in color, but when the offspring of the latter mate with themselves then you'll have dark, inter-

---

9 See source in Sex and Race, Vol. 1, p. 137. 1941.

XLIII. Upper, left to right: Baron de Cotegipe, Prime Minister of Brazil under Dom Pedro II; and Andre Reboucas (1838-1898), one of the greatest engineers of his time. Below: Alberto Santos-Dumont, great pioneer in aviation.

mediate, and light in the ratio of two intermediates to one dark and one light. In other words, all three colors will show up then.

There are those Mendelians who say that this law applies to the mating of unmixed whites and unmixed Negroes. For instance, they contend that if, say, two white men were to have a child each by two unmixed Negro women, a boy and a girl, and these two were to mate then some of the children would be born white, some mulatto, and some black in the ratio of 1-2-1. For instance, Gunnar Dahlberg, great Swedish scientist, who attacks scientific nonsense in his "Race, Reason, and Rubbish," comes, so far as I can see to this conclusion. In one of his illustrated tables, he shows a mulatto couple having children, both white and black.[10]

Now as it happens I know well social life in the island of Jamaica where the upperclass mulatto element is very sensitive about darkness of skin. If a case were to happen where a very dark child were to be born to a mulatto couple it would be regarded as a catastrophe in the family and no power on earth would ever be able to convince the father that the mother was not unfaithful to him. I was acquainted with any number of upperclass mulatto families, some of whom had as many as sixteen children, and I know not one single instance in which a child was appreciably darker than the darker of the two parents.

The story is told of a man who was born much darker than his parents and he explained it by saying that a black man ran after his mother. The retort was, "Yes, and he caught her too."

In fact so firmly is this established that it is used in the law courts to determine paternity in the case of illegitimate birth. For instance, were a light mulatto to be charged with being the father of a child by an unmixed black woman, and the child was not lighter than the mother, he would be acquitted.

I knew well one family in particular where the father was a wealthy mulatto, about five-eighths white and the mother unmixed white, born of Scotch parents on the island. This couple had twelve children, not one of whom was as fair as the mother nor as dark as the father. All were of different shades of color, and had straight hair, and the straight nose of their mother, except two of the girls, the fairest of the children, who had their father's rather Negroid nose.

I have noticed the same in any number of cases where the mulattoes were the offspring of one unmixed white, and one unmixed black parent. I had an excellent opportunity for observing this in Cardiff, Wales, which had a Negro colony of 7,000. The mothers in this colony were originally

10 Race, Reason and Rubbish, pp. 29-30. 1942.

all white—and to a large extent are mostly so now—while the fathers were nearly all blacks. This colony is more than sixty years old, with the result that the mulattoes born there have been mating with mulattoes, and producing so far as I could learn, not whites and blacks, but other mulattoes. In all the hundreds of children there, I saw not one that could be taken for an unmixed black. On inquiry, I was taken to a mother, a white woman, whose ten months' old child showed no trace of white. But even then it was lighter than its father, who was of a very deep black.[11]

Professor Karl Pearson of London asked two medical men who had spent a lifetime of service in the West Indies about this matter of a child being born darker than either of its parents and their replies were firmly in the negative.

As regards mulatto couples producing both whites and blacks, Pearson asked: "Does not this cross usually give a mulatto in color? The theorists says that 25 per cent (of the children) should be pure white skins; 25 percent pure black skins and only 50 per cent mulattoes."

The answer was, "The statement of those whom you call theorists is the most ridiculously incorrect of the lot; indeed it would be very comic to make this statement in public before persons you know. There are now and then slight variations from the usual mulatto brown or mulatto yellow but you may be quite certain that no pure black nor pure white skins come from mulatto and mulatto. You can state this very dogmatically."[12]

In slavery days in the West Indies and the United States when a dark mulatto woman with a dark husband had a very fair child its father was invariably set down as white. Did Nature's process change with the emancipation?

Davenport who studied race-crossing in the West Indies and the South, says similarly, "At Jamaica I asked several highly intelligent colored and white natives if they knew of cases of reversion. All replies agreed in holding the idea mythical."

Pearson is far nearer the truth when he says that the hair, nose, lips are more likely to follow the Mendelian law than color. This is specially true of the lips. I have noticed after a lifetime of observation that in the mixing of white with black, the Negroid mouth is the last feature to disappear, particularly the Negroid length between nose and chin.

---

11 Dr. Parsons relates a similar case in York, England, in 1765, where the white wife of a Negro had a child that was "black though everyone expected it to be tawny." He also reports a singular case in which the color was not evenly mixed, that is, the white mother had a child that was white except for the right buttock and thigh which was black like the father. (Philosophical Transactions, Jan. 31, 1765). For more about the Cardiff Negro colony see my article in The American Mercury, May, 1930.

12 Biometrika, Vol. 6, pp. 349-353. 1908-09.

Since all human pigment is of the same substance—since even the most rabid Hitler Aryan or white Southerner shares with the Negro anywhere from fifteen to forty per cent of identical pigment, it follows that in race-mixing the Negro does not have some coloring foreign to the white to contribute to the offspring, that there must be in the offspring a dilution of pigment, however, unequally partitioned. Furthermore, the offspring of a mulatto and a white quadroon is going to have still less pigment, and so on with the octoroon. How will the supporters of this old superstition of an apparently unmixed couple having a black child explain how one of the partners with all the pigment bred out of him would be able to supply a full quota of it to his offspring.

I maintain that if it were possible for an apparently unmixed white couple to have a Negro baby there ought to be any number of such cases in the South even if it happens in one in every hundred thousand births.

Schienfeld gives a color plate of the chromosomes which shows why "a truly black-skinned child can be produced only if *both* parents carry some Negro skin-color genes, "which he says should dispose of the superstition that some white woman with a "hidden" Negro strain could produce a coal-black baby.[13] A blonde, blue-eyed couple, like an unmixed black one, can produce only their own type. When however, the two are mixed, and then mixed again in certain proportions we may have nearly all kinds of color of skin and texture of hair. Were there no race-mixing there would probably be only white people and black ones on this earth.

I do not wish to be dogmatic but as for myself I simply do not believe that Mendel's law applies to human skin-color. That it does to plants and the lesser animals seems to be proved. Is it not possible that pigment in man follows a different metabolic law from pigment in plants and animals? The latter are often mottled; man rarely is.

While I do not hold that, in some cases, a child might be born slightly darker than the darker of its two parents, I should certainly set down as proof of infidelity a mulatto couple having a white child or a black one. And in the case of a white, or near-white, couple having a legitimate black child I set it down as an impossibility. Thus in the magazine story above-mentioned if the author had made the mother gasp with horror, not so much at the color of the child but at the very evident proof of her adultery it would have been far nearer the truth. Moreover, for a mother to reject her offspring no matter what its color, is monstrous. Birds will hatch and rear the

13 You and Heredity, p. 68. 1939. Snyder, L. H. Principles of Heredity, says similarly "In spite of popular belief to the contrary, it does not appear to be possible for a white woman and a light-skinned Negro to have a black child." (p. 127). See also Dodge: Jour. of Heredity, Vol. 16, 6. 282. 1925, and Fenton, C. L., Our Living World, p. 195. 1943.

offspring of birds of a different kind and color; hens will hatch and rear ducks; dogs will suckle kittens and rear them tenderly; black men and women will lavish care upon their children though born with Caucasian features. This turning away of a mother from her child because of its color is typical of the turning away of the White, from its child, the mulatto. In this respect is seen the superior spirit of Islam, under which the child of a Muslim by a black woman, becomes one of the family and inherits equally with the rest. Under Christianity, as was seen in all the colonies in America— English, French or Dutch—the children of white men by black women were generally thrust back on the weaker group to be exploited. The same holds true in all Christian lands today with special emphasis on British and American ones.

As regards unmixed black couples, they, on the other hand, have been known to produce white children. But these are albinos. They are white only in color; in features and hair they are "pure" Negro. Albinos have been found from time immemorial in Africa. Pearson has given many portraits of them in his "Albinism in Man." Sometimes as happened recently in the South in the case of twins, one is an albino. White parents have also been known to produce albinos, or colorless, children—a fact which confirms Schopenhauer's statement that there is no such thing as a white race. The albino, Caucasian or Negro, is the nearest possible being to a "white" man.

Curly Hair and Negro Ancestry

As regards hair, I noticed in Europe any number of white persons, particularly Irish, Scotch, and Jewish, whose hair was a short, kinky-ish, kind of curl, which though it looked wooly was softer to the touch than that of an unmixed Negro. This was particularly true of one noted Scotch divine I knew.

C. K. Schokking, a Dutch scientist, gives photographs of the members of two families in Holland with hair of this kind but attributes the cause not to Negro origin but to "independent and local" ones. He was able to find "no tradition of Negro blood" in their families, he says.[14] Burlingame, agreeing with him, says that while this so-called "kinky or wooly" hair is "rare among Caucasians," it does occur.[15]

Now I happen to know several cases of very fair persons with this kind of hair, and, who, as in the cases cited by Schokking, had brothers and sisters with straight hair. It also happens that I knew the ancestry of these

14 Hair Mutation in Man. Jour of Heredity, Vol. 25, p. 339. 1934.
15 Heredity and Social Problems, p. 114. 1940.

persons, and that it is Negro, greatly diluted. Since in such cases we attribute the kinky-ish hair to Negro ancestry why say it is different in the case of Caucasians who have the same?

For instance, we know positively that there is some degree of Negro strain, light of course, in the Dutch. Van Herwerden calls attention to the Malayan and Jewish elements, both of which have a Negro strain, that have been absorbed into the Netherland population.[16] But he omits mention of the more direct Negro strain as the Negro soldiers in the armies of Spain, which dominated the Low Countries for centuries. He also says nothing of the Negroes who came from the Dutch colonies of South America, one of which was once northern Brazil. As early as 1653 when the Dutch were settling New York of workmen brought from Holland, five were free Negroes. As for the present day, I, myself, saw scores of Negroes, principally in Rotterdam, some of whom had white wives and mulatto children.

Moreover here is one case from Europe where an English child had the kind of hair described by Schokking and where there is very definite proof of his Negro ancestry. N. B. Harmon of London submitted to the West London Medical Society specimens of hair from the descendants of a Negro who had married a white woman. Of this he says, "A full-blooded African Negro married a Scots woman. She had three daughters by him. The hair of the two elder is shown. Both are frizzy but one much more so than the other. The least frizzy is brownish. The eldest has the typical yellow skin and frizzy, coal-black hair of the mulattoes. She married a Sussex man (white) and had by him six children, five are alive and their hair is shown. The eldest, girl, has brown wavy hair. The second, girl, is a very pretty child with the barest suggestion of quadroon blood. If I had not seen the mother with her I should probably not have thought of any mixture of blood; her fair is fine, dark, wavy brown. The third, girl, has also fine, wavy, lustrous brown hair. The fourth, girl, has beautiful rich-brown, soft, wavy hair. The fifth is a boy; he has a fair almost flaxen hair in very small *tight curls*, but not of the pepper-corn order.

"In this family the black strain has been nearly bred out; the only child who shows any particular *Negroid* character is the fair-haired boy but even his tight curls are not characteristic for *many English boys of his age show the same character.*" (Italics mine).[17]

Euclid said that things that are equal to the same thing are equal to one another. If in a given proved case we see Negro ancestry as the cause of

---

16 Blood-Groups and Interbreeding. Internat. Eugenics Congress III. p. 436. 1923.

17 West London Med. Journal, Vol. 19, p. 205. 1914.

XLIV. Left: Bernardino Rivadavia (1780-1845), First President of Argentina and a mulatto. Right: Emperor Dom Pedro II, who had a very slight Negro strain inherited from his grandfather, John VI, King of Portugal.

kinky-ish hair why should we give a different cause for it in the case of certain others? Does one's ancestry come out of the air as so many geneticists seem to infer, or has it a real foundation in the past? Moreover, the English people, as I have also shown elsewhere, have absorbed a great amount of Negro strain. Incidentally, Joseph Goebbels, great Nazi leader, has this kind of hair, and is also dark-skinned.

I am strongly inclined to believe that all individuals and peoples with naturally curly hair had a Negro ancestor, or ancestors, more or less distant. And I am not alone in that belief.

Chapter Twenty-two

CRITICISMS OF CURRENT RACIST VIEWS

"The cocksureness of the scientific biologist should surely be the cause of the gravest misgivings. The more certain a man is that he is right the more probable is it that he is wrong because it means the facts are as soft clay in his hands and his certainty moulds them to his purpose."—Darbishire

AN analysis of the works of any of the racialists reveals some very queer reasoning. I could cite hundreds of examples but shall confine myself to a few and these are, at that, some of the more reasonable ones.

William McDougall, formerly professor of psychology at Harvard University and now of Duke University, speaking of the difference in moral qualities between the Negro and the Indian repeats the old belief that the Indian is assertive while the Negro is inherently submissive. He says, "The Negro has, in a way, adapted himself to the position imposed on him . . . But the red man has never let himself be impressed into the social system of the dominant whites. In some peculiar way he has proved resistant; he dies rather than submit. Does not this imply some deep-seated moral differences between the two races . . .

"I will suggest merely on the basis of a slight knowledge . . . that the red race is strongly self-assertive, while in the Negro the submissive impulse is strong. The last point may be illustrated by a true story of a Negro maid whose Northern mistress after treating her with great forbearance for a time, in spite of shortcomings, turned upon her and scolded her vigorously. The maid showed no resentment but rather showed signs of a new satisfaction and exclaimed, 'Lor', Missus, you make me feel so good.' Is this not a typical and significant incident? I will even venture to suggest that in the great strength of this instinct of submission we have the main key to the history of the Negro race." He goes on to cite the submission of the Negroes to their chiefs in Africa.[1]

This statement reveals an ignorance of Indian and African history, as well as that of the Negro in the New World.

The Indian was a slave in every country of the New World and like the Negro had to submit whenever superior power was imposed on him. There are several books on Indian slavery which Professor McDougall might have

---

[1] Is America Safe For Democracy? pp. 117-18. 1921.

consulted as J. A. Saco's *Historia de la Esclavitud de los Indios* and A. W. Lauber's Indian Slavery in Colonial Times. As late as 1910, Sir Roger Casement revealed how the Indians of the Putamayo had been reduced to virtual slavery by the Anglo-Peruvian Rubber Company.

Of course McDougall tries to modify his statement by confessing to only "a slight knowledge" of the subject, but what sort of scientist is it who gives permanent form to such indefinite information when there is abundant definite material available, the more so as he is likely to be quoted by other scientists, which actually happens in this case.[2]

Note, also, the air of certainty with which he subtly invests a matter of which he admits he knows little.

On the other hand, I can cite writers, who, speaking from experience, declare that the Negro was more assertive than the Indian. In Volume Two I gave, for example, the opinions of Alexander von Humboldt, the great German explorer, and H. N. Coleridge, both of whom lived among both Indians and Negroes.[3]

The simple truth is that at no time in any part of the New World did the Negro submit quietly to slavery; did he ever miss an opportunity to strike for freedom. Some of the most horrible fights ever recorded occurred on slave-ships on which the Negroes had got the upper-hand, one of which, the revolt on the Amistad, led by Cinque, is a classic. And there were hundreds of revolts from the United States to Argentina, the first occurring in 1522, only twenty years after the bringing in of the blacks. The Negroes of Surinam were the first people of the New World to win their independence. Were they submissive in doing that? The blacks of Haiti under Toussaint L'Ouverture and Dessalines were the first of the Latin-Americans to win their independence. The Maroon Negroes of Jamaica forced the English to grant them virtual independence; the slaves of St. Thomas, Virgin Islands, drove out the Danes and freed themselves; the Negroes of Northern Brazil defeated the whites and formed the republic of Palmares;[4] the Negroes of the Island of St. Vincent, who had been enslaved by the Caribs, said to be the fiercest of the Caribbean Indians, not only defeated them, but absorbed them;[5] the history of the island of Jamaica is studded with slave revolt in which hundreds of whites were massacred—a fact equally true of Cuba, Haiti, Venezuela, and Guatemala; and even in the United

[2] Pitt-Rivers, G. H., Clash of Culture, p. 151, 1927, uses this incident of the Negro maid with apparent approval.

[3] See sources and added quotations in Sex and Race, vol. 2, pp. 10, 12, 75, 77. 1942.

[4] See sources Sex and Race, vol. 2, p. 31. 1942.

[5] Johnston, H. H., Negro in the New World, p. 307.

States where the blacks were greatly outnumbered there were many revolts, the principal of which was that by Nat Turner, who, with his followers killed 61 whites. Aptheker lists 200 plots and revolts of Negroes in the United States between 1526 and 1864.[6]

At Boston in 1770 when the white mob hesitated to attack the British soldiers it was a Negro, Crispus Attucks, who led it on and was thus the first to die in the cause of American independence. Of the five names on the monument on Boston Common reared to the occasion, his name heads the list. Incidentally it was a Negro drummer on the British side who also led on the white British soldiers to attack the Americans in a riot that led up to the clash in which Attucks was killed.[7]

In the United States prior to the second world war there were ten or more riots by Negro soldiers, who charged that they were being ill-treated by the white citizens. The most serious of these were at Brownsville and Houston, Texas, where many whites were killed and wounded. In the Philippines also many Negro soldiers deserted to the enemy. One of the most daring of the Filipino leaders was a Negro deserter, named Fagan.[8]

The African Negro is submissive to his chief because his first lesson is that of obedience. For the warrior the law is iron and in Dahomey, Zululand, and Ashanti, death was the penalty for the slightest disobedience. But though submissive to discipline one may be highly assertive when ordered to act. There is a great difference between one curbed by discipline and the passive resister or the lamb-like person. Morever, for the chiefs to have exercised such power over their followers must not the chiefs, who were also Negroes, been highly assertive?

It is true that certain Indian tribes of the New World, especially those of the United States, did put up a stubborn fight against the white invader but not more so than did the Ashanti, the Zulus, and the Sudanese against the English; or the Dahomeyans and the Islamic Negroes of West Africa against France; or the Congolese against Belgium. The battle of Isandhlwana in 1879 in which Cetewayo, King of the Zulus, annihilated an entire British regiment, armed with the latest weapons surpassed that in which Sitting Bull, Indian chief, wiped out a force under General Custer in 1876. Cetewayo killed 806 whites and 471 of their Negro soldiers, including the Prince Napoleon, heir to the French throne, while Sitting Bull killed 265 whites of which Custer was one.[9]

---

[6] Aptheker, H., Negro Slave Revolts in the United States, pp. 70, 71. 1939.
[7] Kidder, F., The Boston Massacre, pp. 49-50. 1879. According to the testimony at the trial someone called out to this unnamed Negro, "You black rascal, what have you to do with white people's quarrels?"
[8] See sources in the 100 Amazing Facts About the Negro, Proof No. 81.
[9] See ZULUS and CUSTER in Encyc. Britannica.

Another important fact: In America the Indian was on his own soil; he knew the country and had arms such as they were; the Negro in the New World was not only a stranger but he had landed empty-handed even without clothes. Moreover every care was taken to mix up the different tribes so that the Negroes would not be able to understand one another.

The Negroes in Africa, instead of being submissive to the white man, are still very resistant even when they appear to submit and might yet do to the whites in Africa on a continental scale what the Negroes of Haiti did to the French in 1812. In South Africa and parts of East Africa the blacks at this writing are almost in open revolt.

As late as June 1930, European labor delegates discussed at the League of Nations the question of forced labor in Africa, which it was declared was necessary because the Negroes were unwilling to come under white civilization to be exploited even as were the Indians of Sitting Bull's day. But there is this difference: When the Indian objected he was called "the noble Red Man;" when the Africans do the same he is "the lazy nigger."

When McDougall says that Negroes lack assertiveness did he ever see them in their lodges, conventions, debates and Garvey meetings? The chief reason why American Negroes have never been able to unite for their common good is their assertiveness; so many want to be the leader.

Among the most assertive people I know are certain Negroes of the British West Indies, Cuba, and Haiti; and among the most submissive I know are the German and the English lower classes.

As to the case of the Negro maid McDougall mentions, it would be difficult to find a more inept illustration, even assuming that it has not been exaggerated. Many of these Negro maids are perfect tyrants in white households—a type that would not be tolerated in England. The way in which some American servants, colored and white, talk back to their mistresses, has amazed many a foreign visitor.

The Negro woman in this case might even have been mocking her mistress, and later relating it with glee to her friends. But even if she were sincere, it would no more be typical of all Negroes than the cases of those masochistic white men, who have Negro women to whip them, or to inflict on them indignities that cannot be recorded here, are typical of all white men.

Is Negro Blood "Invincible"?

Another sample of the same is from Lothrop Stoddard, Ph. D., Harvard University. He says in support of the alleged inferiority of the Negro, "Of course, the more primitive a type the more prepotent it is. This is why crossings with the Negro are uniformly fatal. Whites, Amerindians, or Asiatcs

XLV. Upper, left to right: Lloyd A. Hall, Consulting Chemist for United States Government, the City of Chicago, and large industrial firms; Edgar P. Benjamin, Attorney and Bank President. Lower: Miles Mark Fisher, Minister and Professor of Ecclesiastical History; G. Luther Sadgwar, artist and art instructor. Center, lower: Berry Armstrong Claytor, expert in Chinese literature for the Library of Congress.

—all are alike vanquished by the invincible prepotency of the more primitive, generalized, and lower Negro blood."[10]

Now prepotency in its biological sense is the power of a certain group or groups to transmit its physical characters to its descendants when crossed with another racial group, that is, according to Stoddard, the offspring of a Caucasian and Negro, would show much more of the Negro. If this were true it would place the Negro nearer the great well-spring of life, nearness to which makes a plant or an animal survive where others perish. Given that vitality, that stamina, that staying power, and a group, when its intellect is developed would come out on top and stay there. Darwin called it "the survival of the fittest."

But as if that were not enough Stoddard adds "invincible" prepotency. What is it to be invincible? It is to be unconquerable. Since when has it become a good thing to possess the vanquishable potency he attributes to the whites, whom he contends throughout his book are a "superior" race?

Moreover nothing is invincible save change, and if, as he argues, that the so-called white race is superior, and hence. should down all the others, what chance will it have against the alleged invincibility of the Negro?

Are "Pure" Negroes" Inherently Inferior?

F. H. Hankins, professor of sociology, Smith University, who is a liberal, but not yet fully divorced from racist doctrine says, "It may well be doubted whether there could be found any pure Negroes, who, if brought up under the most favoring circumstances could develop the intellectual powers necessary to carry on the higher cultural activities of this country."[11]

This is indeed rich. Who runs this country today? Who fills the chairmanship of nearly all the important Congressional committees. Southern demagogues of the type of Cotton-Ed Smith and Theodore Bilbo. Even as regards the Northern politician, history a century hence, is going to record this country as being one of the most stupidly run of all times. For instance giving money to Germany and otherwise helping to build up Hitler and then spending billions of dollars and thousands of lives to pull him down; being Japan's greatest supplier of the materials of war, then spending billions more than was ever had from her to pull her down. Again, there was the plowing-under of crops, the destruction of little pigs, and other government subsidies to bring about an economy of scarcity, while millions of citizens were not getting enough to eat. I maintain that the most benighted

10 The Rising Tide of Color, p. 301. 1921.
11 Racial Basis of Civilization, p. 370, 1926.

African tribe would not be so dumb as to do that. Yes, in our civilization there is plenty of intellect; little of common sense.

White civilization creates a mess with its many wars, and then blunders terrifically in trying to clean up those messes. Mussolini, Fascist monster, was coddled and supported by English, French and American statesmen and capitalists, some of whose sons were killed in the second world war started by Mussolini.

What has saved America so far is by no means the sagacity of its politicians but rather the vastness of its economic resources which permitted it to blunder and waste and still be able to pull through.

Again, why does America have such stringent laws, written and unwritten against all Negroes, mixed and unmixed? Because it believes they could not develop "intellectual powers?" There was George W. Carver, an unmixed black. What chance would he ever have had of getting a high governmental agricultural position? Once, when this great man was invited to speak at a white Southern college, the faculty and most of the students objected so strongly that his lecture was cancelled.

What chance had an American Negro of becoming a Dewey, a Farragut, or a King, when naval regulations compelled him to be only a messman? How could he become an Eisenhower, Mark Clark, or a Patton when until 1943, Negro graduates of West Point were side-tracked to Negro colleges to train cadets there. What, ham-string a man and then blame him for not being a champion sprinter! I know of but one way of finding out whether one is capable of doing a thing or not, and that is to try him. And I am sure, that a scientific experimentalist like Professor Hankins, would have said the same had been dealing with any other group but the Negro.

Furthermore as regards so-called pure Negroes several cases could be cited where they have proved wise and capable heads of states. These are chiefly to be found in Islam, as Kafur, a Negro slave, who ruled Egypt and whose name has become proverbial for wise leadership in the East.[12] Since, however Occidentals are generally unacquainted with Eastern history, I will cite a full-blooded Negro, a slave, who educated himself, and who proved so wise and able a governor that he won even the admiration of his enemies: Toussaint L'Ouverture of Haiti. Governor-General Felix Eboue who did so much for the Allied cause in Africa in the second world war was also an unmixed Negro.

[12] Haas, Jacob de, History of Palestine, pp. 168-170. 1930. See also sketch of Kafur in Rogers, J. A., World's Greatest Men and Women of African Descent. 1932.

White And Negro Intellect Compared

Still another example is that of L. L. Burlingame, professor of biology, Stanford University. Professor Burlingame tries hard to be fair but his mind, it is clear, has been trained along jim-crow lines and despite himself he cannot get out of that groove. In his "Heredity and Social Problems."[83] under the heading "Negro Intelligence," he gives tables of "White and Negro Intelligence" ratings by the United States Army Board in the first world war as follows: New York (white): 58.3; Pennsylvania: 62; Ohio: 62.2; Indiana: 55.9. Those for the Negro in the same states are respectively: 38.6; 34.7; 45.5; 42.2.

He gives also the following Southern States (white): Kentucky: 41.5; Tennessee: 4.0; Alabama: 413; Mississippi: 37.6; Arkansas: 35.6; Louisiana 36.1; Oklahoma: 42.9; Texas: 43.4. Negroes for the same states were: 23.9; 29.7; 19.9; 10.2; 16.1; 13.4; 31.4; 12.1.

As a result of the above, he says, "Note that the whites outscore Negroes in all the states," and then he comes to this conclusion, "In the present state of knowledge it is proper to think that there are probably differences in intelligence between the races."

Since he has based his conclusion on *states* let us look at that angle a little more closely. What do we find? That the lowest Northern state, Indiana, led the highest Southern state, Tennessee. If now we judge intelligence by *states,* as he has done, we could under a heading "White Southern Intelligence," say. "There are probably differences between Northern whites and Southern whites."

Again look at the list for the Negroes and we find that the lowest Northern state: Pennsylvania, led the highest Southern state, Oklahoma. Thus again we could come to Burlingame's conclusion about intelligence and say "There are probably differences of intelligence between Northern Negroes and Southern Negroes."

Look at them again and we find Ohio led New York. Thus we could say that Ohio whites show a difference of intelligence to New York; and so on with each state in their respective sections of the country.

But the comparisons do not end there. Looking at the list again we find that the Ohio Negroes led the whites of all the Southern states and that the Negroes of Indiana led five Southern white states. Now what Professor Burlingame's jim-crow training has led him to do is to take the figures by *states* then as it suits his purpose interpret them by *race.* In a word, he eats his cake and has it, too. If he follows the state line of reasoning he is bound to admit that Northern whites are superior to Southern whites and

13 **Heredity and Social Problems,** p. 240. 1940.

XLVI. Upper, left to right: Milton S. J. Wright, College Professor; and William T. Vernon, Bishop of the African Methodist Episcopal Church, College President, and former Register of the United States Treasury. Below: Isaac Fisher, educator, and noted prize-winning Assayist; and Robert S. Abbott, founder and builder of the Chicago Defender and a civic leader. (See Notes on the Illustrations.)

some Northern Negroes are superior to Southern whites.[14]

But his case becomes even more glaring when we recall that he could have had figures even more typical of the states if he had consulted an easily accessible source: the United States census.

Were it my purpose to take acquired knowledge as proof of inherent "racial" intelligence and then like him limit the figures to what suits my argument I could make out a pretty strong case that Negroes are superior in intelligence to whites. For instance, New York is the most advanced state in the union, but what do we find there? The Negroes, according to the 1930 census (Vol. 2, p. 1229), not only led the whites of ten Southern states in literacy but the New York whites themselves. The figures for illiteracy for New York were: Negroes: 2.5; Whites: 3.6 per cent.

Now why has New York, the most intellectually advanced of the states, so high a percentage of white illiteracy? It has a high percentage of foreign-born whites—Italians, Greeks, Bulgars—who never had an opportunity for education in their native lands. But if a census were to be taken say in 1943, the literacy rate for Negroes in New York might be lower than in 1930, and that of the whites higher. Why? Because war brought in a large number of Negroes from the South where schooling is less than in the North; and because European immigration has been cut down since 1924 and numbers of the illiterate foreign-born whites have died since 1930.

Looking further into the matter of "intelligence" between the whites of the North and those of the South, we find figures that would place the white Southerner occupying an intellectual position to the North exactly analogous to that of the Negro in the white South. Professor J. McKeen Cattell in his "Study of the Distribution of the 1,000 Leading American Men of Science," showed that the state of Pennsylvania alone produced six times more scientific men than the thirteen Southern states; 66 for two Northern states and 60 for the thirteen Southern states combined. As for New York it had 183, or alone more than three times that of the whole South. Again, Who's Who in America (1928-29) gave 5,811 noted persons for New York and Pennsylvania alone as against 4624 for eleven Southern states.

Here as clear as the sun on a cloudless day is the fact that it is not race but environment and opportunity that counts. Professor Lowie cites the case of one single Northern state against eleven Southern ones thus: "Massachusetts produces as many scientists as the South Atlantic states—a cultural

14 Professor Otto Klineberg of Columbia University has shown up the difference between Southern white and Northern Negro in the army intelligence tests even more strikingly. The Negroes of Ohio, he shows, led the whites of Kentucky by more than eight points; while the Negroes of Pennsylvania, New York, Illinois, led the whites of Mississippi, Kentucky, Arkansas, and Georgia. Race Differences, p. 182. 1935.

difference with a vengeance. Do the Bostonian's sex cells carry fifty times as much of the research factor as the Atlantan's? The idea is absurd because there is no appreciable difference in the heredity of the two."[15] If such an enormous discrepancy can be explained by the environment in the case of the whites why, he asks, may it not also be used to explain the difference in attainment between white and black?

In fact environment is so important a factor in developed intelligence that it seems a waste of time to discuss the latter without giving the former the first place, especially in the case of groups. And even of individuals, too. Had Alexander Hamilton remained in the West Indies; had Napoleon never left Corsica; had Andrew Carnegie never left Scotland they would have had the same innate ability but they would never had an opportunity to develop it on the scale they did.

On a visit to the Canadian side of Niagara Falls one summer I saw a sight that symbolized to me the effect of under-privilege on any group. To the right of the falls was an area of grass that was lush and green while below that in an almost straight line across—a color-line so to speak—was another area dry and stubbly. Looking for the cause I saw that the green area was getting the spray from the falls while the dry area was too far down to get any.

A biblical illustration which I think is apt here is that of the parable of the sower. A sower went forth with a bag of seed. Some seeds fell by the wayside, and were eaten by the birds; some fell in stony places, where they were deprived of proper nourishment and withered soon after they had sprouted; some fell among thorns and were choked by them; while some fell on good ground, and bore abundant fruit. Note, however, that all were seed from the same bag, and had the sower taken care to see that all of his seed fell on good ground, the first three cases would not have happened at all.

I have read and consulted dozens of reports of so-called intelligence tests of white and colored children and adults, and it has always struck me that it was the testers themselves who needed to have their intelligence tested. Testing white and colored to see which is superior is like matching a plant that has the freedom of air and sunshine against one forced to do its best in a cellar. Even a half-wit would realize immediately which would show itself superior.

The Negro is repressed on every hand; he lacks the opportunity for education given the whites and even when he gets the education he has the toughest time finding some employer unprejudiced enough to give him a chance to show his talents. Again the wealth per capita of the whites is far

15 Are We Civilized, p. 25. 1929.

in excess of the Negroes. Two or three white men alone, at most five, possess more wealth than all the Negroes put together.

As for the statistics upon which the right-wing sociologists rely so much for proof of their theories these can be juggled or ignored to suit the pattern they wish to present .Such always remind me of the housewife who takes a sample of cloth to the store. She matches and matches, rejecting and rejecting boll after boll of perfectly good cloth until she finds what suits her. There is an old saying: Figures do not lie but liars figure.

This is what I have found. In environments favorable for education, human beings regardless of color, will outstrip those of their "race" who live in less favorable ones. Northern whites outstrip Southern whites; Northern Negroes outstrip Southern Negroes; Southern whites outstrip Southern Negroes; Southern Negroes outstrip the whites of the Balkan States and the Negroes of Northern Brazil, Cuba, and Haiti, where educational advantages are less. The only valid intelligence test would be to match whites and Negroes who have the same opportunity for education and the same degree of wealth and leisure.

100 Negro Millionaires!

Yet another racialist gem is from Dr. H. C. Morton of the very learned Victoria Institute of London, England. In trying to prove the menace of the alleged inferiority of the Negro to white America, he says, "How dire is the peril is shown by the fact that in the '80's, there were over forty Negro millionaires in New York City and today it is estimated there are about one hundred."[16]

A hundred Negro millionaires in New York! Well, Harlem must be swarming with counterfeiters of which the FBI has not yet heard. New York, to the best of my knowledge, has not and never had a single Negro millionaire even among the numbers "bankers." There are perhaps not more than six Negro millionaires in the United States and these are in Oklahoma and Texas.

And so I could go on to cite excerpts like these to fill several volumes. It was this sort of reasoning that aroused the wrath of Schopenhauer. As for myself I have encountered so much of it in books on race by professors, college men, and others who have been *graduated* (a better word is twisted) to fit into a certain scheme that I must confess I have never been able to overcome a certain surprise when I see them manifesting a broad grasp, a wide understanding of life as it actually is, in other words, showing that common sense to be met with sometimes in aged persons who can neither read nor write.

16 Victoria Institute Jour., Vol. 67, p 59. 1935.

Chapter Twenty-three

THE NEED FOR GREATER VISION — THE BAD THINGS SAID ABOUT THE INFANT AMERICA COMPARED WITH WHAT WHITE AMERICA SAYS AGAINST NEGROES

T HERE are human beings, some of them very learned, whose thought processes remind one at times of the rhinoceros. That beast is near-sighted and whenever he senses an object of possible danger beyond his range of vision, he charges blindly at it. In the same way there are those who immediately attack everything that does not happen to fit in with their idea of the true, the beautiful, and the good. The narrowed vision of such does not permit them to see in the tiny seed the giant sequoia that will outlast empires; in the gangling foal, the horse that will one day win the Derby; or in the feeble infant a future Napolean, Theodore Roosevelt, or Joe Louis.

Take the New World. It was nearly two centuries before Europe began to dream of the magnitude of what Columbus had done. Perhaps not a single thinker of the seventeenth century foresaw America's present greatness. In fact some were very pessimistic. Abbe Raynal, when he thought of the slavery of Indians and Negroes, said, "What is all this worth? Nothing! Worse than nothing! The world would have been better off if America had never been discovered and the ocean route to Asia had remained unknown."

Gentry says: "Clearly Columbus had come with a sword, and had but opened a new chapter in the long Iliad of human woes."

"In Europe," says John Fiske, "little heed was paid to America and its discovery except in France. Without knowing much about America, the Frenchmen used to use America to point a moral and adorn a tale." The French aristocrats, he said, lamented that the American Revolution had not only cost France two billion francs, but that America's fight for independence had set a bad example to the French masses and the world.

Voltaire, in Candide, dismissed Canada as "a few acres of snow." The only good that many would admit in the discovery of the New World was the discovery of quinine. Of George III it was said that he thought more of a haunch of venison than his American colonies. As for the attitude of the government itself it was shown in the fact it used the colonies as a dumping ground for its criminals and other human "refuse" as France in our day uses Devil's Island in South America.

When Thomas Jefferson was President he offered to give a building square on Sixteenth Street in Washington to any European nation that would erect a legation buiding on it, but so little was the new republic thought of that not one accepted the offer. Later a similar site was sold to Germany for $125,000.

As for the United States it was singled out for attack. Gustavus Myers in his "America Strikes Back," gives a review of some of the bad things then being said about the United States. Racially, too, Americans were considered the very dregs of the earth. Gobineau, father of the doctrine of white racial superiority, said that the white American population of the 1860's was made up "of the refuse of the ages' and was "an incoherent juxtaposition of the most degraded beings" from which "nothing but the most horrible ethnic confusion would result."[1] Another gloomy writer called the United States "the graveyard of the white race."

The average Englishman entertained great contempt for America and not without cause. Was it not the land on which England was dumping her convicts, prostitutes, rebels and discordant elements? Was it not the land to which the despised, degraded and starving Irish were flocking? The truth is that even from the most charitable middle-class viewpoint, the future of America was unpromising. It was not until the first world war that most Englishmen began to experience a change of ideas towards America. The second world war brought another improvement until this once despised nation is now regarded as the savior of England and the world. The rejected stone has become the head of the corner.

As for Australia, another bulwark of "the master race" idea, the English viewpoint was even worse. Australia was an outright convict dump. The older the Australian family, the more likely it is to be of convict origin. Yet that land with unparallel snobbery now turns up its nose at Negroes and Orientals both of whom had a better moral record than its ancestors.

Now what Europe once said and thought of white America bears a striking similarity to what white America has said and still says of the Negro in certain quarters. The libraries of the United States contain a vast amount of pessimistic matter on this subject. It was not until the Civil War that the

---

[1] For a fuller quotation on this subject by Gobineau and the sources see: Sex and Race, Vol. 2, p. 39. 1942. See also James McSparran's "America Dissected," published in Dublin in 1753, where he warns self-respecting people to stay away from America. He has nothing good to say for the people of North Carolina, whom he finds "rude and illiterate." As for the convicts who are being sent from Ireland to Virginia and Maryland so few of them ever reform he thinks it a "great pity" that "some punishment worse than death or transportation could not be devised for those vermin." (pp. 9, 12.)

XLVII. Upper: George L. Ruffin (1835-1887), Member Massachusetts Legislature and Boston judge; and Jean Arneaux, who won gold medal of the New York Sun as best amateur Shakespearean player in America. Starred in Richard III. Below: Colonel James Lewis, Soldier, Chief of Police of New Orleans, and Surveyor-General of Louisiana. Francis L. Cardoza, Secretary of State of South Carolina (1868-1872) and State Treasurer. Below him: Edward A. Johnson, Historian, College Professor, first Negro Member of New York Legislature.

Negro's stock began to mount a little. What he had done in the Revolutionary War was quickly forgotten.

Some of America's greatest thinkers could see no future for the Negroes and were more than eager to deport him. I shall select two of the greatest of the great: Thomas Jefferson and Abraham Lincoln. Both wanted to colonize the Negro outside of the United States—anywhere so that they could get him out. As president, Jefferson expressed his momentary willingness to act on this as soon as Congress saw fit.

He saw no cultural contribution that the Negro could ever make to America. "Never yet," he said, "could I find that a black had uttered a thought above the level of plain narration; never even saw an elementary trait of painting or sculpture."[2]

But was it the fault of these blacks, condemned by the law of Jefferson's own land, to remain illiterate? Was it also the fault of these blacks that Jefferson did not know that in their native land, other blacks had been and were executing art that was destined to revitalize "white" art—art for which white connoisseurs are now willing to pay more than for Jefferson's autograph. Moreover, two of Jefferson's contemporaries, Rousseau and Chateaubriand, had already seen the value of Negro art. Besides had even the Africans in America executed some of their native art, Jefferson would very likely have considered it crude as he shared the then prevailing view of Africa. He said, for instance, that the ourang-outang "preferred black women to those of his own species."

In fairness to Jefferson, it must be said that it wasn't because he was not kindly and humanitarian. When Abbe Gregoire sent him his work on dis-

---

2 Writings of Thomas Jefferson, Vol. 2, p. 195. 1904. 20 Vols.

Jefferson, in my humble opinion, was superior in his humanitarianism and in his democratic idealism to Lincoln. Lincoln was more of the politician, a very useful quality for his times, I'll admit. He very frankly said that he was a white man first and so acted, the result being that his policy towards the Negro was marked by blundering, which would have been even worse had he lived longer, Negroes would not only have not been given the vote but would very likely have been sent off to die in unhealthy areas of South and Central America.

In the matter of lynching Lincoln also made certain statements that would be viewed with disfavor by liberals today. In the case of a lynching at St. Louis, Mo., while he strongly condemned the practice of lynching, he conceded that the Negro had got what was due him. The lynched man, he said, "had forfeited his life by the perpetration of an outrageous murder upon one of the most worthy and respectable citizens and *had he not died as he did, he must have died by the sentence of the law* in a very short time afterward. As to him alone *it was as well the way it was as it could otherwise have been.*" (Address to Young Men's Lyceum of Springfield, Ill., Jan. 27, 1837.) Italics mine.

I maintain that however "outrageous" a murder it is always a case for the law. Killing is sometimes done in self-defense or under circumstances that admit of extenuation. It is never "as well the way" when the mob handles it.

tinguished Negroes, Jefferson wrote him, "No person living wishes more sincerely than I do to see a complete refutation of the doubts I have myself entertained and expressed in the grade of understanding alloted them (the blacks) by nature, and to find that in this respect they are on a par with ourselves." Jefferson's defect in this respect was his lack of spiritual vision —the vision to see that given the human beings all things are possible, that out of them will come in time great writers, musicians and scientists. Aristotle (384-322 B.C.), who was for nearly two thousand years regarded as the world's greatest scientist, declared that the northern Europeans were "wanting in intelligence and skill."[3] Cicero bemoaned that all that Rome could expect from Britain were slaves who would at best be poor in music, literature, and the arts.[4] Yet Shakespeare, a greater than Cicero or any other Roman writer, arose from these despised Britons.

Lincoln And The Negro

Lincoln, too, while firm for justice to the Negro, spoke even in harsher terms against Negroes than did Jefferson, and was even more eager and active than Jefferson to get them out of the United States. On August 14, 1862, when a deputation of Negroes called on Lincoln at the White House, he spoke in terms that seemed almost to blame the Negroes for the Civil War. He said, in substance, "But for your race among us there could not be war, although many men engaged on either side do not care for you one way or the other. Nevertheless, I repeat without the institution of slavery and the colored race, the war could not have existence. It is better, therefore, for us both to be separated."[5]

Lincoln wrote several nations asking them to take the Negroes off his

[3] Politics, VIII, 7. (trans. Jowett.) Aristotle said, however, that the northern Europeans were "full of spirit." As for the Asiatics he said they were "intelligent and inventive but wanting in spirit."

[4] In his Letters to Atticus, Cicero said, "Britannici belli exitus expectatur: constat enim aditus insulae esse munitos mirificis molibus. Etiam illud jam cognitum est, neque argenti scripulum esse ullum in illa insula, neque ullum spem praedae nisi mancipiis: ex quibos nullos puto, te literis aut musicis eruditos expectare." (Epist. Ad, Atticum I. iv, Epist . 16.) Cicero is frequently quoted as having said also: "The stupidest and ugliest slaves come from Britain." Dan Crawford so quotes him (Thinking Black, p. 26, 1913.) Prof. Ruth Benedict also quotes, "They are so stupid and so utterly incapable of being taught that they are not fit to form a part of the household of Athens." (Race: Science and Politics, p. 10. 1943.) A slave capable of great attainments was a prize. Some of the greatest thinkers of antiquity were slaves. Plato was slave to Anniceris; Epictetus to Epaphroditus; Esop to Iadmon; Terence to Lucanus, and so on. Euclid, great mathematician, was said to be a slave; hence Cicero's complaint that from the British slaves one may expect "no men of letters or any fine hand in music."

[5] Nicolay and Hay. Letters and State Papers of Abraham Lincoln, Vol. 1, pp. 222-25. 1922. 2 Vols.

hands. The Danes in the Virgin Islands, the Dutch in Surinam, the British in Guiana and Honduras, New Granada (now Columbia), Haiti, Ecuador, and Liberia sent in favorable replies. Lincoln selected Haiti, had Congress to vote a first instalment of $500,000 for the purpose, and gave the matter into the hands of Bernard Kock. Lincoln was so anxious to have the Negroes started on their way out that even when Kock was exposed as an unscrupulous adventurer, Lincoln did not withdraw the commission he had given him. Kock, in his greed, had made almost no preparation to house the Negro on the desolate island that had been chosen for them—the Ile de Vache. The colony was a total failure. About 100 of the 500 blacks died from hunger and tropical diseases. Lincoln, finally, had to send a ship for the survivors and the Negroes, who had left American singing hallelujah, glad to go, sang hallelujah, glad to be back.[6]

Luckily, too, for the nation, that Lincoln's project did not work, because we find Lincoln, himself, saying later that but for the aid given the North by the Negro, it could not have won the war. He repeated this four times in his letters. For instance, on September 12, 1864, he wrote as regards the help the Negroes were giving, "Keep it and you save the Union. Throw it away and the Union goes with it."[7] Yet even after the war had been won, Lincoln still toyed with the idea of deporting the Negroes. But for his death he might have sent the Negro soldiers who had fought so gallantly to Panama to dig the canal,[8] where they would have died like flies as did the French in the 1880's.

Even so stalwart an abolitionist as Theodore Parker saw no future for the Negro in America. In 1854, he predicted that "in twenty generations the Negroes will stand just where they are now" and that the Negro in New England would never rise above "the status of a waiter." Yet in 1866, only twelve years later, two Negroes were elected to the Massachusetts legislature.

Jefferson, Lincoln and a host of others would be extremely amazed could they see the Negro today—amazed at their own lack of vision, amazed that their fixed concepts about "race" tied them down so that they could not see that as long as you have Man, himself, no matter what his race or condition, all things are possible. They would be amazed at the number of college graduates, authors, college professors and presidents and scientists, several

6 Nicolay and Hay. Abraham Lincoln: A History, Vol. 6, Chap. 17. 1890; Magazine of American History, Vol. 16, pp. 327-32. 1886; Dyer, B. Persistence of the Idea of Negro Colonization, Pacific Hist. Rev. March, 1943. See also Hispanic Amer. Rev. Vol. 19, pp. 494-503. 1939, on the proposition to colonize the Negroes in Brazil. Another Negro colony in Durango, Mexico, in 1881, met the same fate as that sent to the Ile de Vache.
7 Nicolay and Hay. Letters and State Papers, Vol. 2, p. 576.
8 Butler. Gen. B. F. Butler's Book, p. 904. 1892.

XLVIII. Upper, left to right: Rev. T. Gould and James Steward. Lower: William Steward and Bishop Benjamin F. Lee (See Notes on the Illustrations.)

of whom are instructors and even associate professors in white universities. They would be amazed to learn that Negro illiteracy for the whole nation is lower than that of the native whites in certain Southern states, a people, who, at no time ever had laws passed forbidding them to learn to read.

Nevertheless there are American "statesmen" who still talk seriously of sending the Negroes "back" to Africa. In 1938 and 1939, Senator Theodore Bilbo of Mississippi introduced what he called "The Greater Liberia Act"[9] in Congress asking the United States to buy 40,000 square miles of land in Africa and provide three billion dollars to take Negroes there. Bilbo relied heavily on Lincoln for support but omits to mention the mess Lincoln made with his Ile de Vache project.

In 1865, General Butler told Lincoln that the Negro babies alone were being born faster than the United States would be able to provide ships to take them to Africa. Bilbo said that he would take only 2,500,000, but to provide homes even for these would be a super-gargantuan task. Of course, it is hard to believe that anyone could be so asinine as to take him seriously but Bilbo knew well the mental level of his white constituency and the equally stupid Negroes for whom he said he was spokesman.

Mississippi has 1,074,578 Negroes. Would Bilbo have let that number go out of the 2,500,000? Does the flea wish the dog to migrate and leave him behind? Or the stomach to be separated from the hand? The Negroes of Mississippi don't vote but they are counted for congressional representation. Moreover, what would Bilbo himself do? With his monomania, the Negro, gone, he'd be practically a skull without a brain. And as for the poor whites, most of them would die psychologically. They'd have no one to be better than. No longer would they be able to rub their Aladdin lamp of a white epidermis to feel themselves kings.

Just as America has contributed greatly to the economic betterment of Europe, who once looked down upon her, so has the Negro contributed greatly to the wealth of white America, all of which would have been lost if the policies of Jefferson, Lincoln, and others were followed. Artistically and musically, too, American would have been poorer. As for laughter and comedy, it would even be worse off. American comedy, song, and dance has a decidedly Negro flavor. In a word, it is the Negro who puts the merry in America.

---

9 Congressional Record, May 24, 1938, pp. 7347-7370; April 24, 1939, pp. 4650-4677. The senator claimed that he received 2,500,000 names to petitions of Negroes who wanted to go. I, for one, don't believe he ever received a tenth of that. However, it would have been probably a good thing to have let those go who wanted to go on condition that they sign a pledge never to return, Bilbo with them.

White writers, artists, and comedians have also used Negroes as a stepping-stone to fame and fortune, among them several winners of the Pulitzer Prize. Two of the highest paid comedians—Amos n' Andy—had the Negro as their theme.

When history is written a century hence, the Negro will be given his place among those in the first rank for his role in the building of not only the United States but the rest of the New World. I've given indisputable facts in my "Africa's Gift to America."

Chapter Twenty-four

INCOMPETENCY OF MAN'S KNOWLEDGE

"Man is not and never will be master of Nature." Lowie.

AS regards the mixing of "races" who is the better judge, Man or Nature? Aeons before this planet condensed from gaseous matter; billions of years before life evolved from the lowest form of seaweed; hundreds of millions of years before man developed even the most rudimentary powers of thought, Nature was at work. It is only within the last century, thanks chiefly to Kant, Schopenhauer, Darwin, Spencer, Huxley and thinkers of their type, that man has developed enough mental discrimination to be able to loosen the grip of theology, witchcraft, and other superstition on his throat and is having anything like an opportunity to learn something about himself and his body in relation to the other animals and the forces of Nature.

Hardly more than a century ago the dissection of the human body was frowned on by the church, and was once positively prohibited. The idea was that the human body was "the temple of the living God" and it was sacreligious to dissect God.

How prone is mankind to error, how little able to distinguish the false from the true! A conspicuous example was the premature celebration of peace the world over on November 7, 1918, on a false cablegram.* I never see a blind man go tapping, tapping along the street than I think of the human race in its search for knowledge.

The more I think of it, the more I am convinced that fully half of what the wisest man has in his brain just isn't so. Note the errors in the great books of fifty years ago or less and remember that the writers of today are making similar errors. As for the average human being at least seventy-five percent of his formal knowledge is false, especially if he is newspaper and radio-fed. He has little chance, moreover, to get the real facts about anything as there is a perpetual conspiracy against truth by the powers that be.

One of the most instructive object lessons in the fallibility of the human mind—its incredible imperfections—are the facts presented in Andrew D. White's "Warfare Between Science and Theology in Christendom," or Prof. Lowie's "Are We Civilized?" Both show how the most absurd beliefs—beliefs so ridiculous that few of the most ignorant today would credit them—

---

* The same happened for D-Day, 1944. V-E Day, 1945, was also prematurely celebrated.

XLIX. Upper, left to right: Oscar DePriest of Chicago, former Congressman; and Jean Toomer, poet and novelist. Below: the late John Hope, College President; and Rene W. Merguson, War Correspondent in France (1939-1941), traveller and anthropologist.

were held and defended by the most intellectually active of those times—defended even to the perpetration of the most horrible cruelties. The more I think the firmer grows my conviction that the brain, by which I mean the ability to think, of most human beings was given them not for intellectual pursuits but for elementary needs as food, sex, and shelter, precisely as the so-called lesser animals. The reasoning power of the majority of human beings, could it be visualized, would look like one of those concretized bags of Portland cement one sometimes sees on the city streets. The result is that the beliefs of such individuals are as fixed as the moss in an agate.

The same is true of certain areas in the brains of many of the great scientists. They, too, are to a degree fossilized and like the ignorant and untaught their intellect is a slave to their will.

Persons of this type who are ardent Christians in Europe would be as blindly Mohammedan had they by chance been reared in the East; or Shintoists had they grown up in Japan. The beliefs of most men who live in the same community would resemble so many jellies from the same mold were it possible to visualize them. Were the blacks, or the yellows, or the browns, or the piebalds in power, under the present economic system, we should have the same black, brown, white, or yellow Eastlands, Talmadges, Stoddards, Le Bons, Champlys, and Hitlers, all yelling for their own particular brand of supremacy.

Take the Ku Kluxers and the Garveyites as I knew them in 1921, one shouting for white supremacy in America and the other for black supremacy in Africa. Their arguments were so much of the same pattern that were it possible for them to have exchanged faces they needn't have exchanged brains at all. All that would be necessary would be for the one to use "black" where he once used "white," and the converse. In other words they were but so many Charlie McCarthys on the knees of differing ventriloquists.

Wisdom of Yesterday, the Imbecilities of Today

A few illustrations to show the infantile nature of the intellect in even the wisest: Pliny, the greatest scholar of his day, says in his "Natural History" that hailstones and even lightening will be scared away by a woman's uncovering herself at menstrual periods during a storm. He says further that if she walks in this state through a field of corn that all caterpillars, worms, beetles, and vermin will fall from the corn. A few pages later on he says of the Greeks: "There is no falsehood if ever so barefaced to which some of them cannot be found to bear testimony" and then goes on to say himself: "Another thing universally acknowledged and one which I am ready to accept with the greatest pleasure is the fact that if the door posts are only

touched with the menstruous fluid all the spells of the magician will be neu-
tralized."

The Romans believed that a rooster spoke to a man, and the Jews that a donkey did. This latter belief is still taught in some English and American colleges and it is sacreligious to deny it. Galen and Hippocrates, leading physicians of their day, believed in the efficacy of the number, seven; Bacon, wisest man of his day, held beliefs about magic and omens that most school-boys would laugh at today; John Wesley, Blackstone, Lecky and Sir Matthew Hale all shared the belief of the New Englanders in witches; when Stephen-son told the members of the House of Commons that he could build a railway train to travel twenty miles an hour they talked seriously of sending him to an alienist; large numbers of educated whites will shun Berth 13 on a sleeping-car; flats are rarely numbered 13; the late Bishop Fallows telegraphed Pres-ident Wilson that it was a psychological error to have draft registration day on a Friday. And consider the mistakes of medicine. "For countless years the Augean stables of the materia medica were emptied indiscriminately into the human alimentary canal, weakening and poisoning unlimited hordes of men, women and children," says Dr. Victor Robinson.

Society, in every way, is just as credulous and weak-minded today. We still believe the effusions of the palmist, the phrenologist, and the fortune-teller, reverend and otherwise; the spiritualistic imbecilities of the Oliver Lodges and the Conan Doyles; the pseudo-science of the racialists; fake ad-vertisements in newspapers and over the radio; and the promises of the politicians.

Today, in any country no matter how far advanced scientifically, any charlatan, who has sufficient capital and power behind him, can bring into vogue any kind of false doctrine or phobia that suits his crooked purpose and have men of the highest scientific attainment concocting arguments to prove him right.

A most notorious example of our era was the Aryanism of Hitler, which held for instance that the Jews, who, as a group, are second to none in Ger-many and the world in science, were an "inferior" race. Nevertheless Germany equalled, and perhaps even excelled, every other country in education. And it would have been easy to find great English and American scientists who, had they been living under Hitler, would have been chiming in with the ri-diculous Goebbels and Hausers.

The simple truth is that religion and witchcraft are not alone to blame for spreading superstition as Professor Barzun has so ably shown in his "Race: A Study of Modern Superstition."

There are those who will say: True science has not been guilty. To this the religionist may add: Neither is true religion. But to both one may reply: There can be but one true science, one true religion, namely, that one which by teaching the truth from the start will have the youth growing up accustomed to hearing it. No religion, no science, which is partisan can be the true one. Both must be universal and cognizant of the rights of the individual, regardless of race or religion.

Man, Himself, But a Part of the Universal Law

The true scientist will recognize this fact: The doctrines of evolution and of the survival of the fittest; Mendel's law; the theories of Weissman, Pearson, and Devries, and other scientific postulates, have been deduced from Nature, and not Nature them; he will realize that they function according to the laws of Nature and not Nature them. Mankind is already here, an accomplished fact, and the best that any scientist can do is to endeavor to explain how he got here. And the truth is that it seems to matter little whether the scientist explains man or not for the more he explains, the more he is called upon to explain.

At present we have a number of facts and are merely piecing them together hoping to solve the problems posed by the brain. A pleasant and inevitable diversion! Nevertheless, mankind continues to exist not because of eugenists and reformers in general, but in spite of them.

Before the eugenist could give even a partially correct answer to the question of race-mixture he would have to know tremendously more of anatomy, psychology, and sociology than he now knows. And even then he would fall far short. He would have to know what is back of the life process itself and of death, too, because death is the second most important factor in the perpetuation of life. Were there no death, life would perish.

Will anyone ever know what is back of the life process? Only the ignorant are certain they do because is a pre-determined unfolding. The vast totality of life unfolds forever like a gigantic palm-tree, the outer boughs of which drop off but whose core is eternally fresh.

We cannot fathom the beginning of life for the same reason that one has no memory of his conception, birth, and babyhood, and even if he had his brain would be inadequate to digest all the facts about life and give a correct interpretation of it. Our libraries are filled with millions of books, all containing records of human experience. But what brain is there capable of digesting all those books and giving us a correct interpretation of life, based even on knowledge that Man has conquered? What chance is there then of having a correct interpretation of life since even this which appears possible is impossible? Life leads us always; we do not lead it, delude ourselves as we will.

Many are the guesses at the origin of life. Some biologists tell us, for instance, that the original protoplasm, from which man is supposed to have come, once floated naked in salt water and gradually developed organs of defense. But if the protoplasm were the original and only living thing in the world against what did it develop organs of defense? If it developed organs of defense it must then have had the prevision to see that other rivals would arise out of its loins so to speak. But the protoplasm being perhaps nearest the inanimate, has no intellect, as we understand that term, with which it could have looked ahead, in which case what was said of life being pre-determined would be right.

Man knows next to nothing of the life-force, itself. For instance, the point where the inanimate blends into the animate, that is, the connecting link between so-called non-living matter, like the crystal, and protozoon. There is also a gap between the invertebrate and the vertebrate that many scientists declare has not been bridged, and still another between the lower and higher apes, as well as one between the ape and man. And vaster yet is the gap between intellect and body so far as human knowledge is concerned. Yet many biologists with a great deal of cocksureness lay down laws for the instruction of Nature with her billions of years of experience in breeding.

It was surely this type Shakespeare had in mind when he wrote:

"Man, proud man,
   Drest in a little brief authority,
   Most ignorant of what he is most assured,
   (His glassy essence) like an angry ape
   Plays such fantastic tricks before high heaven
   As make the angels weep."

Placed amid life with its infinite complexity the most gifted biologist is merely an observer and a purblind one. There is no certainty whatever that most of our knowledge is not incorrect and that future generations will not discredit it even as we discredited very much of that of past ones. Who knows but that at any time discoveries might result that will set us facing in the opposite direction, as did those of Copernicus, Leeuwenhoek, Kant and Darwin. As Darbishire says, "The satisfaction of the biologist with our current scientific interpretation of life is the satisfaction of the fool with the paradise which he has built."[3]

In spite of the great progress that has been made in scientific knowledge no one knows the determining essence of good biological value, particularly

3 Introduction to Biology, p. 32. 1917.

where the mixing of the races is concerned. Mankind refuses to mate like the lower animals, a refusal which increases in proportion as he recedes from them. Here the breeder is confronted with the almost unknown quality of Mind and the desire of the individual for that happiness to be found only in the affinity which he selects for himself.

Eugenists are fond of citing in support of their theories the successful breeding of fruit flies, bees, cows, pigs, horses. But in the case of man to have any success in controlled breeding you'd have to return to slavery. Worse, you'd have to put all women in prison from the time they could start bearing children until they became pregnant, when they could be released but only until they could be made pregnant again. Thus while arbitrary interference in mating undoubtedly improves those animals we use for food or profit, it will never work in the case of man. "The brain may devise laws for the blood but a hot temper leaps o'er a cold decree," says Shakespeare. It is only a most arrogant and selfish idiot who tries to dictate to groups of adults where they shall or shall not mate.

The only effective eugenics would be to improve the physique of all human beings by better living conditions so that there would be fewer unfit or diseased persons with whom to mate. This, however, few eugenists would concede since they usually dogmatize in terms of race, "superior" and "inferior," which means privileged and under-privileged.

As for those who are so dogmatic about heredity what do they really know or what can they predict on the period of persistence and degree of distribution of either physical, psychic, and intellectual qualities of parents in their offspring? True, abundant data are available but no sure inferences can be drawn from their varied forms and sources. Numerous volumes exist to prove that heredity is superior to environment and just as many the other way about. Many tell us that the children of thieves invariably develop the habit of stealing at some time in their lives while many are equally emphatic in their assertion that if separated when babes dishonesty will not develop. But it is not a question of heredity or environment but of heredity plus environment. There are innumerable cases where the one sometimes precedes the other but always and everywhere the two are inextricably mixed—so mixed that the honest scientist who attempts to separate them must confess himself baffled.

The eugenists, who are nearly all white, know really little about their own group, and what they know of the Negro is infinitesimal. Herskovits wrote in 1930, "Data on the physical anthropology of the Negroes of the western hemisphere is also sadly lacking. Up to five years ago nothing had been done to study the Negroes of the United States and today little relatively is known of their physical form. Of the West Indies we know less

L. Etta Moten, concert artist, Star of radio, stage and screen. Native of Texas. Scored much success in South America. Her type is called white south of the Rio Grande.

while of the Negroes of Central America and Northern South America we know nothing."[4] Herskovits has probably done more in this field than any other and even that is very little in proportion to what ought to be done.

Yet this lack of information did not prevent a diarrhoea of cock-sure "scientific" pronouncements on "race," evidence of which can be seen in any library. And twenty-nine and a half states of the American union, the Transvaal, and Australia, the legislators of which know about as much of biogenetics as a parrot knows of the construction of its cage; or as the flies buzzing about the ceiling of a Pullman know where the train is going, pass laws against race mixture on the ground that it is harmful biologically.

The right wing eugenists and legislators on "race" even when viewed in the most charitable light are mulish egotists. As for the few who are really sincere they are but the faithful dogs of an exploiting order. Luckily for all of us Nature intends to hold the reins always. Had these people their wish then I would wish to be safely away on some Robinson Crusoe island because they would create chaos; they would upset the delicate balance which it took Nature billions of years to adjust.

Such remind one of Frederick the Great and his prize cherry-trees. Seeing some birds, sparrows, I think, eating the fruit off them, he ordered all the sparrows in his kingdom destroyed. But the following year, he had no cherries at all. The birds, while eating a few of the ripe cherries, had also been eating the insects that ate the young cherries. The farmers, too, complained that the insects had destroyed their crops, and now Frederick had to pay to bring in sparrows.

What would happen, for example, if man had the controlling voice in the determination of sex? There would be at least a great shortage of women as boy babies are most in demand. In parts of the Orient girl babies were hardly considered human and were drowned like kittens and puppies.

The eugenists plan to breed a 100 per cent physically fit race, white, of course. At first thought the idea will seem splendid to some. But is it? Not only is your physically fit individual less considerate of the physical weaknesses of others, but the next war would mean total extinction. The world would certainly have been shot to pieces more in 1914-18 had the number of physically fit been greater. In fact a physical defect can be a salvation. Many a man today is thanking his lucky stars that he had one or more. But for that he might now be a cripple or blind, or insane, or be fertilizing the soil of some far-off land.

[4] American Anthropologist, January to March, 1930.

What is true of this war has been true of all other wars. It is the old men, the women, the physically unfit men, and the children who have always been left behind to carry on civilization while the strong have been engaged in tearing it to pieces.

There are, as was said, forces in Nature, which the human mind will probably never be able to fathom, especially those superficial scientists, who think that by playing on the outside, measuring skulls, leg-bones, etc, they are arriving at an understanding of the inner nature of things and thus have the right to speak as an authority. For instance, anyone who has observed the so-called lower animals, or even the pets in his home, especially cats, will be amazed at their keenness of perception where food and safety are concerned. Cats, even when cut off from all other cats since they were merest kittens, display at times evidences of a certain inner intelligence that seems the despair of even the wisest man. Fabre showed how certain insects will sting other insects in a manner not to kill them but to paralyze them. They will then lay their eggs on the paralyzed insect. Thus, when the eggs are hatched, the young insects will have, not a dead body, but a still living and helpless one to feed on.

Again, fleas, during the summer, will go up four stories of an elevator-less building to reach a cat that never leaves the house. How did the fleas know the cat was there? In Africa, let there be a carcass anywhere around and vultures, so high up in the air you cannot see them, will know about it. How did the vultures know? How did the insects? Instinct, you'll say, but does not instinct imply fore-knowledge? I find it difficult to escape the fact that there is a certain telepathy between unconscious Nature and the lower species that is denied to man. Nature in giving man a higher intellect withheld from him much of the innate intelligence of the animals. A dog or an elephant knows little but that little is really so, while in the case of man if we were to take out of his brain all he has in it that isn't so, we can imagine some brains shrinking to the size of a peanut.

Even the scientist who studies the gene, that is, a minute section of the germ plasm, in its smallest electron would not be able to pierce the inner secrets of Nature and thus be able to say truly whether she is right or wrong in creating certain individuals and peoples. In trying to do this he will find himself up against what for a better name I will call the Mind of the Infinite Unconscious, what the religionist calls God, and which has remained largely a sealed book to the most profound philosophers since the days of the Greeks. Those individuals and peoples whom we like as well as those we dislike were ordained to be born, probably billions of years ago, and the only thing we can do for our own peace of mind is to learn how to get along with them.

"The moving finger writes and having writ
Moves on nor all your piety nor your wit
Can lure it back to cancel half a line."

When we look at the matter in greater detail we find that the whole doctrine of supposed racial superiority when advanced by no matter what group is built upon differences in bodily structure, that is, variation. But since variation is the most obvious thing in nature, mon Dieu, what a field that opens up. Two billion persons on the planet, no two of whom are alike. Ethnology, then, to be scientific, ought to have two billion systems!

This is ridiculous, certain savants will say. But are there not great gulfs fixed, so to speak, between individuals of any same "race" mentally and physically? H. J. Muller says truly, "The natural differences between the races pale into insignificance beside the natural differences between individuals —so much so that an impartial science of genetic improvement could not afford to take the former into account at all in its procedure."[5] Again, Wilhelm Bonger, "The individual differences between members of the same race are so great that those between races themselves are small by comparison." Intellectually, for instance, the difference between Edison or Einstein and a white Georgia fieldhand. To whom is the latter nearer, these two great scientists of his own color, or to the Negro, working in the same field with him? Physically, consider the difference between Schmelling and the average German; or Joe Louis and the average Negro; or Joe Louis and the average white man. Really the whole thing is not even a theory much less a science. As Bonger says, it is only a second-rate religion.[6]

The simple truth is: Some person, with or without the pronouncements

[5] Out Of The Night, p. 120. 1935.

[6] Dr. Bijlmer, Netherlands explorer, who visited Central New Guinea in 1928, found the dwarf Papuans there still living in the Stone Age, and asks whether "the Europeans of the Stone Age, thousands and thousands of years ago" might not have been just such "ordinary people." It is not necessary, however, to go back that far. Conditions that one may call a "social" Stone Age can still be found in certain spots in Europe. As late as 1958 in Paris, the centre of European, if not of world civilization, there was a large cellar where the dregs of the city gathered nightly for shelter on the payment of a few cents. Since the limited space did not permit the "lodgers" to lie down they sat in tightly packed rows on benches and in this position threw their arms and shoulders over ropes stretched from one end of the cellar to the other. Thus they spent the night. The next morning to awaken them the rope was loosened at one end and the human burden fell like lines of filthy clothes.

Now, not half a mile away from these unfortunates were Parisians living in luxurious hotels and palatial homes. Was not the gap that separated the two equal to that between well-to-do natives living in the Papuan seaports and that of the primitives mentioned by Bijlmer? That it was some lack in the mentality of the unfortunate Parisians that made them unable to win at least a little better social condition is evident. In any case there was a tremendous gap between one of these and a member of the French Academy or a banker. In every way, racially and individually, the centuries are contemporaneous.

of the anthropologists, are going to consider themselves superior to others. They were probably doing it back in the Stone Age.

The arguments used in favor of racial inequality in America are of a piece with those used by white against white in Europe, or those used to foster social inequality before "race" was invented. Many persons are inclined to forget that even as the white anthropologists have created divisions to set off Negroes from whites, they have also created divisions to set off white from white, as Nordic, Alpine, Ostic, Dinaric, Mediterranean, etc. In short, in any allegedly superior race you will always find those who consider the greater number of this "superior" race inferior to themselves, the same being identically true within the so-called inferior races. All it sums up to is Ego.

Furthermore, certain members of any "superior" group, in spite of what science may say on the subject, are going to think that certain members of the "inferior" group are superior to some of their own group and like them better than their own kind and even prefer them as mates.

It seems to me that the proper scientific attitude on race is that of Professor J .B. S. Haldane of London University. After a careful study of the subject he said, "The result of our investigation is largely negative," though he thought that some eugenic improvement could be made in the case of defectives, regardless of race. But as regards race mixture he said, "I do not know. I do not think we ought to forbid race-crossing. I do not think we ought to encourage it either, and I do think we ought to study it."[7]

I would like to add this to the above, however. After having studied it —supposing a competent study will ever be made, which I strongly doubt— one should still be neutral. Matchmaking, when undertaken even by scientists, is officiousness. It is high time for people to learn to keep their noses out of other people's love affairs where religion, race, caste, and nationality are concerned.

Havelock Ellis gives the most sensible last word. He says, "The wisdom of man working through a few centuries or in one corner of the earth, by no means necessarily corresponds to the wisdom of Nature and may be in flat opposition to it. This is especially the case when the wisdom of man merely means, as sometimes happens, the experience of our ancestors gained under other conditions or merely the opinions of one class or sex. Taking a broad view of the matter, it seems difficult to avoid the conclusion that it is safer to trust to the conservatism of Nature than the conservatism of Man. We are not at liberty to introduce any artificial sexual barriers into social concerns."[8]

[7] Human Genetics and Human Ideals, p. 172 (In Sir James Jeans: Scientific Progress. 1936. The Sir Halley Stewart Trust Fund Founded for Research Towards the Christian Ideal in Social Life).
[8] Man and Woman, p. 524. 1926.

Chapter Twenty-five

TWILIGHT OF THE BIGOTS, THE HIRELINGS AND THEIR MASTERS

T HE doctrine of white superiority, like other falsities of the past, is headed for the limbo of freak fancies and philosophies. It arose with the spread of the white-skinned variety of humanity into the lands of the darker peoples whose color was used as a badge for their exploitation. In fact, it was so handy that it seemed a veritable "gift from God." Had these peoples also been white, exploitation of them would have passed as soon as they had absorbed enough of the dominant culture to be able to compete with the masters as did the indentured white slaves of the American colonies; or as Irish-Americans, now a power, but whose immigrant ancestors, as Justin Winsor says, were "as unpromising as the dregs of a race could make them." The permanence of the skin-color of the blacks, however made possible permanence of their exploitation whether they went up or down.

So profitable was robbery based on color that it had its learned defenders by the score and an enormous literature arose on the subject. But all such falsities explode sooner or later. Darbishire said that theories are like balloons. "Their makers inflate them; their admirers over-inflate them, and they generally burst from inflation." This is precisely what the Nazis have done. Claiming that they are the only real white people they used the doctrine of white superiority against those whites who had all along been using it against Negroes. It was quite in line with this reasoning that they should call Winston Churchill a mulatto because his mother was American.

But the Nazis did not stop there. With their claim of being "the master race," they made war on the remainder of the white "race," bringing ruin to Europe, the source, the heart of white supremacy. Thanks to the Nazis, therefore, world power has surely passed away from Europe with no possi-

---

1 Several recent writers, as Eric Fischer in his "Passing Of The European Age," have pointed out that European decline is inevitable. As for the United States its future looks doubtful, too. It has been squandering its natural resources at a fearful rate. Already we are told (1943) that America has oil enough only for the next 35 years. As for America's financial wealth consider how much of it has been scattered over almost every country on the globe. On the other hand, Asia and Africa not only have vast human reserves but great sources of untapped mineral wealth. The highlands of Africa, notably those of Ethiopia, are going to see great civilizations of the future because they have not only the climate but the natural resources. Brazil, too, is a nation with a future. The only hope of the white "race" is in peace and friendship with the darker races. As it looks now Russia and Brazil with their policy of racial equality are the hope of the future.

bility of another white racial center arising in any part of the world. European power was built up largely on loot from the Americas, Africa, and Asia. That from the Americas was cut off; and that from Africa and Asia is going to be cut off also because Europe has been too greatly weakened by this war (not to mention the next which seems not far away) to be able to prey as in the past on an aroused and much stronger Africa and Asia. Unless some harmonious, non-exploiting system can be worked out, Europe, in a few centuries more, will sink to the present level of India, which, too, had a civilization as great as Europe's.

With the decline of Europe, which, of course, includes the decline of the British Empire, which has been the great disseminator, if not the originator, of color dissension, the immense tower of race nonsense will crumble in ruins provided that when the non-Nordics come into power, as they inevitably will, they do not imitate all this racial stupidity; that is, create a doctrine of Nordic inferiority, which did exist once but not in an aggravated form. As late as the eighth century there was an Arab school that held that the white man or "red" man as they called him, was inferior. One Arab writer, the greatest of his day and a Negro, actually wrote a book entitled, "The Superiority in Glory of the Black Race Over the White." Today there are millions of colored people—in Asia, Africa, and even in the United States—who will declare that the whites belong to an inferior race. In short we already have a reverse color question in embryo.

With or without Hitler, however, the doctrine of white superiority was bound to be exploded because at no time did it have any more logic than an old wives' tale. For myself I'll say that I have read countless articles and books, pro and con, on anthropology and have attended lectures on the differences between white human beings and black—on pigment, pelvis, liver, weight, heart and kidneys, brain, spleen, racial and sexual differences in hair weight, kinks, color of Negro infants, hearing, ilium, feet, larynx, sweatglands, odoriferous glands, ischomagin groups, blood, muscles of face, protologic pecularities skin and scalp of Negro foetus, face hair, cranial suture closure, and other physical differences and I am bound to say that the whole thing leaves me in a fog. Like Omar Khyyam I listen to the wise and learned then I come out the same door no wiser than I went in; or like Goethe's Faust "who, with ardent labor having studied through" finds himself "with all his lore. Poor fool, no wiser than before." Therefore, I find myself forced to fall back on what I personally *feel* about it, and those feelings have not changed fundamentally from what they were before I began my studies. I believed then that every human being, regardless of color, had a right to one hundred percent courteous treatment and opportunity to develop his better self and his natural gifts and to associate with congenial souls. I still feel the same. I still feel that this should be so whether one's sitting height, or his zygomatic arch, or the rhythm of his pulse, or every other detail of his body be different from that type which for the moment happens to be the ruling race or caste.

And my case is not a whit different from that of the most learned anthropologist. At the bottom of all so-called scientific pronouncement on race, pro or con, lies the student's feelings on the subject.[1a] A scientist has, after all, only a human psychology. The man who thinks narrowly, or is crooked, or a hireling, or who deludes himself into thinking himself broadminded because he speaks lies with brutal frankness, will, if he gets into racial science, be that kind of scientist. Lester F. Ward truly said that if you scratch a savant you'll find a savage. No amount of learning ever takes one away from one's deep, inner self.

On the other hand, the individual who thinks broadly, universally, who sees humanity as one race, who sees in all other human beings a replica of himself, if he enters this field of "science" is also going to use whatever facts he can assemble from Science or from the Bible, as the case may be, to prove the unity of mankind.

In illustration of the first type I shall select two of the finest scientists in the field—men of good heart who give the impression of being really interested in the emancipation of mankind, namely, Professor Jon Alfred Mjoen of Norway and the late Luther Burbank of California.

Mjoen is a world-famed geneticist and miles above such racial quacks as Madison Grant, Lothrop Stoddard and J. C. Curle. With no Negroes about him, Mjoen opposed the crossing of Nordics and Lapps, both of whom are white, on the ground that the Lapps are inferior. When, however, Professor W. C. Castle had him cornered on this subject, he took refuge in racial patriotism. He said: "I do not propose to prevent race-crossings on the ground that we are so much better than the other races. We shall love and protect each of us our own race for the same reason that we love our father and mother because it is our race."[2]

Very touching! Very beautiful! Very loyal! But where, we ask, is all Mjoen's painstaking scientific research when he falls back on sentiment, on racial patriotism? Is not this precisely what the wretched Nazis have done with their "Aryan" patriotism?

Might not also some ignorant Southern Negro or white mountaineer or lyncher have used identical language in talking of their "own" people?

Note that Mjoen classes his so-called race with its good and bad, its rogues, rascals, and jail-birds with his mother and father, because like them

---

[1a] See p. 36 where the great scientist, Henry Fairfield Osborn, does so.
[2] Jour. of Heredity, Vol. 17, p. 181. 1926.

LI. Lucius C. Harper, scholarly editor of the Chicago Defender, influential Negro newspaper. In Latin-America, Spain, Portugal, Italy and France, his type is called white. (See
p. 302.)

they are Nordics. Again, Mjoen is a Mendelian. But Mendel's law shows that both so-called superior and so-called inferior qualities enter into any mixture. Does he, then, like so many other racialists accept Mendel's law, which they usually claim they do, or doesn't he?

Dr. Samuel Johnson called patriotism "the last refuge of a scoundrel." What shall we call racial patriotism? The last refuge of a barbarian.

As regards Burbank, his book "My Beliefs" breathes the very spirit of broad-mindedness and liberality. He speaks like a combination Buddha, Confucius, Emerson and Ingersoll. But with all of this, with all of his scientific research, he announces that "Nature does not approve"[3] the crossing of white with such races as Negro and Mongol.

Does not approve? Ye gods! Was Burbank off on one of Swedenborg's planets when he wrote that? He must have been because there was no one then living who was more competent to speak on what Nature approves and what she does not than he? Did he know that there are millions of mulattoes in the United States? Were these born without Nature's approval? Also in China are tens of thousands of offspring between white men and Chinese while almost under Burbank's nose in California are scores of children by Chinese men and white women.

Nature does not approve of a cross between cat and dog; man and ape or sheep; banana and apple; therefore such blends are impossible. When Burbank says "Nature does not approve" what he really means is *"Burbank does not approve,"* in which case science abdicates and this thinker who would free the world finds himself in the same narrow bin with the Los Angeles waiter who will not serve Orientals and Negroes or the bone-headed congressman whose chief qualification to office is his stock of anti-Negro quotations and arguments.

Truly, as Professor Barzun says, "One comes perilously near to losing his mind wondering just what these race-ridden scientists really mean and want." Schienfield, who is so much more competent to speak on genetics than Burbank, gives a table showing why the "tallest blondest 'Nordic' could mate with the smallest, blackest pigmy and produce children perfectly normal in the eyes of Nature."[4]

H. S. Jennings, another very able geneticist, says likewise, "In the crossing of diverse races there is the same formation of many gene combinations that occurs in the mating of individuals of a given race."[5] Also Professor Castle, "Why, if nature abhors race-crossing, does she have so much of it?

[3] Partner of Nature, pp. 117-18. 1939.
[4] You and Heredity, p. 24. 1939.
[5] Scientific Aspects of the Race Question, p. 70. 1941.

Chapter Twenty-six

RACE, A SPIRITUAL, NOT A SCIENTIFIC PROBLEM

"As a people striving to shape our actions in accordance with the great law of righteousness we cannot afford to take part in or be indifferent to the oppression or maltreatment of any man who, against crushing disadvantages, has by his own industry, energy, self-respect and perseverance struggled upward to a position which would entitle him to the respect of his fellows, if only his skin were of a different hue."—Theodore Roosevelt.

T HE so-called science of race is founded on "racial" differences but since difference is the most obvious thing in Nature and since every individual on the planet differs from every other not only in looks but in psychology racial science can be but *academic;* at best a matter to enliven one's interest regarding his fellow-man. The simple truth is that most of this "science" of race is mere exercise for the pen and the jaw, not to mention boondoggling by scholars who are thereby enabled to get handouts from philanthropists, who had squeezed the money from laboring people. If these superficial differences, called race, did not exist, says Bonger, "The countless laymen and amateurs who now get so excited over race problems would hardly give them any attention."

Is this an argument against the study of so-called racial differences? Not at all. Everything on the planet should be studied and explored. But the trouble began when the anthropologists began to talk of inferior and superior races, when numbers of them sold out to the exploiters of humanity. In fact, the trouble went even deeper because as soon as one begins to talk about superior and inferior quailties whether inside or outside a "race," there are always those inferior creatures—creatures who can only feel themselves big by looking down on others, who will pick up these so-called superior attributes and apply them to themselves. Even some of the great scientists have this inferiority complex as the late Henry Fairfield Osborn, director of the American Museum of Natural History, or Ales Hrdlicka, of the Smithsonian Institution, or Professor Charles Richet, Nobel Prize Winner. In botany and mineralogy, these men would have been real and impartial scientists but the moment "race" entered they were led by their feelings and began to think in terms of inferior and superior with the result that in this respect they sank to the level of the ignorant, race-prejudiced man on the street.

273

I have therefore, decided, after more than forty years of study and reading on the subject that "race" is ethical and spiritual, not scientific. Arguments in favor of racial inequality are capitalistic and as I am absolutely opposed to the exploitation of human beings, no matter how unlike to myself in appearance or point of view, I, therefore favor those who stand for racial equality even when they are academically incorrect, and oppose those who favor racial inequality even when they are academically correct.

"Inferiority" or "superiority" has nothing whatever to do with the question. My dog is hopelessly, immutably inferior to me in nearly every respect, should I on that account give it less than one hundred percent kind treatment?

Though I value as much as any other the good things of civilization I cannot lose sight of the fact that in its present workings, it is more destructive than constructive. The more advanced nations are like a horde of wolves in the chase, the members of which will immediately stop to rend and eat any of the pack that shows signs of weakening—cold, heartless, cruel, grasping.

What deluges of woe have not the leading nations visited upon the darker peoples of the world? What mountains of crime and cruelty mark their footsteps over the earth! The Indian exterminated or herded into cramped corners: the Maori relentlessly butchered; the Australian and Tasmanian blacks killed wholesale like flies with strychnine; India scourged and plundered in the name of a Christian God; China cheated and forced to poison herself with opium; the Eskimo pilfered from; Africa, hospitable Africa, robbed, raped, maimed, her children killed for sport or strewn alive on the bosom of the Atlantic—food for sharks. Brutality, Brutality, unrealizable Brutality! For every ounce of good that the white man's religion or culture has done for the darker races it has exacted a ton of agony. If blood be the price of Culture, Lord God, they have paid in full.

"How the European has been able to establish Colonies," says Nietzsche "is explained by his nature which is that of a beast of prey."

To summarize my conclusions regarding race mixture: Race mixture makes for change and change is inevitable, unpreventable. Whether change in any form—race-mixing, politics, religion, diet—is good or bad depends on those who experience it. Some will welcome it; others will hate it. Some who welcomed it will in time hate it; and some who hated it will in time like it. But as to whether it is good or bad in a universal sense no one knows. Perhaps it is, as Nietzsche says, beyond good and evil.

Man, we are told, evolved from seaweed, a most likely theory. The power of change was great enough to bring him from that state to this. What proof have we that change has lost its potency? Beside such a feat as evolution race-mixture as a form of change is hardly worthy of mention.

Thus I am not interested in whether race mixture is good or bad, whether mixed peoples are superior or inferior to unmixed ones. What I am interested in is that minds will become so enlightened that race-mixture as a form of change may be able to operate on the highest ethical and spiritual lives even when it appears disadvantageous to racial and national prestige.

The developed, if it is to survive, must be reinforced perpetually by the undeveloped, therefore, inasmuch as cultures have their period of birth, development, decline and death like the individuals of which they are composed, it would be no more desirable to have the whole world highly civilized at the same time than it would be to have all the land under cultivation, all the villages swarming with skyscrapers, all the ore in use, or every individual with a brain developed to its limit. In short, the undeveloped peoples, like any other natural resource, are but Nature's reserve—her balance in the bank.

Hence they should not be despised.

There is no individual or aggregation of individuals but were once in a state as infantile and primitive as the lowest now, just as the world's champion pugilist was at one period of his existence so feeble that an aged grandmother could have whipped him.

Patience and kindness should mark all dealing with these primitive peoples. It should be remembered that if there is a law of progress in the universe there is also a law of retardation. It should never be forgotten that Nature seems purposely to create conditions to keep some peoples back until their time shall have come. To some peoples, as to some individuals, she has given too much, and they have accomplished little, as the Tahitians; to others like the Eskimo, she has given too little, and they also, have accomplished little.

Of those who oppose race-mixture I ask: What about the principle of exogamy, or marriage and sexual union outside the tribe or race that has always gone on, as well as what about the almost universal objection to the intermarriage or to sexual unions between near relations. Similarly, to those who say that race-mixing is better than no mixture I will ask what about the principle of endogamy or marriage within the tribe or race, which has always gone on and is the stronger of the two, locally.

Scientific argument in favor of race-mixing or against it is but a development of these two natural laws, which have existed ever since we were in a savage state. Scientific argument in favor of race prejudice, as that

made by Elliott Smith, is but a development of the endogamic principle, plus
a desire on the part of such scientists to look out for their own interests
by standing in with the ruling class. As to our Gobineaus, Stoddards, Hoff-
mans, and Madison Grants, if we were to trace their type back spiritually a
few thousand years we would find that the sole difference between it then and
now is the additional information it has gathered on the subject. In essence,
however, it has remained unchanged by time or the advance of knowledge,
and probably cannot change. In other words you'll find these scientists in
embryo among the most primitive peoples. It is the human will, not knowledge, with which we are dealing.

Stronger peoples have always forced weaker ones to yield them their
labor and their sex at the lowest possible price. Meanwhile they boast of
their alleged superior stock. Since the economic is thus used to dominate
the biologic, how is it possible ever to get an unbiased evaluation of race-
mixture? Thus it should no longer be outlawed and forced down into the
gutter, but be permitted to move on a higher plane. The individual must
be free to marry where he will, inside or outside his "race" and entirely to
the dictates of his or her heart.

Miscegenation is perhaps but a creator of variety, serving as a distri-
butor throughout humanity of those traits acquired by the different races in
their respective environments—traits which it disseminates with as great a
disregard of our changing economic values as a linotype machine distributes
type. There is so far no proof that race-blending produces either inferior
or superior offspring. This would mean in both the cases that the parents
stocks were inferior. Are the proponents of the theory that race-mixing
produces superior children prepared to argue that from two inferior sources
one can get a superior product. Of course, there were such mixed-bloods
as General Dumas, Frederick Douglas, Booker T. Washington and scores
of others who were much superior to both their white fathers and black
mothers but probably a greater number could be cited who rose no higher
than the lower of these two parents. Couples, regardless of color, often
have children inferior to themselves. Great fathers rarely have great sons.

There are two facts about race-mixing that seem certain: It permits
the survival of the white man (in a modified form) in lands with too much
sunlight; and it serves for the multiplication of the species in that it is for
some a natural aphrodisiac—a sexual excitant—for individuals sated with
mates of their own race. It would be interesting to learn the percentage
of adventurers who are lured to foreign lands by prospects of association
with native women. Advertisers for sailors and soldiers go abroad are not
unaware of this.

Given two persons, one white, the other colored, both of equal capabilities, then, as conditions are in America, marriage would ordinarily be to the social and economic disadvantage of the white. If opposers of intermarriage held to this ground their arguments would be valid, but as this sounds commercial, a moral coating is applied and such ideologies as patriotism, white superiority, truth, good citizenship, purity of the home and womanhood are dragged in. The halls of Congress have resounded to much of this.

One who has visualized the flow and reflow of the mixing of white and black through the ages, will find it a perfectly natural process, and one that will go on. Here are two examples that certainly cannot be set down to accident or co-incidence: the coming in of the fairer-skinned Romans and Greeks to mate with Negroes in Egypt at the time when Egypt had become much more black than white; and the importation of the Negro to the New World, there to predominate in the tropical regions and to mix in with the white.

As for those who advocate intermarriage as a solution of the race problem they are not so broadminded as they think. At least this is too much of a concession to color prejudice. Intermixture means a change of racial type and why in a democracy should it be necessary to change one's color in order to get one's rights?

In other ways, too, the race question is so ridiculous that it makes one look silly even to take notice of it. For instance, even as the elephant is afraid of the mouse we find in America that nine-tenths of the nation with the army, the navy, the political machinery, and nearly all the wealth gives the appearance of being afraid of the feeble one-tenth, the Negro.

We are told, too, that white blood is superior, but in the same breath informed that one "drop" of "Negro" blood makes a white man a Negro, which is equivalent to saying that if a citizen has ninety-nine white ancestors and one black, that one drop cancels all that the whites have contributed. Compare that with the Arabs who say that one drop of Arab "blood" makes one an Arab.

While every group has a perfect right to keep to itself if it so decides and to say with whom it will or will not marry, yet the instant it enters the life of another group, so surely does it forfeit that right, and the other group has a right reciprocally to interfere. It is indisputable that in the beginning the black man wished no association whatever with the white, and that the white has forced his company upon him even to the extent of bringing him to America. If the white man will not leave the Negro alone, but wishes to mix with him, the Negro has a perfect right, that is, if there is to be any justice, to say also under what conditions such mixing shall take place.

As for anthropological research while I am strongly in favor of it I do not think that scientific pronouncements are going to help the race question much except in so far as they can be used to influence religious and ethical bodies, labor unions and other organizations, because, in its final analysis, the race question is not scientific, but highly sentimental. And I do not believe it will ever be otherwise because our dealings with others, regardless of race, are too highly charged with likes and dislikes.

To illustrate: The parts of the world in which the race question is most aggravated at the present time are the southern United States and South Africa. Suppose, by way of the impossible, all the students of race were to agree that the Negroes of both regions were superior in every way to the whites, would that alter conditions? I firmly believe it would not make the slightest difference because it is not "race" so much that is involved as vested interests in the labor of the blacks. These vested interests use all their propaganda to keep "race" alive, tempering it, of course, so that the stronger group will not directly attack the exploited group and thus endanger profits.

Therefore Science, like true religion, must come squarely out in favor of the under-dog. It must hammer in, without ceasing, the thought that there is but one race—the human race. It must realize that all its measurements, averages and statistics on "race," even if they were not so self-contradictory, touch only the outskirts of the question because what *might* be true of any group—Slavs, Jews, Negroes, Indians, Caucasians, Mongolians, Eskimos—as regards mentality, intellect, character, height, weight, skull, etc., *is never, never true of the individual members of those groups*. Why not even two peas in the same pod are alike.

It is the individual and his treatment we must never lose sight of.

If the science of "race" is to serve for the betterment of mankind it must ever be inspired by the cool head and the warm heart. Especially the latter. A kind, unselfish deed by the member of one racial group to another will often have a greater effect for good than a whole library of scientific books. Kindness will succeed where formal learning, however great, will often fail. Schopenhauer did not pay it too high a tribute when he said, "As torches and fireworks become pale and insignificant in the presence of the sun so intellect, nay genius and also beauty are outshone and eclipsed by goodness of the heart. Even the most limited understanding and also grotesque ugliness, whenever extraordinary goodness of heart declares itself as accompanying them, become, as it were, transfigured, outshone by beauty of a higher kind, for now wisdom must be dumb. For goodness of heart is a transcendent quality; it belongs to an order of things that reaches beyond this world and is incommensurable with any other perfection."

On the other hand, the most dangerous, the most pernicious and heartless thing in the world is intellect unaccompanied by high morality. This is the lesson the Nazis have taught the world to its bitter cost.

Happily, recent years have seen a change for the better. Anthropology is returning to the noble foundations laid by Blumenbach and Lamarck. We are having an increasing number of these students of man, who are also humanitarians, as Ashley Montagu, Otto Klineberg, Earnest Hooton, H. J. Muller, Ruth Benedict and Margaret Mead.

The good name and the democratic pretensions of the United States are at stake in this matter of Negro treatment. As long as a cultured and refined man who is "colored" is denied the freedom of an ex-convict who is "white" then its democratic pretensions are bare-faced humbug. As long as color distinctions prevail the upholders of the dignified constitution of the United States are co-workers with the miserable jim-crow law makers of the Southern States. As long as human beings continue to be burnt alive on the altar of white "racial superiority" as at Sikeston, Missouri, in 1942, so long will the Statue of Liberty, torch in hand, be also symbolic of the lyncher.

Some day we are going to do for our brains what we do for our houses —give it a thorough cleaning. We are then going to toss out all the beloved rubbish about "race" now cluttering our thinking and preventing the attainment of true brotherhood and peace. Mankind is one. "The earth is but one country and mankind its citizens," says Abdul Baha.

Oswald Spengler in his mighty book, "The Decline of the West," shows the falsehood about race springing out of what he calls the period of Romanticism, and adds, "How utterly unimportant these are for what we call 'race' in higher mankind can be shown by a drastic experiment. Take a set of men with every conceivable race-difference, and while mentally picturing 'race' observe them in an X-ray apparatus. The result is simply comic. As soon as light is let through it 'race' vanishes suddenly and completely."

Here is another test of the oneness of mankind. Go to any large clinic in New York, Paris, or London, and you'll see individuals of the various "races" there awaiting treatment. Are these patients treated according to "race"? No, the Caucasian, Mongolian, Negro, or Indian, or individual from no matter what part of the world, if suffering from the same malady is given the same kind of medicine, which, if he is susceptible of being cured, will cure him regardless of race.

Since, therefore, mankind is so truly one in its organism, must not its thoughts, sentiments, and inherent possibilities be fundamentally the same?

Americans of the future, looking back on our times, are going to marvel, aye, to laugh at our stupidity; how we squabble and fight and kill one another like half-wits over the color of one another's skin, as in Little Rock in 1957.

The solution of the whole question of race is so very simple that I hesitate to give it after all the ponderous tomes on the subject. Nevertheless, I offer it:

Since no man is responsible for his race or his physical appearance, then he ought to be accepted for what Nature has made him. The racially intolerant should remember that what cannot be cured must be endured. Who among us, of normal intelligence, is quite sure that he, himself, is a paragon of beauty, wisdom, and desirability?

The chief goal of life is happiness and when that is attained one can enjoy the maximum of contentment under any color of skin or mixtures of color of skin. The like is true of misery. That the Danes, the Dutch, and the Norwegians had a white skin did not lighten for them one whit the miseries of Fascist domination also suffered by the Ethiopians, who are black.

"Oh blood of the people, changeless tide, through century, creed and race,
Still one, as the sweet salt sea is one, though tempered by sun and place.
The same in the ocean currents and the same in the sheltered sea,
Forever the fountain of common hopes and kindly sympathies.
Indian and Negro, Saxon and Celt, Teuton and Latin and Gaul,
Mere surface shadow and sunshine, while the sounding unifies all.
One love, one hope, one duty theirs! No matter the time or ken,
There never was separate heart-beat in all the races of men."

—*John Boyle O'Reilly.*

NOTES ON CHAPTER SEVENTEEN

APPENDIX TO VOLUME III

It is generally agreed that the Negro had a low rate of insanity during slavery and that this increased after the emancipation. The reason, as I see it, is that when slavery was ended the Negroes either flocked into, or were forced, into the towns, to make a living, where they were subject to the greatly degenerating action of syphilis, alcohol, and bad housing as well as the stress and strain of urban life for which they had not been mentally prepared.

The Eleventh United States Census: Insane, Feeble-minded, Deaf and Dumb, (1890) shows a great increase in Negro insanity in the unsettled years immediately following the emancipation. In 1850 insanity was 175 per million Negroes while that of the white was 766 per million, that is, the Negro rate was one-fourth as much. In 1890, Negro insanity was 886, while that of the white was 1814. The Negro rate had increased until it was now nearly as half as great.

Dr. Benjamin Malzberg (Mental Diseases Among American Negroes: A Statistical Analysis appearing in "Characteristics of the American Negro," edited by Otto Klineberg, 1944), comes to the conclusion that the Negro has now a greater insanity rate for the whole United States. At least so it appears to me. He says, "It is clear, however, that there is a fundamental difference with respect to the incidence of mental disease which is more frequent among Negroes." (p. 394). But Dr. Malzberg's analysis deals almost wholly with New York. He devotes 17 of his 22 pages to New York, and had he called it "Mental Diseases Among New York Negroes" I should have accepted it with little reserve. Had he even said that his conclusions were typical of the Northern Negro, I should not have objected very much. But when he uses New York to typify the Negroes of the nation he does violence to my sense of reality.

Of course he discounts the United States census figures for the nation, preferring those of New York with which he is acquainted. I, myself, do not always like the census figures but faulty as we may deem them to be they are the nearest we have to what is reliable. Moreover, census figures usually show the Negroes on the seamy side. Here is a case they do not. Another factor that inclines me to accept them is a certain consistency that runs through them. The most urban section of the whites and the most urban section of the Negroes are shown to have the greater rate of insanity. For instance, Northern native whites are shown to have a higher rate than Southern native whites.

The Negroes of New York, according to the 1940 census, numbered 517,221 of which only 31,504 did not live in cities and towns. The majority live in New York City. And since urban dwellers are more prone to insanity than rural dwellers Dr. Malzberg tries to equalize by comparing New York City Negoes with New York City whites. However, it seems to me that he should have at least sampled another area for two reasons: First, areas a few hundred miles away for a variety of causes may have widely differing insanity rates as Boston and Philadelphia. Love and Davenport in their report on the first million draft recruits in the first war found a very high rate for the first city and a low one for the second.

Second, the Negroes in the South have a much lower insanity rate than those of the North, therefore it is not logical, to use the New York Negro as also being representative of the South. The 1890 census says, "The ration of colored insane to colored population is more than twice as great in the northern part as in the southern," a fact that has remained largely true. Moreover the proportion of white rural dwellers for New York State far exceeded the proportion of Negro rural dwellers—a fact that should not have been ignored.

Dr. Malzberg chose New York because there was no discrimination there against admitting Negroes to hospitals thus making it "An almost ideal locus for such an investigation." But this statement is based on belief, which some will accept; others reject. My belief is that insane Negroes in the South are more likely to be confined in asylums than white people lest the Negroes damage white property and lives. The South has never been economical where the confinement of Negroes is concerned.

On pages 158-164 of the 1890 report we find the insanity rate for Negroes higher for almost every Northern State and for almost every one of the five ten-year periods of 1850-1890. The exceptions are Massachusetts and Connecticut which had for one or two of the periods a lower rate for Negroes. But in these statistics we also find this: The insanity rate for Negroes in the South was much lower than for the whites there—even the native whites—and the District of Columbia.

As regards this latter statement there are those who will argue, first, that the Negro was better off in slavery; and that second, he had better remain in the South.

Answer: The Negro in slavery had a lower degree of insanity than the white because he had come from a more primitive stock, one less maltreated by civilization. In Volume II of Sex and Race, pp. 155-56, and elsewhere I have shown that the American colonies were a dumping-ground for the human "refuse" of the British Isles. If many Americans were to go back far enough they would find that some of their ancestors in the female line were deported prostitutes. England periodically cleansed herself of street-walkers by shipping them to America. For instance of one ship leaving England in 1692 we read, "For Virginia holding 50 lewd women out of the houses of correction and 30 others who walked the streets at night." (Quoted by Estabrook in First Internat. Eugenics Congress, pp. 398-412. 1923). On the other hand, the Negroes brought from Africa were free of criminal, degenerate stock, and from social diseases except such as they picked up on shipboard from the white crews.

As regards those who might say that the Negro is better off in the South they will also be forced to say that the white immigrant was better off in Europe because what do we find? That the foreign born white not only had a much higher rate than the native white but the Negro also, the sole exceptions for the period 1850-1890, being New Hampshire, Colorado, and New Mexico.

In 1890, the foreign born rate of insanity was nearly three times higher than that of the native white, and more than four times that of the Negro, the figures per million being Negroes, 886; foreign born whites, 3843.

In the District of Columbia the native whites had for the five ten-year periods (1850-1890), the following figures per million respectively: 428; 2093; 2096; 3065; and 4470. The foreign born whites had for the same periods; 610; 5848; 14581; 26048; and 33671. The Negroes had 727; 1886; 1128; 2080; and 2972. This gives the foreign born white seven times the insanity rate of the native white and more than ten times that of the Negro in the District of Columbia for the 1890 period.

Come now to New York State. Here are the figures per million insane: Whites, 770; 1111; 1148; 2763; and 2964. Negroes: 693; 1262; 1522; 2917; and 3924. The Negroes are higher for four periods. But when we compare foreign born whites with native whites and Negroes we find a difference that is almost startling. The figures in this instance are: Native white: 770; 869; 988; 2003; and 2072. Foreign born white: 979; 1813; 2704; 5202 and 5521. Thus in 1890, the foreign born whites of New York had almost double the insanity rate of the New York Negro. Quite a difference when you separate native white from foreign born white!

Now something about later census reports on insanity. These are published under the title "United States Census: Patients in Hospitals for Mental Diseases." I have been able to find those with classifications of race and place of birth for only 1903, 1904, 1910, and 1933. These reports, like those of 1850-1890, show all groups, regardless of color or place of birth, were increasing in insanity.

The 1904 report said as regards the Northern Negro and the Southern one, "In so far as one may judge from a comparison of the figures for the distribution, by color, of the insane in hospitals in 1903 and of the general population in 1900, the same differences still exist." (p. 20) That is, the Southern Negro showed a lower insanity rate than Northern Negroes and the whites in general.

As regards native whites and foreign born whites, the 1904 report says "Of the 140,312 white insane in hospitals on December 31, 1903, 90,297 were natives of the United States, 47,078 foreign born. . . . Of the 46,300 white insane admitted to hospitals during 1904, 31,577 were native, 13,405 foreign born. . . .

"Of the whites at least 10 years of age in the general population of the United States in 1900, 80.5 percent were native and 19.5 foreign born; while of the white insane of known nativity enumerated in hospitals on December 31, 1903, 65.7 percent were native and 34.3 percent were foreign born. Relatively, therefore, the insane are more numerous among the foreign white than among the native." (p. 20).

"The matter of insanity in the foreign born population is largely determined by the nationalities which make up the foreign born population. Thus in Maine and New Hampshire with a foreign population chiefly composed of Canadians, who, as will be shown, exhibit less insanity than most immigrant races, the percentages of insane are relatively higher among the native white than among the foreign born. But the reverse is true, for example, of Massachusetts, Connecticut, New York, New Jersey, and Pennsylvania, which have large contingents of Irish and Germans and to some extent of Scandinavians, who of all foreign born appear to be the most prone to insanity.

"In the states of the South Atlantic division where the foreign born elements are of some magnitude they constitute a disproportionately large share of the insane—for instance in Delaware, Maryland and Florida. This fact also applies to Louisiana and Texas.

"For each state of the North Central division the figures show that the foreign-born whites constitute relatively more to the white insane in hospitals than the general white population. In these states, the Germans, Irish, and Scandinavians are important nationalities among the foreign born whites and as will be shown later, they all send relatively large numbers of insane to hospitals.

"In the Western division also every state has relatively more foreign born among the white insane in hospitals than among the general white population."

The Germans, Irish, and Scandinavians all had a higher percentage of insanity than Negroes both North and South. These, incidentally, are regarded as among the choice Nordic groups for supplying future Americans. The Italians, a not so choice group, had a lower insanity rate than the Nordics.

Coming to 1910 we find the ratios for native white, foreign born white, and Negro proceeding in much the same ratios. On January 1, 1910, the insane in hospitals per 100,000 of population were: Native white: 168.7; Foreign born white 405.3; and Negroes 131.4. Admitted during that year were, per 100,000 of population: Native white: 57.9; foreign born white: 116.3; Negro 44.6. (p. 25). The report adds: "As indicated by the ratios . . . the number of insane of each class to 100,000 of population of the same class the foreign born white in proportion to their numbers contributed more inmates to the hospitals for the insane than any of the other classes. The class ranking next to them is the "other colored," or Chinese and Japanese, who are also mostly migrants. The class having the smallest ratio is the Indian. The ratio for the Negro is smaller than that for the total white and also smaller than that for the total white and also smaller than that for the native white alone. . . .

"The foreign born have unduly large representation in insane asylums." (p. 25).

Of the 54.096 foreign born in hospitals in 1910, the Germans and Irish alone contributed 26,691, or nearly a half.

Just here an important fact about admissions to hospitals of the foreign born, if we say that there was discrimination against the Negro can we also say that there was discrimination against the white foreign born, who as was said has a higher rate of admission than the native white?

In the 1923 report the whites had per 100,000 population: 259.8; the Negroes 192; Indians, 104.5; Chinese, 340.6; Japanese, 148.3. (p. 19).

It is believed, as was said, that Negroes show a lower rate of admissions to insane asylums than whites because the South takes less care of its Negro insane. However, in 1923, we find a higher resident rate in hospitals for the nation of Negroes than of white, the figures being Negro: 644.4; White, 408.8. Negroes admitted to hospitals for insanity would thus appear from this figure to have less chances of being cured.

From what I have been able to gather on this very complicated subject here is the conclusion to which I am inclined. First in insanity is the foreign born white; second, the Northern Negro; third, the native Northern white; fourth, the native Southern white; fifth, the Southern Negro; and last, the Indian. This is consistent, too, with the proportion of urban dwellers in each group.

One important fact in the computation of the insane must not be forgotten, however. Those who can afford it do not generally send their mentally sick to public institutions. This would give the native whites the most in private hospitals, the foreign born whites, next, the Negroes, least.

Dr. Malzberg showed that Negro insanity in New York exceeded that of the foreign born white in the state, even in the case of the Irish. I am inclined to agree with that. Foreign born white insanity was automatically cut down by the law cutting down white immigration in the past twenty years (1924-1944). On the other hand, there was no quota for Negro migrants to the North.

So many factors enter into a mental breakdown of the human organism that it is quite unscientific to say that any group, white or black is, prone to insanity, or even to say that there is "a fundamental difference" in any group inducing this.

Among the factors to be considered, all of which work together at times, are: age; congeniality of surroundings or lack of it; degree of savoir faire in avoiding social diseases and knowledge of a proper diet.

Occupation, too, is important. As regards this the 1904 report said, "The largest percentage of insane, 41.6 is composed of persons returned as laborers and servants. This class constitutes 40 percent of the white insane, 62.5 of the Negro, and 51.5 of the foreign born white . . . 80 percent of the insane was engaged, prior to commitment in occupations described as laboring and servant, manufacturing and mechanical and agriculture, transportation and other outdoor work." (p. 34).

Why the insanity rate is higher among migrants seems to be this: They usually come from the rural districts and the smaller towns where the mental deficiency 'rate is higher than in the city. So long as the mentally deficient remain in their limited accustomed environment they can continue more or less normally; but in the big cities they crack under the stress and strain of the competition. Love and Davenport in their study of the first million draft recruits in the first world war said, "Mental deficiency is more than twice as common in rural than in urban districts and more than twice as common in the average city as it is in the largest cities like New York and Boston." (U. S. Surgeon-General's Office. Bull. 11, p. 134. 1919). Of 500,000 sick reports in the last war, the Negroes had a very slightly higher rate per 1000 mentally deficient than the white, the figures per thousand being: White, 2.80; Negroes, 2.89. (Amer. Academy of Sciences, Vol. 5, 1919, pp. 58-67.)

Here, I think, is clear proof that not "race" but bad, unstable living conditions is what makes for any seeming "fundamental difference" in insanity between one group and another. In the South where the Negro is more settled, where he had a more permanent home life, he had a lower insane rate than the Northern Negro, who is more of a migrant. The native white, and even the children of foreign born whites had a lower rate than the foreign-born white,

for the same reason. It must be remembered that people who are bold enough
to migrate are usually more temperamental than those content to stay at home
and thus more likely to break down mentally. A significant fact is that both the
Negroes and the native whites showed a higher percentage of feeble-minded persons
per million than the foreign born. The obvious reason is the immigration restrictions
imposed by the United States.

There are no magical qualities in "race," most of all where immunity from
disease and insanity are concerned. Indians in the wilds of South America;
Negroes in the wilds of Africa; and Caucasians and Tatars in the wilds of
Asiatic Russia are very little afflicted with insanity. But bring any of these
people into the great industrial cities, subject them to the stern hardships
there, and in time the weakest mentally of their descendants will crack, even
as the mentally weak in a battle will be the first to suffer shell-shock. Even
wild animals degenerate in civilization. Elephants go insane; so do dogs and
monkeys, while the pets in a family will pick up some of his family's diseases.

The title, "Characteristics of the American Negro" is misleading. The ap-
pellation "American Negro" is political and economic, not racial. Since the
"Negro" is not less than 60 percent mixed with white and Indian, while millions of his numbers are from 50 to 100 percent of what is known as "white,"
any thesis or analysis of him based on statistics is necessarily unscientific.
Worst of all, such a title helps to perpetuate an already exploded fiction.

Rejecting the American belief that similarity of color makes for oneness
of interest—an utterly false dogma since the whites of Europe have always
been at war with one another—we find in reality a wider difference between
the native white and the foreign born white than between the native white
and the Negro. The latter is homogenous. He is already American in his daily life
and manners.

Civilization makes for decadence and decadence for increased insanity. Thus
when the primitive stock in the Negro group reaches the same degree of ripe-
ness now generally attained by the Anglo-Saxon or the Jew if he is not reinforced by some primitive Negro stock, say from Africa, not only insanity but
cancer and other diseases that show a metabolic crack-up, will increase also.

For every disease that the unmixed Negro brought with him from Africa he
has acquired at least twenty more in America. It is not a question of Jew
or Latin; Slav or Anglo-Saxon; Native white or Foreign-born white; Northern
Negro or Southern Negro but one of wear and tear on the human organism.
Insanity will be lowered only when human beings are free to lead more congenial, more enlightened lives and when Nature, not race, class, or religion,
selects mates for them.

Syphilis

While on the subject of insanity a word here about its principal cause:
Syphilis. In Sex and Race, Vol. 2, p. 398, I touched on its origin, and cited
Morison and others who attributed it to the Indians, and that it came with
Columbus' men from the New World. However, Professor D. G. Rokhline of
Leningrad University finds evidences of it in Europe long before the dis-

covery of America. He says, "Syphilis has existed in Europe and in Asia in the Middle Ages as well as in the most distant antiquity. Among the most ancient human relics preserved in the Institute of Anthropology and Ethnography of the Academy of Science we have found indisputable syphilitic lesions on a skull of the eleventh to the twelfth century coming from the region of Lake Ladoga." (Russia). He also cites other instances. (La Radio-Anthropologie in **L'Anthropologic,** Vol. 45, 1935.)

Syphilis seems to be a disease bred in the civilizations of temperate climes. Ancient Egyptian civilization lasted for at least 5,000 years but no evdences of syphilis have been discovered there. Elliott Smith and G. R. Dawson who did extensive research on mummies says, "No true case of rickets or syphilitic disease has been found in any ancient Egyptian remains. . . . There was no evidence whatever of any syphilitic injuries to the bones, nor even anything remotely resembling syphilitic injuries to the teeth." Egyptians Mummies, pp. 157-8. 1924.

The same was (and is) generally true of that part of Negro Africa little touched by Arab or white civilization. The great medical missionary, Dr. Livingstone, who journeyed extensively through that region found no syphilis native to it.

Finally, one has to be careful when generalizing racially about syphilis. Certain groups of Negroes have more syphilis than certain other groups the same as among the whites. For instance it was discovered that white railroad employees have a higher percentage of syphilis than laborers, farmers, and businessmen. In a study made at the Mayo Clinic, Rochester, Minn., among railroad men in jobs from which Negroes are barred it was discovered that they had nearly twice as much syphilis per 100 as laborers; and three times as much as businessmen (Jour. of Industrial Hygiene, Vol. 1, 1920). It appears that railroad men, travelling from one town to another, lead more promiscuous lives than other citizens. Away from their wives the railroad men pick up other women at lay-over places, whereas laborers and businessmen are more likely to lead regular home lives. The wives of the railroad men also had a high syphilitic rate. It is likely also that Negro railroad men would show a higher percentage than Negro laborers and Negro businessmen as I have reason to believe they do not lead more temperate lives than white railroad men.

It is possible that certain groups of whites might have a higher syphilitic rate than certain groups of Negroes. Thus, the habit of most sociologists in comparing "race" with "race" is quite unscientific.

SCATTERED NOTES ON SEX AND RACE, VOL. L

(With Chapters to which they are related)

Ancient Egypt and Ethiopia (Chap. 3)

Aristotle (384-322 B. C.), said about the hair of the Ethiopians and Egyptians:
"Why are the Ethiopians and the Egyptians bandy-legged? Is it due to the heat and just as planks are warped when they are dry so are the bodies of living creatures. The hair proves this; for theirs is wooly and wooliness is a curving of the hair." (Problems, xiv, 4. Trans. by W. S. Hett.) Numbers of the natives of the Anglo-Egyptian Sudan still have bent legs. A recent traveller, Felix Shay, mentions this fact observed over two thousand years ago by Aristotle. (National Geographic, Feb. 1925, p. 146). In his Physiognomy (IV) Aristotle also said that the Egyptians and Ethiopians were black. Here is the testimony of one who was on the spot, and who for nearly two thousand years ranked as the world's greatest scientist, at least the Sorbonne so regarded him as late as 1600.

Egypt—The Mamelukes

W. G. Browne says that when the supply of Georgians and Circassians proved "insufficient, or may have been expended, black slaves from the interior of Africa are substituted and if found docile are armed and accoutred like the rest." Travels in Africa. 1799. See also Denon V. Voyages dans La Basse et La Haute Egypte, t. I, Appendix ccxliv. 1807.

Napoleon; Correspondence, Vol. 4, p. 375 speaks of the white and the black female slaves of the Mamelukes.

India (Chap. 5)

On Negro ruling princes in India see Johnston, H. H. Colonization of Africa, p. 92, 1905.

Australia (Chap 6)

On the mixing of white and black in Australia, past and present, P. Hasluck says. "In the later days though casual mating with black women was by no means any less common, regularizing of the match or asking a priest's blessing would probably have been regarded as a sign of the white man's utter depravity." (Black Australians, p. 196. 1942).

Morocco (Chap. 11)

On Empsael, Negro Prime Minister of Mulai Ismael see; Braithewaite, J. History of the Revolutions of Morocco, pp. 120, 177, 178. London. 1729.

Jugo-Slavia (Chap. 11)

As regards the Negro strain more or less distant, which, as I said, is to be found in the Balkans, such having come about largely through Moorish and Turkish invasions of that region, C. L. Sulzberger in an article "Negroes of the Adriatic," in the London Evening Standard, mentions one of the Negro colonies to be found here and there in Europe. He says, "Jugoslavia has two

LII. Crown Prince Frederick of Germany with his sister and one of the Negro pages of the court. By Antoine Pesne (1683-1757).

minorities which are as strange as they can be. One of them is a tiny Negro colony on the Adriatic. . . .

"The Negroes live in a small village near Ucinj, a sea-coast town just north of Albania. They are descended from slaves brought there during the days when Haralampia, the famous corsair, was harrying the eastern Mediterranean. The slaves were used as dowries by rich families. After a number of years they were freed and their children were free. They became peasants, sailors, and sometimes even ship-owners. They are Moslems and have very rarely married white people. Some of them are great dandies. They speak Serbian and live a quiet, isolated life. One of them is an officer in the Jugoslav army. You can see him almost any day strolling down the Belgrade corso with his sword under his arm.

"The most famous member of this colony was Musta, who died in 1900 at the age of 124. . . ."—reproduced in P. T. O. London, Nov. 1939.

As was said before whenever these groups of Negroes are found in Europe they are commonly referred to as slaves, whereas numbers of the free Moors and Turks were unmixed Negroes, and some of them were of high rank. In Cardiff, Wales, there is a colony of 7,000 Negroes. Did these people come there as slaves? No, they settled there only some 70 years ago, being largely the descendants of sailors.

Spain (Chap. 15)

B. & E. Wishaw says," There is still a Negro race at Niebla in the province of Huelva (Spain) with the crisp black curly hair, the large liquid eyes and the blueness under the finger-nails." (Arabic Spain, p. 129. 1912.)

Russia (Chap. 16)

"Mlle. de Protassov, who was as dark and ugly as the Queen of Tahiti, always resided at the Court. She was related to Prince Orloff, who used his influence to get her there." Countess Golovine. Memoirs, p. 44. (Court of Catherine the Great.)

The Negro Caucasians of Russia

In the Soviet Caucasus about fourteen miles from Sukkum on the Black Sea lives a colony of 800 or more Negro families, nearly all unmixed blacks, known as Abhkazians, or Abcausians. That is to say, they are "Black Caucasians.'

They are supposed to have been brought there from Africa by the Turkish feudal lords 300 years ago to work the tobacco plantations, but whatever be their origin the fact remains that Herodotus, the Father of History (484-425 B. C.) records the presence of Negroes in this region, which was then called Colchis, and is still called so.

Herodotus, who saw them said," For my part I believe the Colchi to be a colony of Egyptians because like them they have black skins and wooly hair." (Book II, 104.)

And in 1887, two thousand years later, we find the eminent anthropologist,

Ernest Chantre, speaking of the mixed Negro strain of some of the tribes of Colchis. (Recherches Anthropol, dans le Caucase, Vol. 4, p. 11, 1887.) Abhkazia, or Abcausia, was united to Colchis under the Byzantine emperors, says Chantre. And as I showed in Sex and Race, Vol. I, Chap. 11, there was much Negro strain in the Byzantines. The same was true of the Turks, who succeeded the Byzantines. That there has always been a Negro strain in the peoples of the Caucasus seems evident. Moreover, the word, Caucasus, itself, is of Ethiopian or Negro origin, according to two distinguished authorities, Jacob Bryant and Gerald Massey. Bryant says it comes from the Ethiopian, Cush. "Co-Cusus"—the temple or places of Cush, son of Ham (Analysis of Ancient Mythology, Vol. 5, p. 103. 1807.) Massey says, "Even the word, Caucasian, tells of an origin in the Kaf or Kaffir. Philosophy will support ethnology in deriving from Africa. . . ." (A Book of the Beginnings, Vol. 1, p. 18.

Otto Hall of New York City who spent several weeks among these Russian Negroes tells me that they are collective farmers, whose principal crop is tobacco from which a kind of Turkish tobacco is made. Most of them are jet-black, though some show Turkish and Armenian mixture. They are mountaineers, are generally tall, and are great horsemen, being able to perform most of the Cossack feats. They eat barbecued wild-mountain goat, cornmeal mush, and drink vodka.

Eugene Gordon, another American, who visited them, describes the region in which they live as having such tropical plants as bananas and palms, while the "air is heavy with the scent of tropical flowers." He adds that "the Abhkazian Negroes, shortly before the 1917 Socialist Revolution were allowed by their princely owners to occupy small strips of land." (Daily Worker Mag. Sept. 18. 1943.) See also David Tutaeff, "The Soviet Caucasus," p. 79. 1942.

Afghanistan

M. Ilin (Men and Mountains, p. 135. 1935) tells of seeing people in Afganistan black as Negroes.

Portugal (Chap. 15)

(Research on Portugal contributed by James M. Ivy)

On Negro strain in ancient Portuguese. "This pendulousness (between Europe and Africa) is accentuated in the Upper Paleolithic epoch, a period, probably, in which there was considerable ethnic and cultural infiltration from Africa (Capsienses). This penetration left permanent traces, more frequently localized in the southern zones. Other indications of African penetration during this period may be seen in the representations of capsiense sculptural art of the Peninsula depicting women with prominent buttocks. They remind one of the steatopygy of the Bushmen and the Hottentots."—Gilberty Freyre, Casa Grande, pp. 140-41.

"Feminine figures predominate in the Aurignacian sculpture, which makes one suspect that they must have been symbols of fecundity; and these figures of women generally show huge, pendent dugs, a wide space between the ilias crest, more or less prominent bellies, well-marked external genital organs, and especially a prominence of the buttocks which reminds one of the well-known steatopygy of the Bushmen and Hottentot women of South Africa."

Antonio Augusto Mendes Correa: Os Povos primitivos da Lusitania, p. 163. Porto: 1924.

On the more recent Negro strain in the Portuguese. Excerpts from J. A. Pires de Lima: **Mouros, Judeos e Negros na Historia de Portugal** (Moors, Jews, and Negroes in the History of Portugal) Porto: 1940.

"Furthermore, the Negroes were almost always treated very kindly, and the people usually addressed them with the diminutive, 'See the little black!'"

"There were many families, and often aristocratic ones, who bore such names as **Préto, Negro Negrão, and Negreiros** (terms for Negro)", p. 16.

"The amount of Jewish and Negro blood absorbed by the Portuguese in the past has been exaggerated by foreign scientists. This is done in an attempt to belittle us." p. 22.

"Leite de Vasconcelos lists many names of Hebraic origin and then tells us that by the end of the sixteenth century Lisbon had a population of 200,000 inhabitants. One third of these were Negroes; while another third consisted of New Christians." (Note: Cristaos Novas of New Christians were converted Moors.)

Camões, Lirica de Camões (ed. de Rodrigues e Vieira). Coimbra, 1932. "Endechas a Barbara escrava" ("Laments of the Barbarous Slave Woman").

Many popular songs and sayings also refer to Negroes in Portugal: e. g., Marujinho (Little Sailor), O Preto (The Black).

Large number of Negroes came into the Peninsula with the invasion of Hannibal. p. 57.

In the 8th century Arabs invaded the Peninsula and brought in many Negroes. p. 57.

Negroes entered Portugal in very large numbers during the period of the Discoveries (Descobertas). p. 57.

de Lima asserts that Clenard exaggerates when he says that in the 16th century the number of Negroes and Moors exceeded the number of free Portuguese. p. 57.

Negroes in Portugal were not held in lifetime slavery. After seven years of service they were free. (Link: Travels in Portugal, pp. 154, 203-04, 420. 1801.)

References to Negroes in Portugal in Portuguese literature:

Garcia de Rezeñde, Miscelânea e veriedade de Historia. Coimbra. 1917. 58-59, 189. He refers to the great influx of Negroes and its sad consequences.

"Three of the great figures of Portuguese imperialism were of mixed-blood. Vieira (João Fernandes Vieira, 1613-1681), and, according to some, Anchieta (José de Anchieta, 1533-1597) and Pombal (Sebastiõ José de Carvalho e Mello, conde de Oeiras, marques de Pombal, 1699-1782), three great expressions of imperial Portugal, had Negro blood. This was due not only to the culture of the Portuguese, but to their imperialism as anthropocentrism as distinguished from the present-day ethnocentric imperialism of the British, North Americans, Germans, Italians, and Japanese."

Gilberto Freyre, **Uma Cultura Ameaçada: A Luso-Brasileira** (A Culture

Threatened: The Luso-Brazilian), Recife, 1940, a lecture delivered before the Gabinete Portuguese de Leitura, Pernambuco, June 2, 1940, p. 38.

This quotation is preceded by several paragraphs in which Freyre points out the two characteristics of Portuguese character: their boldness in facing the unknown, their intellectual curiosity, and their conservatism. Then he criticizes those who attribute Portuguese pioneering and originality to the Nordics. He points out that these discoveries were often made by men who were a mixture of white, Jewish, Moorish, and Negro.

Freyre, writing, of course, for a Brazilian public already familiar with the ethnic melange that were the Portuguese, takes the Negroidism of the Portuguese so much for granted that he doesn't go into lengthy detail. But here is a quote from the **Casa Grande** on the point.

"In place of the idea of race superiority so noticeable in the English colonizer the Portuguese colonizer of Brazil substituted the criterion of purity of faith. It was faith, and not blood, that he defended against the contamination of the heretics. He made religious orthodoxy, rather than race, the basis of political unity. But we must not confuse this criterion of prophylatic selection, quite legitimate in view of the ideas of the period, similar to our modern ideas of eugenics, with outright xenophobia." p. 135.

SCATTERED NOTES ON SEX AND RACE VOLUME II
(With Chapters to which they are related)
Latin America
(Research on Latin-America contributed by James W. Ivy)

Brazil (Chap. 3)

"A veritable melting pot of races, our country was from the very beginning of its formation the center for the meeting of three distinct races, two of which were very different. Probably the ethnic origin of no people has resulted from the mixing of such radically racial elements. Our ethnic mixtures acquired in Brazil an intensity and a complexity of which our Latin brothers on the continent know nothing. . . . Among us, on the contrary, the Negro, the Indian, and the white were profoundly mixed, crossing and re-crossing in every possible sense, whites with blacks, blacks with Indians, and then all three re-crossing again, in every part of the country. (Oliviera Vianna. Evolução do povo brasileiro. 2 a. edicao, p. 123).

"One of the most peaceful conquests of science appears to be the establishment of the truth of the essential unity of mankind. Even the materialistic theories of Darwin and his successors are in agreement with the Bible on this.

"Throughout pre-historic times Negroes, and not the white, have been the rulers of the earth. Unfortunately archeology is limited in its researches to the borders of an age which dates back for millenniums. Whence came the primitive colonizers of Europe? In relatively recent epochs, no doubt from Asia; at earlier periods, however, Africa must have been the cradle. Saint Yves d'Alveydre, curious French author of the celebrated **Mission of the Jews**, tells how the Cushites, who after crossing the Mediterranean and invading and conquering France, showed their disdain for that race, which was inferior because of its skin and eye color, by dubbing them with the name of the most degrading white thing they could think of: **scytha**. In the language of the Cushites **scytha** meant spittle. This same name had been given by the ancestors of the Abyssinians to the Celts.

"The Negro type is almost as common in India and Asia as the brown, only the latter have straight hair. The early inhabitants of India according to the **Vedas** used to go on great marauding expeditions which often carried them as far as the shores of the Mediterranean. The brown pigmentation of the Greeks was, therefore, a result of the Hindu blood brought in by these conquests. Greek theogony was likewise a symbolic adaptation and an anthropomorphic incarnation of the cosmogic myths of India.

"Easily open to maritime invasion the shores of the Mediterranean received a large dosage of African blood through its commerce. Pre-history, therefore, teaches us that African blood is without question to be found in the peoples living on the shores of the Mediterranean. On this concept, or rather historical fact, there is virtual unanimity of opinion. Gobineau and Ripley recognized it years ago when they ascribed an Afro-European origin to the Aryan language, which proves that the assimilation of both elements was already complete.

"From this Negro influence in Europe, at one time very widespread, but now disappeared to leave only a few traces in the swarthy pigmentation of certain ethnic groups, we can draw three conclusions: First, the African mixture was not inferior, since there was once no more noble race than the Mediterranean; secondly, the progressive Aryanization of Brazil, an example set by Europe, is a fatal and inevitable consequence; and thirdly, Europeans and Africans are close relatives." (Baptista Pereira, Pelo Brasil Maior, Sao Paulo: Companhai Editora Nacional, 1934, pp. 274-275.)

This quotation is one section of a lecture on "Brazil and Race" and much of it, of course, does not mention the Negro, but in his summary of his lecture Pereira states:

Let us make a synthesis of the principal ideas in this essay.

We have proved

The unity of mankind;

The futility of race prejudice;

The impotency of both anthropology and ethnography in its attempts to isolate individual characteristics as a basis for doctrines of inferiority and superiority;

The purely theoretical nature of the conjectures about primitive peoples and primitive migration;

The bankruptcy of Gobinism and Nordic superiority;

The indisputable mongrelization of almost all peoples;

The influence and penetration of Negro blood in all civilizations;

The Afro-European character of Greek and Latin civilization, and hence:

The recency of white hegemony and

The role of Portugal as an agent in establishing it;

And finally the lack of foundation for the accusation that Brazil, because of its absorption of "inferior" blood, is degenerate and therefore not worthy of leading in the vanguard of civilization. (Ibid., pp. 307-308)

Slavery—Jealousy of the Slave Mistresses

"It is a fact generally observed in slave societies that the mistress is more cruel in her treatment of slaves than the master. It is a fact confirmed by our chronicles, our folklore, our oral tradition, and travelers. There are on record not two or three, but scores of cases of the cruelty of the senhoras de engenho toward defenseless slaves. Young wives who had ordered that the eyes of beautiful slave maids be plucked out and brought to their husbands at dessert time in a sweet-meat dish, floating in still fresh blood. Baronesses through jealousy or spite would order the sale of fifteen-year-old mulatto girls to old libertines; others would knock out the teeth of their slaves with shoe heels; or order their breasts cut off, their fingernails torn out, their faces or eyes burned; a whole series of tortures the motive for which was almost always jealousy of the husband, sexual hate, and the rivalry of woman with woman.

"Among Brazilians," wrote Burlamaqui at the beginning of the nineteenth

century, "a woman who suspected her husband or lover of illicit sexual relations with a female slave commonly used such phrases as: 'I'll fry her,' 'I'll
roast her,' 'I'll burn or cut off such and such a part of her.' etc." (Freyre,
Casa-Grande, p. 249.)

From Aluizio D'Azevedo, O Mulato, "Domingas was stretched motionless on
the ground completely naked, her head shaved, her hands tied behind her back,
her feet in stocks, and her genital parts burned with a red-hot iron." (p. 56-67
1941. 11th ed.

Domingas was the slave woman, mistress of Jose da Silva, and mother of
the mulatto Dr. Raimundo Jose da Silva. Da Silva's wife Quiteria suspected
the relationship and meted out this punishment one day when her husband
was absent.

Background explanation for the quotation from Azevedo's **The Mulatto:** Dr.
Raimundo de Silva, the offspring of a white, Jose Pedro de Silva, by his slave
mistress, Domingas, now a **formado** of Coimbra, traveled and wealthy returns to
his home town of Maranhão. He is elegant, handsome, well-mannered, well-
educated and very charming to the ladies. He falls in love with Ana Rosa the
daughter of Manoel Pedro da Silva, a Portuguese. Ana Rosa had been reared
upon her mother's death by Pedro's mother-in-law D. Maria Barbara, a member
of one of the old families of the town and full of prejudices of white purity. She
always bragged about her Portuguese ancestors, á la Back Bay; disliked Negroes and
always referred to mulattoes as **goats** (Cabras). Naturally she would be horrified
at the idea of any member of her family marrying one of Negro descent, even
at the idea that Dr. Raimundo should marry his cousin Ana Rosa. Raimundo, I
should have said, is **formado** in law. Now in this passage Manoel has been forced
to give Raimundo an answer to a question which Raimundo has been pressing on
him for a long time: the request for the hand of his daughter. The passage shows
how during the middle of the XIX century in Brazil, old families were scrupulous
to retain their "purity" and their prestige. Prejudice against Dr. Raimundo is
primarily one of class rather than one of race. Raimundo lacks class even though
wealthy, travelled and educated because he and his mother were freed at the
baptismal font.

"So you promise," questions Manoel, "not to be shocked by what I'm going
to say?"

"I swear I won't. Speak right out!" answers Raimundo.

Shrugging his shoulders and fairly hissing out the words with a sort of
self-confident air, Manoel explained:

"I refuse my daughter's hand because you are a . . . well . . . how shall I
put it? . . . well . . . you are the offspring of a slave. . . ."

"I-I . . . I'm the son of a slave?"

"Yes, you are a colored man; unfortunately that's true."

Raimundo turned livid.

"Well, you see, friend, personally I don't refuse you Ana Rosa's hand . .
uh! . . . uh . . . it's the family. My own family is very scrupulous in this
respect and Maranhense society is the same way. It's all nonsense I agree.
I even go so far as to call it a silly prejudice, but you can't begin to imagine

how mulattoes are scorned in this community. They would never forgive me if I permitted such a marriage. Furthermore, I'd have to break a promise . . . the promise I made to my mother-in-law never to give her granddaughter in marriage to any but a legitimate white, a Portuguese, or at least to the descendant of a Portuguese. I admit you are a very dignified and respectable young man, but . . . well . . . you got your freedom at the baptismal font, and in Maranhão no one can ever forget that." (p. 251).

On Count Gobineau, originator of the doctrine of white superiority.

"In 1868 Gobineau was in Brazil as minister of Napoleon III. He paints Rio de Janeiro as a backward city swollen with a large colored population. During his stay he got to be intimate with only one Brazilian, Dom Pedro II, and their sympathetic friendship was cemented by a mutual interest in letters and the arts. Yet even this friendship, as his private correspondence shows, did not soften Gobineau's prejudice against us, since he did not want to vegetate in a Negro country.

"A personal misfortune must have contributed much to his antipathy for Brazilians. As an exile in a tropical country, Gobineau, the elegant diplomat with the fine physiognomy and the Aramis-like head, was missing those amorous facilities which had been so freely furnished by other countries to which he had been accredited, and therefore he got himself involved in an unfortunate predicament in a Rio theater. One night at the theater, so goes the tradition of the period, Gobineau thought he had met in a certain Brazilian lady a substitute for his absent Duchesse de Chevreuse and therefore attempted to speak to her without introduction. But a member of a prominent family, Viscount de Saboria, without attaching the slightest importance either to Gobineau's Viking ancestry or his twenty-four Scandinavian quarterings, slapped the Count. This angered the Aramis-Norman-Viking. **Pays de sauvages!** he muttered in the lobby as he passed his handkerchief over his smarting face. Only in a country of barbarians would a savage "coon" (**moreno,** literally brown) have the temerity to exhibit such disrespect for a grandson of Odin, and moreover toward one who is an intimate friend of the Emperor.

"From then on Brazilians were on the Index. His racial theories, helped along by his wounded pride, incandesced and vulcanized themselves into an implacable hatred. And this is the reason why Mr. Gobineau has never seen Brazil otherwise than as a country of Negroes, which suggested to Lapouge the ridiculous doctrine that they would eventually come to dominate the whites and that Brazil would in a short time be Africanized into a South-American Congo.—Pereira, op. cit., pp 235-237.

Cuba

"The Cuban is one of the most mixed-blooded peoples. Each of the major racial strains before arrival in the island was itself a complex mixture of dissimilar elements. Perhaps the Indians were the most homogenous; the Negroes, on the other hand, were taken from every African coast and from all parts of the interior; from the coast of Mauretania, from Senegambia, Guinea, Gabon, Congo and Angola on the Atlantic side and as far as the ports of Zanzibar and Mozambique on the Indian Ocean. Africans of many different melanoid races arrived in the slave ships, and curious paradox, many Negroes who came to Cuba such as the Congoes and the Bantus can no longer be classified as such according to the anthropologists. Furthermore it is not the exceptional ethnologist who claims that all African tribes have some admixture of white blood. . . .

"The blacks came to Cuba at first from Spain, herself abundantly supplied with slaves from Guinea and Congo. . . .

"The Negro's contribution to Cuba is not a mean one. Aside from his tremendous capacity for work, which made Cuba's economic incorporation into world civilization possible, and his zeal for liberty, which hastened national sovereignty, the Negro's cultural influence can be detected in our cooking, in our vocabulary, in our verbosity, in our oratory, and in our "maternalism." and even in that healthy reaction which we call **choteo** (satirical jesting), but above all in art, in religion and in the tone of our collective emotionalism.

"As for our arts, music belongs to him. The extraordinary vigor and captivating originality of Cuban music is a mulatto creation. In fact all music of original beauty which has been America's gift to the Old World is a combination of black and white elements. Even Gobineau, the high priest of "racism," conceded the Negroid race's sovereignty in esthetic matters." (Fernando Ortiz, Phylon, First Quar. 1944, pp. 35-6.

Chile (Chap. 4.)

Benjamin Subercaseaux (**Chile o Una Loca Geografia**): "Our present population, which. I know not why, is considered by many to be almost clean of all aboriginal blood, is in reality full of it." He also mentions the little Congoblacks of the Azapa. Valley.

Argentina

"At the beginning of the eighteenth century Buenos Aires had 20,000 Negro slaves out of a total population of 40,000." (Baptista Pereira, **Pelo Brasil Maior,** p. 42.)

L. L. & J. S. Bernard, "The Negro in Relation to other Races in Latin America," "The warden of the national prison of Buenos Aires is a mulatto and he is also a professor in the University of Buenos Aires. . . . Rivadavia, one of the great figures in Argentine history, was a mulatto." (Proceedings National Acad. of Science, Vol. 5. No. 3. p. 316. 1928.

Luis Alberto Sanchez: "Some assert that Bolivar had Negro blood and Rivadavia, the first president of Argentina, was undoubtedly a mulatto." Antioch Review, Fall of 1942, p. 360.

Uruguay

For additional information on Negroes in Uruguay from 1680 to 1830: see "Negroes in Uruguay" by Ildefonso P. Perez, Phylon, 3rd Quar. 1943. He says, "It is unquestionable that the black race forms a very important nucleus of the population of Montevideo from 1777 to 1830, at times a third part, and that its impact was felt in various aspects of the life of the city." (Montevideo.)

Cuba (Chap. 7)

Jose Vasconcelos: La Raza Cosmica (p. 157):

"Cuba es mulata; aunque hay alli mucha gente blanca, se siente la influencia del negro" as well as Luis Araquistain's **La Agonia Antillana** (p. 184): "Esta es le gran tragedia racial de Cuba: su creciente africanization?" (This is the great tragedy of Cuba: its increasing Africanization).

The Dominican Republic (Chap. 8)

Pedro Henriquez Urena (1885) is of Negro descent; he's rated one of the best critics in Spanish-American literature, and filled the Charles Eliot Norton Chair. of poetry at Harvard last year. Max Henriquez Ureña is his brother. Both of them are from Santo Domingo where nearly everybody has more than a dash of Negro blood.

Latin America (Chap. 12)

Louis Quintanilla, A Latin American Speaks, p. 6-7. 1943. "Roughly speaking, there are substantially fewer than twenty-five million Whites in Latin America out of a total population for the twenty republics of one hundred and twenty-five million. In other words, Latin-America is only one-fifth White. Only Chile, Costa Rica, Argentina, and Uruguay are predominanlty white."

The more I study Latin American life the more I become aware of the tremendous influence of the Negro in Latin-American development and culture. His influence there seems to have been greater even than it is in the States. And I have also noted that the good neighbor policy is leading to a systematic suppression of the truth of the tremendous importance of the Negro in South America. For fear of wounding American sensibilities I suppose, most writers on Latin America (and most of them are very superficial) make few references to the Negro or his status in those countries. Nor will they admit the fact that the majority of South Americans are colored people: mestizos and mestizos, Indians and Negroes.

Mexico (Chap. 6)

Arno Fouche, a white engineer of New York, who lived many years in Mexico says that two or more of the recent presidents of Mexico had a Negro strain: "Such an excellent mixture," he says, "are the **triquenitos**, consisting of three blood origins, Spanish, Indian and Negro. The presidents, Porfirio Diaz, and Victoriana Huerta were of colored descent, partly. I met the former's daughter, Senorita Juanita Concha at the Teatro de los Heroes in Ciudad Chihuahua, shortly before her retirement from the stage and marriage to one of the wealthiest ranchers of Rosario, Argentine. She was a phenomenal coloratura of light and grand opera. . . ." (Letters to J. A. Rogers).

NOTES ON RACE MIXTURE IN THE LEEWARD ISLANDS, BRITISH WEST INDIES

(Chap. 10)

Contributed by J. R. Ralph Casimir, Dominica, British West Indies.

"Charles Louis Corriette, Dominica planter, on a trip to Europe, some six years ago brought back a German wife. They are still together and have one child. Frederick E. Degazon, of St. Lucia, has an English wife. They have two children. He was formerly Crown Attorney in Dominica and is now of St. Lucia. Edward Fadelle, Dominica planter and engineer, has an English wife. Dr. Boyd of Dominica, Government Medical Officer of Nevis, B. W. I., has an English wife. So has Dr. K. M. B. Simon, Government Medical Officer of Dominica Miss "Pep" Lartigue, colored, of Dominica, married a United States marine last year. Dr. R. L. Renwick of Grenada, Government officer of Dominica, has an English wife. Dr. E. B. Garrard, an Englishman, resident in Dominica, married a colored woman fifteen years ago and has had three children by her. Both are alive.

"Solange Bellot, colored daughter of John Bellot, wealthy mulatto merchant and planter, owner of several estates in Dominica and Martinique was married to Dr. Hilaire Thaly, white. They had two sons and one daughter. One of the sons, Daniel Thaly is an M.D., a poet of distinction, and a Chevalier of the Legion of Honor. He was for a time Government Medical Officer of Dominica."

ANGLO-SAXON AMERICA

Tennessee (Chap. 15)

For additional facts on miscegenation in Tennessee see: A. A. Taylor, "Negro In Tennessee, 1865-1880, pp. 288-9. 1941.

North Carolina (Chap. 15)

For additional information on race-mixing in ante-bellum North Carolina see J. H. Franklin: The Free Negro in North Carolina, pp. 35-39. 1943. The writer gives instances from the records of mixed marriages and of white women, the wives of white men, bearing mulatto children. "That Negroes were still marrying whites toward the end of the colonial period," he says, "can be seen by the statements of petitioners to the General Assembly, who, in 1775 asked that the tax on interracial marriages be reduced."

Boston and New York (Chap. 30)

For the latest figures on mixed marriages in Boston and New York City, together with the proportion of white men who marry Negro women and Negro men who marry white women with their place of birth and occupation see chapter; "Negro-White Intermarriage in Recent Times." in Klineberg, O., Characteristics of the American Negro, pp. 177-300. 1944.

New Jersey and New York—Voodoo (Chap. 33)

For additional information on white women who go to, or take part in voodoo rites in Harlem, and a fuller story of "Dr" Hyghcock, Negro voodoo doctor of Malaga, N. J. as told in the chapter, Religion and Miscegenation, Vol. 2, see story of one of the white girl devotees of Dr. "Hyghcock" in True Magazine, Sept. 1938, with pictures.

Delaware (Chap. 35)

For a composite race in America see C. A. Weslager, "Delaware's Forgotten Folk: The Story of the Moors and the Nanticokes," 1943. Illustrations of these mixed-bloods show them from the apparently unmixed white to dark mulatto and the Negro-Caucasian-Indian.

Canada (Vol. 2, Chap. 36)

Ida Greaves says of the marriage of whites and Negroes in Canada, "About half of the intermarriage of both male and female is with British stock, somewhat more men than women appear to marry into the French race and the next largest percentage of intermarriage is with Indians while there are scattered instances of marriages with German, Dutch, Ukrainian, Icelandic and Jewish peoples. The proportion of intermarriage naturally differs with the opportunity of contact and is therefore greater in cosmopolitan cities than in rural districts. It is said, for instance, that 40 percent of the Negro men in Montreal are married to white women and of 23 children born of Negro mothers in the city in 1926 only 14 had Negro fathers." (The Negro in Canada. McGill Univ. Studies, No. 16.)

NOTES ON RACE MIXTURE FROM A LETTER FROM REV. GEORGE SINGLETON,

Editor of the Christian Recorder, December 30, 1942: (Chap. 30).

"The first Bishop elected in the African M. E. Church was the Reverend Daniel Coker of Baltimore, Md. His mother was a white English woman, and his father a Negro. He was not 'consecrated,' (1816) but Allen was in his stead. Several reasons have been alleged. A persistent tradition is that he was too 'white.' He had a brother by the same name. There is a white lady at this writing who is 'passing' for Negro and working in our church. Another white lady is a member of Bethel in Chicago. I received a white woman into my church while pastoring in Springfield, Illinois. She was from Indiana. I performed the marriage ceremony for two friends, one colleague school teacher, in South Carolina. They obtained their license as "White." They are living in Detroit, where the man has a position as "White" in a large automobile plant. I have another good friend, an eminent Surgeon, with whom I served in World War I. His Caucasian friends take him for one of them. He goes to Washington, D. C. and mingles with them. Again, he mingles with Negroes as one of them. It is interesting to talk with him.

Dr. X was compelled to leave Columbia, S. C. a few years ago because a white lady was so infatuated with him. But why go on? The whole story will never be told. I was doing a thesis in the University of Chicago, and found in the sources reference to a son of President Andrew Jackson. He was waiting table in New Orleans. My authority is Frederick Law Olmsted.

"One of my classmates in South Carolina was a very fair girl from Abbeville, S. C. Her mother was beautiful and very fair. Her friend was a prominent white man in the town. This girl never wanted for anything. Finally ¡her white father sent her to Cornell University where she received her master's degree. She is at present Dean of Women at .... University.

"I have a friend in Columbia, S. C., the wife of a prominent Dentist. She hails from Springfield, Illinois. Before he died her father told me that he was a direct descendant of George Washington. Traced it back to Virginia. Another friend, a young minister's wife in Ohio is a descendant of Nathaniel Greene of Revolutionary fame."

NOTES ON THE COLORED BRANCH OF THE HARPER FAMILY IN AMERICA (Chap. 30)

Contributed by Lucius C. Harper

ROBERT AUGUSTUS HARPER, our grandfather.

His mother, Elizabeth Betsy Keating, was owned, and brought to America from San Domingo, by Robert Parson, Scotch-Irish, and well-to-do gentleman of leisure who displeased Southern hospitality generally. He settled in Augusta, Georgia, around 1827.

Being intelligent, he entertained the intelligensia of that day. The story goes that one of the founders of Harper's Magazine, a young man came South to visit him; lived with the Parsons for the summer and while there met this comely colored girl—Elizabeth Betsy Keating—in the household. After his return to New York City, this son (Robert A. Harper) was born and named after Parson (Robert, his first name), Augustus, for Augusta, Ga., and Harper after the publisher.

My sister tells me we have in our family one of the first copies of Harper's Magazine. Robert A. Harper, the old "Augusta Log" shows opened one of the first book ·stores in that city. The Harper Brothers' Art Store, now operating on Broad Street in Augusta, is the outgrowth of this venture, which to date is 95 years old, and has been in control of the family since its founding. Robert A. Harper, however, was not listed as "colored" in the old "Augusta Log" which was a sort of catalogue of the early business pioneers of that city. But, of course, he was.

In recent years an Augusta daily newspaper reprinted some of the early history of the city from that "Log," and those reading it would have thought Robert A. Harper was a white man. But they re-copied it as it was originally compiled.

Robert Harper became a famous musician in the South. He sold and introduced the first Stradivarius violins in that section of the country. In his youth he was apprenticed to the Cherchin Piano Company of New York, and whenever they made the sale of a piano in the South, he was sent to instruct the sons and daughters of the old aristocracy there. He compiled a book of his visits to these plantations or mansions, with the fees he obtained and the like. He stayed in the mansions as a sort of guest while instructing. The book contains an old remedy which eradicated the smallpox epidemic that prevailed throughout the South during his time.

He organized an orchestra and is accredited with composing the Oglethorpe March, the famous Georgia theme song. Leaders of the Confederacy used his orchestra almost exclusively for the grand balls and the like. He later organized a Drum and Bugle Corps of the young colored boys who were the offsprings of white and black unlicensed unions. Fathers of these boys did not wish to grow up amid conditions of the slavery, and Harper used this Drum and Bugle Corps as a sort of "Underground Railroad" to get them out of the South to Quaker schools then in and around Pennsylvania. He would take them on a tour, and leave six or eight in northern schools and repeat this plan until he had satisfied the boys' fathers, who, of course, paid him liberally for his services. Many of these boys finished reputable northern colleges, including the University of Pennsylvania, and some of their names are to be found as leading politicians of the South during the Reconstruction Era. Some, of course, were light enough in color to go over to the white side, but for many years thereafter corresponded with him at his book store in Augusta.

Before his death he acquired much real estate in Augusta, and a half block from the old Harper homestead, which still stands at 913 Ninth street, and is today occupied by his heirs, is a canal which the old map of Augusta shows that Harper granted the city the right to "cut it through his estate" with the proviso that a large portion of his estate be exempt from taxes. This agreement prevailed so long as he lived, but was changed after his death through legal technicalities.

Of the 42 descendants now surviving, 7 have gone over on the white side and are holding responsible positions in big white commercial concerns around New York, California and Massachusetts. All are married into white families; five have children, comprising in all 14—eight boys and six girls.

(Lucius C. Harper is editor of the Chicago Defender. He is most strikingly of the type that throughout Latin America, and even in Spain, is called white —a reason, incidentally, why I asked him for this sketch. His account of the members of his family who have crossed over to the white and whose descendants are now enumerated as such could be told in endless versions. He died since this was written.)

ADDITIONAL CASES OF MIXED ROMANCE (Chapter 34)

(From the New York White Press).

Miranda Foote, heiress of Galesburg, Illinois, who was married to "China" Crawford, Negro stable-boy, and disowned by her parents, died in misery and poverty. Crawford, who was a gambler, ran through his white wife's money. (N. Y. Pess, Feb. 13, 1898, p. 14).

Mrs. Dinnie C. Provost, wealthy society woman of Brooklyn, N. Y. was married to James A. Cutlar, Negro bicycle instructor, Nov. 20, 1896. Cutlar worked for one Schwallanbach, owner of a bicycle establishment, and used to give lessons to Mrs. Provost. They used to take long rides together and she fell in love with him. Schwallanbach said that he hired Negro instructors in order "to obviate any familiarity between our customers and our instructors." Mrs. Provost, who was 35, and seven years older than Cutlar, had inherited a fortune from her first husband besides being rich in her own right. (N. Y. World, Oct. 27, 1897. The story has two pictures of Mrs. Provost and one of Cutlar).

George A. Fleishman, prosperous farmer of Fulton, N. Y., married his Negro housekeeper, Minnie Coleman. His pastor, John G. Cornwell, white Southern, refused to perform the ceremony, and the couple went to Syracuse.

William S. Horton, rich plumbing contractor, asked annulment of his marriage on the ground that his wife deceived him as to her color. She had told him that she was Spanish and French but he learned from a tombstone maker in Bridgeport, Conn., that her mother (or grandmother) was colored. Mrs. Horton did not contest the suit (N. Y. World, Apr. 26. 1910, p. 4).

Mabel Williams, white governess in a rich family of Norfolk, Va., eloped to New York with William Morse, a coachman to a society doctor, She met Morse while the doctor was making a professional call on the family for which she worked. (N. Y. World, Sept. 29, 1900).

Mrs. Julia McFarlane Gerhart, of New York, was married to her Negro butler, William Kellogg. At her death, he inherits her property (New York World, April 5, 1913, p. 3).

The New York World, April 3, 1910 (p. 2) relates how a colored woman inherited a large slice of the fortune of Lord Delaval Beresford of England. When Lord Beresford was killed in a railroad wreck, Dec. 23, 1906, in Texas, his brother, Lord Charles Beresford, claimed his huge fortune, which included vast holdings in Mexico. However, the colored woman (name not given) was able to produce witnesses that the deceased lord had introduced her to several persons as his wife, thus establishing her as his common-law wife. She was awarded money and property totalling $500,000 by the courts.

The New York Press, May 15, 1901, devotes two columns of its front page to the remarkable story of a white society girl who was engaged to the most prominent dentist in the United States and how the latter finally confessed that he was of Negro ancestry.

The society girl was Lizzie Rector of Jersey City, N. J. The dentist was Thomas J. Wilkerson, president of the United States Dental Association, graduate of New York University. Dr. Wilkerson was described as tall, athletic, handsome, moving in the best circles and of charming personality. "He told Miss Lizzie," says the account, "that generations back there had been an African strain in his family. He had lived the life of a white man among gentlemen. To all practical purposes, he was a white man in manners, in habits, and looks. But he felt that honor demanded that he tell this woman of the taint in his ancestry."

The engagement was broken off in consequence.

WHITE SUPREMACY VERSUS RUSSIA AND BRAZIL

Brazil and Russia, particularly the latter, are seen as menaces to white supremacy by many. Among the writers expressing this view are J. C. Curle and John Clark Epps. Curle says: "Half the races of the world, colored as well as white, are pouring into Brazil. Germans, Italians, Portuguese and Russians are balanced by Syrians, Levantines, Chinese and Japanese, none of them show colour prejudice so that you have pure white, brown, yellow, native Brazilian, and African Negro spawning freely in almost gorgeous infinite permutations. Stand with me in those gorgeous forests behind Rio de Janeiro, where orchids hang from the trees and water rushes down, and watch the married couples who come walking by. A blond German passes with a Brazilian girl; a Syrian with a woman three parts Indian; an Italian with another of the same and a Brazilian and a Chinaman with two elegantly dressed Negresses. They are human beings and physically fine; they mean well by each other and by Brazil but they are piling up a ghastly reckoning against the future and dealing Evolution deadly blows. Brazil is glorious. I like her people. But this miscegenation horrifies me and must lead to a vast futility.

"Brazil in fact is preaching the Communism of color." (Our Testing Time, pp. 112-13. 1926).

Clark says: "Among my fellow-workers in the factory and those among whom I ate and slept in a community boarding house, I met men and women from all parts of the earth and of every shading of races. There were white men from Detroit and other American cities; black Negroes from America, one even from South Africa; a strange dark fellow from Mexico; Chinese from Canton; Japanese, native Siberians; Hindus, and all the varied conglomerations from the vast Russian hodge-podge of peoples. Two black-skinned Russian men had white Russian women 'companions,' a very dark Hindu had a red-haired German girl. . . .

"The thing that struck me at once was the feverish desire of the comrades to show how international they were by hurrying into these mixed companionships . . . the younger Communist women besieged every unattached man of color so that the latter never lacked opportunity to find white companions. . . .

"I see Communist Russia gathering up the far flung forces of the colored sections of humanity and molding those pliant masses into a mighty weapon with which to storm the citadel of Western civilization and culture in a fierce fanatical effort to obliterate all that it holds worthy. One billion human beings, mostly of the colored grades of humanity, are being beckoned to by Bolshevism to come forward and join her legions." (White Race Herald, Oct. 1930, pp. 4-5

NOTES ON BEETHOVEN

Because Beethoven was German and because his portraits are usually shown with a white tone and abundant hair nearly every one thinks of him as white. Beethoven lovers are certain of this and are generally amazed and even indignant when told that he was Negroid in color and features. However, there is not a single shred of evidence to support the belief that he was a white man neither from those who knew him nor from his biographers.

Beethoven's Color According to His Contemporaries

Fischer: "Rounded nose, black-brownish complexion." (Translated by Robert Haven Schauffler; Beethoven The Man, Vol. 1, p. 1. 1929).

Carl Czerny: "His beard—he had not shaved for several days—made the lower part of his already brown face still darker." (Beethoven: Impressions of his contemporaries, arranged by Oscar Sonneck, p. 26. 1926).

Grillparzer: "Dark." (Ibid, p. 154.)

Bettina von Arnim: "Brown." (Ibid, p. 77.)

Weber: "Dark red." "Hair bristly." (Ibid. p. 161.)

Schindler: "Red and Brown." (Ibid. p. 166.)

Rellstab: "Brownish." (Ibid, p. 180.)

Gelinek: "Short, ugly, dark." (L. Nohl: Beethoven Depicted By His Contemporaries, p. 37. 1880.)

The only one of Beethoven's contemporaries who describe him as being of a color that might be interpreted as white was Sir Julius Benedict, who said he was "very red." Benedict, however, wrote his impressions more than twenty years after he had seen Beethoven once. Beethoven's face had a ruddy tint which was accentuated by his walks in the open air. I have seen mulattoes with this ruddy complexion which in winter could be called "very red."

Beethoven's Color According to His Biographers

Fanny Giannatasio del Rio: "Beethoven could not possibly be called a handsome man. His somewhat flat broad nose and rather wide mouth, his small piercing eyes and swarthy complexion, pockmarked into the bargain, gave him a strong resemblance to a mulatto." (An Unrequited Love; An Episode in the Life of Beethoven, p. 60. 1876.) Fanny Giannatastio was in love with Beethoven. Her husband kept a boy's home where Beethoven sent his nephew. Her diary was published after her death and was dedicated to Queen Victoria.

May Byron: "Swarthy." (A Day With Beethoven, p. 9. 1927). The word swarthy comes from the Anglo-Saxon, sweart, black. This word in various forms has the same meaning in several North European languages, as in the German, schwarz.

Alexander Wheelock Thayer, in his description of Beethoven, cites the following story from Andre de Hevesy, another of Beethoven's biographers, who had it from Carpani. The story is about Haydn, Beethoven's teacher.

"Everyone knows the incident at Kismarton, or Eisenstadt, the residence of

Prince Esterhazy, on his birthday. In the middle of the first allegro of Haydn's symphony, His Highness asked the name of the author. He was brought forward.

" 'What!' exclaimed the Prince, 'the music is by this blackamoor. Well, my fine blackamoor, henceforward thou art in my service.'

" 'What is thy name?'

" 'Joseph Haydn.' " (Beethoven The Man, pp. 27-8. 1927.)

Carpani says of this that Haydn's color gave strong reason for the Prince's remark and that Haydn was thereafter called "The Moor." As late as the last century, the word "Moor" was used to describe Negroes in all the countries of Western Europe. Shakespeare uses the words "Moor" and "Negro" synonymously (Merchant of Venice, Act iii, sc. v. 42.) In Germany, the Negro was called "Mohr," in France, "Maure" or "Mor"; in Sweden, "Morian,' etc.

Thayer, by way of illustrating how dark and Negroid Beethoven was, used the above-mentioned incident concerning Haydn, and adds that Beethoven "had even more of the Moor in his features than his master," that is, Haydn. He adds that Beethoven's "nose, too, was rather broad and decidedly flattened." (Life of Beethoven, Vol. 1, p. 146. 1921.)

Thayer adds: "A true and exhaustive picture of Beethoven as a man would present an almost ludicrous contrast to that which is generally entertained as correct. As sculptors and painters have each in turn idealized the work of his predecessor until the composer stands before us like a Homeric god — until those who knew him personally, could they return to the earth, would never suspect that the grand form and more noble portraits are intended to represent the short, muscular figure and pock-pitted face of their old friend." (Ibid, p. 245.)

Frederick Hertz says, "Beethoven was short and corpulent; he had coal-black hair; dark eyes and skin. His face was quite ugly with strong protruding jaws (prognathy), receding forehead and flat, thick nose. One may easily trace in Beethoven slightly Negroid traits." (Man kann in Beethoven Physiognomie leicht negerahnliche Zuge finden—Rasse und Kulter, p. 164. 1925.) The translation is Race and Civilization, p. 123. 1928. (A. S. Levitius.) On page 178 Hertz also says, "Beethoven with his Negroid traits."

Brunold Springer in his "Racial Mixture As a Basic Principle of Life," (as reported in the New York Times, July 1, 1940, in an article entitled "Negroid Blood in Hitler's Aryans") mentions Beethoven as one of the great Germans who was of Negro ancestry. This book, according to the Times, was published in Berlin.

Emil Ludwig says, "His (Beethoven's) face reveals no trace of the German. . . . He was so dark that people dubbed him **Spagnol** certain that there was a mixture of Spanish blood in this half-Netherlander as in so many others." (Beethoven, pp. 8, 15. 1943.)

Other writers here and there have also, like myself, been struck by Beethoven's Negroid appearance. J. W. Chadwick says that Frederick Douglass, great mulatto abolitionist, bore "a certain resemblance" to Beethoven. (A Life For

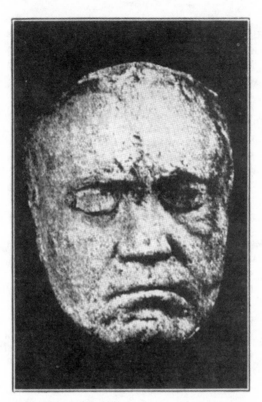

LIII. Beethoven at the age of 42. (Full view of life mask taken by Klein in 1812.)

Liberty, p. 197. 1899.) W. E. B. DuBois, writing of George Bridgetower, Beethoven's mulatto companion and accompanist, says, "And the unexplained complexion of Beethoven's own father." (The Negro, p. 141. 1915.) W. C. B. Sayers says of Coleridge-Taylor, noted English mulatto composer, "The story is told of a playful prank of Mr. Henry Down's who decorated the large bust of Beethoven in the Conservatoire with Coleridge-Taylor's sombrero. It was a small hat for a large head but it helped to show the remarkable resemblance that existed between the sovereign composer and the colored one. This likeness in brow and the outlines and general expression of face has been remarked in later photographs of Coleridge-Taylor." (Samuel Coleridge-Taylor, p. 72. 1915.)

In short, there is no evidence whatever to show that Beethoven was white.

Beethoven's grandfather came from Louvain, Belgium, which with Holland had been ruled for centuries by Spain. The Spaniards of that time not only had considerable Negro strain from the Moorish invasion but they had unmixed

Negroes in their armies. For further details on this see: Sex and Race, Vol. 1, p. 169, 2nd ed., or p. 162, 1st ed. For Beethoven's Belgian ancestry see: R. V. Aerde: Les Ancetres Flamands de Beethoven, 1928, and E. Closson, L'Element Flamand Dans Beethoven, 1928.

As regards Goethe, great German writer, who is also said tto be of Negro descriptions of him is a sketch from life by Letronne and engraved by Hofel. Done in charcoal it showed Beethoven dark, that is, more like the descriptions of his color. However, in some books this picture has been changed somewhat. The charcoal has been rubbed out giving quite a different aspect to his face. One of the latter appears in Emil Ludwig's Beethoven. Compare this, for instance, with a reproduction from the original in Paul Bekker's Beethoven, p. 80, pt. 2, 1911 (German edition).

Finally, the Negro strain in Beethoven comes out clearly in his life-mask at the age of 42, and even more in his death-mask.

As regards Goethe, great German writer, who is also said to be of Negro ancestry, see Sex and Race, Vol. 1, p. 118, 2nd ed., for source on Goethe's ancestry. Hertz says, "It is indeed very significant that many race dogmatists find in Goethe non-Teutonic, Oriental traits. . . . Almost all anthropologists hold Goethe for a non-Teuton. . . . (He had) "a distinctly dark complexion." (Race and Civilization, pp. 326, 128, 123. 1928.) In Goethe's ancestry are two members called "Mohr," the German word then used for "Negro."

MAMMY PLEASANT *(Chap. 34, p. 350)*

"Mammy" Pleasant, a Negro woman, is, without doubt, one of the unique and amazing women in the history of California, if not of the United States Arriving in San Francisco as a cook, she became a dominant figure in politics and high white society. She was also the "housekeeper" of one of the richest men of the city, ruling his household, his white wife and the children.

Later, she fought in the courts one of the richest men of her time, if not the richest, United States Senator William E. Sharon of Comstock Lode fame, a power in Wall Street and politics, and won, though the decision was later reversed.

She is also said to have been the chief financial backer of John Brown, whose raid on Harper's Ferry brought the discussion over slavery to a showdown that ended in the Civil War and the emancipation of the slaves.

Mammy Pleasant's power, it is said, originated in her voodoo practices and her sale of love charms to wealthy white debutantes and their mothers. As a midwife for these families she also acquired secrets that gave her power over them.

Even before her death, at the age of eighty-seven, she had become a legendary figure so that the stories about her conflict in some of their details. Some reports are that she died poor; others very wealthy.

First, an account from two persons who knew her. Amelia Neville says (The

Fantastic City, p. 126, 1932): "She was one of our figures of mystery, a shrewd old Negress who had made a fortune in mining stocks and gained a neat profit on the side from the sale of love charms to enterprising young ladies desiring the favor of wealthy gentlemen. But her reticence concerning her affairs was complete. She was the despair of cross-examiners.

"One saw her picturesque and solitary figure passing through streets of the financial district. She had been born in slavery but she walked like a duchess,

LIV. "Mammy" Pleasant

tall and slim. In all the years I saw her, she never varied the style of her costume, a long, full-skirted gown with kerchief crossed over her bosom and a wide black hat over her head, such a costume as she might have worn in New Orleans, where she was given her freedom before the war.

"Promoting romance and gambling in stocks were mere avocations—Mammy Pleasant was by vocation a housekeeper and lived at the home of Judge Bell." Judge Bell—Colonel Thomas Bell was a Scotsman who had taken $20,000,000 from the Comstock Lode. "Mammy" Pleasant, by all reports, dominated him, his wife, Theresa, and her six "children." Mrs. Bell in dying said in her will, however, that she had never had a child, and that the six Bell children should not be permitted to share in her fortune as they had all been brought into the house by "Mammy" Pleasant.

Hallie Q. Brown, a colored elocutionist, who won much fame in Europe and America in the 1890's and 1900's, who has a sketch of Mammy Pleasant in her unpublished book, "Travels and Noted People," says, "Mammy Pleasant was notorious in all that that term implies. I first saw her at my recital. She came forward and made herself known. I knew her relatives. She was not a beauty as some have written. She was rather tall, slender, with sharp features, keen black eyes, very dark, almost black. She wore a purple silk dress, black velvet cape, purple bonnet and strings tied under her chin. She invited me to come to see her but my friends advised me not to go. But I went as I had a purpose—I had recently come from Birmingham, Alabama, from where a young teacher had run away in disgrace and her parents, hearing that she was with "Mammy" Pleasant, asked me to inquire about her when I went to California." (Letter to J. A. Rogers, June 22, 1943.)

A clipping from a San Francisco daily (probably the Call), reproduced in the Indianapolis Recorder, September 30, 1939, says: "In a little graveyard down in Napa have just been laid to rest the remains of the most remarkable colored woman in California, if not in the United States, Mammy Pleasant. Dying a few years ago in this city, of old age, her demise brings to mind many sensational cases in which she figured prominently—notably John Brown's Harper's Ferry Raid.

"To Mammy Pleasant is given credit for backing this historic movement. Unto the day of her death its tragic outcome weighed heavily upon her. But it was her connection with affairs involving many of California's wealthiest people that she gained her later and greater renown.

"Born ninety years ago, she married a wealthy Cuban in her early twenties. Her husband died and left her a comfortable fortune. Soon after his death she became acquainted with Garrison, Phillips and other noted abolitionists, and through them she became interested in the anti-slavery movement. In 1848, she went to California.

"When Sarah Althea Hill began her famous suit against Sharon, Mammy Pleasant was her principal adviser. She welded a mysterious influence not only over the Hill woman but over others of equal talents, including a number of millionaires.

"Recently she was offered $50,000 if she would subscribe to certain facts concerning a certain prominent San Francisco man, but she declined with the remark that she had never needed money badly enough to betray a friend.

"Mammy Pleasant left an estate valued at $300,000 to friends who had taken care of her during her declining years."

Herbert Asbury (Barbary Coast, p. 14, 1933), telling of the great trouble in getting servants in San Francisco during the California gold rush, and the airs that most domestics had put on, says, "A notable exception to this foolery was Mammy Pleasant, a gigantic Negress from New Orleans, black as the inside of a coal-pit, but with no Negroid features whatever, whose culinary exploits were famous. She said flatly that she was a cook, and would be called nothing else. She arrived in the early part of 1850, preceded by her reputation, and was besieged by a crowd of men, all anxious to employ her, before she had so much as left the wharf at which her ship had docked. She finally sold her services at auction for five hundred dollars a month, with the stipulation that she would do no washing, not even dish-washing. This was the highest wage paid to a cook, although several others received as high as three hundred dollars a month."

Mammy Pleasant's greatest notoriety came in the very sensational "Rose of Sharon" case in which she financed her protegée, the beautiful Sarah Althea Hill, against Senator Sharon, who Sarah claimed had married her privately, and then had thrown her out without a cent. The case rocked San Francisco society and reverberated over the nation.

Everett Wilson (True Detective Magazine, April 1940), writing of Mammy Pleasant's role in this case, says, "More than one San Franciscan was asking, Where does Sarah get the money to live in that house on Rincon Hill and to carry on her legal battle? . . .

"The answer now came in hushed whispers that gained more and more credence, 'Mammy Pleasant!'

"Mammy Pleasant! It was a name used only in discreet whispers in San Francisco—until it was shouted later in the Sharon litigation and in another famous court battle only a few years ago.

"Mammy Pleasant, tall, dusky giant, had come to San Francisco no one knew exactly when. She was part West Indian and part Cherokee. She had been a friend of John Brown in Civil War days. She let it be known that she was a sorceress, an obi-woman, steeped in the voodoo lore of the West Indian jungles.

"She worked herself into the homes of the top families in post-pioneer days as nurse and maid or midwife. Such was her strange and compelling power that she stepped into the innermost confidences of those families. She was the custodian of a rattling closetful of skeletons.

"As the children she brought into the world grew to girlhood and became society belles, Mammy Pleasant was the confidant of their love secrets. Drawn by a strange attraction, they came to the gaunt conjure-woman for advice and sympathy. Some even beseeched her for magic charms and love potions. Many firmly believed that she had supernatural powers.

"But voodoo lore was not Mammy Pleasant's only stock in trade, and the fortune she salted away swelled out of all proportion to the usual income of a conjure woman. She was in addition an extortionist, using her vast store of family secrets, as the years went on, for evil purpose.

"Then, too, she was an engineer of blackmail. She picked on likely young girls who came to her for advice, and got them under her weird power. She introduced them to wealthy and philandering men. After that she promoted and financed their romances, staking the girls to jewels if they had no money for finery. Soon the jaws of the blackmail trap would close and Mammy Pleasant would get her fat cut of the profit."

This was the reason, it was alleged, why Mammy Pleasant was interested in the golden-haired Southern beauty, Sarah Althea Hill. She had financed her romance with the Senator and was financing the legal battle. "She was going after the biggest game of her career. When Sharon's love for his inamorata turned to disgust or disinterest and the latter could milk him of no more money, the gaunt witch had disdained secret shakedown methods and had dared to gamble all on dragging the silver millionaire into court, while she coached her protege from the sidelines," says Wilson. When Mammy Pleasant was called to the stand, she proved more than the match for the high-priced Sharon lawyers.

Sarah Hill, after one of the bitterest and most slanderous cases ever fought in court won, being proclaimed the legal wife of Senator Sharon on Christmas Day, 1884, and as wife of Sharon and entitled to a share in his vast wealth. A year later, however, Senator Sharon died and on September 24, 1888, the court ruled against Sarah's claim.

Mammy Pleasant's greatest claim to fame was her financing of John Brown.

Earl Conrad in an article "She Was A Friend of John Brown (Negro Digest, December 1940) says,"

"Mrs. Pleasant was a politically powerful person in the history of California. Arriving thtre in the period of the gold rush of 1849 she grew up with the State to become a business woman who warranted the respect of every figure of importance, and a person of some notoriety as well, for her operations in real estate and her influence on many prominent private lives. "Mammy" Pleasant, as she became known, was famous, chiefly, for her relationship to the rise of the Barbary Coast. Taking a cue from the rough-riding white men who amassed fortunes by any and all means, Mrs. Pleasant plunged into Barbary Coast operations, and became wealthier and more influential than most of her teachers. Despite this fame, or notoriety as it was regarded in California, she will doubtless be remembered chiefly, if not only, for the contribution that was the high mark of her life, her association with the commander of the Harper's Ferry expedition.

"Mary Ellen was born in Philadelphia probably in the year 1814, a free Negro. Her mother was a Louisiana Negro and her father a Kanaka. At the age of seven she was sent to Nantucket where she was placed at work in a huckster shop. This early experience seems to have set the tone for her later business sagacity. Later she went to Boston to work, and this city, with its flourishing abolition movement at the time, represented a turning point in her life. While employed in boot-binding and vest-making she met and married her first husband, a wealthy Cuban named James W. Smith. Smith was an abolition sympathizer, and the friend of William L. Garrison, Wendell Phillips, Lewis Hayden and others. Often the abolition leaders came to the Smith home, and Mary naturally became absorbed in the question of the freeing of her people. Mr. Smith died in 1844, and his last request was that his wife devote a portion of the money that he left to the cause of emancipating the slaves. As a result of the sale of bonds bequeathed to her Mary came into possession of about $45,000.

"A few years later, in 1848, she married John J. Pleasant. Together they went to California, where they invested the money in real estate. Mrs. Pleasant operated a boarding house in San Francisco, and to this board came Newton Booth, one of many men afterwards distinguished in the economic and political scene, who was elected Governor of California even as he stayed at the Pleasant home.

"Throughout this period Mrs. Pleasant kept in touch with the East Coast abolitionists, Garrison and Phillips. She subscribed to **The Liberator,** and

studied carefully the operations of Brown in Kansas. In 1858 she decided
to go east and meet the Old Man and give him funds to continue his work.
It is doubtful whether she then knew that Brown contemplated any raid in
the Virginia region.

"It is a matter of record that she drew a large-sized United States Treasury
draft early in the Spring of 1858, and that she sailed to the east. She arrived
in New York, converted her draft into a Canadian draft, and immediately
headed for Chatham, Canada. She wrote to persons who could place her in
touch with John Brown, and soon a meeting occurred. According to Mrs.
Pleasant, one night in her room she turned over the whole amount of her
check to John Brown and his son. Although the matter of the amount of
money passed over to Brown has been questioned. . . ."

After the capture of John Brown, Mammy Pleasant returned to California
and kept her part in the affair a secret. The federal government was round-
ing up all who had aided John Brown. Mrs. Pleasant ascribes her escape from
implication to the fact that a letter she had written to John Brown promising
"more money and help," and signed with her initials, "M. E. P." was taken
for "W. E. P." She made her "W's' like an "M.

Mammy Pleasant kept the secret until the closing years of her life then
on October 20, 1901, she sent a telegram to Sam P. Davis, editor of the Car-
son City (Nevada) Appeal and Also Comptroller of the State of Nevada who
had been writing stories of her behind-the-scenes roles in Coast politics, to
come to California. There she told him her story.

"Sam Davis,' says Earl Conrad," checked on her story. He hunted up
Jason Brown, then living in California, and Jason said that it was true
John Brown received a considerable sum of money from a colored woman in
Chatham in 1858. Davis visited Sarah Brown, a daughter also living in Cali-
fornia, and she too affirmed that John Brown, had received a large sum from
a colored woman at that time and place he never revealed the woman's name.
Davis wrote to Chatham, Canada, and learned that there was on file there a deed
showing the transfer of property—four lots, in September of 1858, to Mary Pleasant,
and there was another record again 1872 when the property was conveyed to James
Handy, a San Francisco man.

"Mrs. Pleasant said to Sam Davis, 'I felt very bad over the failure of my
mission, but never regretted the time or the money I spent on the trip. It
cost me, all told, about $40,000. It seemed at first like a failure, but time proved
that the money was well spent. It paved the way for the war and the war freed
the slaves. I always felt that John Brown started the Civil War and that I helped
Brown more than any other one person financially. I wish I had given more. When
I die, all I want on my tombstone is: 'She was a friend of John Brown.'

"Then came her death and burial: and if a tombstone was placed over her
grave, with the inscription that she desired, there has been no sign of it in
recent years.

"As a 'mystery' woman with a background reaching back into misty legend,
'Mammy' Pleasant's career in California has caught the imagination of novel-
man, across the Bering Straits from ice-bound Siberia?

ists, playwrights and newspaper feature writers. There's Charles Dobie's **Less than Kin,** a romance with a 'Mammy' Pleasant plot that has gone through several editions, and who has not seen 'The Cat and the Canary' on the legitimate stage or in one of its several movie productions? 'Mammy' Pleasant is the black housekeeper who appears here and there when least expected and it is this character that holds the lines of the popular old melodrama together.

"But, as a character who exerted a powerful influence on affairs on the West Coast and on the anti-slavery contest in the east, she might have been neglected for all time except for one woman, a white woman, who had a vague memory of 'Mammy' Pleasant as she moved about San Francisco just before the close of the old lady's long life. Impelled by a great curiosity this writer, Mrs. Stella Ingrim Brown of San Jose, California, began to gather every scrap of information available about the activity of the colored woman who wielded power and wrought strongly three quarters of a century ago. The untimely death of Mrs. Brown a couple of years ago cut short the work on a definitive life of the most unusual Negro woman of the Pacific Coast, contemporary of Harriet Tubman and Sojourner Truth, though working in a different field.

"Mr. Boyd B. Stutler, the historian who visited Mrs. Pleasant's /grave, has thoroughly investigated her claims to association with John Brown, and he in convinced that she played a part in his campaign." (Note: The Negro Digest in which this article appears is a defunct publication of that name.)

Charles Dobie who knew Mammy Pleasant devotes a chapter to her in his book, "Pageant of an Francisco," pp. 317-323 (1939). He quotes Zoe Battu about her, "Her life made her mercilessly calculating and shrewdly realistic; at the same time it gave her a large tolerance. And she had a certain goodwill and generosity to everyone.

"Her great lust and mania were for power. She valued money only as a means to an end."

SOURCES OF THE BELIEF THAT HAM BECAME BLACK
BECAUSE HE WAS CURSED BY NOAH

The belief that the descendants of Ham, that is, the Egyptians and Ethiopians, became black because Ham was cursed by Noah, originates in the Talmud, Midrash, and other rabbinical writings of from the second to the fifth centuries A. D.

There are three principal versions of this legend, all of which have a basis in sex relations.

The chief one is that Noah forbade all the persons and the animals in the ark to have sex intercourse. Ham disobeyed the order; the dog followed his bad example; and then the raven. As a result all three were cursed: Ham was made black; the dog was attached to the body of the female after intercourse; and the raven which had incited the other animals to have intercourse was punished by being made "to copulate through his mouth." (Sanhedrin 108b).

Louis Ginzberg (The Legends of the Jews, Vol. 5, p. 56. 1925) says, "The older sources (Sanhedrin 108b; Br. 36:7. Yerushalmi Ta'anit I, 64d; Tan. Noah 12) state that three were punished because they did not observe the law of abstinence while in the ark. Ham, the dog, and the raven. Ham became the ancestor of the black (colored) race. . . ." (See also Vol. 1, p. 166 of this work).

Another version is that Noah was drunk and while he was lying on the ground spilling his semen Ham laughed at him while his other sons, walking backward so as not to see his nakedness, covered him with a garment. This is, in part, Biblical. (Genesis X, 22, 23). As a result Noah cursed Ham by having the curse fall on his son, Canaan (Gen. X, 25). The reason for this says Ginsberg is that "to Ham, himself, he (Noah) could do no harm for God had conferred a blessing upon Noah and his three sons as they departed from the ark. Therefore he put the curse upon the last born son of the son that had prevented him from begetting a younger son than the three had. The descendants of Ham, therefore, through Canaan, have red eyes because Ham looked upon the nakedness of his father; they have misshapen lips because Ham spoke to his brothers about the unseemly condition of his father; they have twisted curly hair because Ham turned and twisted his head round to see the nakedness of his father." Because Ham did not cover his father "naked, the descendants of Ham, the Egyptians and Ethiopians, were led away captive into exile by the King of Assyria while the descendants of Shem, the Assyrians, even when the angel of the Lord burnt them in the camp were not exposed their garments remained upon their corpses unsinged." (Vol. 1, pp. 169-170).

The Midrash Rabbah, Genesis, Noah, chap. 37, gives a different version. It says that in the quarrel between Noah and Ham, the former said, "You have prevented me from doing something in the dark (sc. cohabitation) therefore your seed will be ugly and dark-skinned. Rabbi Huja said: Ham and the dog copulated in the Ark therefore Ham came forth black-skinned while the dog publicly exposes its copulation." (p. 293. 1939. I. Epstein, editor).

Ham, one part of the legend goes, prevented Noah from having sex relations by castrating Noah while the latter was in the ark. Another part of the legend says that it was not Ham, but a lion, that struck Noah in his privates, mutilating him, as Noah was leaving the ark. When Noah got drunk, as the fable goes, and started to cohabit, he forgot his injury, with the result that his semen was scattered over the ground. In this humiliating state Ham laughed at him. (See also HAM in **Jewish Encyclopedia.**)

In other words, this twisted legend, which has no more scientific foundation than the Uncle Remus stories of Brer Rabbit, was firmly believed in for centuries by supposedly intelligent white Americans and is still accepted by millions of them. Moreover as I showed (Sex and Race, Vol. I), Noah's alleged curse actually worked in reverse because the sons of the alleged Shem became slaves to the mythical Ham for over four hundred years in Egypt.

This rabbinical concept of how Negroes became black was written long after the Jews had left Egypt and were in Europe at which time, the Jews, who were very likely a black people originally, had become fairer through mixing with lighter-skinned Asiatics and Europeans. The whole story evidently had its basis in the rivalry over the land of Canaan, which the Jews claimed that God had given them as an inheritance forever or more likely because the Egyptians had made concubines of the Jewish women. Placing a curse on a people is still used as a justification for taking what they have and otherwise exploiting them.

This myth becomes all the more contradictory and ridiculous when one recalls that the thing held most sacred by the Jews, the holy fire in which Jehovah used to make himself manifest, as in the burning bush of Moses, was black (Ginzberg, Vol. 2, p. 303). Add to this that in Daniel (VII, 9,) Jehovah, "the Ancient of Days" is pictured as having "the hair of his head like the pure wool." That is, according to Jewish legends he was both black and wooly-haired.

The rabbis also taught that "Cain's face turned black." (Ginzberg's Legends of the Jews, Vol. I, p. 108; V, p. 137). But it happens that the West Africans who had, it appears, an ancient Egyptian connection, teach the opposite, namely, that Cain was originally black but that when he killed Abel and God shouted at him in the garden he turned white from fright and his features shrank up. (Winwoode Reade "Savage Africa, p. 24. 1864) and other sources.

NOTES ON THE ILLUSTRATIONS

Who Is A Negro? What Is A Negroid?

As to who or what is a Negro the scientists are in as hopeless a muddle as they are over what constitutes "race." The more conscientious they are the more perplexed are they.

The same is true as to the difference between the words, "Negro" and "Negroid." Just when Negro ceases and Negroid begins no one seems to know, especially since in the United States individuals who are sometimes fairer and more Caucasian in features than some white people are called Negro, while in Africa coal-black people with wooly hair, but with regular features, we are told, are not Negro, but Negroid. For instance, Cust is quoted in the Century Dictionary regarding who are really Negro. "The tribes of North Guinea are the representatives. . . . When these characteristics are not all present, the Race is not Negro, though black and wooly-haired.' That is, the vast majority of the people of Africa could not be classed as Negro, and perforce, much less so the colored people of the United States.

Other scientists use the word "Hamitic" to avoid the use of Negro and Negroid. This is even worse because so-called Hamitic is a language classification like "Aryan" or "Semitic." As a Frenchman or an American can be of any color so a "Hamite" may be white or black.

The Watussi, an East African people, with black skins and wooly hair, are called Hamitic and are said to have "little in common" with Negroes racially. On the other hand in the United States if one of one's thirty-two direct ancestors was a Negro and all the others white, we are told by the politicians who direct the United States census and certain professors of anthropology in big universities that such a one has much in common with Negroes.

In archaeology and ancient history one finds the same mess. For instance Elliott Smith held that the Natufians, a prehistoric race, that once inhabited Palestine had Negroid features but were not Negro. The same is said of the Bushmen, a prehistoric people, that once roamed over southern Europe and Africa as far as the Cape. A people, white, mulatto, and black, closely intermingled as are those of North Africa, are all called Caucasian; while the people of Mauritania, an almost black people with frizzly and often wooly hair, are called white. Note, however, that though these scientists lay great stress on the word "Negroid" they do not use "Caucasoid" to distinguish peoples as the Sicilians and Kabyles, who, in the majority, are as far removed from the Scandinavians as the Mauretanian is from the Congolese.

Nott and Gliddon in their "Types of Mankind" fixed their own definition of "Negro." Amenophis III, they said, showed no "Negro admixture." Darwin differed with them. "When I looked at the statue of Amdunophis III," he said, "I agreed with two officers of the establishment, both competent judges, that he had a strongly marked Negro type of features.' |Descent of Man, Pt. 1, p. 172.

1874.) I might add here that the mummy of Amenophis II, his grandfather is quite black. Felix Shay (National Geographic Maga. Feb. 1925, p. 130) calls it "blue-black." I have seen mummies of a yellow ivory tint, also.

Again Reisner calls the portraits of two members of the family of Cheops, builder of the Great Pyramid, Negroes, while Flinders-Petrie, another great Egyptologist, says they are not. (G. H. Beardsley. The Negro In Greek and Roman Civilization, p. 12, 1929). And so on with innumerable other cases.

In other words, current definitions of what is a Negro is not founded on Nature, but created for political and economic use. The United States Bureau of Census has one definition; certain of the states as South Carolina, Florida, Oregon, and Virginia, also have others; while individual Americans still have others. It seems to me so far that the person best qualified to give a scientific definition of what is a Negro is a lunatic in a padded cell. (See also my discussion of this in Sex and Race, Vol. 1, pp. 37-39. 1941.)

I have, however, used the term, Negro, though it is to the last degree incorrect, for the reason that long usage has made it the best known one for a certain aggregation of human beings, which comprise nearly all the so-called races. As long as we have a certain condition we must have a name by which to call it. And the mere fact that a condition is unpleasant will also make its name unpleasant. Thus "Negro" serves for this purpose as well (or as badly) as any other. A shift to "colored," or some other name will not help, therefore. It is not the name but the treatment that hurts.

As for "Negroid" the type so called is really mulatto, or show evidences of white mixture, which in America is simply called "Negro" even by the scientists. Therefore to simplify matters I have just used "Negro," and whenever I use "Negroid," I also mean "Negro."

I.

Some of the Germans, for reasons given in Volume One, were very dark. Henry Swinburne, Englishman, who visited Cologne in 1780, described the Elector, or ruler, of that part of Germany as "a little hale, black man." (Courts of Europe, Vol. 1, p. 371. 1841).

XIII.

See page 65 of this work. This picture has a religious connotation but African princes, or other dark-skinned men called princes, were once considered romantic in England. In Anna M. Mackenzie's Slavery, or The Times, the Uncle Tom's Cabin of 1793, Adolphus, the African prince, son of King Zimza, marries a charming English heiress, and it is not the prince who is regarded as being honored but the white heiress (Whitney, L. Primitivism and the Idea of Progress, pp. 89-90. 1934). Omai, South Sea prince, brought to England by Captain Cook, was a great favorite with the ladies. So, also was Prince Lee Boo. (History of Prince Lee Boo. 1821). George A. P. Bridgetower's father was called "The African Prince"; and so was Ira Aldridge, famous Shakespearean actor, American Negro, whose father was said to be a Foulah king. Other cases could be cited.

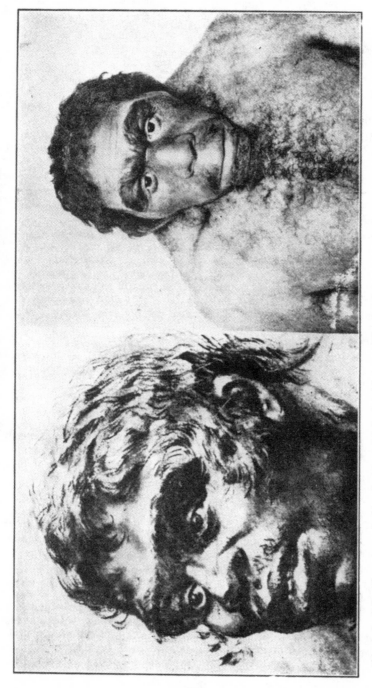

LV. Left: Palaenthropus, or Prehistoric Man of Palestine (Courtesy Illustrated London News). Right: Reconstruction of Neanderthal Man, or The First Known German (Courtesy Field Museum, Chicago). As regards skin-color and hair, nothing is really known of what they were like in primitive man. There are no known surviving traces. The hair was probably of the pepper-corn variety, like that of the Hottentot-Bushman. The Willendorf Venus, oldest known representation of the human form of about 15,000 to 20,000 B.C., shows hair of this latter type. (See Illus. No. 5, Sex and Race, Vol. I. Also J. R. Marett, p. 220).

XXVI.

Gerald Massey says, "The Dea Multimammia, the Diana of Ephesus, is found as a black goddess, nor is the hue mystical only, for the features are as Negroid as were those of the black Isis of Egypt." (A Book of the Beginnings, Vol. 1, p. 18. 1881. See also: Sex and Race, Vol. 1, p. 279, 2nd ed. for a Negro Madonna).

When St. Paul attacked the worship of Diana, "the magnificence of her whom all Asia and the world" worshipped—he and his companions were mobbed (Acts 19:23-40). The later Diana of the Greeks, called Artemis, was transformed into a white woman, but in some cases she still remained black as the statue of her in the Museo del Conservadores, Rome; and that in the Museo Campano at Capua, where she is shown on horseback. (See also McClintock and Strong's Cyclopedia of Biblical etc. Literature (DIANA).

Mylitta was probably connected with the intermixing of blacks and whites because the word "Mulatto" is derived from her (G. P. Rawlinson's Herodotus, Vol. 1, p. 444. 1859). This word probably passed into the Berber language where it is "mulati," from which the Spaniards and the Portuguese very likely had it. (Weiner, L. Mayan and Mexican Origins, p. 93. 1926). Webster's Dictionary says that it is derived from the Spanish **mulo,** mule, which is evidently wrong as there were mulattoes long before the time of Spain or Portugal. **Mulier,** Latin for woman, probably has the same origin. At least it certainly isn't derived from "mule."

XXVII.

As regards the Black Madonna of Alt-Otting see American Notes & Queries Feb. 1943, p. 175; also Sex and Race, Vol. 1, Appendix Pt. 2, The Black Madonna and the Black Christ.

VXIX.

Harry P. Howard, an American, who lived many years in China and Japan, things that Hirohito, present Emperor of Japan, also shows a Negroid strain. He is, he says, "distinctly Negroid in appearance; travelling incognito, he would have considerable difficulty in getting a drink in some Southern states." (America's Role in Asia, p. 162. 1943). He speaks also of the mixed white and Negrito (little Negro) strain of the Japanese. Japan still has a very Negroid people: The Eta, who are very likely the descendants of the little Negroes who are said to be the first inhabitants of the islands.

For an article on the Etas of today see "The Ghettos of Japan," by Albert A. Brandt in Coronet, pp. 3-6, June 1944. (See also Sex and Race, Vol. 1, Chap. 6).

XXXI.

Note the resemblance of the man, upper left, to that of Ay, father of Queen Tiyi in Pl. XXVII of this book, upper left.

XLVI.

Milton S. J. Wright is head of the Department of Economics and Political Science, Wilberforce University. He received his Ph. D. from Heidelberg University, where he was such a brilliant student, that he attracted the special notice of Adolf Hitler, when the latter visited Heidelberg in 1932. Hitler invited him to the Europaische Hof, the town's leading hotel, entertained him at dinner together with other members of the Nazi party, and interviewed him on the race question for two hours. He also invited Dr. Wright to visit the Brown House at Munich, an invitation he did not accept. (For an account of this interview see: Pittsburgh Courier, May 20, 1942). Dr. Wright has filled other important positions as Dean of Sam Huston College, Texas; and Advisor on Negro Affairs for the United States, Department of the Interior.

Incidentally, I know also a Negro woman, born in Africa, wife of the Liberian Consul-general at Hamburg, who was received as a social equal in Nazi circles. She showed me photographs of same. She was once entertained at dinner by Goering's wife and sat in the same box at the opera with her. Hitler's attack on Negroes was poltical, not racial and fanatical, as that of the average Southern white. See Hitler's own pronouncement on this as quoted in Sex and Race, Vol, I, p. 18, 1941.

XLVIII.

The Gould and Steward families are descendants of Elizabeth Adams, white granddaughter of John Fenwick, one of the Lords Proprietors of New Jersey, who married a Negro, named Gould, and was disinherited in consequence. The descendants of this couple now in live in Gouldstown, N. J., while others have intermarried with whites and their offspring are scattered in the white race." Several Negro members of this family have attained distinction. among them being a bishop and a United States army chaplain. (Steward, W. & T. G., Gouldstown, pp. 12, 50, 51. 1913.

What is said of the Goulds can be said of many other Negro families, except in the latter case, the white ancestor is usually male. One may meet such families who claim descent from George Washington, Thomas Jefferson, Henry Clay, John Adams, Robert E. Lee, Andrew Jackson, Woodrow Wilson, and other illustrious persons.

LVIII.

As regards the peopling of the so-called New World, it seems to me, whether we believ in Atlantis or not, there was once a land-bridge between Africa and America and another between America and Asia. The West Indies Islands are very probably the remains of a sunken continent; likewise the islands of the Pacific.

Man is not the only creature in the "New" World to be accounted for. The "New" World had nearly all the animals of the "Old." Are we to assume, according to the orthodox scientific theory of the peopling through Alaska, that the dinosaurs, elephants, and other huge beasts of the "Old" World also arrived in boats, like man, across the Bering Straits from ice-bound Siberia?

"A SUNKEN CONTINENT."

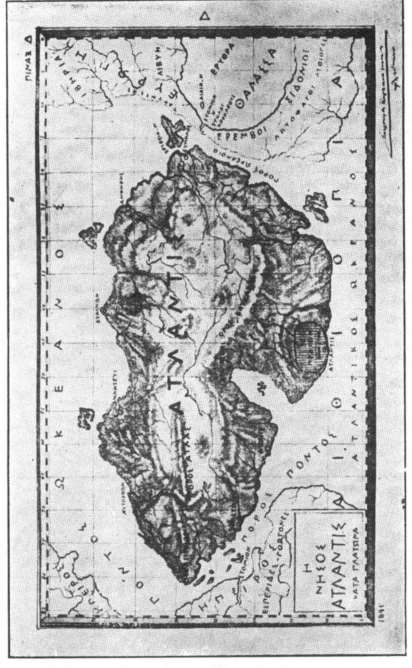

LVI. The Legendary "Atlantis" as conceived by Patrocie Campanakis, Greeg geographer. He places it between Africa and Central America and shows that what are now the West Indies were part of a great land mass. (See also Notes on the Illustrations).

It seems to me that, even assuming that there was no land bridge and that the Americas are the younger of the two great land masses that Man could have arrived in America from several sources, that is, from Africa, from the Pacific Islands, and through Alaska.

Primitive man, we know, could cross vast stretches of ocean without a compass and in boats that were really canoes. The Polynesians performed feats that were almost miraculous in this respect. Uenga, a twelfth century sea-rover, crossed 4000 miles of the Pacific Ocean, 2500 of which from Rapa to Rapa-nui (or Easter Island) were made with no intervening stopping place. Karika, another Polynesian, made even longer voyages all with no compass or log book, but aided only by the stars, the sun, and the flight of birds. Since it was possible to cross to Easter Island, why was it not possible to reach the coast of Chile, also, since there are intervening islands?

As regards Africa, the distance is only 1600 miles with the midway islands of St. Paul and Fernando Noronha. In any case it is as easy to accept the theory that man came to the New World from Africa as that he crossed Bering Strait and journeyed over the great mountains and glaciers of Alaska, and over 15,000 miles by land until he reached the tip of South America.

It is popular also to think of the so-called Indian as of Mongolian type but only some of them were. Early America had a great variety of peoples, some of which were white, or almost white, and others distinctly Negro. Victor Larco Herrera in "Cobrizos, Blancos, y Negros," makes out an excellent case, together with illustrations, that copper-colored, white, and black people lived in early America. Other Latin-American archaeologists have also given what seems to be sound proof that Negroes were in America before Columbus, especially in the tropical and semi-tropical regions.

Alfonso Toro, one of Latin America's leading archaeologists and historians mentions the "Negro warrior god" of ancient Mexico, Ek-ahau. He says, "Other gods of war were the Negro captain, Ek-ahau, who gives orders to six Negroes, terrible warriors." (Compendio de Historia de Mexico—Historia antigua—p. 44. 1926).

J. A. Villacorta also mentions Negroes in ancient Guatemala. He quotes the Mss. of Chichicastenango and mentions "the whites and the blacks" who lived in that region, speaking different languages, etc, and of "the Negro chiefs who appear in the role of "conquerors" (vencedores). This writer gives Negro figures from the ancient monuments (Arqueologia Guatemalteca, p. 331-37. 1930).

For sources from other writers see; Sex and Race, Vol. 1, Appendix, Pt. 1.

Also so hard-headed a scientist as Sir G. Elliot Smith believes that America was known to the ancients and that the South Sea islanders reached America by way of the middle Pacific. He says, "There can be no reasonable doubt that Asiatic civilization reached America partly by way of Polynesia as well as directly from Japan and also by the Aleutian route.

"The immensely formidable task of spanning the broad Pacific to reach the coasts of America presents no difficulty to the student of early migrations." **(The Influence of Ancient Egyptian Civilization in the East and in America** in John Rylands Library Quar. Bull. Vol. 3, pp. 48-77. 1916-17). See also Simoens

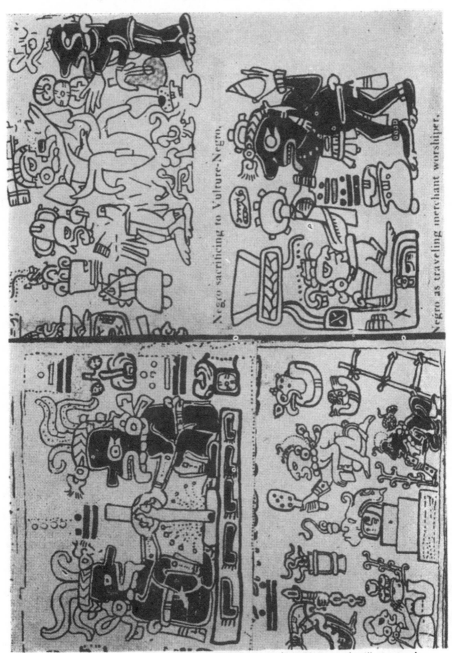

LVII. Negroes on the Ancient Mexican Monuments. (See Note on the Illustrations).

LVIII. Negro Stone Heads from Mexico (Courtesy American Museum of Natural History). Centre face, right, is detail from gigantic head found at La Venta (National Geographic, Sept. 1943).

da Silva A. C.. Points of Contact of the Prehistoric Civilizations of Brazil and Argentina with those of the Pacific Countries, (1922); as well as A. Mattos, Prehistoria Brasileira (1938).

A. Hyatt Verill (The American Indian, 1927) discusses the theory of the arrival through Alaska and asks among other things why if the Indian came from Asia through Alaska did he leave what is now the United States and go all the way to Central America to found his only civilizations.

But whatever be the truth I, personally, find the orthodox scientific theory of the peopling through Alaska as incomplete as the Atlantis or the Pacific theories. Of course, the specimens of early man found so far are much older in the New than in the Old, but I wonder whether if Columbus, instead of arriving from the Old World had come from the New World whether the names would not have been reversed.

People have got into the habit of thinking of "New" and "Old" but is it not possible that some day this idea may be overthrown by accidental discoveries? If the New World had a tropics, a million years ago, and there is no doubt of that, I believe that just as there were tropical plants and animals there, so there was tropical man also.

Of course, the question of where New World man came from is academic to the highest degree. It enters the political and economic fields actively however when the matter of the Negro is brought in. Exploiters of Negro labor and the inheritors of the belief that Negroes were always a slave race will oppose vigorously the idea that the civilization of Central America with its great pyramids could have come by way of Africa. I quoted the case of Ignatius Donnelly, who, in saying that Africans did reach America and gave portraits of Negroes from the ancient American monuments to prove it, said that such Negroes were "slaves."

LVII.

Picture: Upper left: Negroes drilling fire. Lower left is described by Antonio Villacorta as "El Dios Negro que toca un instrumento de viento figurán dose tambien el sonido." (Soc. Geografia e Historia de Guatemala, Anales, Vol. 7, 1930-31, p. 42.) Right: see Weiner L., Mayan and Mexican Origins, Chap. "The Black God," pp. 98-105 & PL. LXII, LXIII, LXIV, LXXXV. The Black God, which has red lips, is Ekchuah. See also Harvard Univ. Peabody Museum of American Archaeol. Papers, Vol. 4. No. 1, pp. 34-37. 1904-1910.

END OF VOL. III

BIBLIOGRAPHY

The books and articles consulted in this work are too many to be given here. See Index of Authors and footnotes for a partial list of them. Below is given a list of books and articles which deal wholly or much with the miscegenation of whites and blacks.

I. WORKS ON MISCEGENATION

Abel, W. Bastarde am Rhein. Neues Volk. February 1934.

Aikman, K. B. Race mixture with some reference to Bible history. Victoria Institute Jour. London. Jan. 1935.

Baldwin, L. F., From Negro to Caucasian. San Francisco. 1929.

Barker, J. Ellis. Colored French Troops in Germany. Current History, July 1921.

Black, Stephen. Black men, White women. English review. London. October 1919.

Calhoun, Arthur W. Racial Association in the old South (In Social History of the American Family Vol. 2) 1917.

Champly, Henry. White women, Colored men. Long & Co. London. 1936.

Chavez-Gonzalez, R. A. El mestizaje y su influencia en America, Guayaquil.

Croly, David G. Miscegenation. 1864.

Day, Caroline B. A Study of Negro-White Families in the United States. Peabody Museum of Harvard University. 1932.

Davenport, Charles B. Race-Crossing in Jamaica. Carnegie Institution. 1929.

Dover, Cedric. Half Caste. Secker & Warburg. London. 1937.

DuBois, W. E. B. Social Equality and Racial Intermarriage. World Tomorrow. March 1922.

Eve (Woman's Illustrated Daily) Paris. February 20-March 29, 1920.

Fantham, H. B. Notes on some cases of racial intermixture in South Africa. S. African Jour. of Science. Vol. 24, 1927.

Some further cases of physical inheritance of race mixture observed in S. Africa. Vol 26. 1930.

Finch, Earl. Effects of racial miscegenation (In G. Spiller: Universal Races Congress, pp. 108-112.) London. 1911.

Findlay, George. Miscegenation. Pretoria. 1936.

Fischer, Eugen. Die Rehobother Bastards. Jena. 1913.

Fletcher, M. E. Report on an investigation into the colour problem in Liverpool and other ports. Ass'n. for the welfare of helf-caste children. 1930.

Fournier-Gonzáles, G. La raza negra es la mas antigua raza de las razas humanas. Valldolid. 1901.

Frazier, E. Franklin. The free Negro family. Fisk University Press. 1932.

Grentrup, Theo. Die Rassen mischehen in dem deutschen Kolonien. 1914.

Guenther, Hans F. K. Rassenkunde des jüdischen Volkes. Munich. 1930.

Herskovits, Melville. The American Negro. Knopf. 1928.

Holm. J. J. Holm's Race Assimilation. Atlanta. 1910.

Jenks, A. E. Legal status of Negro-White amalgamation in the United States. Amer. Jour. of Sociol., March 1916.

Klineberg, Otto. Characteristics of the American Negro. Harper. 1944. (pp. 277-300 gives figures and other details on mixed marriages).

Lacerda, Joao, B. The metis, or half-breeds of Brazil. (In G. Spiller; Universal Races Congress, pp. 377-382) London. 1911.

Lima, Oliveria. Racial intermarriage in South America. Missionary Review. July 1924.

Marett, J. R. de la H. Race, sex, and environment. Hutchinson. London. 1936.

Plaatje, Solomon. The mote and the beam, South Africa. 1921.

Powell, John. The last stand. Richmond Times-Despatch. Feb. 16-28. 1926.

Reuter, Edward B. The Mulatto in the United States. R.G. Badger. Boston. 1918.

Rheinische Frauenliga. Farbige Franzosen am Rhein. Engelmann. Berlin. 1921. (This work which is published in English, French, Dutch, Italian and Spanish gives cases of alleged rape on German women by colored French soldiers stationed on the Rhine. The French edition L'Afrique sur le Rhin, Leipzig, 1923, gives a list of brothels maintained in Germany for the colored troops).

Schuyler, George S. Racial intermarriage in the United States. Haldeman-Julius Blue Book 1387.

Shapiro, H. L. Descendants of the mutineers of the Bounty. Honolulu. 1929.

Storms, J. C. Origin of the Jackson Whites. 1936.

Woodson, Carter G. Beginnings of the miscegenation of Whites and Blacks. Journal of Negro History, Oct. 1918. pp. 335-359.

Indian-Negro-White Mixture

Estabrook, Arthur H. Mongrel Virginians. Williams & Wilkins. Baltimore. 1926.

Foster, Laurence. Negro-Indian relationships in the South-East. Philadelphia. 1935.

Harrington, W. R. The Shinnecock Indians. Amer. Museum of Natural Hist. Anthrop. Papers. Vol. 22. 1924.

Jenks, A. E. Indian-White amalgamation. Bull. No. 6. University of Minnesota studies in social science. 1916.

Johnston, J. H. Relations of Negroes and Indians. Jour. of Negro Hist. January 1929.

LaFarge, Oliver. The changing Indian. 1942 (See chapters by Frank Lorimer and H. L. Shapiro).

Porter, Kenneth W. Relations between Negroes and Indians. Jour. of Negro Hist. July 1932.

Powell, John. The last stand. Richmond Times-Despatch. Feb. 16-28. 1926. (See also Chap. 35, Sex and Race, vol. 2).

Weslager, C. A. Delaware's forgotten folk. Univ. of Pennsylvania Press. 1943.
Woodson, Carter G. Negroes and Indians in Massachusetts. Jour. of Negro Hist. January 1920.

Novels

Azevedo, Aluizo. O mulato. Rio de Janeiro. 1927.

Brady, Cyrus T. A doctor of philosophy. Scribner. 1903.

Cather, Willa, Sapphira and the slave girl. Knopf. 1940.

France, Anatole. Balthasar. Paris. 1889.

Garnett, David. The sailor's return. Knopf. N. Y. 1925.

Goll, Claire. Le Nègre Jupiter Enleve Europa. Paris.

Howells, William D. An imperative duty. Harper & Bros. New York. 1892.

Insua, Alberto. El Negro que tenia el alma blanca. Madrid. 1923.

Kearney, Belle. A slaveholder's daughter: an autobiography. Abbey Press. 1901.

Lemaire, Madeline. Blanche et noir. Paris.

Majette, Vara A. White blood. Stratford Co. Boston. 1924.

McKay, Donna. A gentleman in a black skin. William Faro. 1932.

Maupassant, Guy de. Boitelle. Paris.

Merrick, Leonard. Quaint Companions. Dutton. 1924.

Ross, Albert (pseud.) A Black Adonis. 1895.

Royer, L. C. Lat Maitresse noire. Paris.

Smith, Lillian. Strange fruit. Raynal, Hitchcock. 1944.

Spencer, Edward. Tristan; story of a marriage of black and white. Galaxy magazine, January-February, 1867.

Sutherland, Joan. Challenge. Harper and Bros. 1926.

Steen, Marguerite. The sun is my undoing. Viking. New York. 1942.

Townsend, Wm. C. Love and Liberty. Abbey Press. 1901.

White, Robb. Run Masked. Knopf. New York. 1938.

Wood, Clement. Deep River. Godwin. 1934. (This novel is a departure from the usual ones dealing with miscegenation in the United States).

Plays

Anicet-Bourgeois. Le docteur noir. Paris 18. (This play translated into English and called "The Black Doctor" was played by Ira Aldridge in London in July 1841.

Braddon, Mary E. The octoroon. New York. 1862.

Boucicault, D. L. The octoroon. New York. 186...

Hughes, Lanston. Mulatto. (unpublished).

Marlowe, Christopher. Lust's Dominion, or The lascivious queen. London. 1657.

O'Neill, Eugene. All God's chillun got wings. Boni & Liveright. New York. 1924.

Shakespeare, Wm. Titus Andronicus.

Poems

Cleveland, John. (1613-1658). A fair nymph scorning a black boy courting her. London. 1687.

Herbert, George. (1583-1633). The Blackamoor and her loves. (See Sex and Race, vol. I, pp. 84, 259-260, and vol. 2, pp. 217-219 for other poems.)

II. SOME BOOKS AGAINST RACISM

Barzun, Jacques. Race: A study in modern superstition. Harcourt Brace. 1937.

Benedict, Ruth F. Race: Science and Politics. Modern Age. 1940.

Blum, Leon. Contre le racisme. Paris. 1938.

Dahlberg, Gunnar. Race, reason and rubbish.

Finot, Jean. Race prejudice. Dutton. 1906.

Hertz, Frederick. Race and civilization. London. 1920.

Hirschfeld, Magnus. Racism. London. 1938.

Huxley, Julian. We, Europeans. J. Cape. 1935.

Inman, Frederick W. Biological politics as an aid to clear thinking. J. Wright. 1935.

Lakhovsky, Georges. La civilisation et la folie raciste. Paris. 1939.

Linton, Ralph. The study of man. New York. 1935.

Maggiore, Guiseppe. Razza e fascismo. Palermo. 1939.

Miller, Hermann J. Out of the night. Vanguard Press. 1935.

Montagu, M. F. Ashley. Man's most dangerous myth; The fallacy of race. Columbia Univ. Press. 1942.

Myrdal, Gunnar. An American dilemma. Harper Bros. 1944.

Seligmann, H. J. Race against man. Putnam. 1939.

Smith, F. Tredwell. An experiment in modifying attitudes towards the Negro. Columbia Univ. Press. 1943.

Russell, Bertrand. An outline of intellectual rubbish.

III. BOOKS FAVORING RACISM*

Céline, L. F. Bagatelles pour un massacre. Paris. 1927.

Champly, Henry. White women, colored men. Long & Co. 1936.

Curle, James H. Our testing time. Doran & Co. 1926.

Cox, Earnest S. White America. Richmond. 1923.

Gauch, Hermann. Neue Grundlagen der Rassenforschung. 1933.

Gould, Charles W. America: a family matter. Scribner. 1920.

Grant. Madison. Passing of the great race. Bell. 1924.

Guenther, Hans F. K. Rassenkunde des jüdischen Volkes. Munich. 1930.

Sayers, J. D. Can the white race survive? Washington, D. C. 1929.

Schultz, Alfred P. Race or mongrel? Page & Co. 1903.

Smith, William B. The color line. Phelps and Co. 1905.

Stoddard, Lothrop. Rising tide of color. Scribner. 1923.

* The number of books favoring racism by American and English writers has declined and even seems to have passed out of fashion since the rise of Hitler and his doctrine of "the master race," to which he arrogates the Germans and from which he excludes all other whites.

INDEX TO VOLUMES I, II and III*

Authors and Painters

* 12 pages were added in various places in the second edition of Vol. I. Therefore this index will not always be accurate for the first edition of Vol. I.

INDEX CONTINUED ON NEXT PAGE

INDEX TO VOLUMES I, II and III
NAMES MENTIONED

INDEX CONTINUED ON NEXT PAGE

INDEX TO VOLUMES I, II and III
SUBJECTS

ALSO BY J. A. ROGERS

Sex and Race, Volume 1
ISBN 978-0-8195-7507-4

Sex and Race, Volume 2
ISBN 978-0-8195-7508-1

Africa's Gift to America
ISBN 978-0-8195-7516-6

The Five Negro Presidents
ISBN 978-0-9602294-8-2

100 Amazing Facts about the Negro
ISBN 978-0-9602294-7-5

Nature Knows No Color-Line
ISBN 978-0-8195-7510-4

From Superman to Man
ISBN 978-0-9602294-4-4

Books available from Hopkins Fulfillment Services,
Customer Service, P. O. Box 50370, Baltimore, MD 21211-4370;
phone: 1-800-537-5487; or visit www.HFSbooks.com